Colonialism and Culture

THE COMPARATIVE STUDIES IN SOCIETY AND HISTORY BOOK SERIES

Raymond Grew, Series Editor

Comparing Muslim Societies: Knowledge and the State in a World Civilization
Juan R. I. Cole, editor

Colonialism and Culture
Nicholas B. Dirks, editor

Constructing Culture and Power in Latin America
Daniel H. Levine, editor

Colonialism and Culture

Nicholas B. Dirks, Editor

Ann Arbor

THE UNIVERSITY OF MICHIGAN PRESS

1995   1994   4   3

Library of Congress Cataloging-in-Publication Data

Colonialism and culture/Nicholas B. Dirks, editor.
        p.   cm.—(The Comparative studies in society and history
book series)
    Includes bibliographical references and index.
    ISBN 0-472-09434-3 (alk. paper).—ISBN 0-472-06434-7 (pbk. :
alk. paper)
    1. Colonies—History. 2. Europe—Colonies—History.
3. Indigenous peoples—History. 4. Culture—History. I. Dirks,
Nicholas B., 1950-   . II. Series.
JV305.C65   1992
325'.3'09—dc20   92-3315
                                                        CIP

Foreword

For more than thirty years, *Comparative Studies in Society and History* (*CSSH*) has published articles about human society in any time or place, written by scholars in any discipline and from any country. Those articles, inevitably reflecting the changing methods and interests in their authors' specialized fields of research, have presented new evidence and new techniques, challenged established assumptions, and raised fresh questions. The series of books entitled Comparative Studies in Society and History extends and refocuses the discussions begun in some of the most stimulating essays.

The editor of each volume identifies a field of comparative study and presents contributions that help to define it, selected from among the articles that have appeared in *CSSH* from October, 1958, to the present and from scores of manuscripts currently being considered. Written by scholars trained in various traditions, some of whom were born before 1900 and some after 1960, the essays are chosen for their contribution to what the editor perceives as an important continuing dialogue. The volumes in this series are thus not just anthologies. Each contains specially commissioned essays designed to suggest more fully the potential range of the topic. In addition, the articles taken from *CSSH* have been revised by their authors in light of the larger project. Each volume is, therefore, a new work in the specific sense that its chapters are abreast of current scholarship and, in its broader purpose, a cooperative enterprise reconsidering (and thereby reconstructing) a common topic.

Having established a theme and identified scholars to address it, the editor then invites these colleagues to join in exploring the ramifications of their common interest. In most instances this step includes a conference in Ann Arbor, attended by contributors and other scholars, where issues of conceptualization, interpretation, and method can be debated. Sometimes the volume's topic is made the basis of a graduate course, with contributors giving a series of lectures in a seminar lasting a term or more and attended by a variety of interested specialists. The book, which started from an indirect dialogue in the pages of *CSSH,* thus takes form through direct encounters among scholars from different disciplines and specializations. In open-ended and lively discussion, individual manuscripts are criticized and new suggestions tested, common concerns identified and then matched against the criteria of different disciplines and the experience of different societies. Reshaped by the community it has created, each volume becomes a statement of the current state of scholarship and of questions raised as by-products of the process in which general problems are reformulated while individual essays are reconsidered and revised.

By building from discussions conducted over the years in *CSSH,* this series extends the tradition represented by the journal itself. A scholarly quarterly is a peculiar kind of institution, its core permanently fixed in print, its rhythmic appearance in familiar covers an assurance of some central continuity, its contents influenced by its past yet pointing in new directions. *CSSH* seeks to create a community without formal boundaries—a community whose membership is only loosely determined by subject, space, or time. Just as notes and references embed each article in particular intellectual traditions while stretching beyond them, so the journal itself reaches beyond editors, contributors, and subscribers, speaking in whatever voice unknown readers respond to whenever and wherever they turn its pages. The resulting dialogues are not limited to any single forum, and the journal changes from within while balancing between venturesomeness and rigor as old debates are refined and new problems posed.

The books in this series further the aspirations acknowledged in the opening editorial of *CSSH,* in which Sylvia Thrupp declared her belief that "there is a definite set of problems common to the humanities, to history, and to the various social sciences." Changes in the way these problems are conceived and in the vocabulary for expressing them have not lessened the determination to reject "the false dilemma" between "error through insularity and probable superficiality." Insistence upon thorough, original research has been the principal defense against superficiality, emphasis upon comparison the means for overcoming insularity. Many of the articles published in *CSSH* are systematically comparative, across time and between societies, and that is always welcome; but many are not. Each published article is chosen for its scholarship and imagination as well as for its broad implications. For the contributors to and readers of that journal, comparison has come to mean more a way of thinking than the merely mechanical listing of parallels among separate cases. Articles designed to speak to scholars in many disciplines and to students of different societies are recognized as intrinsically comparative by the nature of the problem addressed, structure, and effect.

Every piece of research deserves to be seen in many contexts: the problems and concerns of a particular society, the immediately relevant scholarly literature with its own vocabulary and evidence, the methods and goals of a given discipline, a body of theory and hypotheses, and sets of questions (established, currently in vogue, or new). It is also impossible for any prescription to delimit, in advance, how far subsequent comparisons of similar problems in different contexts may reach. For the past twenty years, *CSSH* has placed articles under rubrics that call attention to a central comparative theme among related studies. In addition, an editorial foreword in each issue notes other sets of connections between current articles and earlier ones, inviting additional comparisons of broad themes, specific topics, and particular problems or methods. A variety of potential discourses is thus identified, and that open-ended process has culminated in this series of books. Some of the volumes in the series are built around themes for comparative study that have always been recognized as requiring comparison; some address topics not always recognized as a field of study, creating a new perspective through a fresh set of questions. Each volume is thus an autonomous undertaking, a discussion with its own purposes and focus, the work of many authors and an editor's vision of the topic, establishing a field of knowledge, assessing its present state, and suggesting some future directions.

The goal, in the quarterly issues of *CSSH* and in these books, is to break out of received categories and to cross barriers of convention that, like the residual silt from streams that once flowed faster, have channeled inquiry into patterns convenient for familiar ideas, academic disciplines, and established specialties. Contemporary intellectual trends encourage, indeed demand, this rethinking and provide some powerful tools for accomplishing it. In fact, such ambitious goals have become unnervingly fashionable, for it no longer requires original daring or theoretical independence to attack the hegemony of paradigms—positivism, scientism, Orientalism, modernization, Marxism, behavioralism, and so forth— that once shaped the discourse of social science. Scholars, however, must hope that the effort to think anew also allows some cumulative element in our understanding of how human societies work. Thus, these books begin by recognizing and building from the lasting qualities of solid scholarship.

A lot of that scholarship has been about cultural difference, a topic that for centuries has stimulated influential works. Somewhat surprisingly, current explorations contain much that is new, for the study of colonialism and culture moves beyond typologies of otherness, theories of evolution, and models of modernization to encompass the preoccupation of today's scholars with the cultural role of power and with the reflexiveness of scholarship itself. Questions newly posed have created a distinctive field of study, one quite different from the observations of travelers, the accounts of empire builders, the studies of earlier anthropologists, or the polemics on imperialism written by its advocates, critics, or victims.

Issues addressed in Nicholas Dirks's introductory essay in this volume continue to be discussed throughout the book. The sensibilities and the modes of analysis associated with literary studies have become important to research in anthropology and history, as the essays by Dirks, Vicente L. Rafael, Michael Taussig, and Timothy Mitchell demonstrate. Richard Helgerson's comparison of two sixteenth-century works, with which the book begins, impressively illustrates the fruitfulness of this approach. What the age of discovery discovered was Europe.

The ambiguous connections of commerce and culture, a theme in all of the essays, are confronted in Mitchell's chapter on the world as exhibition and on culture as commodity. And those connections are exposed, in action and from a very different perspective, in Frederick Cooper's essay on the discipline of labor. Cooper's study shows how the imperatives of capitalism were interpreted in the colonial situation—as does David Ludden's analysis of the claims made for economic development in modern India, claims with all sorts of social, cultural, and political implications that confounded change and continuity.

These chapters are also about state making and the kinds of protest it provoked, which is Michael Adas's central concern. His close reasoning about protest, which is both embedded in culture and provoked by change, contributes to a broad literature on the politics of peasant societies. Throughout the book, state making is seen as a universal phenomenon but not a single process. By emphasizing complexity and contingency, the essays in *Colonialism and Culture* can also grapple fruitfully with issues of power, another theme that runs through every chapter. No longer identified simply as compulsion or measured through confrontations, power is here shown to be subtler, more pervasive, and more surprising in its effects than the mere application of force or imposition of culture. Ann Laura Stoler's chapter, a model of this approach, studies how the markers of cultural difference, with gender the most salient and effective, were used to generate and reconstitute those differences.

This book thus illustrates the special appeal and significance of its topic. We are drawn to think yet again about colonialism and culture because their interaction reveals so much that societies and scholarly projects normally keep offstage. Where two rivers flow together, it is often possible to observe currents otherwise imperceptible; and the studies in this volume treat the unspoken values, hidden assumptions, and buried connections out of which states are made and power is simultaneously exercised and thwarted. Similarly, reflection on how these cultural encounters should be studied and on where there is ground solid enough to support a scholarly stand becomes in fact a comment on issues central to all the human sciences. Readers of Gyan Prakash's essay will find exposed there the (European) cultural history of the history of (Indian) culture, the instrumental accounts from several sides of imperialism and of nationalism, and the paradoxes and contradictions of recent campaigns for liberation from these frameworks. They will also find a telling expression of some of the intellectual dilemmas of the late twentieth century, dilemmas that ironically lead back to the opening essay of this volume.

Raymond Grew

Acknowledgments

Grateful acknowledgment is given to *Comparative Studies in Society and History (CSSH)* for permission to reproduce the following articles in revised form:

"From Avoidance to Confrontation: Peasant Protest in Precolonial and Colonial Southeast Asia" by Michael Adas first appeared in *CSSH* 23:217-47 under the same title.

"From Little King to Landlord: Colonial Discourse and Colonial Rule" by Nicholas B. Dirks first appeared in *CSSH* 28:307-33 as "From Little King to Landlord: Property, Law, and the Gift under the Madras Permanent Settlement."

"Orientalism and the Exhibitionary Order" by Timothy Mitchell first appeared in *CSSH* 31:217-36 as "The World as Exhibition."

"Writing Post-Orientalist Histories of the Third World: Indian Historiography Is Good to Think" by Gyan Prakash first appeared in *CSSH* 32:383-408 as "Writing Post-Orientalist Histories of the Third World: Perspectives from Indian Historiography."

The following are reproduced in unrevised form:

"Confession, Conversion, and Reciprocity in Early Tagalog Colonial Society" by Vicente L. Rafael originally appeared in *CSSH* 29:320-39.

"Rethinking Colonial Categories: European Communities and the Boundaries of Rule" by Ann Laura Stoler originally appeared in *CSSH* 31:134-61.

"Culture of Terror—Space of Death: Roger Casement's Putumayo Report and the Explanation of Torture" by Michael Taussig originally appeared in *CSSH* 26:467-97.

Contents

Introduction: Colonialism and Culture

Nicholas B. Dirks

"Europe is literally the creation of the third world."

—Frantz Fanon

In the opening chapter of *A Passage to India,* E. M. Forster carefully describes the geographical setting of the novel. The landscape "presents nothing extraordinary," nothing, that is, except the Marabar Caves. Although the caves provide the only visible wrinkle, they also contain the ambivalent space of the echo, the space in which the psychosexual fears of a British memsahib become projected onto the dark, glassy walls of colonial terror. Hallucinations of violation become inscribed in the fact of rape, at once the inverted metaphor of exploitation and the patriarchal pillar of colonial honor. The "events" at the caves disrupt the narrative and display the terrible totality of a colonial world; there are, in the end, only the colonizers and the colonized.

Forster asserts that colonialism is more than just a narrative of momentary disarray, for colonialism has become nature itself. The landscape tells all: the Indian city of Chandrapore "seems made of mud, the inhabitants of mud moving. So abased, so monotonous is everything that meets the eye, that when the Ganges comes down it might be expected to wash the excrescence back into the soil. Houses do fall, people are drowned and left rotting, but the general outline of the town persists, swelling here, shrinking there, like some low but indestructible form of life." Anticipating Said's critique, Forster ironically notes that whatever cultivated decoration might have marked the natural contours of mud and water "stopped in the eighteenth century, nor was it ever democratic." Otherwise, it is all nature at its lowest ebb.

The prospect alters, however, from the vantage of the civil lines, the official British cantonment; "viewed hence Chandrapore appears to be a totally different place. It is a city of gardens." Nature has given way to culture. The vista becomes now a "tropical pleasaunce washed by a noble river." Although irony steeps all of Forster's prose, he suddenly tightens the noose: "As for the civil station itself, it provokes no emotion." In truth, as Forster goes on to show, tremendous emotion cathects around the issue of rape, both for Adela, who has mingled fear with desire, and for the Collector and his crowd, who have reacted to the "crime" with racial hatred.

Although the trial seems to produce justice, it ruptures the appearance of friendship between Aziz and Fielding and does not vindicate the colonized. The novel concludes with a kind of natural closure that reiterates the inscription of colonialism in India's landscape. For in spite of an extraordinary past of intimacy and support, Aziz and Fielding could not be friends, would not be friends, not until the Indians had driven "every blasted Englishman into the sea." In the words of the final paragraph: "The horses didn't want it—they swerved apart; the earth didn't want it, sending up rocks through which riders must pass single file; the temples, the tank, the jail, the palace, the birds, the carrion, the Guest House . . . : they didn't want it, they said in their hundred voices, 'No, not yet,' and the sky said, 'No, not there.'" Not until the antinomy of native nature and colonial culture was dissolved through the closure of colonialism itself would Aziz and Fielding be in a position to engage with each other as genuine friends.

If Forster's writing inscribed colonialism and its antinomies so dramatically into the very contours of the natural world, his poetic conceit was appropriately chosen.[1] Nature, after all, is the world that is given, exempt from the capacity of humans to shape it and of historical processes to change it. And though nature seems invariably to stand in some kind of opposition to culture, it is also the case that culture is a way of talking about nature; culture, in the anthropological sense, is the congeries of values, beliefs, practices, and discourses that have come to carry the force of nature. Nature itself, as well as the various forms of nature's opposition to culture, appear to anthropology as the residues of cultural construction. Poetic conceits aside, Forster was writing the ethnography of British colonialism in India. For Forster, nature was a way of talking about culture.

In both metropolitan centers and colonial peripheries, the anthropological givens of culture have been transformed over and over again by colonial encounters. Often, these transformations seemed overdetermined, for culture in places such as India became, through colonial lenses, assimilated to the landscape itself, fixed in nature, and freed from history. Thus, castes, villages, and tribes were seen as the scientific axioms of a millenial geology of colonial spaces, the social facts of colonial control and the ideological means by which histories of colonial conquest were erased. For colonial rulers, the culture and nature of the colonized were one and the same.

Although colonial conquest was predicated on the power of superior arms, military organization, political power, and economic wealth, it was also based on a complexly related variety of cultural technologies. Colonialism not only has had cultural effects that have too often been either ignored or displaced into the inexorable logics of modernization and world capitalism, it was itself a cultural project of control. Colonial knowledge both enabled colonial conquest and was produced by it; in certain important ways, culture was what colonialism was all about. Cultural forms in newly classified "traditional" societies were reconstructed and transformed by and through colonial technologies of conquest and rule, which created new categories and oppositions between colonizers and colonized, European and Asian, modern and traditional, West and East, even male and female.

The anthropological concept of culture might never have been invented without a colonial theater that both necessitated the knowledge of culture (for the purposes of control and regulation) and provided a colonized constituency that was particularly amenable to "culture." Without colonialism, culture could not have been so simultaneously, and so successfully, ordered and orderly, given in nature at the same time that it was regulated by the state. Even as much of what we now recognize as culture was produced by the colonial encounter, the concept itself was in part invented because of it. Culture was also produced out of the allied network of processes that spawned nations in the first place. Claims about nationality necessitated notions of culture that marked groups off from one another in essential ways, uniting language, race, geography, and history in a single concept. Colonialism encouraged and facilitated new claims of this kind, re-creating Europe and its others through its histories of conquest and rule.

If colonialism can be seen as a cultural formation, so also culture is a colonial formation. But culture was not simply some mystifying means for colonial conquest and rule, even as it could not be contained within colonized spaces. Culture was imbricated both in the means and the ends of colonial conquest, and culture was invented in relationship to a variety of internal colonialisms. Colonial theaters extended beyond the shores of tropical rivers and colonized spaces, emerging within both metropolitan contexts and the civil lines of colonial societies. Culture became fundamental to the formation of class society, the naturalization of gender divisions in Western bourgeois society, and to developing discourses of race, biology, and nationality. At the same time, metropolitan histories were both sustained and heavily influenced by colonial events; sexuality in Sumatra, torture in the Congo, terror in the Marabar Caves—were all displacements of the fault lines of expanding capitalism at the same time that they became fundamental moments in the unfolding narrative of the modern.

The parallel mutualities of colonizers and colonized on the one hand and colonialism and culture on the other make it more difficult than ever to devise historical narratives of cause and effect. If culture itself, as an object of knowledge and a mode of knowledge about certain objects, was formed in relation to colonial histories, it is all the more difficult to recognize the ways in which specific cultural forms were themselves constituted out of colonial encounters. This task becomes even more daunting when we realize that these cultural forms became fundamental to the development of resistance against colonialism, most notably in nationalist movements that used Western notions of national integrity and self-determination to justify claims for independence. In turn, Western colonial nations did not simply exploit colonized nations for economic profit, but depended upon the process of colonization and colonial rule for securing the nation-state itself: developing new technologies of state rule, maintaining and deepening the ruptures of a classed, patriarchal society during a time of reform and democratization, consolidating Western control over the development of world capitalism, even achieving international cultural hegemony in areas ranging from fashion to the novel—bringing both colonialism and culture back home.

Looking at colonialism as a cultural project of control thus focuses attention on the interdependency of these terms, on the complex interplay of coercion and hegemony, on the categories of thought that generally orient scholarly considerations of colonial history or historical anthropology. Linking culture and colonialism does not efface the violence of colonialism. Not only does this linkage preserve a sense of the violent means by which colonialism was effected and maintained, it allows us to see anew the expanded domains of violence, to realize that cultural intervention and influence were not antidotes to the brutality of domination but extensions of it. Representation in the colonial context was violent; classification a totalizing form of control. Brute torture on the body of the colonized was not the same as the public exhibition of a colonized body, but these two moments of colonial power shared in more than they differed. And torture became terror through the culture of colonialism itself.

Now that decolonization and the twentieth-century transformations of the world order have rendered colonialism a historical category, linked to the present more by such terms as *neo* and *post* than by any formal continuity, there is both license and risk in our collective interrogation of the colonial past. Colonialism is now safe for scholarship, and culture seems an appropriate domain in which to measure the effects of colonialism in the contemporary world. Is it possible that, in calling for the study of the aesthetics of colonialism, we might end up aestheticizing colonialism, producing a radical chic version of raj nostalgia? Is it likely that by linking colonialism and culture, we might ignore the extent to which colonialism became irrelevant due to transformations in the world economy having to do with the hegemony of superpowers and the internationalized structures of late industrial capitalism? Might we become so complicit in the displacements of postmodernity that we fail to recognize the informal continuities between the colonial past and the new world order present?

These are questions and worries that we should not let slip away. However, there are opportunities in the present intellectual conjuncture that we should not lose. For the first time it seems possible to imagine dramatic transformations in certain academic landscapes: the traditional analytic antinomies that have shaped questions and discourses in the past are being reformulated and sometimes dissolved. Colonialism can be seen both as a historical moment—specified in relation to European political and economic projects in the modern era—and as a trope for domination and violation. Culture can be seen both as a historically constituted domain of significant concepts and practices and as a regime in which power achieves its ultimate apotheosis. Linked together, colonialism and culture can be seen to provide a new world in which to deploy a critical cartography of the history and effects of power.

This new cartography might cast perspective on the history of the old cartography, returning us to the age of the Enlightenment itself. We all know that the Enlightenment was the age of discovery and reason. It was also the age when reason was idealized as a quality or attitude that could transcend social and historical particularities. Reason made discovery the imperative of Western thought, but was neither dependent on discovery nor driven by it. What gets lost in this account, however, is that colonialism provided a theater for the Enlightenment project, the grand laboratory that linked discovery and reason. Science flourished in the eighteenth century not merely because of the intense curiosity of individuals working in Europe, but because colonial expansion both necessitated and facilitated the active exercise of the scientific imagination. It was through discovery—the siting, surveying, mapping, naming, and ultimately possessing—of new regions that science itself could open new territories of conquest: cartography, geography, botany, and anthropology were all colonial enterprises. Even history and literature could claim vital colonial connections, for it was through the study and narrativization of colonial others that Europe's history and culture could be celebrated as unique and triumphant.

As the world was shaped for Europe through cartography—which, writ large, included ships logs, narrative route maps, the establishment of boundaries, the textualization of treaties, the composition of epics, the fighting of wars, the raising of flags, the naming and appropriation of newly discovered spaces, the drawing of grids, the extermination of savages (and the list could go on and on)—so also it became peopled by classificational logics of metonymy and exclusion, recognition and opposition. Marking land and marking bodies were related activities; not only did land seem to determine much of a putatively biological nature, bodies themselves became markers of foreign lands. Before places and peoples could be colonized, they had to be marked as "foreign," as "other," as "colonizable." If geography and identity seem always to have been closely related, the age of discovery charted out new possibilities for this relationship.

Colonialism therefore was less a process that began in the European metropole and expanded outward than it was a moment when new encounters within the world facilitated the formation of categories of metropole and colony in the first place. But colonialism was not only good to think. The world was full of incentives for accumulation of all kinds, from knowledge to spices, from narratives to military command posts. There were compelling reasons to invent systematic beliefs about cultural differences, uniting such disparate projects as the precarious formation of national identity and the relentless exploitation of economic resources.

Colonialism was neither monolithic nor unchanging through history. Any attempt to make a systematic statement about the colonial project runs the risk of denying the fundamental historicity of colonialism, as well as of conflating cause with effect. It is tempting but wrong to ascribe either intentionality or systematicity to a congeries of activities and a conjunction of outcomes that, though related and at times coordinated, were usually diffuse, disorganized, and even contradictory. It could be argued that the power of colonialism as a system of rule was predicated at least in part on the ill-coordinated nature of power, that colonial power was never so omniscient nor secure to imagine itself as totalizing, and that while colonial rulers were always aware that their power was dependent on their knowledge, they themselves were never similarly aware of all the ways in which knowledge was, in any direct or strategic sense, power.

Neither, however, was colonial power fragile, least of all for the colonized. Colonial self-representations have too often been reproduced in postcolonial scholarship, wherein colonialism is viewed as a veneer, the thinness of which is indicated by the relatively paltry numbers of Europeans who actually ruled over imperial frontiers. Arguments about colonial fragility were first weakened by counterarguments that stressed the collaboration of colonial elites,[2] though these arguments have been shown subsequently to demonstrate more about colonial contempt for the colonized than about the sinuous and hegemonic character of colonial power.[3] The sedimented effects and legacies of colonial power are now attested to by a great variety of writings, ranging well beyond the scholarship in this volume to the proliferation of lamentations, from Fanon to Rushdie, that reveal the extent to which colonialism lives on in postcolonial societies and psyches.

Hegemony is perhaps the wrong word to use for colonial power, since it implies not only consent but the political capacity to generate consent through the institutional spaces of civil society, notably absent in the colonial context. Nevertheless, colonialism transformed domination into a variety of effects that masked both conquest and rule. Not only did colonial rulers align themselves with the inexorable and universal forces of science, progress, rationality, and modernity, they displaced many of the disruptions and excesses of rule into institutions and cultures that were labeled as tradition. Colonialism came to be seen as ascendent and necessary precisely through the construction of the colonial world, with its naturalized oppositions between us and them, science and barbarity, modern and traditional. And in this construction, consent was less the issue than the reality of power itself.

An example of this process can be seen in the history of the caste system in India. For anthropology, for social theory, and for contemporary political practice in India, culture in India seems always to have been principally defined by caste. Caste has always been seen as central in Indian history, and as one of the major reasons why India has no history, certainly no sense of history. Caste defines the core of Indian tradition, and caste is today—as it was throughout the colonial era—the major threat to Indian modernity. However, I have argued elsewhere that much of what has been taken to be timeless tradition is, in fact, the paradoxical effect of colonial rule, where culture was carefully depoliticized and reified into a specifically colonial version of civil society. In ethnographic fieldwork, in the reading of texts traditionally dismissed as so much myth and fabulous legend, in reconstructing the precolonial history of Indian states and societies, in reading colonial texts, and in charting the contradictory effects of colonial rule, I found that the categories of culture and history subverted each other, opening up supplemental readings of "caste" that made it seem more a product of rule than a predecessor of it.[4]

Such an argument need not accord total power to the British, nor suggest that caste was invented anew by them. Rather, the point is that caste was refigured as a "religious" system, organizing society in a context where politics and religion had never before been distinct domains of social action. The religious definition of caste enabled colonial procedures of rule through the characterization of India as essentially about spiritual harmony and liberation; when the state had existed in India, it was despotic and epiphenomenal, extractive but fundamentally irrelevant. British rule could thus be characterized as enlightened when it denied Indian subjects even the minimal rights that constituted the basis for the development of civil society in Europe. This is also not to suggest that one culture simply gave way to another, nor that the politics and historicity of caste in the seventeenth century were the same as the politics and historicity of caste today. Rather, salient cultural forms in India became represented as nonhistorical at the same time that these representations were only made possible under the historical conditions of early colonialism. In the colonial era, the colonizers and the colonized were increasingly implicated in new discourses on social identity that led to subtle shifts in social relations and political control. The success of colonial discourse was that, through the census, landholding, the law, inter alia, some Indians were given powerful stakes in new formulations and assumptions about caste, versions that came increasingly to resemble the depoliticized conditions of colonial rule. These versions were then canonized in the theoretical constructions of caste by anthropology, first in the hands of colonial administrators, later in the imaginations of such powerful thinkers and academics as Louis Dumont. Caste became the essence of Indian culture and civilization through historical process, under colonial rule.

This reference to anthropology reminds us that Western scholarship has consistently been part of the problem rather than the solution. When Edward Said published his pathbreaking *Orientalism,* he articulated the most compelling polemical critique of the implication of scholarly discourses in colonial legacies that has so far been made. During the last decade, it has been impossible to engage in the study of the colonial world without either explicit or implicit reference to his charge that not only our sources but also our basic categories and assumptions have been shaped by colonial rule. Said has made the case that the Orient, qua Orient, was constituted as an effect of the collaboration of power and knowledge in the West, a collaboration most significantly made possible by the colonial era. When Said used the term *Orientalism,* he meant it in a number of interdependent senses. These senses included the general tendency of thought, found throughout colonial establishments, in which the Orient was made to be Europe's other, a land of exotic beings and exploitable riches that could service the economy and the imagination of the West. Orientalism also refers to a much more sophisticated body of scholarship, embodied in such practices as philology, archaeology, history, and anthropology, all glorifying the classical civilizations of the East (at the same time they glorify even more the scholarly endeavors of the West that made possible their recuperation) but suggesting that all history since the classical age was characterized by decline, degradation, and decadence. Orientalism, whether in the guise of colonial cultures of belief or of more specialized subcultures of scholarship, shared fundamental premises about the East, serving to denigrate the present, deny history, and repress any sensibility regarding contemporary political, social, or cultural autonomy and potential in the colonized world. The result has been the relentless Orientalization of the

Orient, the constant reiteration of tropes conferring inferiority and sub-ordination to the East.

But if Said's influence has been pervasive, so also is the concern to move beyond his general critique, both in the sense of breaking down the monolith of colonialism, and in engaging more directly than our Orientalist forebears the brute realities of an Orient that resists reification in Western discursive or political formations. There is a search both for voices outside and voices raised against those of the Orientalist establishment. There is worry that if we accord totalizing power to such entities as the West, or the Orientalists, we will misunderstand and misrecognize the spaces of resistance, at the same time that we unwittingly align ourselves against those spaces. Within the last few years there has been growing attention not only to the question of the politics of knowledge, but to the politics of thinking about power and resistance. However, at the same time that there is renewed concern to identify and even celebrate resistance, there is similar concern to avoid the pitfalls of romantic affiliation against forces that we resist far too often in vain.

The articles in this volume consider the cultural dynamics of colonial conquest, the cultural forms and effects of colonial rule, and the colonial cultures of response and resistance among both colonized and colonizer. These questions are not altogether new, but there are significant differences from earlier discourses on colonialism, particularly in the social sciences, and the way most of us pose them here. In taking the domain of culture as the locus of influence and change, for example, we signify an important shift in concern. A conference or volume such as this one as recently as ten years ago would, in all probability, have focused on the economic and political impact of colonialism, and would likely have used the term *imperialism* rather than colonialism. In earlier academic days, scholars interested in the cultural implications of colonialism would have concentrated on elites, been drenched in modernization theory, and preoccupied with the elegantly framed tensions between the pulls of tradition and the inexorable rush of modernity as experienced by the key political-intellectual figures of the Third World: Gandhi, Nkrumah, or Sukarno.

Clearly, we now mean something different by the term *culture,* and clearly we have serious reservations about the assumptions of modernization theory. Clearly also, when we take culture as a site of intervention, dislocation, and struggle, we seek to identify and analyze a new set of issues and problems. Influenced by such variable figures as Marx, Benjamin, Gramsci, Williams, Foucault, Derrida, and Said, we take colonialism as an important subject in its own right as well as a metaphor for the subtle relationship between power and knowledge, between culture and control. To invert the phrase I used earlier, many of us now believe that colonialism is what culture is all about. And if this is so, there are grounds to suggest that the interdisciplinary study of colonial histories and societies provides the basis for major theoretical advances in the elaboration of a new, critical "historical anthropology."[5]

In part, this volume is meant to explore the cultural character of colonial influences; in part, we mean to critique those forms of colonialist self-legitimation that take us beyond earlier agendas having to do with the exploration of forms of economic exploitation or political domination. These objectives are not specific to those of us working on colonialism, and we have all been influenced by a wide range of theoretical shifts in the academy as well as by a heightened concern about our own implication in various forms of academic neocolonialism. Thus, for example, some of us attempt to explore the fact that our new "cultural" concerns have a lot to do with the recuperation of forms of experience that have rarely been the subject matter or legitimating conceit of academic discourses. Feminist concerns and theoretical perspectives, for example, have encouraged academics to attend to certain of these other worlds not only because they are there but because "history" has too often been defined by public events and political pasts, domains of experience from which women (or various subaltern groups) have typically been excluded. In what is perhaps a parallel phenomenon, current concerns of postcolonial intellectuals (e.g., Said, Spivak, Nandy, Bhabha, Rushdie, and before them Fanon, Cesaire, and Memmi) draw our attention to the cultural dislocations brought about by colonialism for both the colonized and the colonizers.[6]

There are no doubt many dangers in this conjuncture. For example, there are serious consequences in taking colonialism as our only subject, as such a move can make us ignore precolonial history, or various aspects of change that might have little to do with the structures of colonialism or the colonial subject except in so far as that subject has been appropriated by or become accessible to the colonial gaze. As mentioned earlier, the use of colonialism as a general rubric may encourage the view that colonialism is a single, metahistorical formation, rather than a heterogeneous and historically specific set of phenomena. In addition, our move to think about colonialism side by side with culture might make it more difficult to balance the political and economic aspects of social change under and after colonialism with the more subtle cultural and social effects of colonial intervention. Furthermore, although our discourse about colonialism is predicated on our sympathy with (and implication in) the postcolonial predicament, we still write in established Western institutional contexts (from university positions, in *CSSH*); what does this imply about the voice and ground of our own academic and political practices. Equally perplexing is the transnational context in which theories about colonialism, postcolonialism, and cultural studies are generated; what does it mean that Edward Said, or Ranajit Guha and the Subaltern Studies collective of Indian historians, take the very same texts by Gramsci, Foucault, or Williams as fundamental that are recited everywhere else in the Western academy. We ignore at our peril the manifestations of the postcolonial predicament in provincial universities in Asia or Africa where these theorists would all signify elitist forms of exclusion, new Western forms of domination. There are local political and cultural movements that would view poststructuralist critiques with alarm; take, for example, feminist agitations against the revival of sati in India that frequently invoke old colonial texts of moral outrage as supports in their struggle. Even within the discourses of the Western academy, we might ask about the residual disciplinary implications of this study of colonialism; despite all the gestures being made by students of literature toward history and society, or by students of history and society toward textuality and discourse, we still reproduce the division between the humanities and the social sciences in most of our professional activities. These questions proliferate with the fury of colonial discourses themselves. They provided the basis for lively and often impassioned discussion during the conference that spawned this volume.

If, in the present intellectual climate, it would be absurd to attempt to write anything resembling a master narrative of colonial history, the same is also true for the conference in which the articles published here were discussed. But there were certain recurrent concerns that echo the questions I have raised, that helped produce my sense of what this collection of articles might signify. There was deep and abiding concern about the political economy of academic production, so much so that one session was characterized by a member of the audience as an "orgy of reflexivity."[7] Perhaps the basis for all this worry was that participants felt somehow that it had become not only safe but profitable to pontificate about the horrors and the excesses of colonial power. Was there yet another form of neocolonialism operating within the conference itself, where the surplus value of colonial terror could be marketed in the specious currency of the academy. And, in what is a refrain common in many academy conferences of late, was there not extraordinary delusion in the exclusive academic reference and provenance of our debates. Some worried that the only real politics in the conference were academic politics.

At the same time, the diversification and internationalization of the academy, as well as the sense that colonialism was not yet completely dead, not merely a convenient foil for the displacement of our own politics, kept drawing the discussion out of its moments of reflexive anxiety. There was general recognition that the historiography of colonialism had been reanimated by critical concerns from a wide variety of academic disciplines, from postcolonial intellectual voices both within and without the academy, and by movements such as the Subaltern Studies collective of Indian historians. Indeed, even the attention we gave to the cultural dislocations of colonialism, what has been called the "postcolonial condition," was rooted in a discursive energy that had clearly penetrated and unsettled the normal concerns of the Western academy, even capturing headlines, as in the recent controversy over Rushdie's *Satanic Verses.* In the end, it came as something of a shock to realize that some of the Subaltern historians were, in many ways, simply reproducing the history of social history in the West, recuperating silenced voices and excluded histories by extending the net of the [once] "new social history" from Europe and the United States to India.

This is not to say that the East is bound forever to play the farce to Europe's tragedy, repeating in tragicomic mimesis the historical failures of the West. The voices of the postcolonial world are new; the challenges to the normal procedures of academic reason are genuine; the politics of academic engagement with changing contours and contexts of academic production are different than they have ever been before. Furthermore, in the conference, we were all aware of how provisional and partial was our capacity to understand the collisions of context and reference that came with our new concerns. The fact, for example, that Subaltern historians must wrestle with the multiple social histories of nationalism in the context of colonialism immediately changes the character of the historiographic enterprise surrounding the study of the rise of the nation. And, while Subaltern Studies history may seem simply like more good social history to some in the Western academy, in India today it is often seen as antinationalist history. Nationalism is not simply a movement that took place to gain freedom, it is a system for organizing the past that depends upon certain narratives, assumptions, and voices, and that continues to have important stakes throughout the social and political order. In India, at least, the politics of the academy can never be separated from politics outside its own institutional confines.

Thus, throughout the conference, we were constantly told to put things back into context, at the same time that we were provided with example after example that deconstructed the conceit of context. We were impressed with the need to interrogate the politics of writing, when both the questions we were writing about and the larger politics of scholarship itself seemed constantly to overtake the projects—individual and collective—that had been brought together in the conference room. We kept trying to find ways to rescue subaltern voices among the colonized, only to find that colonialism was about the history by which categories such as the colonizer as well as the colonized, elite as well as subaltern, became established and deployed. We found that, in examining the cultural effects of colonial rule in various parts of the globe, we constantly confronted the repressive character both of all cultural regimes and of any attempt to normalize the domain of culture itself. Order and control, whether in a specifically colonial situation or in a variety of postcolonial contexts, were seen as the effects of the excess of power, and this image of excess seemed always to bleed into our sense of what culture was all about.

We also found that, when thinking about power, it was always necessary to think about resistance. This was so for different reasons. Some felt that attending to resistance was the only way to counter complicity in power's complacent self-representations; others felt more utopian forms of identification with the struggles of all resistance movements. But the question was inevitably sharply debated. Seeing resistance where previously it had not been recognized, as some among us urged, following the suggestions of James Scott, seemed perilously romantic to some and dangerously unpolitical to others.[8] And while not wishing to align our scholarship with power itself, many of us feared that the glorification of resistance trivialized the all-pervasive character of power, particularly in colonial regimes. During these discussions, it became clear that one of the problems with the selection of the essays in the volume had to do with the absence of any explicit consideration of nationalism. Nationalism was recognized both to have constituted the single most important site of resistance to colonialism, at the same time that it provides the most salient demonstration of the power of colonialism to reproduce itself, spawning myriad clones in new nations throughout the postcolonial world that have often been as repressive as the worst colonial regime.

And so we debated the narratives of colonialism—the narratives we encountered in archives or fieldwork, the narratives we produced: the narratives of colonial tea parties, police stations, marriage regulations, museum exhibitions, legal and property systems, revenue and labor policies, plantation regimes, atrocity reports, and historiographies. In reflecting about the writing of our histories and our anthropologies, often in having to confront writings that we thought we had left behind years before, we ultimately recognized the power of writing, the force of representation. The conference did not end with despair about powerlessness, but a recognition that if we built our own narratives around the aura of power, we had to accept the consequences. At the very least, we all agreed that our narratives operated in the spaces we could open up between power and resistance, between scholarship and critique, between colonialism as a historical moment and the academy as our institutional context, between culture as a sign of difference and culture as a project of control, between Ann Arbor in May and the postcolonial world that we came from and went to. We agreed that, if there was a politics in what we were writing about, there was certainly a politics in how we were writing about it.

When Europeans in the sixteenth century wrote and published accounts of their many overseas voyages, they not only described the newly discovered and rediscovered lands of America, Asia, and Africa, they also provided a highly significant and influential representation of Europe itself. One striking element in at least some of these writings is the clear emergence of the nation as the principal actor in Europe's expansion. And if the nation realized itself through travel, it also had its origins in empire. As the nation imagined itself through texts, maps, and consuming desires both for foreign adventures and distant goods, the colonial era began. Taking Camões's Lusiads and Hakluyt's Voyages as its main texts, the article by Richard Helgerson examines this originary moment for European nation-ness.

In the Lusiads, Helgerson sees an attempt to deny the commercial identity of Portuguese expansion. Camões uses epic form to express the ethos and to serve the interests of the feudal aristocracy. By bringing merchants into the nation and gentlemen into the trade, Hakluyt tries rather to reconcile opposing class interests. He combines epic fragments and commercial letters in a collection that grants comparable status to each. The result of this representational project is a new respect for merchants in a national community that comes to define itself in economic terms, a community that by the eighteenth century can appropriate even the Lusiads as an "epic of commerce." This commercial turn does not, however, establish a final interpretive settlement. Indeed, at the height of the "new imperialism" of the nineteenth century, Hakluyt's Voyages was itself renamed "the prose epic of the modern English nation." It is by such namings and renamings that the ideological project of the nation proceeds. Rather than being repositories of fixed and retrievable meanings, Helgerson argues that these texts have historical lives; that the texts are scenes of contestation—sites of cultural production and reproduction.

European expansion also encoded older justifications for travel and conquest. Colonial power sought not only natural resources and strategic positions, but also native souls. The colonial project of missionization and conversion is the site for Vicente Rafael's nuanced discussion of Christianity in early Tagalog colonial society. For the Spaniards, conversion represented the ultimate form of conquest. To convert was to submit to God's dominion and, by implication, to a host of mediating authorities, including the church and its priests. But even as submission through belief was totalizing, belief itself depended upon a range of understandings, communicated and organized by translation. And in translation, conversion was not always what it seemed.

Rafael documents what was lost and gained in translation, concentrating on the reiterative moments of confession that inscribed conversion into the routine relations between colonizers and colonized. Tagalog subjects maintained certain meanings, resisting Spanish concepts of conversion and perpetuating indigenous concerns to mediate authority and hierarchy through relations of exchange and debt. Rafael argues that Tagalog conversion "involved confession without 'sin,'... submission without translation." Thus the translation of power enabled the hollowing out of authoritative claims, the resistance of translation made possible newly contested and provisional forms of submission. The weapons of the weak[9] were deployed through the slippage of words and meanings in a colonial field of power relations.

The question of resistance comes up more directly in Michael Adas's consideration of avoidance and confrontation in precolonial and colonial Southeast Asia. Adas's important article, the first of the articles reprinted here to be published, proposed that there were a variety of forms of resistance in precolonial regimes that provided peasants with strategies and opportunities to simultaneously resist authority and fashion some degree of control over their lives. Adas was concerned to show that there was more to resistance than rebellion, that peasantries were anything but passive when they engaged in such quotidian acts as flight, foot-dragging, and pilfering. Adas further argued that some of these modes of protest were distinctly suited to precolonial political regimes, where limited bureaucratic resources for control and surveillance were additionally weakened by underpopulation and the small scale and reach of much political power. Colonial rule both led to structural changes that made some of the modes of protest more difficult and introduced more pervasive and intrusive forms of state power. Direct confrontation became increasingly necessary, and costly, as colonial state apparatuses began to bear down with new military might on the peasants as producers of revenue for colonial expansion and consolidation.

Adas has written an addendum to his article for this volume, in which he questions the sharp and sudden distinction he once made between precolonial and colonial regimes, and addresses a more general concern about the focus on everyday resistance that has been generated by the important work of James Scott during the last decade. This last concern, a principal topic of discussion during the conference, raises a larger issue about the relation between definitions of resistance and understandings of power. While it seems clear that the expansion of the category of resistance to include forms of avoidance as well as a whole range of indirectly articulated expressions of discontent, disbelief, and refusal has been of tremendous importance in moving us beyond what Adas correctly characterizes as the "somewhat romanticized vision of the peasantry as a class prone to confrontational protest and highly susceptible to mobilization in revolutionary movements," some of the participants in the conference were concerned that perhaps the pendulum had swung too far. Has resistance become a category that perversely reinscribes a bourgeois commitment to individual agency instead of dismantling power itself, as is often claimed? If Gramsci's theory of hegemony may put too much stress on the need for consent, Foucault's proposals about discursive power dispel the need to find either consent or its opposite. Though some found this latter view incontestable, others continued to worry about the consequences, epistemological as well as political, of adhering to any totalizing theory of power.

Nevertheless, there are clearly times and spaces when power itself appears as a totalization, perhaps nowhere more saliently than in what Michael Taussig has called "the space of death." Taussig's moving tale of torture on the rubber plantations of the Putumayo suggests the limits of classical political economy in explaining the heart of darkness, wherein "rational" explanations and polite incomprehension seem equally out of place. Taussig seeks to turn the hallucinatory quality of accounts of total horror against itself, to find the appropriate tone for a poetics of subversion. In the end, the article moves uneasily at an angle to the narratives that "are in themselves evidence of the process whereby a culture of terror was created and sustained."

If the space of death alerts us to those moments when rationality is most helpless, the culture of terror reminds us that culture consists of webs of meanings that may be saturated with violence and fear. Torture is practiced on the bodies of the Indians, but it is also disseminated and embodied through gossip, rumor, hearsay, and narration. The descriptions of torture reveal excesses that turn the projections of wildness and savagery back from the jungle and its inhabitants onto the torturers themselves. Culture is seen both as horrific excess and as societal self-fashioning, for the history that constructed the categories of rational and wild, civilized and savage tells Conrad's story over and over again: the heart of darkness is at once the collective psyche of the colonizer and the totalizing culture of domination enabled by colonial rule. Thus, Conrad's craft becomes Taussig's concern, for in writing about torture, even more so in writing about the writing of torture, it becomes increasingly difficult to write against torture.

If the excess of colonial rule seems most apparent in stories of torture, India has traditionally provided counternarratives of imperial bequest. Britain provided technological infrastructures such as the telegraphs and the railways that lasted well beyond the "transfer of power."[10] Even more saliently, Britain installed the institutions of administration and law that imparted the capacity for self-governance as well as the necessary basis for modern, democratic civil society. Law not only provided the means for the regulation of order and the protection of civil rights, it underwrote the establishment of a new rule of property, with private ownership and public markets in land. Surely this legacy provides a different, even redeeming, sense of colonial history.

The article by Dirks demonstrates, however, that the introduction of law in colonial India was by no means a completely enlightened affair. Law established a discursive arena in which the contradiction of colonial rule—for example, that while property was introduced, a "free market" was both carefully regulated and massively constrained, or that while the old regime was dismantled, political concerns led to the maintenance of theatrical forms of kingship and truncated versions of tradition—were allowed to flourish. Even the British inability to control the continuous "alienation" of lands by local lords unable to adjust to new standards of management and rule was converted, through legal process, into yet another colonial opportunity to sustain the fiction of its own powerlessness.

Dirks argues more generally that colonial discourse was effective precisely because discourse was not mere language. Rather, he suggests that discourse cannot be separated from the conditions under which truth is regimented and revealed, conditions that are imbricated in and produced by the institutional structures of everyday life. In the case of India, these institutional structures were fundamentally changed by colonial rule. Paradoxically, these structures often changed most dramatically precisely when colonial discourse portrayed things as unchanged. Dirks thus also argues against recent trends in Indian historiography that view colonialism as far less important than the spread of world capitalism or the gradual transformation of the world under a set of universalizing global processes.

If capitalism cannot explain all of colonial history, it is nonetheless crucial to look at the ways in which colonialism introduced capitalist forms, for example, a wage economy, into a variety of colonized locales. Fred Cooper, in an article written specifically for this volume, exposes some of the contradictions involved in the colonization of time by colonial power in Kenya, focusing on British attempts to induce African workers to adapt to the work rhythms of industrial capitalism. In concentrating on dockworkers, strikes, and changing perceptions of different kinds of labor discipline, the article decisively dispenses with any fixed sense of how labor was understood by colonized workers and organized by colonial capitalists. Cooper is careful not to contrast precolonial and colonial modes of work too starkly, making clear that colonial rule worked to maximize control over certain portions of the African work force at the same time that it used contradictions in local economic structures and imperatives to curtail African resistance. In fact, Cooper demonstrates that this process involved the mobilization of a new form of colonial discourse that separated the capitalist domain more sharply than ever before from the undisciplined work culture outside it. Thus, academic accounts stressing the dualism of the African economy are seen to reflect colonial transformations rather than precolonial realities.

Dualism has been one of the core words of the postcolonial development regime, and reflects yet another of colonialism's most dramatic legacies: development itself. David Ludden's article, also written for this volume, examines the way in which the idea of development emerged out of colonial concerns that the state monitor production, collect revenue, assemble data, and manage the economy. Development was thus linked in instrumental ways to the growth of the modern state, the preoccupations of colonial rule, and a general commitment to economic progress. Perhaps most critically, within the development regime, agriculture becomes a science of production rather than a site for social relations. In the end, Ludden argues, development has become such a secure category of the modern that it has disguised its own colonial roots as well as its total dependence on state centralized power and the hegemony of the West.

If studies of law, labor, and agriculture in colonial theaters reveal the importance of discourse and the construction of new categories, the examination of colonial exhibitions by Timothy Mitchell provides the basis to scrutinize the precise forms of representation and knowledge elaborated by the colonial order. Mitchell writes that the West put the Orient on display in various European exhibitions as the West's great "external reality." Mitchell demonstrates that these exhibitions epitomized a developing Western experience of order and truth, thus linking the colonial project with the development of modern techniques of representation and meaning. Once again, colonialism is not mere epiphenomenon, here securing modern epistemes along with the natural resources and labor power that have previously exhausted explanations of colonial exploitation.

Mitchell stresses that Orientalist knowledge was markedly pictorial. Noting, as one example, that Edward Lane, author of *Account of the Manners and Customs of the Modern Egyptians* (1835), began his career not as a writer but as a professional engraver, he cites an Egyptian who wrote, "Every year that passes, you see thousands of Europeans traveling all over the world, and everything they come across they make a picture of." But both pictures and accounts seem to have been always already composed, elaborating earlier pictures and citing previous citations with the full hubris of colonial omniscience. In the World Exhibition held in Paris in 1889, a group of Egyptian Orientalists were invited to view themselves as they really were, and were thereby humiliated at the same time they learned the certain limits of their participation in any forum of Orientalists in the age of colonial domination. The modern duality between representation and reality seems to have depended on a colonial world in which it was clear who was the master and who the slave. Perhaps we can now better understand why Derrida has defined metaphysics as "the white mythology which reassembles and reflects the culture of the West."

If the relation between colonizers and colonized can be likened to Hegel's division of the world into masters and slaves, it is also clear that colonialism played a critical role in the development of class and gender hierarchies within the world of the colonizers themselves. Ann Stoler argues for an anthropology of colonialism in which we trace the ways in which the category of the colonizer was produced through the colonial encounter. Stoler suggests, on the basis of her work on plantation culture in Sumatra, the importance of colonial history in the actual creation and specification of new classes and constituencies within the colonial elite, as well as important shifts in the meaning and use both of gender and of sexual politics.

Stoler examines the historical backdrop of a colonial world in which European plantation employees were either prevented or discouraged from marrying, instead engaging in concubinary relations with Javanese women. Only after 1920 were these regulations relaxed, and white women incorporated into a new regime of civilized European colonial society. Although European women have typically been accused of being a conservative force in colonial situations, Stoler demonstrates that these women were imported precisely to enforce racial boundaries and police the European community. Concerns about racial purity sometimes conflicted against, and at other times augmented, concerns about poor and ill-bred Europeans, who posed a constant threat to the superior self-image of Europeans and the consequent elision of class differences among the colonizers. Sexual politics were thus defined in relation to the exclusion and enclosure of the colonial categories of race and class.

Taussig, Mitchell, and Stoler all show how colonialism was not some historical process that simply took place in colonial locales, but rather was fundamental to the construction of modern selves and societies in the metropole as well as the colony, constantly reiterating the story told by Helgerson. Prakash shows this to be so for the way we write histories of the world as well. He begins by asking how we might write histories of the Third World that somehow escape from the binary oppositions that, since Said's *Orientalism*, have been recognized to have constructed most such histories in the past. In particular, Prakash proposes a postfoundationalist approach to the writing of history, based on a critique of the way in which Indian historiography has always relied upon certain foundational categories and procedures: for example, the nation, civilization, or class. Prakash has proposed that a post-Orientalist historiography "visualizes modern India, for example, in relationships and processes that have constructed contingent and unstable identities," thereby displacing "the categories framed in and by that history." Prakash praises the work of historians in the Subaltern Studies collective in regard to their disruption of colonialist and nationalist essentializations of Indian civilization or nationality, but questions their "resurrection of culture and tradition as an originary ground for contestation." Post-Orientalist historiography, he suggests, must instead "take the forms of knowledge, culture, and 'traditions' canonized by colonial and hegemonic Western discourses as issues of inquiry."

In taking Said as the benchmark for current critical historical and anthropological writing about the Third World, Prakash and the rest of the authors in this volume do not take Said as the last word. First, the culture in the title of this volume is not the culture of Western literary studies, but rather the congeries of belief, value, assumption, and habitus identified by anthropology. Even if, as I suggested earlier, anthropology and its study of culture can be linked to the history of colonialism, from the perspective of the Western academy, anthropology does genuinely democratize and universalize (through the recognition of difference) the Arnoldian assumption that culture is a privileged domain of human expression. Second, the authors in this volume all assume that Orientalism has been as subject to change, contest, and instability as Prakash's postfoundational sense of Indian historiography. Indeed, it has only been because of this contingent historicity that Orientalism—as a body of scholarship, as a colonial attitude, and as a Western or modern belief system—has itself been implicated in the complex and contradictory history of colonialism. As Fanon enunciated with particular clarity, Orientalism and its own Western self-fashioning has been as dependent on the colonial encounter as the constructed verities of the East. Nevertheless, our revisionist sensibility takes from Said the conviction that this encounter was framed by and riddled in the fundamental fact about both colonialism and Orientalism: domination.

But domination never occurs outside history, and domination is never so totalizing as to be secured without continual struggle, contest, and the will to mastery. Thus, Orientalism's history is what explains Orientalism's power; it was only because colonial rule and attitudes changed that Orientalist knowledge, although it never directly reflected the brute reality of an Orient outside relations of power, could both facilitate colonial rule and be implicated in the production of Orientalist effects. India as a society in which history was irrelevant and in which caste as a religious system explained most everything became "true" because of the specific collaboration of knowledge and power that took place in the context of colonial rule.

And so colonialism remade the world. Neither Europe nor the Third World, neither colonizers nor colonized, would have come into being without the history of colonialism. As this volume makes clear, the effects of colonialism are both more thorough and more disguised—at once all-embracing and yet often intangible—because of the ways in which the cultural predicates and categories of our world have been reshaped through colonial encounters. Perhaps we can only fully appreciate Forster's dramatic vision of the colonial world now, in the aftermath of colonialism, when he supposed it would be possible to engage in genuine human intercourse across colonial categories. But once etched by hundreds of years of history, the world is slow to revert to its previous form. The postcolonial world is one in which we may live after colonialism but never without it. Colonialism continues to live on in ways that perhaps we have only begun to recognize.

This volume reflects and represents a moment of struggle in the human sciences, a moment when, as scholars, we are attending to the extraordinary dislocations of colonialism for our own senses of self and society.[11] As we look back on a colonial world, we look out on a world where colonialism continues to have profound effects. Despite decolonization, certain destinies and identities seem fixed, while others seem chaotic, disorderly, unfixed. Colonialism is coming back to haunt "new nations," where shifting identities and precarious polities are anchored against the modern by the reinvention of forms of tradition that too often clearly betray the traces of a colonial past. Colonialism has also not vanished from former colonial powers, where debates over nationality and multiculturalism mask increasing anxiety over the categories and identities of race, language, culture, and morality.[12] The postcolonial predicament carries its history with it, inverting Marx by making new histories out of old farces.

NOTES

The conference on Colonialism and Culture would not have happened without the invitation, encouragement, and inspiration of Raymond Grew who, as editor of *Comparative Studies in Society and History* (*CSSH*), had already played an important role in many of these articles. I am also grateful to Nicola Beisel, who worked hard to make the conference possible in a great variety of ways. I am indebted to all the participants, who were persuaded at short notice to attend and defend articles that had already been published in the journal. David Ludden and Fred Cooper both wrote new articles for the conference. Richard Helgerson, who did not attend the conference, graciously has allowed me to publish an article here that he previously delivered at a workshop on a similar theme that I organized at the California Institute of Technology in the spring of 1987. I am also grateful to Ruth Behar, Fred Cooper, Geoff Eley, and Roger Rouse for agreeing to participate in the conference as discussants. This volume, and this introduction in particular, owes much to all the participants in the conference, colleagues and students alike, who made the gathering one of the most memorable of its kind that any of us ever attended. I should add here that all the participants were invited to revise their articles if they so chose. Timothy Mitchell, Gyan Prakash, and I revised the basic text of our articles; Michael Adas added an addendum. The articles by Vicente Rafael, Ann Stoler, and Michael Taussig are published here as they were initially published in the pages of *CSSH*.

    1. I am not suggesting that Forster fully anticipates later critiques of colonialism, least of all critiques from a variety of colonized subject positions. A careful reading of the text would question the way in which "India" is permitted to speak through Aziz—the exemplary educated native radicalized by exposure to the contradictions of civil society in a colonial situation. Further, Aziz is a Muslim, who seems to be able (for Forster) to speak for "India" as a nascent nation at least in part because of the glories of Mughal political history; Godbole—the representative Hindu—speaks for an entirely different India, the Orientalized India of the inscrutable, religious, apolitical East.

2. See, for example, J. Gallagher, G. Johnson, and A. Seal, eds., *Locality, Province, and Nation* (Cambridge: Cambridge University Press, 1973).

3. See Ranajit Guha, "Dominance without Hegemony and Its Historiography," *Subaltern Studies* 6 (Delhi: Oxford University Press, 1989).

4. See my *The Hollow Crown* (Cambridge: Cambridge University Press, 1987) and "Castes of Mind," *Representations,* no. 37 (Winter 1992).

5. The identification of "colonial discourse" as an important site of study has been of immeasurable value in opening up the concerns of literary studies in recent years under the important influence of writers such as Edward Said, Homi Bhabha, and Gayatri Chakravorty Spivak. But the limits of this enterprise correspond to the boundaries that continue to separate most of the work in literary studies from what historians and anthropologists can do; this volume seeks to show what can be accomplished when historical anthropology takes up the theoretical challenges of critical theory. There are a number of precedents for this enterprise, perhaps most conspicuously the work of Bernard Cohn (see *An Anthropologist among the Historians and Other Essays* [Delhi: Oxford University Press, 1987]).

6. See Robert Young, *White Mythologies: Writing History and the West* (London: Routledge, 1990).

7. The source of this phrase was Geoff Eley.

8. James Scott was invited to attend the conference, but was unfortunately unable to do so.

9. The phrase, of course, is James Scott's.

10. The official British characterization of India's independence; as Peter Fay has pointed out, the phrase conveniently conceals India's nationalist struggle for independence.

11. I am not using colonialism here in the broad sense that is employed in some literary or cultural studies circles, that is, to stand as a metaphor for cultural domination based on categories of ethnicity, race, and so forth. As informative as these analogies are, they have a tendency to appropriate the historical experience of colonialism for specific contemporary concerns within the United States or England, thus ironically reproducing certain operations of colonialism itself.

12. See, for example, Talal Asad, "Multiculturalism and British Identity in the Wake of the Rushdie Affair," *Politics and Society* 18, no. 4 (December 1990): 455–80.

Camões, Hakluyt, and the Voyages of Two Nations

Richard Helgerson

Everyone knows what Columbus did in 1492, but not everyone remembers what he did in 1493. He wrote an account of his voyage and made it available for publication. In the course of the next several centuries, just about as many voyages were written and published as were made. And the written voyages were scarcely less important in the transformation of Europe and the rest of the world than were the actual ones. As Daniel Defert has remarked, "In this literature Europe becomes conscious of itself, writes its own description, and understands itself increasingly as the guiding principle of a planetary process, no longer simply a region of the world."[1] But the Europe that knew itself in this way was, by this very fact, already significantly unlike the late fifteenth-century Europe from which Columbus had originally sailed. All through the centuries from 1492 to the European empires of the nineteenth century and on into the postcolonial world of the present, Europe has undergone a constant, if uneven, process of practical and ideological adaptation to the new conditions discovered or created by its own expansionist activities. But never has that adaptation been more rapid, more intense, or more far-reaching than in the first century following Columbus's voyage. And in that period, the single, most important feedback mechanism, the most important source of information about the newly discovered and rediscovered worlds, and the most important body of self-representations of Europeans in the act of encountering and exploiting those distant regions was the printed voyage. In these books, Europe first saw the other, but here it also first saw itself interacting with that other and thus first saw itself *as* an other—other, that is, than it had been or had thought of itself as being before.

My subject is this process of self-representation and self-alienation in two major European texts of the latter part of the sixteenth century: the great Portuguese national poem, *The Lusiads* by Luís de Camões, an epic account of Vasco da Gama's first voyage to India, and Richard Hakluyt's massive, three-volume gathering of the *Principal Navigations of the English Nation*. What sets these two works apart from most earlier sixteenth-century travel narrratives is the featured place each gives to the nation. As Hakluyt's title suggests, the English nation is the prime actor in his book, as the Portuguese nation—ancient Lusitania—is the main actor in Camões's. Whatever else they may be doing, both Hakluyt's *English Voyages* and *The Lusiads* are actively engaged in the ideological construction of the nation. This in itself is a project of major significance and is, I would argue, inextricably linked to the process of European expansion. One cannot, of course, say what would have happened had there been no New World or had the Europeans not discovered it. But it is, I think, clear that, as things did happen, European state and nation formation occurred in relation to and as an effect of Europe's expansion. In that process, books like *The Lusiads* and the *English Voyages* had their part. What interests me in this essay is, however, less their common participation in early modern nation building than the marked differences between the two in their representation of the nation, for those differences reveal something of the profound ideological dislocation entailed by Europe's nationalist and expansionist remaking of itself.

Class, Nation, and Camões

"As armas e os barões...."[2] These opening words of *The Lusiads* announce the poem's genre and its subject. This is to be a Virgilian epic concerned with military accomplishment. But Camões has significantly altered Virgil's formula. "Arms and the men" takes the place of "arms and the man"—"Arma virumque." Despite the narrative centrality of Vasco da Gama, *The Lusiads* has no single hero. Instead, it celebrates the deeds of a nation. There is, however, a peculiar and distinguishing exclusiveness to Camões's concept of the nation. For him, Portugal is identified with its *barões*—not its "men" or even its "heroes," though the word is often translated in both ways, but its "noblemen," its "barons." In choosing this term and making it plural, Camões enforces both the aristocratic and the nationalist ideology already strongly associated with the classical epic. But that very emphasis betrays a tension, an uncertainty imperfectly masked by assertiveness.

Camões had good reason for uncertainty. Despite his claims, Gama's voyage does not quite satisfy the requirements of either class ideology or literary decorum. A classical epic, as the Renaissance understood it, was, above all, a poem of war. And the feudal nobility was just as firmly identified as a class devoted to war. But, as Voltaire objected, Gama never fights.[3] The arms are there. They are often mentioned, occasionally shown off, even fired once or twice. But except for a minor skirmish, they are never used in battle. "I came, I saw, I went home again" might have been Gama's summary of his experience. So crucial was that coming and going to the Portuguese empire as it developed in the seven decades between Gama's voyage and the publication of Camões's poem that Camões could hardly have put any other event at the center of his narrative. But still the very act of representing the Portuguese nation in an epic poem centered on an essentially peaceful, if hazardous, maritime voyage of discovery raised a potentially troubling question. Is this a properly heroic action, an action worthy of a class devoted to war? Is the nation that takes its identity from such an action a truly noble nation?

One way to deal with this problem, the way adopted nearly a century later by Milton in *Paradise Lost*, would have been to write a heroic poem against the ideology of the heroic poem, to turn the genre against itself, to sing a "better fortitude...unsung." This Camões does not do. Though he talks no less than Milton of his rivalry with the ancient poets and of the rivalry of his heroes with theirs, his "outro valor" (1.3) is not fundamentally "other." It is, rather, the same valor enacted on a larger stage. In keeping with this conservative intent, Camões attempts rather to conceal than to expose and exploit the difference between generic expectation and the story he has to tell. Gama's first voyage may have been marked by no significant battle, but it followed from many battles, the several centuries of heroic warfare by which Portugal was reclaimed as a Christian kingdom from the Moors and retained its autonomy from the encroachment of its Castilian neighbors, and it was itself followed by a no less glorious series of battles in the Indian Ocean and the Far East. The greater part of four of *The Lusiads*'s ten cantos is given over to the recital of these events, and Gama's involvement as narrator, listener, and even participant helps divert attention from the incongruous peacefulness of his first voyage.

That incongruity does, however, hint at a still more fundamental suppression, a more significant refusal to acknowledge what the poem and the poet cannot help but know. What both know—what we all know—is that the Portuguese sailed around the Cape of Good Hope and across the Indian Ocean in search of a more direct access to the much-desired wealth of the Orient. For that purpose, war was initially not needed, and even subsequently it remained subordinate to a mercantile motive. It is this "base" motive, this quest for "vile reward" (1.10) that Camões will not acknowledge, whether in his heroes or in himself.

Rumors of wealth do nevertheless echo through the poem. Again and again we hear of the gold and spices, the medicinal drugs, and precious jewels "que produze o aurífero Levante" (2.4). Indeed, in its descriptions of Calicut (7.35, 41), Jiddah (9.3), and Malacca (10.123), *The Lusiads* goes so far as to present the outline of a theory that would equate long-distance trade with communal well-being, suggesting (perhaps subversively) in two of those instances that trade has "ennobled" the city that engages in it.[4] Clearly the hope of such wealth and such nobility is what makes the Portuguese so eager to reach the Indian coast. Others, even in the poem, have no difficulty discerning this motive. The natives of Mombasa suppose Gama seeks "the rich merchandise of the golden East" (2.4), and the merchants of Jiddah recognize in him a rival for their Indian trade (9.4). But these perceptions are not shared by the Portuguese themselves. If commercial gain is their goal, they never say so, nor does their poet. Instead, they repeatedly and insistently proffer a set of quite different motives, motives more compatible with the crusading ethos of a Christian *barão*. Gama and his companions voyage in search not of wealth but rather of honor, conquest, and the opportunity to spread the Christian faith.

The closest Camões comes to allowing the expression of a commercial interest occurs in a passage so hedged in with qualification and denial that it deserves some particular attention. At his first meeting with the Zamorin, the ruler of Calicut, Gama offers a "commercial" pact, a treaty of "peace and friendship" (7.62). Whatever the historical Gama may have meant (the passage comes from Camões's chronicle sources), can the heroic, antimercantile Gama of this poem really mean it? There is reason for thinking he does not. The offer contradicts not only the general spirit of the poem but also both the narrator's flat statement earlier in the same canto that the Portuguese have come "to plant the law of Christ and to give new customs and a new king" (7.15). But if he does not mean it, why does he say it? Is his offer merely a diplomatic lie, like the earlier lie he told the King of Malindi to avoid leaving his ship? I don't think so. It is rather a contradiction forced on Camões by the contradictions in his ideology and his material. Both the facts of history and the logic of his narrative require that Gama meet the Zamorin. When they meet, Gama must have something to say about why he is there. Unprepared to fight (and in history not having fought), he can hardly announce his "true" reasons: conquest and conversion. So Camões lets him say what the historical Gama is supposed to have said and then does what he can to remove the force of that saying. He has Gama conclude his description of the trade agreement that is to bind the Portuguese king and the Zamorin with the unlikely but ideologically saving claim that "yours will be the profit, his the glory will be found" (7.62).[5]

The word *profit—proveito—*is as strongly negative a term in Camões's lexicon as *glory* and *fame* are positive. Desire for profit grows in the "base heart" (8.59) of the heathen ruler; the noble-hearted Portuguese seek only fame. Or at least in the ideal time of *The Lusiads,* a time less historical than mythic, they sought only fame. When, however, Camões considers his own age and his own experience, the sharp distinction between "them" and "us" breaks down. "No more, my Muse, no more," he concludes in Sir Richard Fanshawe's translation,

> . . . my harp's ill strung,
> Heavy, and out of tune, and my voice hoarse:
> And not with singing but to see I've sung
> To a deaf people and without remorse.
> Favor (that wont t'inspire the poet's tongue)
> Our country yields it not, she minds the purse
>   Too much, exhaling from her guilded mud
> Nothing but gross and melancholy blood.[6]

"She minds the purse / Too much." Portugal is overcome by a "gosto da cobiça" (10.145). "Favor," the gratuitous reward characteristic of a noble and courtly society, the reward figured in the Isle of Love to which Venus leads Gama and his men, is denied. Instead, values that Camões never clearly defines but that seem strongly marked by a mercantile spirit have taken over.[7] Intent not merely on representing a Portugal that is, a Portugal that prefers *gloria* to *proveito,* Camões aims to bring such a nation into existence by showing it an ideal image of its heroic and nonmercantile self. From this perspective, his misrepresentation even of the past, his suppression of the commercial motive that directed the Portuguese to the Indies and the Far East, comes to seem a hortatory representation of what should have been and what should be—if, that is, Portugal is to deserve a poet like Camões.

Camões's own densely conflicted subjectivity is the measure of the distance between the actual Portugal and its heroic ideal. In the poem, only the Zamorin, caught between fear of invasion and hunger for profit, possesses a similarly rich and troubled inner life. As for Gama, the poet's surrogate both as narrator of Portuguese history and as recipient of prophetic inspiration, he is as transparent as a ghost. He has no existence apart from the mission of state that fills him.[8] He is brought into his own historical narrative, the account of himself and his nation that he gives the King of Malindi, as a function of a royal proclamation, itself the product of a god-sent dream. A heroic national destiny thus chooses its protagonist all unawares. For Camões it is just the other way around. As numerous passages of complaint and admonition make clear, he must invent from often resisting and unsuitable material a nation that will justify his heroic literary undertaking—an undertaking defined by the ancient antipathy of the epic to commerce.[9]

This, however, is greatly to exaggerate the hold of the past, and particularly of the literary past, on the present. A modern cultural movement, born in the very Italian centers of commerce whose monopolistic control of the eastern trade Portugal was successfully supplanting, was responsible for the renewed prestige of Greek and Roman literary forms. In imitating the ancients, Camões imitated the Italians. "*Os Lusíadas* is," as C. M. Bowra has remarked, "in many ways the epic of Humanism."[10] But in being the epic of humanism, it is also the epic of an intense conflict in cultural values made more intense by the Portuguese expansion. In the course of the sixteenth century, according to the report of the modern economic historian of the Portuguese empire, Vitorino Magalhães-Godinho, "opposition continued without respite between the anticommercial attitude and ideological system on the one hand and the pursuit of profit and the effort to create material goods on the other."[11] On one side Godinho lets us hear the aristocratic archbishop, Dom Frei Bartolomeu, charging that "where there is a crowd of merchants and merchandise, cupidity, the root of all evil, is never absent," and, on the other, the apothecary-adventurer, Tomé Pires, answering that "trading in merchandise is so necessary that without it the world could not go on. It is this that ennobles kingdoms and makes their people great, that ennobles cities, that brings war and peace."[12] Both voices speak in *The Lusiads,* but not with equal strength or authority.

"Of this country," Camões wrote sometime during his lengthy stay in India, "I can tell you it is the mother of corrupt villains and the stepmother of honorable men. For those who throw themselves into the pursuit of money always bob to the surface like inflated bladders, while those who take as their motto 'To arms, Mouriscote' . . . wither before they ripen."[13] Castilian *hidalgism* finds its Portuguese counterpart in the *fidalgism* of a passage like this. The "To arms, Mouriscote"—"à las armas, Mouriscote"—is particularly revealing. Taken from a Spanish chivalric poem, the line points to the nonhumanist literary sources of Camões's aristocratic ideology. Like Cervantes's mad *hidalgo,* the *caveleiro fidalgo* Luís de Camões sees himself and his experience through eyes trained by much reading of chivalric romance, and he projects that vision onto his poem.[14] The romantic tale of the Twelve of England, the perilous encounter with the giant Adamastor, the enchanted visit to the Isle of Love—episodes like these belong rather to the world of Rodomonte, Ruggiero, and Orlando than to that of *pius* Aeneas. In *The Lusiads,* these two worlds, the world of chivalric romance and the world of Roman epic, coalesce to exclude still more powerfully base mercantile cupidity. Literary reminiscence does difficult political work.

When Gama offers the Zamorin the profit of their trade and keeps only the glory for the king of Portugal, he imagines systems of value that never touch. Glory is as clean as a poem, as clean as Gama's transparent self. But in sixteenth-century Portugal things were messier. Overseas trade was a crown monopoly in which both king and nobles participated actively. This monopolistic policy, like Camões's poem, had an exclusionary intent. It kept the middle class weak and allowed the nobility, as Oliveira Marques has written, "to invest their new capital in land, in building . . . and in luxuries. As a result, the feudal structure of the country . . . was not essentially shaken by expansion."[15] Still, the threat of mercantile contamination persisted. The king of Portugal had himself "become a merchant"—a merchant whose commercial identity figured in his very title.[16] After Gama's voyage, kings of Portugal styled themselves lords "of the conquest, navigation, *and traffic* of Ethiopia, Arabia, Persia, and India" ("domin[i] . . . conquistae, navigationis, *et commercii* Aethiopiae, Arabiae, Persiae, atque Indiae"). And the taint of so prevalent an activity inevitably marked the Portuguese people as well. By the early seventeenth century, a French visitor to India could say of them that they were "good merchants and good sailors, and that's all."[17] What a blow such a remark would have been to Camões. But by the time it was made, he had died and Portugal had fallen under the sovereignty of the king of Spain.

The preservation of Portuguese national autonomy, the exclusive identification of the nation with its aristocratic governing class, and the equally exclusive identification of that class with a heroic crusading ethos—these were the prime elements in the ideological program of *The Lusiads*. Many things would have urged this program on Camões: his own class identity, his experience as a soldier and government agent in North Africa, India, and China, the epic and romantic models on which he drew, the centuries of anti-Moorish warfare that had characterized Portugal's history, and the very real menace to class and to nation posed by both Portugal's geographic location and the effects of its rapid and enormous mercantile expansion. Like the other coastal peoples of Iberia—the Galicians, Catalonians, Valencians, and Andalousians—the Portuguese were constantly threatened by Castilian aspiration to peninsular hegemony. But unlike the others, the Portuguese had succeeded in preserving their independence by adopting the warrior mentality of their inland rivals.[18] Or so Camões seems to have thought. That is why he puts such emphasis on the shared crusading zeal of the two Iberian nations *and* on the many wars waged between them.[19] Portugal maintained itself by being more Castilian than the Castilians. But could it continue to do so as the center of a vast commercial empire?

As an extension of intra-Iberian rivalry and of anti-Moorish warfare, Portugal's penetration into the Indian Ocean fits the heroic pattern of its feudal history and thus deserves the epic representation Camões gives it. But as a commercial venture, it undermines the very basis of aristocratic Portuguese self-understanding. And though Camões chooses not to dwell on the simultaneous overseas expansion of Spain, preferring to compare Gama and his Portuguese successors with the heroes of Homer, Virgil, and Ariosto than with Columbus, Cortés, or Pizarro, the vast territorial conquests of the Spanish, their establishment in the New World of a quasi-feudal system of land tenure, and their haughty disdain for trade must have made Portugal's commercial empire seem still less ideologically defensible. The Portuguese had won half the world but lost their own aristocratic souls. Some such suspicion combined with his own unhappy experience in the East, experience that seems to have included open conflict with the Portuguese trading community in Macao, goes far toward explaining why Camões expresses such ambivalence about the seagoing venture that forms the main subject of his poem.

It is in these terms, rather than merely as a conventional moral attack on overweening ambition, that I would read the famous episode of the old man of Restelo who erupts suddenly into the poem at the end of canto 4, just as Gama is departing for India.[20] Though this "reverend father" seems to object to *any* venture in search of fame and is as resolute in his neglect of the mercantile motives of Gama's voyage as is Camões himself, he does make a distinction between the traditional struggle against the neighboring infidels, which he allows, and this new undertaking, which he rejects. And he prophetically mocks that royal title, borne by the kings of Camões's own time, in which, as we have noticed, conquest, navigation, and trade were so compromisingly mixed. "Do you seek," he asks, "an uncertain and unknown fate so that fame will exalt and flatter you, calling you, with extravagant plenty, lord[s] of India, Persia, Arabia, and Ethiopia?" (4.101). Is it really fame itself the old man objects to, or rather this new commercial renown, renown tinged with infamy? When the poet addresses his readers and particularly his king, the difference between the two sources of fame is made clear, as is his preference for one over the other. He passionately attacks the corrupting influence of money and calls, with equal ardor, for renewed war against the Islamic rulers of neighboring North Africa.

Never has a king followed the recommendation of a poet with greater fidelity than King Sebastião followed that of Camões. But then the recommendation may itself have been made with a knowledge of the king's projects. Among the many pressures shaping *The Lusiads* there was also this: *The Lusiads* was written as a courtly poem in search of royal patronage, a poem that fit itself to the tastes of its dedicatee—who, in this case, was already bent on doing precisely what his poet told him to do. In 1578, six years after the publication of Camões's epic, King Sebastião led a great army to destruction on the sands of Alcazarquivir, where Sebastião himself died. Just two years later, after the brief reign of the tubercular Cardinal-King Henrique, Philip II of Spain assumed the Portuguese crown. Not until 1640 did Portugal regain its autonomy, and by then its place as the dominant European power in the Orient had been taken by the Dutch, a nation that was winning its independence from Spain just as Portugal was losing its own independence. In its commercial expansion, republican Holland was, moreover, as eager to suppress all signs of aristocratic identity as Camões had been to suppress the marks of trade. The Dutch avoided territorial acquisition, made little attempt to spread their Protestant faith, called even their de facto colonial administrators "merchants," and produced no epic poem celebrating their overseas accomplishments.[21] They thus exemplify the triumph of those values Camões opposed just as clearly as Don Sebastião does the defeat of those he supported.

This crushing verdict of history has not, however, been ratified by the Portuguese people, who have embraced *The Lusiads* as their national poem—the prime literary representation of who they have been, who they are, and who they should be. Not even Shakespeare's position in the English-speaking world can rival that of Camões in his homeland. Statues of him are everywhere. Streets, squares, and ships are named for him. A national holiday commemorates him. His epic is the one inevitable school text. Illustrations of it decorate hotels and offices. Newspapers and magazines devote extensive space to its discussion. There can be few examples in history of a poet or of a poem more intimately linked with the identity of a nation than Camões and *The Lusiads* have been with that of Portugal.[22] Through the dark decades of subjection to Spain and the long centuries of colonial rule in Africa, Asia, and South America, the Portuguese were sustained and inspired by Camões's vision of their heroic destiny—a vision that even in 1572, when the poem was first published, blatantly contradicted the reality of its author's experience.

Commodity and Vent

Camões died on June 10, 1580. Philip II became king of Portugal two months later. Anticipating both events, Camões wrote, "All will see that so dear was my country that I was content to die not only in, but with it."[23] But as one career ended, another began. In England, the younger Richard Hakluyt responded to Portugal's loss of autonomy with his first surviving work, "A Discourse of the Commodity of the Taking of the Strait of Magellanus." What to Camões must have seemed a consequence of the ignominious defeat of Portuguese chivalry, chivalry he had urged onto the field where it perished, was to Hakluyt a threat of national isolation. "The peril that may ensue to all the princes of Europe if the King of Spain be suffered to enjoy Portugal with the East Indies is...a matter of great and grave consideration," he wrote. And the menace to England was particularly keen. "Whenever the rule and government of the East and West Indies and their several isles and terrritories shall be in one prince, they neither will receive English cloth nor yet care for any vent of their commodities to us, having then so many places of their own to make vent and interchange of their commodities."[24] Unlike Camões, Hakluyt thinks in economic terms, in terms of "vent" and "commodity." And these are the terms that continue to dominate the various collections of voyages that he published over the next two decades.

In a brief and informal memorandum like the "Discourse on the Strait of Magellan," this economic conception of the nation appears in its least qualified form. It is equally clear in the writings of Hakluyt's elder cousin and namesake, Richard Hakluyt of the Middle Temple, under whose tutelage the editor of the *Principal Navigations* began his geographical studies. "Since all men confess (that be not barbarously bred) that men are born as well to seek the common commodity of their country as their own private benefit..." begins one of the elder Hakluyt's several important notes of instruction. And before many lines we discover that "of many things that tend to the common benefit of the state... no one thing...is greater than clothing [i.e., trade in cloth]" (*Corr.*, 1:184). There then follows a detailed discussion of English cloth making and the ways it may be improved by a close study of the Turkish trade. This particular document was addressed to "a principal English factor at Constantinople." The elder Hakluyt's other papers, most of which his cousin published in one or another of his collections, have a similarly practical intent. They concern North American colonization, Persian dye stuffs, the northeast passage, the Levant trade, and the Virginia enterprise, and are all directed to those immediately involved. But whatever the particular object, the general understanding remains the same. Commerce is the life of both England and the world.

In both its representation of England and its representation of the world, the younger Hakluyt's *Principal Navigations* conveys a similar message. Its size (834 folio pages in the 1589 edition, expanding to over 2,000 in 1598-1600), the number of voyages it records (93 in 1589, 216 in 1598-1600), the number of supporting documents it prints (159 in

1589, 378 in 1598–1600), its historical scope (1,500 years in the first edition, 1,600 in the second), and its geographical coverage (the greater part of the known world in both editions) testify to England's "great trade and traffic in trade of merchandise" (*Corr.*, 1:55) and work to augment that trade by inspiring and informing future enterprisers and adventurers.

I do not mean to suggest by this that every one of those voyages and every one of those suporting documents concern trade. Many obviously do not. As Hakluyt himself points out in his preface to the 1589 edition, most of the medieval English voyages he prints were directed to the Holy Land and were undertaken, whether by pilgrims or crusaders, "principally for devotion's sake according to the time" (*PN*, 1:xxv). Nor are such uncommercial motives confined to the Middle Ages. Even the elder Hakluyt, in his pamphlet for the Virginia enterprise, could list as the first three "inducements to the liking of the voyage":

1. The glory of God by planting of religion among those infidels.
2. The increase of the force of the Christians.
3. The possibility of the enlarging of the dominions of the Queen's most excellent Majesty and consequently of her honor, revenues, and of her power by this enterprise. (*Corr.*, 2:327)

But if motives like these, motives that would have pleased even Camões, head his list, they are followed by twenty-eight others that concern commercial activity. And this latter group determines all the elder Hakluyt's practical advice. When, for example, he catalogs the various "sorts of men which are to be passed in this voyage," he specifies thirty-one different skills and trades, from fishermen and salt makers to shipwrights and painters, but he includes no minister of the gospel (*Corr.*, 2:336–38). Conversion, if it is to happen at all, will follow and serve commerce rather than the other way around.

A similar seeming complexity of motive in the work of the younger Hakluyt generally resolves itself in a similar way. He charges, for example, in the dedication to Philip Sidney of his first collection, the *Divers Voyages* of 1582, that "if hitherto in our own discoveries we had not been led with a preposterous desire of seeking rather gain than God's glory, I assure myself that our labors had taken far better effect."[25] But, as the context makes clear, *gain* here means short-term gain of the sort Frobisher's men sought in hunting for gold rather than finding out the northwest passage, and *God's glory* means the long-term gain that would come from well-established colonies and secure commerce with the East. It is in this, as well as in the more obvious spiritual sense, that, as Hakluyt goes on to say, "Godliness is great riches and that if we first seek the kingdom of God all other things will be given unto us." Those "other things," the "lasting riches [that] do wait upon them that are zealous for the advancement of the Kingdom of Christ," evidently include not only the treasure of heaven but also "the most noble merchandise of all the world," the trade of Cathay.

To dismiss such religious claims as mere humbug would surely be wrong, though Hakluyt himself, when referring to the Spanish and Portuguese, had little compunction about doing so. The Iberians, "pretending," he says, "in glorious words that they made their discoveries chiefly to convert infidels to our most holy faith (as they say), in deed and truth sought not them but their goods and riches." Coming just a few lines after his own glorious words, this charge can as easily confirm as erase our doubt. But even if Hakluyt could himself see through motives like those he professes, that does not make the profession any less necessary or any less significant. Resistance to an open acknowledgment of commercial designs, like the resistance we encountered in Camões, exists too, though at a much lower level, in Hakluyt. And when the audience becomes socially more elevated, as it is in the letter to Sidney, the level of resistance also rises. Addressing a merchant of London in his notes on the Turkish trade, the elder Hakluyt easily and perhaps automatically drops all mention of propagating the faith. Finding a vent for English cloth is service enough to the commonwealth. But when he or his cousin writes for a larger, more general audience, especially one that includes members of the landowning aristocracy, they become aware that something else needs to be said. If their conception of the nation is fundamentally economic, it is not a conception they can always admit—not even, I would guess, to themselves.

The Hakluyts were not alone in this difficulty. In sixteenth-century England, the mercantile community itself lacked a conceptual vocabulary that would have allowed it to assign special value to its own activities. So concludes an impressive recent study by Laura Stevenson of merchants and craftsmen in Elizabethan popular literature. While the older, negative stereotype of the merchant as a greedy usurer waned in the last decades of the sixteenth century, no more favorable image emerged—or rather none that would serve to distinguish merchants from the aristocratic leaders of society. Instead of praising merchants for their diligence, thrift, or financial talent, as their successors a hundred years later would do, Stevenson's popular authors "praised them for being 'magnanimous,' 'courtly,' 'chivalric' vassals of the king." As she demonstrates, "the labels Elizabethan authors attached to men of trade...reveal that they never sought to consolidate the social consciousness of these men by appealing to bourgeois values. Elizabethan praise of bourgeois men was expressed in the rhetoric—and by extension, in terms of social paradigms—of the aristocracy."[26]

Writing an epic poem addressed to a crusading king, Camões had good reason actively to suppress the commercial side of Portugal's overseas expansion. But even without such reason, in less obviously class-minded genres and addressing an audience that included many merchants, Elizabethan writers fell back on a strategy not altogether unlike his. Where he celebrates a mercantile voyage of discovery in terms borrowed from epic warfare, they dress merchants themselves in the rhetorical (and sometimes in the literal) garb of chivalric knights. For at least a few years, "gentle" merchants and clothiers in armor appeared as familiar figures in the popular literature of Elizabethan England. Clearly, the producers of these images—poets, players, printers, preachers, and pamphleteers—felt some need to show the leading members of the urban commercial class in a more positive way than had been customary. The extraordinary growth and diversification of the English economy, particularly as a result of increased overseas trade, required new forms of expression, as they required new forms of economic organization. On the organizational level, the rapidly proliferating array of joint stock companies met this need. On the expressive level, the merchant heroes of Elizabethan popular literature performed an analogous function. The one provided capital; the other, ideological support. But economic reorganization seems to have been easier than social revaluation. For all their debt to predecessors such as the Merchant Adventurers, the joint stock companies set an essentially new course from which there was no turning back.[27] The merchant hero was, in contrast, an unstable and short-lived paradox, an attempt to deny change even while expressing it, a reassertion of traditional social values and a familiar social hierarchy in the very midst of their subversion.

In its representation of commercial activity, Hakluyt's *Voyages* managed to slip past the conceptual barriers that otherwise confined not only the popular writers studied by Stevenson but also Hakluyt himself, barriers that could make him prefer "glory" to "gain" in a way strongly reminiscent of Camões. Far the greater part of its first two volumes— those concerned with voyages to the north and northeast and to the south and southeast[28]—are given over to the activities of merchants, their agents, and their "servants." And even in the thick, third volume, which deals with the New World in the west, an area where gentlemen and mariners were the dominant figures, merchants play a conspicuous role. Furthermore, the voices we hear in all three volumes are often those of the merchants themselves, for their reports are among the most frequent documents in Hakluyt's collection. They are thus doubly brought into unaccustomed prominence, both as actors and as authors.[29] Sometimes they earn the right to this attention, as do the merchant heroes of Elizabethan popular literature, by behaving as aristocrats. Merchant ships engage in battle against "strong and warlike" opponents (*PN*, 1:xliv), and the merchants themselves not only fight valorously but also perform with dignity and skill as ambassadors before monarchs all over the world. But they accomplish even these "gentle" actions in the course of avowedly commercial voyages, and they spend far more of their time acting specifically as merchants: finding out likely trade routes, analyzing markets, securing charters and commercial privileges, ordering and carrying goods, mastering foreign systems of coinage, weight, and measure, setting up "standing houses," hiring factors and other employees, and engaging in actual trade. In no body of writings published in England in the sixteenth century—and, so far as I know, in none published elsewhere in Europe— were merchants and their doings presented more fully or more favorably or with less ideological constraint than in Hakluyt's three volumes of *Navigations, Voyages, Traffics, and Discoveries.*[30]

Something powerful and powerfully disruptive goes on in Hakluyt's text as a result of his larger project of demonstrating and encouraging English expansion, something that he could not himself have easily acknowledged. To what should we attribute this feat? In part, at least, to the fact that Hakluyt was not really trying. Unlike Stevenson's popular writers, Hakluyt had only incidentally undertaken the task of praising merchants. His intention was rather to describe the world and to show England active in it. And for that purpose, mercantile voyages were among his richest sources. To omit them would be to leave large gaps in his description. But including them inevitably altered the picture. Not only did they make it more complete, they changed its essential character. Seen through the eyes of merchants, the world emerged as a vast network of markets offering unlimited commodities and vent, and England itself emerged as the aggressive commercial entity required from the first by Hakluyt's strategic thinking. As Hakluyt formulated his argument in the early "Discourse on the Strait of Magellan," what mattered most to England was finding buyers for its cloth and suppliers for its needs. In his various prefatory addresses to the *Voyages,* a strong but less sharply defined English presence in the world seems enough. But whichever way he puts it, mercantile activity assumes a prominence that can hardly help but upset the usual assessment of the relative importance of various social groups within the English polity. If England's "wealth and honor," as the tirelessly repeated formula has it, depend above all on overseas trade, then it follows that merchants are exceptionally important Englishmen, perhaps no less important than their traditional superiors, the landowning gentry and aristocracy.

Gentlemen and Merchants

People of all sorts, from the queen and her councillors to common soldiers and seamen, contributed to the Elizabethan expansion. But the initiation, organization, and financing of most voyages remained in the hands of just two groups, merchants and gentlemen. Voyages to Russia, Turkey, and the East Indies were primarily the work of the merchants. Gentlemen, particularly west country gentlemen connected to the Gilberts and Raleighs, dominated the attempts at western planting.[31] The two Hakluyts were similarly divided. The elder Hakluyt did most of his consulting for the eastward-bound merchants; his younger cousin did most of his, particularly in the 1580s, for gentlemen with colonial designs in the west. The *Principal Navigations,* shaped by its scientific goal of describing the whole world and by its nationalist ambition of showing England active everywhere, represented both groups and both regions.

The differences between merchants and gentlemen should not be exaggerated. As William Harrison remarked, merchants "often change estate with gentlemen, as gentlemen do with them, by a mutual conversion of the one into the other."[32] And members of both groups participated in many of the same projects. Nevertheless, a sense of class difference persisted. Harrison insists on it and so do those other Elizabethans who tried to describe the social structure of their country, Richard Mulcaster, Sir Thomas Smith, and William Camden. However they chose to divide the various categories of Englishmen—and they by no means agreed about every detail—each located gentlemen and merchants in quite distinct classes and each made it clear that the former was superior to the latter. Such differences in status were, moreover, seen to be seconded by differences in interest, even with regard to a common undertaking like overseas expansion—as this account of a text reprinted by Hakluyt suggests.

> In 1583, writing in support of a project for the colonization of Newfoundland, Sir George Peckham considered it "convenient that I do divide the adventurers into two sorts: the noblemen and gentlemen by themselves, and the merchants by themselves." He said he had heard that in fact two companies were going to be established, one for each class. And he shaped the propaganda accordingly. For the gentry he stressed the fine climate, the conditions favorable to landowners, the crops that could be produced, and the excellent hunting. . . . For the merchants he provided a list of over seventy commodities which could bring them profit.[33]

Theodore K. Rabb, from whose book *Enterprise and Empire* I have taken this summary of Peckham's views, argues that, though Peckham may have been wrong about the gentry's hunger for land, he was right that fundamental differences separated them from merchants as investors. Where merchants were motivated by a relatively uncomplicated desire for profit, gentlemen needed the impulse of glory. Gentlemen chose to support riskier and more glamorous ventures: exploration and colonization rather than settled trade. And they were more strongly influenced by ideas of national enterprise. As Rabb points out,

> One needs only to turn from the minutes of the staid and solidly merchant East India Company to the records of the exuberantly hopeful and optimistic Virginia Company to appreciate the difference. The great trading corporation pursued its profits singlemindedly. Discussions of national prestige were entirely absent: in fact, it had to be reminded by the government of its national obligations; and even the tracts written in its behalf dealt more with economics than glory. The literature relating to the Virginia Company, on the other hand, was full of the most lofty and ambitious sentiments: Indians were going to be converted, Spain was going to be frustrated, and England's fame was going to be spread abroad.[34]

Such differences in content were associated with different generic forms. Dedicating his edition of Peter Martyr's *Decades* (1587) to Sir Walter Raleigh, Hakluyt promises that Raleigh's endeavors in Virginia will win him, "if not a Homer, yet some Martyr—by whom I mean some happy genius—to rescue your heroic enterprises from the vasty maw of oblivion" (*Corr.,* 2:369). Heroic enterprises demand a heroic treatment. Hakluyt himself worked to make sure the demand would be met. Several years earlier he had recruited his Oxford "bedfellow," the young Hungarian humanist Stephan Parmenius, to memorialize in Latin verse the Newfoundland expedition of Raleigh's half-brother, Sir Humphrey Gilbert. Both Parmenius and Gilbert died on the voyage, but Parmenius's embarkation poem, *De Navigatione,* survived to appear in the *Principal Navigations,* where it was joined by another heroic poem, George Chapman's *De Guiana, Carmen Epicum,* an English blank-verse celebration of Raleigh's "discovery" of Guiana.

These poems bear a striking resemblance to Camões's *Lusiads*—a resemblance that testifies not only to the persistence of heroic convention but also to a shared aristocratic ideology. When Chapman addresses "you patrician spirits that refine / Your flesh to fire," he makes clear the class bias common to all three; and when he attacks "gold-made men as dregs of men," he expresses the antimercantile attitude that is the reflex of that bias (*PN,* 10:448). Each poem is, furthermore, marked by the same stylistic as well as social elevation, the same proclamation of inspiration, the same prophetic vision of empire, the same rarified evocation of boundless wealth, the same neglect of commerce, the same nationalist emphasis, and the same identification of the nation with the monarch and the arms-bearing nobility. Whatever the differences between Portugal and England, between Camões and Hakluyt, they have at least this much in common. Nor is the epic strain in the *Principal Navigations* confined to these isolated bits of verse. Elements of it recur in many of the individual voyages and in Hakluyt's own prefatory statements, where he can, for example, link Raleigh's colonial enterprises with the medieval "heroical intents and attempts of our princes, our nobility, our clergy, and our chivalry" (*PN,* 1:lxv) in much the way that Camões linked Gama's voyage with the crusading warfare of Portugal's feudal nobility.

But in Hakluyt's case, the volume he introduces with these evocations of aristocratic glory is filled with records of mercantile profit and loss. Though recognized by no system of poetics, commerce, like conquest, has its genres, and they too are amply represented in Hakluyt. At the opposite pole from the epic poem, with its elaborate narrative structure and its careful hierarchical ranking of gods and heroes, is the bare list of commodities to be bought or sold in some distant part of the world. Here, as in the still more frequent commercial letters and notes, the profit motive is taken for granted and all attention is focused on the practicalities of trade.

Consider, for example, this brief extract from a letter sent by John Newbery from Babylon to Master Leonard Poore in London:

> Since our coming hither we have found very small sales, but divers say that in the winter our commodities will be very well sold. I pray God their words may prove true. I think cloth, kerseys, and tin have never been here at so low prices as they are now. Notwithstanding, if I had here so much ready money as the commodities are worth, I would not doubt to make a very good profit of this voyage hither, and to Balsara, and so by God's help there will be reasonable profit made of the voyage. But with half money and half commodity may be bought here the best sort of spices and other commodities that are brought from the Indies, and without money there is here at this instant small good to be done.

The letter concludes with a list of "prices of wares as they are worth here at this instant":

> Cloves and maces, the batman, 5 ducats.
> Cinnamon, 6 ducats, and few to be gotten.
> Nutmegs, the batman, 45 medines, and 40 medines maketh a ducat.
> Ginger, 40 medines.
> Pepper, 75 medines.
> Turbetta, the batman, 50 medines.
> Neel, the churle, 70 ducats, and a churle is 27 rottils and a half of Aleppo.
> Silk, much better than that which cometh from Persia, 11 ducats and a half the batman, and every batman here maketh 7 pound and 5 ounces English weight. (PN, 5:455–56)[35]

In itself there is perhaps nothing very remarkable about this letter. How else would one expect a merchant to write? But still, this representation of the world as a great field of commodities, each in flux, each identified for the "instant" by exotic measures of quantity and price, is as much the product of cultural work as an epic poem. One is as ideological as the other. In place of the epic's resistance to social change, its attempt to figure the present as a version of the mythic past, the commercial letter makes all value depend on a constantly changing market, a market whose very operative terms—*batman, medine, churle, rottil*—suggest acceptance of a kind of cultural dislocation that the epic refuses. Or perhaps it would be better called cultural undifferentiation, for, in a letter like this, we see something of what Marx talked of as the abstracting and undifferentiating force of money. Here, the world of distinct and differentiated objects and cultures, including the distinction of self and other, begins to melt before the common denominator of ducats and medines. This melting is not unresisted. Newbery can still distinguish between what English goods will bring on the Babylonian market and what they are really worth. But even this is a long way from the absolute differentiation of them and us that Camões or Chapman attempt to erect and maintain.

In directing critical attention to this letter, I am granting it a privilege not ordinarily accorded commercial documents. This is the kind of treatment that in our culture is reserved for poems. But in his own time, Hakluyt already did something very like this. By printing both poems and letters in the same format—and notice (fig. 1) what a handsome format it is—and the same collection, he implicitly assigns comparable status to each. Gilbert's voyage to Newfoundland with its accompanying embarkation poem and the Newbery-Fitch voyage to the East Indies with its accompanying commercial letters appear as equivalent parts of a single expansionist project. Both are voyages of the English nation.

Class differences do nevertheless persist in the reception of Hakluyt's text, as they did in the communal enterprise he represented. In the 1840s, to take an example from a period two-and-a-half centuries after the original publication of the *Voyages,* the Hakluyt Society was founded, according to D. B. Quinn, as "a typical expression of Free Trade optimism." But no sooner had the Society's first publications appeared than they were roundly damned by J. A. Froude, the Victorian "prophet of imperial revival," who rather hailed the *Voyages* as "the prose epic of the modern English nation"—a kind of Camões for the nascent British Empire. Hakluyt changed, as Quinn puts it, "in the period of the new imperialism of the late nineteenth century from the great Free Trader"— in effect, a merchants' Hakluyt—"to the protagonist of nationalistic

Giles Porter and maſter Edmund Porter, went from Tripolis in a ſmall barke to Iaffa, the ſame day that we came from thence, which was the 14 day of this preſent, ſo that no doubt but long ſince they are in Ieruſalem: God ſend them and vs ſafe returne. At this inſtant I haue receiued the account of M. Barret, and the reſt of the rings, with two and twentie duckats, two medines in readie money. So there is nothing remaining in his hands but a few bookes, and with Thomas Boſtocke I left certaine ſmall trifles, which I pray you demaund. And ſo once againe with my hearty commendations I commit you to the tuition of the almightie, who alwayes preſerue vs. From Aleppo the 29 of May 1 5 8 3.

Yours aſſured, Iohn Newberie.

Another letter of Maſter *Newberie* to the aforeſaide M. *Poore*, written from *Babylon*.

MY laſt I ſent you, was the 29 of May laſt paſt from Aleppo, by George Gill the purſer of the Tiger, which the laſt day of the ſame moneth came from thence, & arriued at Feluge the 19 day of Iune, which Feluge is one dayes iourney from hence. Notwithſtanding ſome of our company came not hither till the laſt day of the laſt moneth, which was for want of Camels to cary our goods: for at this time of the yeere, by reaſon of the great heate that is here, Camels are very ſcant to be gotten. And ſince our comming hither we haue found very ſmall ſales, but diuers ſay that in the winter our commodities will be very well ſold, I pray God their words may prooue true. I thinke cloth, kerſies & tinne, haue neuer bene here at ſo low prices as they are now. Notwithſtanding, if I had here ſo much readie money as the commodities are woorth, I would not doubt to make a very good profite of this voiage hither, and to Balſara, and ſo by Gods helpe there will be reaſonable profite made of the voiage. But with halfe money & halfe commoditie, may be bought here the beſt ſort of ſpices, and other commodities that are brought from the Indies, and without money there is here at this inſtant ſmall good to be done. With Gods helpe two dayes hence, I minde to goe from hence to Balſara, and from thence of force I muſt goe to Ormus for want of a man that ſpeaketh the Indian tongue. At my being in Aleppo I hired two Nazaranies, and one of them hath bene twiſe in the Indies, and hath the language very well, but he is a very lewde fellow, and therefore I will not take him with me.

The beſt ſort of ſpices at Babylon. Balſara. Ormus.

Here follow the prices of wares as they are worth here at this inſtant.

CLoues and Maces, the bateman, 5 duckats.
Cynamom 6 duckats, and few to be gotten.
Nutmegs, the bateman, 45 medins, and 40 medins maketh a duckat.
Ginger, 40 medins.
Pepper, 75 medins.
Turbetta, the bateman, 50 medins.
Neel the churle, 70 duckats, and a churle is 27 rottils and a halfe of Aleppo.
Silke, much better then that which commeth from Perſia, 11 duckats and a halfe the bateman, and euery bateman here maketh 7 pound and 5 ounces Engliſh waight. From Babylon the 20 day of Iuly, 1 5 8 3.

The prices of ſpices at Babylon.

Yours, Iohn Newberie.

Maſter *Newberie* his letter from *Ormus*, to M. *Iohn Eldred* and *William Shals* at *Balſara*.

RIght welbeloued and my aſſured good friends, I heartily comend me vnto you, hoping of your good healths, &c. To certifie you of my voiage, after I departed fro you, time wil not permit: but the 4 of this preſent we arriued here, & the 10 day I with the reſt were committed to priſon, and about the middle of the next moneth, the Captaine wil ſend vs all in his ſhip for Goa. The cauſe why we are taken, as they ſay, is, for that I brought letters from Don Antonio. But the trueth is, Michael Stropene was the onely cauſe, vpon letters that his brother wrote him from Aleppo. God knoweth how we ſhall be delt withall in Goa, and therfore if you can procure our maſters to ſend the king of Spaine his letters for our releaſement, you ſhould doe vs great good: for they cannot with iuſtice put vs to death, It may be that they will cut out our throtes, or keepe vs long

in

Fig. 1. John Newbery's letter to Leonard Poore as it appeared in the second edition of Richard Hakluyt's *Principal Navigations of the English Nation* (1599). Huntington Library.

empire"—a gentlemen's Hakluyt.[36] Nor, though Froude's characterization of the *Voyages* as the prose epic of the English nation has been so often repeated and elaborated that it has attained almost the status of unquestioned fact, did that transformation quite settle the issue. Reviewing the secondary literature on Hakluyt, L. E. Pennington has noticed a continuation into our own century of the split between commercial and imperial readings. "Insofar as historians of all shades have generalized on Hakluyt's motives, they have," Pennington writes, "tended to divide into two camps: those who have seen his thinking as essentially concerned with the high strategy of international politics, usually with religious overtones"—the gentleman's version—"and those who have viewed him as essentially a pragmatist interested in promoting the economic advancement of England"—the merchants' version.[37]

A shifting and unstable system of differences thus yields a certain measure of continuity. Different social classes, different motives for expansion, and different representational practices in the sixteenth century are at least partially replicated in nineteenth- and twentieth-century differences in reading. Free traders and imperialists repeat, albeit with significant changes in emphasis and ideological commitment, the differences between merchants and gentlemen that divided both Elizabethan culture and Hakluyt's text. The *Principal Navigations,* like Camões's *Lusiads,* is a scene of ongoing struggle, a place of cultural production and reproduction. And, like *The Lusiads,* it defines the field of contest in national terms. The nation thus emerges as a transcendent and itself uncontested point of reference. In this, the two achieve a similar end. But Hakluyt differs from Camões in making trade and traders so obvious and so valued a part of the nation. What Camões excludes, he includes. Without denying difference, his book bridges it. The *Principal Navigations* brings merchants into the nation and brings gentry into trade. Given the ideologically dominant position of the erstwhile warrior aristocracy, this is an accomplishment of considerable moment, one that significantly redrew the parameters of social consciousness, helping to bring about the nineteenth- and twentieth-century arguments over trade and conquest reported by Quinn and Pennington. And if Hakluyt did not himself quite make all this happen, his book nevertheless provides the most notable testimony to an enabling change in which it undoubtedly participated.

In this changing cultural milieu, even the gentleman initiators of overseas projects could occasionally accept an economic explanation of their behavior. Chapman may have sung the glory of Raleigh's Guiana expedition in a way that etherealized gold and left little place for trade, but Raleigh himself was sometimes inclined to confound the motives of conquest and commerce and to blur the line between gentlemen and merchants. "Whosoever commands the sea, commands the trade," he wrote in his *Discourse of the Invention of Ships,* "whosoever commands the trade of the world, commands the riches of the world, and consequently the world itself." And in discussing the possibility of a royal marriage with a family descended from merchants, he remarked, "It is true that long ago they were merchants; and so was King Solomon too. The kings in old times . . . traded with nature and with the earth, a trade by which all that breathe upon the earth live. All the nobility and gentry in Europe trade their grass and corn and cattle, their vines and their fruits. They trade them to their tenants at home, and other merchants adventure them abroad."[38] Where all wealth (and indeed all life) derives from trade and where all men are traders, an economic conception of the nation is "natural" and inevitable. That Raleigh and his various supporters, including Chapman and Hakluyt, were not always consistent in maintaining such a conception is again testimony to the strength of the aristocratic ideology against which it was struggling to assert itself. But Hakluyt's *Voyages* does represent, despite all the countermoves it contains, a fundamentally new alignment of power in England, one in which merchants and mercantile activity had an ever-increasing share.

Spain's Tyrannical Ambition

In Raleigh's heady talk of commanding the world through trade, an aristocratic idea of universal conquest piggybacks on a mercantile notion of universal commerce. For sixteenth-century Englishmen, both were conditioned by the preeminent accomplishment of Spain. When the Merchant Adventurers gathered in the 1550s to consider the decline in their trade, the example of Spain suggested a remedy. When Hakluyt urged action in the Strait of Magellan and the northeast passage, Spanish hegemony required his bold response. When Raleigh undertook to settle Virginia and exploit Guiana, Spanish success and the Spanish threat shaped both his plan and his rhetoric. Like Portugal, which fell to the dynastic claims of Spain, and Holland, which came into existence in opposition to Spanish overlordship, England necessarily defined itself and the character of its overseas expansion in terms of its relation to Spain.

For England, as for Portugal and Holland, simple freedom from Spanish dominance was the first requirement of national self-realization. And that freedom was far from secure. Once in the course of England's sixteenth-century expansion it had virtually been lost, and in the year before the *Voyages* first appeared it was again severely menaced. In 1553, Sir Hugh Willoughby and Richard Chancellor sailed from an England ruled by the staunchly Protestant boy-king Edward and the anti-Spanish regent Northumberland. Two years later, Chancellor returned to find the throne shared by the half-Spanish Mary and her Spanish husband, Philip. In that latter year, Richard Eden, who in 1553 had dedicated his first book on America to "the right high and mighty prince, the Duke of Northumberland," brought out his *Decades of the New World* with a dedication to the "potentissimus ac serenissimus Philippus, ac serenissima potentissimaque Maria." "Stoop, England, stoop," Eden wrote in his address to the readers, "and learn to know thy lord and master, as horses and other brute beasts are taught to do."[39] Only Queen Mary's infertility and death saved England from the accomplishment of that beastlike humiliation. But in the 1580s, the execution of another Queen Mary, Mary Queen of Scots, raised once again the menace of Spanish rule—this time through armed invasion. Little more than half a century earlier the great empires of Mexico and Peru had fallen to Spain, and within the previous decade a similar fate had overtaken Portugal and its East Indian possessions. Why not England? With the defeat of the Armada, the most pressing threat passed, but through the remainder of Elizabeth's reign, war with Spain continued to be the prime conditioning element in England's expansion.

The ideological relation of England to Spain was further complicated, as was that of neither Portugal nor Holland, by an awkward mix of similarity and difference. Like Spain in both religion and aristocratic heritage, Portugal could figure itself, as in *The Lusiads,* as a rival in a common imperial project. Unlike Spain in both religion and class structure, Holland could develop as Spain's antithesis, as a bourgeois commercial nation with no imperial ambition. Neither of these positions quite suited England. England was Protestant and had an active, if not fully acknowledged, merchant class. But it was also a nation with a strong aristocratic identity and tradition, a nation whose most glorious memories were of feudal conquest and crusading zeal. England could thus feel comfortable neither in a complete repudiation of the Spanish model nor in an unqualified imitation of it.

Two arguments for American colonization, Sir George Peckham's "True Report of the Newfound Lands" and Hakluyt's own "Discourse of Western Planting," reveal both the intensity of the preoccupation with Spain and the conceptual problems that arose from it. Emulation is the theme of Peckham's "Report." "Why," he asks, "should we be dismayed more than were the Spaniards, who have been able within these few years to conquer, possess, and enjoy so large a tract of the earth...? Shall we...doubt [God] will be less ready to assist our nation...than he was to Columbus, Vasques, Nunes, Hernando Cortes, and Francis Pizarro?" (*PN,* 8:123-24, 131). But if Spain provides the model, it has also made that model suspect. As a member of a prominent Catholic family, Peckham says little of that darker side of Spain's accomplishment. For him, it is enough that Spain has spread the Christian faith abroad and increased its own wealth at home. England should, he suggests, do likewise. But even Peckham feels compelled to argue at length and with much biblical citation for the lawfulness of colonization. Hakluyt's account of Spanish behavior in the New World suggests why Peckham might have felt such justification needed. Quoting freely from the recently translated *Relacion de la Destruycíon de las Indias* of Bartolomé de las Casas, Hakluyt proclaims the "most outrageous and more than Turkish cruelties" of the Spanish "in all the West Indies" (*Corr.,* 2:257). "The Spanish," he says, "have not done in those quarters these forty years be past, neither yet do at this present, ought else than tear [the Indians] in pieces, kill them, martyr them, afflict them, torment them, and destroy them by strange sorts of cruelties, never either seen or read or heard of the like...so far forth as of above three millions of souls that were in the Isle of Hispaniola...there are not now two hundred natives of the country" (*Corr.,* 2:258).[40]

Spain's destruction of the New World natives was only the most dramatic example of a tyranny that seemed intent on spreading itself over the entire world. This ambition, Hakluyt shows, is no more than what the Spanish have themselves advertised. In the dedication of his *Decades,* Peter Martyr advised Emperor Charles that, from the wealth of the Indies, "shall instruments be prepared for you whereby all the world shall be under your obeisance,"and Gonsalvo de Oviedo, in his *History of the Indies,* told the emperor much the same: "God hath given you these Indies...to the intent that your Majesty should be the universal

and only monarch of the world" (*Corr.*, 2:244–45, 312). Coming into
the gallery of the governor's house in San Domingo half a century later,
Drake and his men found an emblem to the same effect, the arms of
the king of Spain with "a globe containing in it the whole circuit of
the sea and the earth whereupon is a horse standing on his hinder
part within the globe and the forepart without the globe, lifted up as
it were to leap, with a scroll painted in his mouth, wherein was written
these words in Latin: *Non sufficit orbis,* which is as much to say as
the world sufficeth not" (*PN,* 10:114). Drake's bold depredations in the
Caribbean and the Pacific mocked this overweening ambition, and the
various English schemes for western planting, Hakluyt's among them,
were meant to bridle it still more effectively. But both depended for
their particular rhetorical force on being seen as parts of a movement that was essentially different, one that had no such universalist
ambition.

For a country whose only overseas possession was the often rebellious
neighboring island of Ireland, first conquered centuries earlier, such
renunciation would, one supposes, have come easily. But that appears
not to have been the case. No one was more eloquent or outspoken in
his condemnation of Spanish ambition than Raleigh, but surely his
notion of commanding the world by controlling the seas bespeaks an
imagination infected with ideas of universal conquest. Knowledge of
Spain's triumphant accomplishment could turn even a poetic meditation
on England's past into a fantasy of what might have been. Had only
the English managed to avert the civil wars of the fifteenth century,
Samuel Daniel writes in the 1595 edition of the poem he devoted to
those wars, they, not the Spanish, would have "joined the Western
Empire" to their continental conquests and would now be in position
"to march against the Earth's terror Ottoman."

> The proud Iberus' lord not seeking how
> T'attain a false-conceived monarchy,
> Had kept his barren bounds and not have stood
> In vain attempts t'enrich the seas with blood.[41]

England's loss was the Spaniard's gain. But from this heroic and aristocratic perspective (Daniel imagines Essex and Mountjoy in the role of
conquering protagonists of England's imperial glory), there is no essential
difference between England and Spain.

In its very form, its systematic representation of the whole of a hitherto
unknown world, a book like Hakluyt's expresses and inspires similar

dreams of universal dominance. From the first, something of this sort had been the effect of the new maps and globes that began appearing in the wake of Columbus's discoveries. One maker of those early maps, Robert Thorne, an English merchant "who dwelt long in the city of Seville in Spain," wrote Henry VIII in 1527 to urge that he occupy some of the new "empty" space. "Out of Spain they have discovered all the Indies and seas occidental, and out of Portugal all the Indies and seas oriental. . . . So that now rest to be discovered the . . . north parts, the which, it seemeth to me, is only your charge and duty"—a duty imposed, Thorne argues, by the "natural" desire of "all princes . . . to extend and enlarge their dominions and kingdoms" (*PN,* 2:161, 159). From the new cosmography, conquest follows inevitably. If one European prince does not seize the great unclaimed regions of the newly mapped world, another will. Hakluyt's own global imaginings, beginning with his "Discourse of the Strait of Magellan" and continuing through the two editions of his *Principal Navigations,* similarly derive from this new, map-conditioned sense of the world, a sense that his work made more widely available in England.

But in Hakluyt that sense is qualified, as it is not in Thorne or Daniel or Peckham, by a sense of England's difference from Spain. Hakluyt's England defines itself in opposition to Spanish tyranny, Spanish cruelty, and Spanish ambition. And for that purpose, the inclusion of so many mercantile voyages is crucial. If Spain's behavior in the New World has given conquest a bad name, trade has not been similarly tainted. "For who doubteth," writes Peckham, "but that it is lawful for Christians to use trade and traffic with infidels and savages, carrying thither such commodities as they want and bringing from thence some part of their plenty" (*PN,* 8:97)? In a letter to the Emperor of China concerning the "honest and lawful custom of traffic in all countries" (*PN,* 11:420), Elizabeth herself confirms such ideas. The pursuit of trade rather than conquest becomes a sign of England's virtuous difference.

No one in any document gathered by Hakluyt argues for free and unrestricted trade, though Hakluyt himself does use the term "free trade of merchandise" (*PN,* 1:xlviii). But this trade, like all other between civil states, is licensed and privileged by royal charter. It is made free by proper authority. What was so offensive about the Spanish was their absolute denial of trade to such vast and lucrative markets. "For the conquering of forty or fifty miles here and there and erecting of certain fortresses, [they] think to be lords of half the world, envying that others should enjoy the commodities which they themselves cannot wholly possess" (*PN,* 6:141). It was in testing the limits of this Spanish prohibition that John Hawkins, carrying a cargo of slaves to the settlements of the Caribbean, had his celebrated conflicts with the Spanish, conflicts that did much to inflame anti-Spanish feeling. Against such tyrannical intransigence even piracy, like that of Hawkins and Drake, seemed well justified.

Drake's daring and successful raids on Spanish settlements and shipping contributed greatly to England's sense of maritime accomplishment—as did the defeat of the Armada and the burning of Cadiz. Heroic encounters of this sort fill Hakluyt's *Voyages,* particularly in its much enlarged second edition. If England in the sixteenth century never succeeded in establishing a permanent settlement of its own in the New World, it nevertheless managed to humble the proud Iberian conquerors, thus proving Hakluyt's contention that Spain's "might and greatness is not such as *prima facie* it may seem to be," for "some of his countries are dispeopled, some barren, some...far asunder also held by tyranny" (*Corr.,* 2:251). What Drake and the others exposed was not merely the material weakness of the Spanish Empire—a "dissembling and feeble scarecrow" (*Corr.,* 2:252) upheld only by American gold—but the weakness of tyranny.

In his "Description of Florida," translated by Hakluyt and four times published at Hakluyt's instigation,[42] René Laudonnière makes that anti-imperialist argument in historical and theoretical terms. Travel "into far and remote regions" for the purpose of trade or the exportation of excess population serves, according to Laudonnière, the genuine interests of the traveling country. Travel for the purpose of planting, as the Romans did, "not only their ensigns and victories, but also their laws, customs, and religion in those provinces which they had conquered by force of arms" is ultimately self-destructive. It leads to the "ruin and overthrow" of the country that undertakes it. "These," he claims with obvious reference to Spain, "are the effects and rewards of all such as being pricked forward with their Roman and tyrannical ambition will go about thus to subdue strange people: effects, I say, contrary to the profit which those shall receive which only are affectioned to the common benefit, that is to say, to the general policy of all men, and endeavor to unite them one with another as well by traffic and civil conversations, as also by military virtues and force of arms, whenas the savages will not yield unto the endeavors so much tending to their profit" (*PN,* 8:446–47).

Laudonnière's may seem a distinction with little difference. In each case, one people subjects another to its will—if necessary, by force of arms. But to Laudonnière (and presumably to Hakluyt) the difference was large and essential. Where the Romans (and Spaniards) pursued (and pursue) "universal monarchy," Laudonnière would seek only mutual profit, "an end so much more commendable as it is far from all tyrannical and cruel government" (*PN,* 8:447). Trade does not alone define this antityrannical overseas project. Finding a home for excess population, bringing the "strange ... country to civility," reducing "the inhabitants to the true knowledge of our God," all figure in Laudonnière's program, as they do in Hakluyt's. But since these goals are also shared by the Romanlike imperialists, trade remains the chief distinguishing sign. Here, without quite rejecting values such as those that shaped Camões's *Lusiads,* Laudonnière sets them on their head. To seek profit, he seems to suggest, is the best way to temper an excessive desire for glory, the "Roman and tyrannical ambition ... to make [one's] name immortal" (*PN,* 8:447).

In these texts, one sees the emergence of an anti-imperialist and even antiaristocratic logic of bourgeois nationalism. But if Hakluyt would seem at times to be approaching an argument of this sort, an argument that would set trade and nation *against* conquest, settlement, and imperial dynasty in much the way that he sets England against Spain, he never reaches it. The strength of the dynastic conception was too great, the association of honor and conquest too firm, the practical dependence (in at least some parts of the world) of even trade on settlement and armed coercion too obvious for him to tie the nation exclusively to trade. Nevertheless, his book does make it possible to imagine an England not merely competing with Spain for the same prize of universal dominance, but opposing itself to empire and working instead to construct a world of distinguishable and sovereign economic entities—that is, a world of nation-states—capable of entering into relations of trade with commercial England. Pushed by the need to differentiate England from tyrannical and Catholic Spain, Hakluyt's text moves toward an anti-imperialist— indeed, anticolonialist—logic of economic and cultural nationalism. This is the Hakluyt the Hakluyt Society was founded to perpetuate. And though it is not the only Hakluyt, it is one that arises almost inevitably from the textual practices by which his book did its promotional work.

Posthumous Writings and Rewritings

Any one of a large number of books from the next couple centuries— starting with Samuel Purchas's massive continuation of Hakluyt, *Hak-*

luytus Posthumus, or Purchas His Pilgrims—might be taken as evidence of the change of attitude brought about by Hakluyt's *Voyages* and by the commercial expansion to which it contributed. But none that I know registers that change more unequivocally than Thomas Mun's *England's Treasure by Foreign Trade,* the treatise that gave mercantilist theory its classic formulation. Written in the mid-1620s, though not published until 1664, Mun's little book brings into sharp focus ideas of class and nation that we have seen emerging in Hakluyt.[43]

For Mun, as for Hakluyt, the traditional ruling class, the landed artistocracy, provided the inevitable standard of value. If merchants are to be honored, it is as members of a "noble profession."[44] But now, as was never possible in Hakluyt or in the work of those Elizabethan contemporaries of Hakluyt, the popular writers who praised merchants, men of trade are preferred to nobles, and they are preferred not for their magnanimity and valor, but for qualities intrinsic to their commercial activity, for diligence, thrift, and worldly knowledge. Indeed, Mun presents such qualities as autonomous and self-sufficient. No other set of duties than the specifically commercial ones he enumerates need be considered in defining either the ideal merchant or the true national interest. And from this it follows that merchants, not aristocrats, are the proper governors of a modern state. "It is therefore," he writes, "an act beyond rashness in some who do disenable their counsel and judgment (even in books printed) making them uncapable of those ways and means which do either enrich or impoverish a commonwealth, when in truth this is only effected by the mystery of their trade." The defensive edge in this last sentence is sharpened by Mun's characterization of England as a country where the traditional nobility does not practice trade and where those who do are "not so well esteemed as their *noble vocation* requireth."[45] But clearly the very existence of his treatise, the very fact that in England in the 1620s such thoughts were thinkable, suggests that a significant change in the estimation of merchants had already taken place.

And that change depended in its turn on another, on one so successful that, unlike the somewhat tendentious claim for merchants, it required no argument. Throughout his book, Mun simply assumes that the nation, as a purely economic unit, should be the basis of all calculations of relative honor and worth. The balance of trade is always the balance of a nation's trade. The nation is always the entity enriched or impoverished by a surplus or deficiency of exports. There had been medieval anticipations of this idea. The anonymous fifteenth-century *Libelle of English Policy,* first printed by Hakluyt, is one of the clearest. And it was, of course, to go on dominating economic thought for centuries. Adam Smith's *Wealth of Nations,* to cite only the most conspicuous example, both accepts it and, in its chapter "Of Colonies," makes explicit the anti-imperialism latent in the notion of economic nationalism. National prosperity, Smith argues, derives rather from trade—now explicitly free trade—than from the maintenance of monopolistic political and economic control over conquered and colonized territories. The establishment of colonies—Hakluyt's plantations—is in this view only a way of extending the world system of trading nations, a way of expanding the field in which commercial activity can take place.[46]

Neither this economic understanding of a nation's interest nor the accompanying sense of the superiority of merchants appears in anything like an unqualified way in Hakluyt, whether in individual voyages and documents or in the collection as a whole. Nor does the clear expression of these ideas, when it does finally come, settle the issue. As the reports of Quinn and Pennington on the nineteenth- and twentieth-century reception of Hakluyt suggest, powerfully conflicting groups and interests continued to struggle for interpretive possession of his text—just as they struggled for the domination of overseas activity itself. But for such ideas to emerge at all, representations like Hakluyt's were needed. Their depiction of merchants as rightful and important emissaries of the nation enabled the kind of positive statements and grand schematic elaborations that we find in Mun, Smith, and the many other economic theorists of the last four centuries.

In one of those odd convergences by which history constantly rewrites itself, the representational and ideological systems that found expression in Hakluyt even managed to produce a wonderfully apt misreading of Camões. In 1776, the year of both *The Wealth of Nations* and the American Declaration of Independence, William Julius Mickle, Camões's only eighteenth-century English translator, advertised *The Lusiads* as "the poem of every trading nation, ... the epic poem of the birth of commerce."[47] How, one wonders, could any reader of Camões, much less a translator, so miss the point? But in 1776, in an England that controlled the Indian commerce Gama had opened, trade *was* the point. So massively overdetermined was Mickle's reading that it appears almost with an air of inevitability. Two centuries of overseas trade and, no less important, two centuries of discourse prompted by trade had made Camões's anticommercial meaning as invisible to Mickle as Mickle's meaning would have been to Camões or his original courtly Portuguese readers. Nor is *The Lusiads* a wholly innocent victim of this bizarre twist in the hermeneutic spiral. Commerce and its relation to national identity are, after all, central to *The Lusiads*. It is simply that Camões worked to suppress what Mickle strove to exalt. Much the same can be said of their mutually contradictory understandings of Portuguese history. In Mickle's view, Prince Henry the Navigator was "born to set mankind free from the feudal system and to give the whole world every advantage, every light that may possibly be diffused by the intercourse of unlimited commerce" (xii). Camões, on the contrary, saw the spread of that very feudal system and the religion that supported it as Portugal's mission. But, again, both accept that the point at issue was as much the structure of power at home as its extension abroad.

The differences between the aristocratic Portuguese poet and his middle-class English translator over issues whose stake they nevertheless identify alike includes their sense of the heroic genre in which both wrote—the genre to which, as we have seen, Hakluyt's *Voyages* has, in the last century-and-a-half, been regularly assimilated. To Camões, an "epic of commerce" would have seemed a ridiculous paradox. He seized on the ancient heroic genre precisely because it so obviously legitimated the military ethos of the feudal nobility to which he belonged. For Mickle, who bemoaned "the uncommercial and dreadful consequences of wars unjustly provoked" (cv), the revival of ancient learning, signaled by the return of the epic, served rather to bracket the dark age of feudalism between two periods of enlightenment and trade. But on the incompatibility of commerce with the feudal system and the resulting impossibility of basing a stable literary or national identity on some combination of the two, they would have agreed.

More eclectic than either and more deeply involved in the practicalities of overseas expansion, Hakluyt would not easily have accepted this agreement. Nevertheless, his text is caught, as theirs are, in the historic conflict of classes, of interests, and of representational forms by which the world of Camões's nostalgic imagination gave way to the eighteenth-century world of Mickle and his contemporary Adam Smith. To call that text "the prose epic of the modern English nation," as J. A. Froude and a host of imitators have done, may be to misname it almost as badly as Mickle misnamed *The Lusiads*. Yet it is by such misnamings that the ideological construction of the nation—and the powerfully hidden reaffirmation that prior to and independent of all its constructions the nation does, in fact, exist—goes on. And even the misnamings are the products of material and textual forces not unlike those that produced the works they misname.

To say this may, however, seem to suggest that, against these misnamings, we might set true names. In conclusion, I want to dispel this positivist implication, for in this discursive field there are no true names. What is at stake is not truth but success. Do the names stick? Do men and women behave as though they lived in the kind of community Camões or Hakluyt or Mickle or Froude name? From Columbus on, written voyages tell not only what happened when some captain and crew sailed to some distant land. They also tell what world those happenings require and suppose: what structures of identity, what division of power, what representational practices—all matters that Europe's expansion could not help but unsettle. For Europe to transform itself from its medieval isolation and marginality to the position of world dominance that it is only now beginning to lose demanded much prospective and retrospective renaming. It is to this process that Camões, Hakluyt, and their interpreters have contributed. They enforced the emerging nationalist bias of Europe's expansion and struggled over the nation's identity. In our own age of decolonialization and international economy, even the positive side of this accomplishment begins to appear increasingly problematical. Though nationalism may still be the most powerful ideological force in the world (Europe's most widely accepted cultural export), nations no longer seem quite so natural as they once did. But that, I would suggest, is all the more reason for questioning the ideological strategies of the texts that first helped elevate the nation to the privileged position it has so long enjoyed.

NOTES

This chapter is a shortened version of a chapter from my book *Forms of Nationhood: The Elizabethan Writing of England* (Chicago: University of Chicago Press, 1992). Copyright © by the University of Chicago Press 1992.

1. Daniel Defert, "The Collection of the World: Accounts of Voyages from the Sixteenth to the Eighteenth Centuries," *Dialectical Anthropology* 7 (1982): 16. See also Defert's "Collections et nations au XVIe siècle," in *L'Amérique de Théodore de Bry,* ed. Michèle Duchet (Paris: Editions du CNRS, 1987), 47–67.

2. *Os Lusíadas* is quoted from Luís de Camões, *Obras completas,* ed.

Hernani Cidade, 5 vols. (Lisbon: Livraria sá da Costa, 1946–47). Quotations are identified in the text by canto and stanza. Except where otherwise indicated, translations are based on those of Leonard Bacon, *The Lusiads* (New York: Hispanic Society of America, 1950).

3. Voltaire is quoted by William Julius Mickle in the introduction to his translation, *The Lusiad; or, The Discovery of India. An Epic Poem* (Oxford: Jackman and Lister, 1776), cxxii. It should be noted that on the subject of Camões, Voltaire is not a very reliable witness. His objection in this instance has, however, been repeated with greater respect for Camões's text by Georges Le Gentil (*Camoëns: L'Oeuvre épique et lyrique* [Paris: Hatier-Boivin, 1954], 51–52).

4. "Calecu ... / Cidade já por trato nobre e rica" (7:35) and "Malaca por empório ennobrecido" (10:123).

5. David Quint discusses this line in a brilliantly suggestive article on the ideological differences between epic and romance, "The Boat of Romance and Renaissance Epic," in *Romance: Generic Transformation from Chrétien de Troyes to Cervantes,* ed. Kevin Brownlee and Marina Scordilis Brownlee (Hanover, N.H.: University Press of New England, 1985), 178–202.

6. Sir Richard Fanshawe's translation of *The Lusiads,* ed. Geoffrey Bullough (Carbondale, Ill.: Southern Illinois University Press, 1963), 334.

7. See, for example, his execration on gold (8:96–99) or his account of Cupid's campaign against those who give their affection to things designed "for use and not for love" (9:25).

8. That this thinning out of "heroic subjectivity" was the product of the exigencies of the early modern state is argued by Neil Larsen and Robert Krueger in "Homer, Vergil, Camões: State and Epic," *I & L: Ideologies and Literature* 2, no. 10 (1979): 69–94.

9. On this antipathy, see Quint, *Boat of Romance,* 187–89.

10. C. M. Bowra, *From Virgil to Milton* (London: Macmillan, 1945), 138. See also the essays collected in *Camões à la Renaissance* (Brussels: Editions de l'Université de Bruxelles, 1984).

11. Vitorino de Magalhães-Godinho, *L'Économie de l'empire Portugais aux XVe et XVIe siècles* (Paris: S.E.V.P.E.N., 1969), 834–35.

12. For Pires, I follow the translation of Armando Cortesão, *The Suma Oriental of Tomé Pires* (London: Hakluyt Society, 1944), 1:4.

13. "Da terra vos sei dizer que é mãe de vilões ruins e madrasta de homens honrados. Porque os que se cá lançam a buscar dinheiro, sempre se sustentam sobre água com[o] bexigas; mas os que sua opinião deita *á las armas, Mouriscote* ... antes que amadureçam, se secam" (*Obras completas,* 3:245–46).

14. In the opening chapter of *O Strange New World* (New York: Viking Press, 1964), Howard Mumford Jones describes how Europeans' reading of romance conditioned their response to the New World. See also Irving A. Leonard, *Books of the Brave* (New York: Gordian Press, 1964).

15. A. H. de Oliveira Marques, quoted by Larsen and Krueger, "Homer, Virgil, Camões," 83.

16. Richard Hakluyt, *The Principal Navigations Voyages Traffiques and Discoveries of the English Nation,* 12 vols. (Glasgow: MacLehose, 1903–5), 2:165. Subsequently cited as *PN.* An instance of the Portuguese king's title can be found at *PN,* 5:63.

17. François Pyrard de Laval, quoted by Magalhães-Godinho, *L'Économie,* 834.

18. Pierre Vilar discusses the relation between the "dry and warlike" Spain of the interior plateau and the "rich and fleshy" surrounding provinces in the first chapter of his *Histoire de l'Espagne* (Paris: Presses Universitaires de France, 1958).

19. Bowra remarks (*Virgil to Milton,* 91) that "in the southwestern corner of Europe the Portuguese nation ... had to secure its independence against two main enemies, the Moors and the Spaniards. That is why the three battles which Camões presents at some length are Ourique, where in 1139 the nation was born in battle against the Moors, Salado, where in 1340 Affonso IV helped the King of Castile to rout the Moors, and Aljubarrota, where in 1385 João I defeated a Spanish attempt to conquer Portugal."

20. For a recent discussion of this episode and the varying interpretations of it, see Gerald M. Moser, "What Did the Old Man of Restelo Mean?" *Luso-Brazilian Review* 17 (1980): 139–51.

21. See J. H. Parry's chapter, "The Sea Empires of Portugal and Holland," in *The Age of Reconnaissance: Discovery, Exploration, and Settlement* [1963], rpt. (Berkeley: University of California Press, 1981), 242–57.

22. Two volumes prepared to commemorate the 400th anniversary of Camões's death testify to his extraordinary place in Portuguese culture: *Estudos sobre Camões: Páginas do diário de noticias dedicadas ao poeta no 4° centenário da sua morte* (Lisbon: Imprensa Nacional, 1981) and *Camões e a identidade nacional* (Lisbon: Imprensa Nacional, 1983). The first is a collection of articles that appeared in a leading Portuguese newspaper; the second, a collection of addresses by some of Portugal's most prominent writers and intellectuals.

23. Quoted by Aubrey F. G. Bell, *Luis de Camões* (Oxford: Oxford University Press, 1923), 65.

24. *The Original Writings and Correspondence of the Two Richard Hakluyts* (London: Hakluyt Society, 1935), 1:139, 143. Subsequently cited as *Corr.*

25. *Divers Voyages Touching the Discovery of America* (1582), sig. 2ᵛ. *Divers Voyages* has been edited in a facsimile edition with an introductory volume entitled *Richard Hakluyt, Editor,* by David B. Quinn (Amsterdam: Theatrum Orbis Terrarum, 1967).

26. Laura Caroline Stevenson, *Praise and Paradox: Merchants and Craftsmen in Elizabethan Popular Literature* (Cambridge: Cambridge University Press, 1984), 6.

27. For a history of the joint stock companies, see William Robert Scott, *The Constitution and Finance of English, Scottish, and Irish Joint Stock Companies to 1720,* 3 vols. (Cambridge: Cambridge University Press, 1910–12).

28. The order of these volumes changed from the first to the second edition. In the first edition, the southern voyages come first; in the second, the northern voyages take their place.

29. Hakluyt's successor, Samuel Purchas, remarked on the role merchants play in books like the ones he and Hakluyt assembled. "Soldiers and merchants [are] the world's two eyes to see itself," he proclaimed on the title page of his *Pilgrims* (1625) and in the body of the work he said that "the actors" of the voyages he was collecting are "the authors, and the authors themselves the actors of their own parts, arts, acts, designs" (*Hakluytus Posthumus, or Purchas His Pilgrims* [Glasgow: MacLehose, 1905–7], 2:286).

30. As if in response to the large amount of commercial material that his project compelled him to print, Hakluyt inserted the word *traffics* into the title of the second edition. The title of the first edition had referred only to navigations, voyages, and discoveries.

31. Kenneth R. Andrews discusses these differences in *Trade, Plunder, and Settlement: Maritime Enterprise and the Genesis of the British Empire, 1480–1630* (New York: Cambridge University Press, 1984), 9–10, 17–22.

32. Quoted in Stevenson, *Praise and Paradox,* 80. See also Stevenson's useful discussion of the various Elizabethan descriptions of the class divisions of England (79–91).

33. Theodore K. Rabb, *Enterprise and Empire: Merchant and Gentry Investment in the Expansion of England, 1575–1630* (Cambridge, Mass.: Harvard University Press, 1967), p. 35.

34. Rabb, *Enterprise and Empire,* 39–40.

35. Of the unfamiliar terms in this passage (*batman, medine, turbetta, neel, churle,* and *rottil*), the *OED* defines only three, *batman* ('an oriental weight'), *medine* ('a silver half-dirhem'), and *neel* ('obs. form of *anil*'), and quotes this passage as the earliest instance of each. Among themselves, Elizabethan merchants spoke a language that was not altogether English.

36. D. B. Quinn, "Hakluyt's Reputation," in *The Hakluyt Handbook,* ed. D. B. Quinn (London: Hakluyt Society, 1974), 1:147–48.

37. L. E. Pennington, "Secondary Works on Hakluyt and His Circle," in *Hakluyt Handbook,* 2:588–89.

38. T. Birch, ed., *Works of Sir Walter Raleigh* (London: R. Dodsley, 1751), 2:80, 1:276–77. I owe these quotations from Raleigh to Christopher Hill, *Intellectual Origins of the English Revolution* (Oxford: Clarendon Press, 1965), 165–70, where Hill discusses Raleigh's ideas concerning commerce and labor.

39. Richard Eden, *The Decades of the New World,* rpt. in *The First Three English Books on America,* ed. Edward Arber (Birmingham: [Turnbull & Spears,

Edinburgh], 1885), 52 (in quoting Eden's Latin, I turn his datives into nominatives). Despite the apparently pro-Spanish content of Eden's dedication and preface, it seems likely that his purpose was to goad Englishmen into competing with the Spanish in the New World.

40. Hakluyt's part in the spread of anti-Spanish propaganda has been discussed by William S. Maltby in *The Black Legend in England: The Development of Anti-Spanish Sentiment, 1558-1660* (Durham, N.C.: Duke University Press, 1971), 61-75.

41. Samuel Daniel, *The Civil Wars,* ed. Lawrence Michel (New Haven: Yale University Press, 1958), 311.

42. In French in Paris (1586); in his own English translation in London (1587); in Theodore de Bry's illustrated Latin version in Frankfort (1591); and again in English in the second edition of the *Principal Navigations* (1600).

43. On the date of composition of *England's Treasure,* see B. E. Supple, "Thomas Mun and the Commercial Crisis, 1623," *Bulletin of the Institute of Historical Research* 27 (1954): 91-94; J. D. Gould, "The Trade Crisis of the Early 1620s and English Economic Thought" and "The Date of *England's Treasure by Forraign Trade,*" *Journal of Economic History* 15 (1955): 121-33, 160-61.

44. Thomas Mun, *England's Treasure by Forraign Trade* [1664], facs. rpt. (Oxford: Economic History Society, 1928), 88.

45. Mun, *England's Treasure,* 3 (italics in original). Quint (*Boat of Romance,* 195-96) finds similar sentiments expressed still more openly in Lewis Roberts's *Treasure of Traffic* (1641): "It is not our conquests, but our commerce; it is not our swords, but our sails, that first spread the English name in Barbary, and thence came into Turkey, Armenia, Moscovia, Arabia, Persia, India, China, and indeed over and about the world." Quint comments: "Insisting that the true heroes of exploration are merchants, Roberts provides an alternative"—an alternative, we might add, that Hakluyt had a large share in making available—"to an aristocratic ideology which interprets the discoveries in terms of imperial conquest."

46. The term *world system* alludes to Immanuel Wallerstein's two volume work, *The Modern World-System* (New York: Academic Press, 1974 and 1980). These volumes provide an excellent introduction to the origins and consolidation of what Wallerstein calls "the European world-economy."

47. William Julius Mickle, *The Lusiad* (London, 1776), cxlvii.

Confession, Conversion, and Reciprocity in Early Tagalog Colonial Society

Vicente L. Rafael

If one were a Tagalog convert to Christianity in the seventeenth or early eighteenth century, one would have probably been compelled to go to confession at least once a year. Confronting the Spanish priest, one would be subjected to his anxious probing in the vernacular as he proceeded through a checklist of possible transgressions against each of the Ten Commandments. Such checklists in the local language, called *confessionarios,* were common throughout the colonial period.[1] Compiled by missionaries skilled in Tagalog, they were designed to serve as mnemonic devices to aid Spanish clerics in eliciting the confessions of their native flock.

The questions contained in the *confessionarios* systematically delved not only into sinful acts, but into the sinful thoughts, words, and desires that informed the commission or contemplation of such acts. Whether these involved paying homage to the spirits (*nono*) of this forest or that river, or employing the services of a shaman (*babaylan*) for some curing ritual or the interpretation of dreams—sins against the first and second commandments, respectively—the confessor demanded no less than an unconditional recounting of sins by way of a rigorous accounting for them.[2] A Tagalog male, for example, would have been beset by the following sort of questioning, remarkable not so much for its luridness as for its typicality, with regard to the sixth commandment.

355. Have you committed a sin with some woman?

. . . .

366. How many times did you sin with her?

367. You say that you always saw each other alone, well then, how do you expect me to know how many times those were?

368. If you can't give me the exact number of times, give me a rough estimate, tell me more or less how many times?

369. And if you can't tell me this, tell me how many years, or months, or weeks, or days has it been since you started sinning with her.

370. And during this entire period, how many times a week did you sin with her? Was it every day, or every other day, or what?

371. And aside from all those times you slept with her, did you not at other days and hours also cavort and play around in a wanton manner?

372. And during those moments of playing around didn't you at times just verbally joke around, and at other times embrace each other, and kiss each other, and touch each other, touching every single part of your bodies without reserve?

373. And did something dirty come out of your body?

374. And did you cause her to emit something dirty, too?

375. How many times did you play around in this manner, for example, within a week? And how many times did each of you have an emission? Because not only is this a sin, indeed, it is a very serious sin.

376. Aside from all this, I also suspect that every time you saw her or thought of her, you also lusted for her. Wasn't this the case?

377. And because of your lust, did you do anything to your body, any kind of lewdness? And did your body emit something dirty?[3]

What is curious about this passage is the way in which the priest's discursive drift mimics the sexual act it is hunting down. Interest in the quantity of transgressions leads to a feverish desire to learn of their quality. This periodically climaxes, as it were, with the questions, "And did something dirty come out of your—or her—body?" Here, the authority of the confessor seems to come precisely from being able to locate those moments when the male convert squandered what should have been held in reserve, to be deposited only for the purpose of reproducing other potential converts. What is implicit in this and other similar exchanges is the sense of "You wasted yours while I still have mine." That is, the sense, on the confessor's part, of being able to have the means with which to track down each and every single thought, word, and deed that led the convert to lose his "property"—a property that, having originated with God, should have been used only for the purpose of reproducing a surplus that could then be returned to Him. And having located those moments of loss, the priest, through the penitent, could then initiate their recuperation into a narrative of sin, an admission of guilt, and the submission to (and hence affirmation of) God's laws. What was lost could thus be recovered in language. By insisting on the translation of the past into a comprehensive tabulation of discrete acts and desires, confessional discourse substitutes for the imagined experience of previous transgression the current act of its retelling. The confession that the priest extracts from the penitent is thus the result of a labor of accounting for and recounting the past. This narrative product is then delivered by the agency of the priest back to the supposed origin of all property, indeed, the final owner of all the means with which to secure property: God the Father.

I begin this essay with the preceding note on confession mainly because it suggestively encapsulates, from the missionary point of view, the more salient features of the larger process of conversion that, in large measure, determined the shape of Spanish colonial rule in the Philippines. It is this process of conversion—as a historical phenomenon that had an explicit though highly unstable linguistic basis—that I wish to examine here.

Conversion entailed evangelization—literally the dissemination of God's Word, which is none other than Christ. As the Son of God, Christ is believed to be the special Sign of the Father's authority. The sacred Sign in turn provided men and women with the privileged means with which to purchase salvation—the sacraments. These were meant to serve as the codes that were to effect the conversion of bodies and souls into the elements of God's Word.[4] To avail oneself of the sacraments is precisely to take on the Sign of God, that is, to confess one's inherent sinfulness and hence one's ultimate and unending dependence upon an omnipotent Father through the Son and the Son's chosen representatives on earth.

In the early colonial period (late sixteenth to the early eighteenth century), the chosen representatives of the Sign happened to be Spaniards.[5] As proponents of a revitalized Catholicism and envoys of an expansive Castilian monarchy, the Spanish missionaries sought to capture not only native bodies but, more important, native minds and souls. Because of this, they desired not only the external submission of the conquered populace but their internal accession to the king's will to the extent that it was reflective of God's. The politics of evangelization insisted that the relationship between ruler and ruled be determined by the uncompromising surrender of both to one God and to His laws.[6] Conquest through conversion was thus idealized as the totalizing hierarchization of everything and everyone under a single ruler at once present and absent in His vast realm. To convert was then to accept God's domination via a mediating chain of representatives: the sacraments, the liturgy, the church, and its priests.

It is worth noting, however, that in the history of Spanish-Tagalog encounters one of the conditions that made possible this dialectic of submission was a process of linguistic exchange, that of translation. As with the Indians of the New World, the *indios* of the Philippines were subjected to the faith in their own language. The translation of Christian doctrine into the vernacular was a key feature of evangelization. And among the various languages in the archipelago, Tagalog, which was spoken in the most populous and fertile areas adjacent to the colonial capital of Manila, received the most sustained attention from the missionary writers. Indicative of this are the numerous grammar books, called *artes,* and dictionaries, called *vocabularios,* published in this vernacular, along with devotional literature in translation by Spanish priests.[7] The fragment of the *confessionario* text included above is an example of this prodigious production.

The translation of the doctrine into the Tagalog vernacular, however, resulted in the transformation of the language itself. Highly charged words such as *Dios, Espiritu Santo, Cruz, Jesu Christo,* and so forth, which the Spaniards felt had no direct equivalent in the local language, were kept in their untranslated forms. In the interest of conversion, translation prescribed, just as it proscribed, the language in which the natives were to receive and return God's Word. Such is suggestive of the incipient politics of translation where conversion was concerned and becomes apparent from even the most cursory reading of the missionary grammar books published from the seventeenth century.

In the Tagalog *artes* for example, what is immediately striking is the use of the Latin and Castilian languages as the principal points of reference in reconstructing Tagalog grammar. The linguistic machinery of Tagalog is structured in terms of *nombres, verbos, adjectivas, pasivas, activas, acusativos, imperativos, preteritos,* and so forth. It is as if the missionary, in order to understand Tagalog, had first to superimpose on it the grammatical grid of another language, Latin.

The absence of Tagalog terms in the designation of Tagalog grammar is a curious circumstance. The impression one gets from reading missionary-composed *artes* is that grammar, as such, did not exist for the Tagalogs before the missionaries began writing about the language. In order to use Tagalog as a tool of conversion, the missionary writers, it seems, had first to determine its parts. But they did so precisely by relocating the native language in the complex grid of Latin and Castilian discourse. The linguistic apparatus of Latin and Castilian were made to act on Tagalog, precipitating it as a useful instrument for evangelization. In doing so, the missionaries were following the tradition laid down by Antonio de Nebrija's 1492 grammar of Castilian, which had established Latin as the grammatical basis for the reconstruction of the Spanish vernacular.[8] They learned Tagalog only by first encoding it within a historically and genetically alien structure. Such a move was conceivable on the basis of what the Spaniards believed was the existence of a nonarbitrary hierarchy of languages. Latin was seen to serve as the structural model for the recodification of all the vernaculars in the world to the extent that it was the universal language of the Church. In Spain itself, while Castilian became the dominant language of the *imperio,* Latin continued to function as the privileged means for communicating what the Augustinian theologian-poet Fray Luis de Leon called the *gravedad,* or gravity, of the Same Truth.[9] That Tagalog should be organized around the matrix of Latin was thus a function of the Spanish belief in the proximity of Latin to God's Word.

But while Tagalog was encoded with reference to Latin grammar, its translation was expressed in Castilian. *Vocabularios* as such were always Castilian-Tagalog or vice versa, never Latin-Tagalog. In this sense, Castilian occupied the mediating position between the language of God and that of the *indios,* serving as a passage from Latin grammar to Tagalog speech. This was why Castilian words could fill in for terms lacking in Tagalog where the translation of the faith was concerned. For the missionaries, *Dios* could not be translated into *bathala* (deity), *binyag* (to give one a new name) into *bautizar.* Castilian thus initiated not only the movement of translation; it also instituted a notion of untranslatability. What this underscores is, once again, the Spanish investment in a linguistic hierarchy wherein only certain words were adequate to express Christian concepts. The activity of translation coupled with the notion of untranslatability resulted in the subordination of Tagalog as a mere derivative of Latin and Castilian; it became, therefore, merely an instance of the divine production of signs in the world. Just as conversion and colonization were meant to reclaim the fallen souls of the natives by subduing them in accordance with the laws of God and king, translation was believed to be instrumental in construing the local language as yet another set of signs that could be returned—or "reduced," as the Spaniards were wont to say—to the putative source and final destination of all things: the Father.

Given the foregoing considerations, it is not unwarranted to find a pervasive complicity between language and power where conversion is concerned. As we saw earlier, confession, the epitome of conversion, was meant to compel the native penitent to produce a past in relation to the Christian history of salvation. Confessional discourse was structured in such a way that the convert's narrative of sin was filled with the syntax of Christian wishfulness. Similarly, the coherence of Tagalog as a linguistic system could be made apparent only when it had been converted into the grammatical grid of Latin. In both confession and translation, the Spanish priest and language played a peculiar role. Together they served as the third term working to achieve the transposition of native speech into the structure of Latin on the one hand, and the conversion of native bodies into suppliant speakers of God's Word on the other. Thus did a linguistic hierarchy predicate the politicoreligious structure of authority within the colonial context. Just as the working of conversion betrayed the Spanish concept of submission, the operation of translation and its negative underbelly, untranslatability, encoded Spanish ideas regarding the representation of power.

But what of the Tagalogs? Confronted with Spanish attempts to encode their bodies, souls, and language as aspects of the divine Word, how did they respond? We know from missionary accounts that, despite an initial and short-lived reluctance, the overwhelming majority of Tagalogs "readily received" Christianity.[10] What might conversion to the faith have meant for them? What drew them to the signs of Christianity in the absence of external and purely coercive Spanish measures? Did the terms of Tagalog submission coincide with or substantially differ from missionary expectations, and how and to what extent?

Although admittedly these are broad questions to which comprehensive answers are not possible, I can sketch some ways in which the problem of Tagalog response to conversion might be approached.

Students of Philippine history are aware of the difficulties involved in arriving at distinctly native responses to Spanish rule prior to the nineteenth century. The vast majority of sources for the early colonial period were written in Spanish by and for the colonizers rather than the colonized. The tendentiousness of these documents thus tends either to obscure native perceptions or subordinate these to Spanish intentions. There are, however, also those reams and reams of devotional texts— *confessionarios,* prayer books, sermons, catechisms, and so forth— written in the vernacular by the missionaries that were meant to solicit and maintain native adherence to the faith.

What I want to suggest here is the possibility of reading these missionary texts in Tagalog against the grain of their ostensible meaning— that is, to read them not simply in terms of the message that the Spaniards intended them to convey, but in terms of how they might have been received by the Tagalogs who heard them. This textual strategy is warranted by a feature that Tagalog shares with all other languages: the arbitrary connection between a word and its range of possible referrents. As evinced in the *vocabularios* compiled by the missionaries, the native vernacular tended to give rise to associated references in addition to the Spanish-Christian meanings that they were meant to translate. This is further complicated by the fact that clerical discourse in Tagalog was often permeated with untranslatable words having no prior link to Tagalog culture. Breaking into the fabric of the vernacular, these opaque words lent themselves to a semantic drift that did not guarantee the appearance of the message of Christianity. The point to be stressed here is the possibility of detecting a Tagalog response operating within the structure of their language as it was recorded by the missionary lexicographers—a response that would alternately invite and evade the force of the Christian message that the vernacular was conscripted to bear. In such a way would language put into question rather than, as the Spaniards expected, merely affirm the project of conversion.

To convey a sense of this circumstance, we might first examine the missionary practice of grafting untranslatable Christian-Spanish words into the vernacular text. As noted earlier, this was meant to safeguard the purity of the concepts behind these terms from any possible confusion with existing native beliefs. Yet, their insertion into the vernacular texts necessitated their subjection not only to the syntax of Tagalog but also to its unforseeable semantic effects. As signifiers with no definite signifieds in Tagalog, such words lent themselves to a whole range of associations. Once again, we can turn to the *confessionario* quoted above, that from Fray Sebastian Totanes's *Manual,* to see how this works. In this instance, it is helpful to see both the Tagalog and Spanish texts, bearing in mind that the English translation tries as closely as possible to approximate the Tagalog rather than the Spanish text. The following is what the missionary is advised to say about communion to a convert receiving last rites:

66. Anacco, tayong lahat na Christiano,y, ynootosan nang P. Dios at nang Santa Iglesiang Ina nating maquina-bang cun magcocomul-gar touing mey pang-anib ang ating buhay.... Ytong paquinabang na yto,y, pinangalang *Viatico,* na cun baga sa uicang Tagalog ay Bauon nang mey paroroonang malayo. Pabauon nga nang Santa Iglesia sa tauong mey saquet na malubha ytong camahal-mahalang na Sacramento nang pagcocomulgar, nama-catatapang at macalala-cas sa taou sa pagcacabanalan at sa paglalaban sa manga tocso nang diablong maraya.	66. Hijo mio, Dios nuestro Señor y la Santa Iglesia nos manda comulgar quando hay peligro de muerte. . . . A este comulgar llaman Via-tico, que quiere decir: Provision para el que tiene que hacer Viage largo. Provee la Santa Iglesia al Hombre enfermo con este San-tissimo Sacramento para el Viage dela eter-nidad para fortalecerle en la Fe, en la Esper-anza, y en la Charidad, para que exercite las Virtudes y resista con valor a las tentaciones de demonio.	66. My child, all of us who are Christians are ordered by our Lord God and by our Mother Church to avail ourselves of commun-ion every time our lives are in danger. . . . This useful thing is called *Viatico,* which in the Tagalog language is the *bauon* of those who are going on a long jour-ney. This is the provi-sion that the Mother Church gives to the seriously sick person, this most blessed Sacra-ment of communion, that endows one with bravery and strength in order to reach holiness and to fight against the temptations of the devil.[11]

In listening to the priest's talk, the convert about to receive communion as part of the last rites is bombarded with a remarkable number of untranslatable words. Against the impending threat of death, the Spanish formulation is unequivocal in situating ritual discourse as that which brings to the convert the Sign of God, the *Viatico,* or host. It is the host that ransoms the individual from the finality of death as it fortifies him or her in faith, hope, and charity with which to resist the devil.

In the Tagalog text, however, while the word *Viatico* is retained, it slides into the register of *bauon,* which is the food that one takes on a journey. The nature of this journey is itself problematic. Whereas the Spanish speaks of it in terms of eternity (*eternidad*), implying the abolition of prior history, the Tagalog is rendered as *paroroonang malayo,* long journey, which leaves unspecified the points of departure and arrival. What the *Viatico* as *bauon* does is similarly equivocal. In the Tagalog, it gives one neither "faith, hope, and charity" (*Fe, Esperanza y Charidad*) but "bravery" and "strength." The words used here are *tapang* and *lacas,* respectively, neither of which contains any kind of moral or theological connotation. Instead, *tapang* and *lacas* both denote the capacity to release energy, which, in the passage above, is directed at achieving *cabanalan,* 'holiness,' and resisting *tocso,* 'temptation.' Yet the word *cabanalan,* from the root word *banal,* also means "to become disconcerted, disjointed, confused"; *tocso,* on the other hand, also refers to questions, interruptions, and jokes. There is a sense, then, in which the Tagalog text could be read in a way that would be considerably at odds with Spanish expectations. The appearance of *Viatico* leads one to think not of the means to transmute death into the passage to eternal life, but of provisions to be taken on an indeterminate journey. These provisions could be valued for the protection they supply against the danger of interruptions and confusions outside, particularly from the confusion of "spirits" believed to cause illness, and from the interruption of life by death.

In another passage, Totanes's text speaks of the efficacy of evoking the "sweet names" (*catamistamisang pangalan / dulcissimos nombres*) of Jesus and Mary in resisting temptations of the body. It urges the convert to

Gamitin mo,t, houag bitiuan iton sandata, at manalo ca ngani sa lahat na manga caauay mo.... Si Jesus nang si Jesus, si Maria nang si Maria ang iyong uiui-cain, ang iyong tuturan sa caybuturan nang loobmo at sa bibigmo naman.... Magpa-Jesusmaria nang Magpa-Jesusmaria ca	Usa de esos poderosa arma, no la sueltas no la dejes, y venceras ciertamente a todos sus enemigos.... Jesus-Maria, JesusMaria es lo que en cada respira-cion has de decir con el corazon, y con la boca tambien.... Repite continuamente estas Santisimos y Dul-cissimos Nombres de	Use these and do not let go of this weapon, so that you might tri-umph against all your enemies.... Jesus and Mary, Jesus and Mary is what you should say, and what you will have in each breath of your soul and on your mouth as well.... Repeat again and again Jesusmaria, Jesusmaria

| hangan sa dica mapat- | Jesus y de Maria mien- | while you have the |
| dan nang hininga. | tras tengas vida. | breath to do so.[12] |

Here, the names of Jesus and Mary are regarded as powerful weapons that can be used to ward off the threat of danger. Their efficacy consists entirely in their repetition not as two names but one, *JesusMaria.* The repeated utterance of the name drains it of any extralinguistic content to the point of converting it into an opaque sign that shelters the speaker from external harm. What this amounts to is a recasting of the Christian Sign into something that can be torn away from the linguistic commerce that originates from and returns to the Father. It is instead rendered into an amuletlike object that does not result in the subjection of the speaker to the language of God. In fact, the very opposite occurs. The name of the Sign is converted into a weapon that distances the self not only from the claims of death, but from the law that pretends to control it.

All of this is suggestive of some of the ways in which the idea of untranslatability tends to undercut rather than promote the comprehension of the Christian concept when it is transferred onto the vernacular. Similarly, the translation practice of adapting native terms to fit Christian contexts added a further problematical dimension to the project of conversion. In illuminating this point, it is instructive to look at Spanish attempts to translate the Tagalog terms of reciprocity.

Inhabiting the vernacular texts that the priest addressed to the converts is a notion of reciprocity that is culturally specific to the Tagalogs. In communicating humankind's generalized indebtedness to the Father for having made of His Son the "gift" that ensured their salvation, Spanish writers constantly employed the Tagalog idioms of *utang na loob,* 'debt of gratitude,' and *hiya,* 'shame.' In numerous devotional texts, one's submission to God and dependence on Christ were invariably phrased in terms of an *utang-na-loob* relationship, while sorrow and repentance for one's sins were rendered as a feeling of *hiya* for having been remiss in paying one's debts to the Father. Similarly, God is said to have given His own *loob* to the converts through Christ, expecting them to return their own *loob* to Him. Damnation, in this case, is the permanent separation of human from divine *loob,* thus marking the end of all *utang-na-loob* ties between the two.[13]

As parts of a constellation of "values" among the peoples in the Tagalog areas, *utang na loob* and *hiya* have attracted considerable attention from scholars since the 1960s. Among the most influential works are those written by Charles Kaut and Mary Hollnsteiner.[14] Set along the lines of structural-functionalist theory, their analyses of these values have been rightly criticized for being ahistorical. As Reynaldo Ileto has cogently pointed out, studies of *utang na loob* and *hiya* that exclude history end up depoliticizing reciprocity by failing to consider the place of conflict in the Tagalog processes of exchange and indebtedness.[15] Ileto goes on to resituate these ideas of reciprocity in the peasant movements of the late nineteenth and early twentieth centuries. He convincingly demonstrates the revolutionary potential of *utang na loob* as constantly invoked in the Tagalog literature of this period, as well as in the writings of messianic leaders as they rallied followers in a series of uprisings against Spain and later the United States. But while Ileto's work is a significant departure from Kaut and Hollnsteiner, it nonetheless tends to join them in regarding the *loob* in *utang na loob* as a privileged, a priori entity.[16] In this sense, *loob* is regarded as connoting the core of Tagalog being, as that which is part of, yet apart from, processes of exchange.

It is of critical importance to hold on to Ileto's insight regarding reciprocity as that which is always predicated on the possibility of conflict and disruption. However, in considering the historical effects of *utang na loob* and *hiya* in the context of conversion, it is important to try to circumvent partially both a phenomenological and a purely operational definition of *loob,* one that designates the "inside" that is staked in a Tagalog debt transaction. This might be done by reexamining *loob* first of all as a linguistic fact, as a signifier that attaches itself to a variety of mutually exclusive signifieds. It is the process of making *loob* into a motivated sign that precisely lends it value and force, situating it as a cultural term in a larger historical field. However, in tracing the diverse meanings of *loob,* we also get a sense of its semiotic instability, which Spanish translations sought to limit but could not fully contain.

In the missionary texts, *loob* is charged with the task of carrying the weight of such Western concepts as soul, will, and conscience. *Loob,* along with a host of other Tagalog terms—*sisi* ('repentance'), *casalanan* ('sin'), *aua* ('pity'), to cite only a few—were meant to bear the burden of all those cherished metaphysical and theological concepts that would allow for the imposition of Spanish rule both inside and outside the natives' minds. However, if we turn to other sorts of missionary texts— the *vocabularios* and the early twentieth-century *diccionarios* modeled after them—we get a sense of the semantic diversity of *loob.* In the 1613 *vocabulario* of Fray Pedro de San Buenaventura, *loob* is defined as 'inside,' 'to go inside,' and 'an interior room in a house,' in addition to the Spanish constructs 'will' and 'heart.' In Fray Juan de Noceda and Fray Pedro San Lucar's 1745 *vocabulario* and Pedro Serrano-Laktaw's 1914 *diccionario,*[17] these definitions appear along with other connotations of *loob.* On the one hand, it is defined as *lo mas interno,* the most interior part of the person, hence the seat of taste and desire; on the other hand, it is also the mere inside of any object, as in *looban,* the inside of a house, the ground on which it is built, the floor of a building, the yard that marks off the space between house and street. In this sense, *loob* is not a privileged inside that defines being, but an inside that signals an interval separating one object from another, or one part of the object from its other parts. *Looban* can also function as a verb to mean the act of attacking and sacking a house. Rendered as *ipaloob* or *pagpapaloob,* it pertains to the insertion of one object into another, its enclosure and concealment from the gaze of those outside. The verb form of *loob* indicates the consequence of a prior displacement of objects from the outside, either through exchange or robbery. There is a sense, then, in which there is nothing natural or spontaneous about what is inside, for what is inside is constituted by things that have been shifted there from the outside or *labas.* The "inside" and "outside" thus tend to be situated in terms of one being at the interval of the other. This is further reflected by the inflection of *loob* into *pangloob,* 'under clothes,' which serves as an interior layer between the outer clothes and the body. It is also the same word used to mean the inside of a cage used for fishing along a river bank, and as a kind of trap for rats. This is a further extension of the sense of *loob* as the space for the containment of things that come from the outside.

However, it should be noted that the inside of things is also thought of to lend itself to a similar process of displacement outside. This is shown by the fact that *loob* is at the root of one of the words for 'to give,' *ipagcaloob,* while the word for gift itself is *caloob,* literally part of the inside of something. From this it seems that *loob* is juxtaposed with, rather than dialectically opposed to, *labas,* 'the outside.' In being attached to the word for debt (*utang*), *loob* figures as both the site and the object of exchange. It is constituted by objects in circulation just as it functions to represent the desired form of circulation. *Utang na loob* from this perspective is not only a debt of gratitude but also a debt of, from, and for the inside, as indicated by the particle *na*. The *loob* that is staked in a debt transaction is therefore an inside that is also an interior surface, a container as well as that which is contained, but only to the extent that it is already oriented toward an external process of exchange.

Loob is important not because it invariably designates a soul—as the Spaniards would have wanted it to—at the core of being. Its significance lies in the way it marks out the space within which objects and signs from the outside could be accumulated and from which and toward which they could be issued in payment of a debt. In *utang-na-loob* transactions, the *loob* that one places in circulation is one that is detachable and reattachable, not one that sums up the self in its totality. This is to say that where the Tagalog idea of indebtedness is concerned, *loob* is precipitated in the process of exchange, not prior to it. It is, therefore, not an anterior state that stands in a superior position to the mechanism of debt transactions. Rather, it is that which can be known and realized only in the process of indebtedness. To reduce *loob,* as the Spaniards did, to a question of intentionality and the locus of guilt and repentance would be to assume that it stands behind and above the terms of reciprocity. But as the various inflections of *loob* suggest, what is implicated in *utang-na-loob* transactions is neither an originary source of gifts nor a privileged interiority accountable for its debts.

If a sense of subjectivity does not determine exchange, constraining one to enter into a reciprocal network of indebtedness with others, what does? In the context of *utang na loob,* it is the concept of *hiya*. From the early seventeenth century to the present day, *hiya* has been defined as the appropriate affect that accompanies indebtedness. Yet, it is also that which arises from the sensed exclusion from a circuit of debt relations.

Often translated as 'shame,' *hiya,* like *loob,* can take on a wide variety of significations. The feeling of *hiya* is one that is also characterized by irritation and vexation at being made into an object of amusement or into a foil for someone else's aggrandizement. The act of subjecting one to this state of shame is called *hiyaiin,* that is, to mock, to jest, to disconcert and confuse, and, figuratively, to slap and trample upon. To this extent, to be in a state of *hiya* is to be in a vulnerable position as one available for an other's blows, whether physical or verbal. For this reason, the feeling of *hiya* involves experiencing a certain kind of embarrassment that arises from being unduly overwhelmed (*empachar*). The negative aspect of *hiya* appears as the sense of being unable to fend off signs that come from the outside by performing a response adequate to what one has received, that is, the sense of the unregulated and undeserved reception of signs and things from the outside. The displeasure produced by the feeling of *hiya* therefore comes from being made to think of all the things one would have wanted to give back in return but cannot, as well as all those things that one would have wanted to receive but is no longer able to request.

But insofar as *hiya* is an essential component of *utang na loob,* it also has a positive register. This is shown by the term *magbigay hiya,* 'to render respect,' 'to consider and honor someone.' Reflective of this is the Tagalog saying, *Ang tauong kulang sa hiya, walang halaga ang wika,* 'One who lacks *hiya* is one whose words have no value.'[18] *Hiya* gives value to words proferred in discursive exchange, just as it is the dominant affect that arises from sensing one's failure to return what has been received. Here lies the ambiguity of shame. On the one hand, it is the condition of possibility for indebtedness whereby to have no *hiya* is to have no *utang na loob.* Indeed, as studies of Tagalog reciprocity indicate, the worst denigration possible is to characterize an individual as being *walang hiya,* 'without shame,' which is synonymous with *walang utang na loob,* 'without any sense of indebtedness.' On the other hand, *hiya* also represents the rupture in debt transactions, filling one with confusion and a deep sense of helplessness in relation to the outside. *Hiya* thus colors the entire spectrum of indebtedness, signaling both its operation and its failure. It is from fear of public shame, that is, of being excluded from a network of exchange vis-à-vis the outside, that one accedes to *utang-na-loob* ties, for without the fear of *hiya,* the *labas,* or outside, would remain unknown. Consequently, the *loob,* or inside, could never be put into circulation. Participation in exchange is conceivable only to the extent that one is successful in blocking the surge of *hiya. Utang-na-loob* ties are valued precisely insofar as they allow one to contain the negative and undesirable affect and effect of *hiya,* converting them instead into an element that infuses what is given up in return. Reciprocity in terms of *hiya* and *utang na loob* is thus ordered toward anticipating and domesticating the ever-present possibility of being deluged by an uncontrollable rush of signs from the outside. For if one were incapable of knowing *hiya,* one would end up being "shocked" by it to the point of being cut off from exchange. And without exchange, no sense of an inside, or *loob,* would emerge.

What I want to hypothesize here is that, to the extent that Christianity was phrased in the idiom of *hiya* and *utang na loob,* Tagalogs felt constrained to attend to it. Caught up in what seemed like an unending stream of unfamiliar and untranslatable words put forth in the familiar terms of reciprocal obligation, the natives "converted," that is, availed themselves of the sacraments as a way of entering into a debt transaction with the Spaniards and their God. The Tagalog interest in contracting Christianity stemmed from their fear of being overcome by *hiya*—of being barraged by gifts and signs that they might not be able to "read" and would be unable to "control." Yet the terms of this contract differed between ruler and ruled. The Tagalog notion of reciprocity spelled a crucial difference in the terms of indebtedness that conversion entailed. One way of getting a sense of that difference is to consider the matter of confession.

The validity of confession, as we have seen, largely depended on a procedure of accounting for one's sins. However, while insisting on a rigorous accounting, the missionaries also demanded that the conversion of sins into a narrative be as straightforward and free from deviation as possible.[19] But as missionary accounts indicate, native converts tended to be much more concerned with the possibility that confession presented for embarking on a discursive exchange than with getting to and at the point of that exchange. Why this should be the case has to do with the nature of payment involved in *utang-na-loob* relationships.

Studies of Tagalog reciprocity have often stressed the seeming inequality built into debt transactions. The hierarchy that is precipitated by indebtedness is based on the sensed incommensurability between the gift received and the gift returned, particularly if the former is an unsolicited one.[20] Prototypical of this is the debt relationship obtaining between mother and child. The child is said to have an *utang na loob* to its mother (and never the reverse) by virtue of having received from her the unexpected gift of life. It is assumed that the child will never fully be able to repay this debt. Instead, it is expected to spend its life giving token recognition of this debt to the mother by means of what might be described as partial payments in the form of respect (*paggalang*). But respect as a form of token recognition tends to be most explicit on the level of discourse. This is evinced by the use of words of deference when addressing the mother—or any other parental figure—such as *ho* and *po*. These terms are usually attached to words directed to the figure of authority, as in *Ano po ang gusto ninyo?* 'What do you want (sir/madam)?' By themselves, *ho* and *po* refer to nothing in particular. Only when they are inserted in the interval—or *loob*—of words directed at one's parents and elders do they take on significance in that they convey the existence of respect. To this extent, they are also the signs of the existence of *utang-na-loob* ties that would otherwise remain unarticulated. Aside from this expression of deference, children usually do not have set tasks around the household. Only when they have become adults are they expected to take care of their parents. The burden of indebtedness thus falls upon the child who, even as he or she enters adulthood, never stops owing his or her *loob* to the parent. As Hollnsteiner puts it, "Nothing [the child] can do during its lifetime can make up for what [the mother] has done for it."[21]

The intrinsic inequality of debt relationships comes across as benign where a mother and her child are concerned. However, it can take on much more pressing political overtones when it is transferred to other social contexts. For example, where the traditional forms of landlord-tenant ties are concerned, Hollnsteiner makes the following pertinent observations.

> In the landlord-tenant relationship . . . the tenant knows he cannot approach anywhere near an equivalent return. As long as he fulfils his expected duties towards his landlord and shows by bringing a few dozen eggs and helping out in festive occasions that he recognizes a debt of gratitude (*utang na loob*), he may continue to expect benefits from his landlord. The tenant receives uninterrupted preferential treatment despite the fact that he never reciprocates with interest and never reverses the debt relationships.[22]

The hierarchical relationship between landlord and tenant (at least on a conceptual level) arises because of the inability of the latter to override the gifts of the former. What underwrites the continuation of exchange between the two is the nature of the payment. The tenant is expected to do no more than render token signs of his or her indebtedness to the landlord. Partial payments ensure that a continuous flow of gifts from above will accrue to those below. Such payments have no set form. Neither are they subject to a rigorous schedule. Instead, the nature and frequency of payments depend more on the creditor's whim and the debtor's resources. Reciprocity in this case maintains a hierarchy to the extent that the full payment of debts can always be—indeed, must be—deferred.

The imperative to defer full payment in favor of tokens of indebtedness makes for a peculiar contract. Among the Spaniards, the contraction of debt obligations between two parties was always articulated with reference to a third party that stood outside the exchange yet determined its contours. Whether figured as God, the king, the state, or the law, this third agent served as the central figure in all negotiations, acting as the origin, interpreter, and enforcer of the terms governing exchange. It was thus invested with the sense of being the source of hierarchy just as it was the source of all gifts. It was also within the province of the transcendent third term to insist on specific kinds of payments in return for the benefits it had given its subjects. In the context of Spanish colonization, these payments would consist of such things as taxes, forced labor, the ritual observance of sacraments, and so forth. Furthermore, the specified amounts of payments were always coordinated with a time-table of sorts: monthly tax rolls, weekly masses, or annual confessions. This made for a system of indebtedness that was posited on the possibility and inevitability of full payment, for ultimately all debts contracted by the individual within the law culminated in death. Death was the last horizon of exchange. And where evangelization was concerned, it marked the moment of irrevocable reckoning of all of one's accumulated debts in the presence of an infinite creditor.

In *utang-na-loob* ties, in contrast, the tripartite structure of the Spanish contract gives way to a different configuration. The contracting of debts, given the nonoriginary source and destination of gifts (*loob*) and the practice of token payments, is premised not on the sanction of a transcendent third term but precisely on its elision. The possibility of eliding the third term has a linguistic basis. Like other Malayo-Polynesian languages, Tagalog has two pronouns to indicate the first person plural, we. These are *cami,* the 'exclusive we,' and *tayo,* the 'inclusive we.' *Cami* is that which makes it conceivable to articulate a transaction between a self and an other that arises from the exclusion of a third party. In this case, one speaks of maintaining *utang-na-loob* ties that are predicated upon a negative consideration of those who are outside such ties. Such is indicated in expressions recorded in eighteenth-century dictionaries, as in *Cami,y, nagpapapautangan nang loob,* 'We are indebted to each other (and not to them)' or 'We are contracting debts with one another (and not with them),' and *Hindi nagpapautang loob siya sa aquin,* 'He or she does not want to be indebted to me.' The forging of obligations thus becomes a matter between *loobs* rather than between individuals before the law.[23]

The effect of this elision is to render the hierarchy obtaining in *utang-na-loob* ties explicitly arbitrary. This is to say that relationships of indebtedness are not instituted by an absolute source of debts making itself felt through a progressive chain of signs. The arbitrariness of hierarchy in this instance comes from the tenuous link it is thought to have with the figure of authority from which gifts come. The token payments of debts are made not in order to memorialize authority and thereby consolidate hierarchy. Rather, token returns are meant simply to loosen the pressures from above, resulting in the deflection of the full force of hierarchy.

Conversely, the failure to make partial payments signals one's failure to "read" in the gift the return that is demanded, leading to the outbreak of *hiya*. It is the moment when one is taken up by a violent onrush of signs that makes it impossible to have a sense of *loob* that could be offered in exchange. Hollnsteiner, in discussing a Visayan analogue of *hiya, way ibalus,* cites a popular saying.

A beggar prays for the good health of whoever gives him alms, and a dog barks for his master, but a *way ibalus* does not even have a prayer or a bark for his benefactor.[24]

This indicates that the eruption of *hiya* leaves the individual speechless, utterly unable to return that which has been received from the other. It is in the interest of containing *hiya* that one is thus constrained to reciprocate a gift and thereby elude the potentially confounding and disconcerting force of hierarchy. Tagalog reciprocity, then, is a matter of "reading" into the gift that one receives not so much its source but, more important, the return that is expected. Within a Christian-colonial context, the idea of *utang na loob* furnished the Tagalog converts a way of conceiving relations of inequality that would sporadically displace the demands issuing from the totalizing hierarchy of Spanish Christianity.

This was perhaps why the Tagalogs responded enthusiastically to the signs of Christianity, particularly to the sacraments, such as penance. Missionary writers often spoke of the avidity with which native converts turned to confession. The idiom of *utang na loob* and *hiya* riveted the natives' attention not to its sacramental value, however. Instead, it drew native converts toward the discursive machinery of confession as a means of contracting and extending ties of reciprocity with those who had a surplus of signs. By availing themselves of the sacraments, Tagalogs afforded themselves opportunities for negotiating around Spanish demands and thus avoiding the shock of *hiya* when confronted by them. It was perhaps because of this that hearing native confessions was, as the Jesuit Murillo Velarde writes, "to enter into a labyrinth without a clue."[25] Upon asking for an exhaustive accounting of the penitent's past, the missionaries were beset by a series of digressions, non sequiturs, and even displays of braggadocio. Fray Blancas de San José's exhortations to the Tagalogs give ample evidence of this.

> Despite all the admonitions and examples of the Priest, why do so many of you persist in such twists and turns, in such obscurities and deviations in your *loob* so that your sentences are contaminated with these same obscurities; how you should be ashamed (*mahiya*) of yourselves for engaging in riddles (*nagbobogtongan*) during confession.[26]

The twists and turns of native confession are said to take on the quality of riddles (*bogtong*). Native riddles were recorded by missionary lexicographers in their efforts to illustrate word usage in Tagalog. The riddles seem to have existed prior to the Spanish conquest, and they continued in circulation, many remaining unchanged, throughout the Spanish period and up to the present day. Such riddles, or *bogtong,* were also staple components of Tagalog literature during the Spanish colonial period, and the Spanish accounts note their popularity. Tagalogs were given to trading riddles in a game called *magbogtongan* during fiestas, funeral wakes, weddings, and even while engaged in such mundane tasks as tending their fields. These games were not contests in the sense of having winners and losers; rather, the delight in trading riddles came from the way in which they presented an opportunity for showing one's ability to generate semantic slippages that decontextualized words from their everyday usages. We see this in the following examples.

Riddle. A little lake bounded by a bamboo fence.
Answer. An eye.
Riddle. By day a bamboo tube, by night a sea.

Answer. A sleeping mat.[27]

The responses "eye" and "sleeping mat" have no necessary connections to a "lake bounded by a bamboo fence" or "bamboo tube" and "sea." The pleasure of *bogtongs* comes from the way they shift the referent of a word away from its functional connotations, creating for it another constellation of associations. Hence, "mat" is seen not in association with sleeping but with the sea at night, and "eye" is brought in touch not with seeing but with the bounded area of a lake. By converting the discourse of sin into a game of *bogtongan,* the native penitent took confession to be an invitation to display his or her ability to return conundrums in exchange for other conundrums received from the priest. In lieu of a straight narrative, the confessors got back what seemed a bewildering show of the penitent's verbal dexterity.

Adding to this bewilderment was the natives' propensity to tell not their own sins but those of others.

> And others seriously go astray when they tell to the Priest the sins of their wives, or their sons-in-law, or their mother-in-law, while their own sins rarely cross their lips; the only reason why they go to the Priest is in order to denounce to him all the people they dislike.[28]

What occurs here is that the self that confesses turns its focus not on its own sins but on those of others. Rather than assume the responsibility for one's sins—as the acts that originate from one's "own" *loob*—there is a move to appropriate even the sins of others as offerings that might appease the figure of authority. In other passages, Blancas complains of the tendency to blame others, including neighbors, wives, and even the *demonio,* for one's sins. Tagalog penitents thus were far from attaching a sense of ownership to their sins inasmuch as sins were not attached to a soul but to the *loob*. This suggests that the imperative for the internalization of guilt and repentance prescribed by the missionaries was liable to be circumvented by the natives. Instead, confessional discourse remained suspended in the economy of *utang na loob* and *hiya.* From this perspective, it is not surprising to hear that confession was used as well for displays of braggadocio.

> One other great error that others commit in their confession is that they only speak of their great deeds, while never speaking about their

sins [and] the only reason they go [to confession] is to honor their own goodness.[29]

To brag about one's goodness (*cabanalan*) results in bypassing the demand for a narrative of sin. In effect, it subverted the entire conceptual apparatus of confession. Instead of submitting to the law in recounting accumulated transgressions against it, native penitents converted confession into a receptacle for boasting and protestations of innocence. In this sense, the *loob* that is offered as payment for one's debt in confession ends up submitting to the representatives of the law while simultaneously relegating the law itself into the margins of exchange.

To the Spanish demand that converts make their bodies speak the language of God, the Tagalog tendency was to respond by performing token payments designed to appease the figures of authority and deflect the force of hierarchy. This involved eluding the internalization of the interrogative language of the law carried by the insistent voice of the dominant other. The turn to confessional discourse—as most probably to the other sacraments—was motivated in part, as I have argued, by the fear of *hiya* and the desire to establish *utang-na-loob* ties with those at the top of the colonial hierarchy. From this perspective, it is possible to postulate the emergence of one type of Tagalog conversion: one that involved confession without sin, of submission without translation. Conversion where the Tagalogs were concerned during this period would then have occurred as an *après coup* response to the unsolicited and therefore "shocking" gift of signs that the Spaniards "bestowed" on them. In taming this shock, Tagalogs resorted to the familiar terms of *hiya* and *utang na loob* that accompanied the transfer of Spanish signs in the vernacular. Converting conversion and confusing confession, Tagalogs "submitted" while at the same time hollowing out the Spanish call to submission.

NOTES

1. See John Phelan, *The Hispanization of the Philippines: Spanish Aims and Filipino Responses, 1565–1700* (Madison: University of Wisconsin Press, 1959), 65–67.

2. See Vicente L. Rafael, *Contracting Colonialism: Translation and Christian Conversion in Tagalog Society under Early Spanish Rule* (Ithaca: Cornell University Press, 1988), 84–109, for a more thorough discussion of the procedures

of accounting and the internalization of guilt with regard to confessional discourse.

3. Fray Sebastian Totanes, *Manual tagalog para auxilio a los religiosos de esta provincia de S. Gregoriao Magno de Descalzos de N.S. Padre S. Francisco de Philipinas* (Sampaloc: Convento de Nuestra Señora de Loreto, 1745), 133–37.

4. Catholic theology regards Christ Himself as the source and author of all the sacraments; they were codified into a set of seven distinct rituals by the Council of Trent. Their crucial importance lies in their function of bringing God's gift to bear on the convert. Sacraments are signs valued for their capacity to make transparent the source of all gifts. Their power is such that, in accordance with the Thomistic formulation, "they effect what they signify; they are signs that cause what they signify and cause by signifying" (A. M. Amado, "Sacraments of the Church," in *New Catholic Encyclopedia* [New York: McGraw Hill, 1967], 4:808). In their ritual performance, sacraments are thus the codes that constitute their own utterance so that the articulation of each sacrament brings with it the articulation of the entire history of Christianity.

5. The combined effects of Spanish racism, royal legislation, and the absence of adequate institutions for training natives for the priesthood made it impossible for a native clergy to emerge prior to the second half of the eighteenth century. See Horacio de la Costa, S.J., "The Development of the Native Clergy in the Philippines," in *Studies in Philippine Church History,* ed. Gerald Anderson (Ithaca: Cornell University Press, 1969), 65–104.

6. The record of the conflicts and their resolutions between Spanish ecclesiastical and civil authorities with regard to such things as the collection of tribute, the solicitation of native submission, and the extraction of *corvée* labor from the natives testifies to persistent attempts to instill the primacy of evangelization in the spread and consolidation of Spanish rule in the Philippines. See "Actas del Primer Sinodo de Manila (1582–86)," *Philippinana Sacra* 4, no. 12 (September–December, 1969): 425–537; John Schumacher, S.J., "The Manila Synodal Tradition: A Brief History," *Philippine Studies* 27 (1979): 285–348. The ideological supremacy of evangelization received, of course, its most explicit expression in the institution of the *patronato real* (i.e., the royal patronage of the Church in the Indies). See Costa, "Development of Native Clergy," 69–71.

7. Phelan, *Hispanization,* 50–51; Schumacher, "Manila Synodal Tradition," 309; Rafael, *Contracting Colonialism,* 23–54. For Tagalog, the exemplary *arte* was that of Fray Francisco Blancas de San José, *Arte de la lengua tagala* (Bataan: por Tomas Pinpin, 1610); while the most significant *vocabularios* were that of Fray Pedro de San Buenaventura, *Vocabulario de la lengua tagala* (Pila: por Tomas Pinpin, 1613) and the two volume compilation of Fray Juan de Noceda and Fray Pedro San Lucar, *Vocabulario de la lengua tagala* (Manila, 1754; 3d ed., Manila: Imprenta de Ramirez y Giraudier, 1860).

8. Ig. González-Llubera, ed., *Gramática de la lengua castellana* (London: Oxford University Press, 1926), first published in Salamanca in 1492.

9. See Carlos Noreña, *Studies in Spanish Renaissance Thought* (The Hague: Martinus Nijhoff, 1975), 189–97.

10. See, for example, the accounts of Diego de Bobadilla, S.J., "Relation of the Philippine Islands, 1640," in *The Philippine Islands, 1493–1898,* ed. Emma Blair and Alexander Robertson (Cleveland: Arthur H. Clark Co., 1903–9), 64:295ff.; Pedro Chirino, S.J., *Relacion de las Islas Filipinas* (Rome: n.p., 1604); Pedro Murillo Velarde, "Jesuit Missions in the Seventeenth Century," in *Philippine Islands,* ed. Blair and Robertson, 64:32ff. Using far less military force than they did in the New World (and meeting with much less resistance from the natives as well), the Spaniards succeeded in converting over half a million people in the islands while retaining less than 300 missionaries by the first half of the seventeenth century. Whatever reluctance existed on the part of the lowland, non-Islamised populace seems to have been overcome rapidly. This was particularly true among the Tagalogs. See Phelan, *Hispanization,* 8–9, 56.

11. Totanes, *Manual,* 36–37.

12. Totanes, *Manual,* 50–51.

13. See, for example, the devotional texts of Fray Alonso de Santa Ana, *Explicacion de la doctrina christiana en la lengua tagala* (Manila, 1672; Manila: Imprenta de los Amigos de Pais, 1853), 112; Fray Pedro de Herrera, *Meditaciones cun manga mahal na Pagninilay na sadya sa Sanctong Pag Eexercicios* (Manila, 1645; Manila: La Imprenta de la Compania de IHS, 1762), folio 8; Fray Francisco Blancas de San José, *Librong Pinagpapalamnan yto nang aasalin nang taoung Christiano . . . ,* 3d ed. (Manila: n.p., 1662), 282–83; 370. For a more thorough listing of other devotional texts popular in the seventeenth century, see Rafael, *Contracting Colonialism,* 84–109.

14. Charles Kaut, *"Utang na Loob:* A System of Contractual Obligations among the Tagalogs," *Southwestern Journal of Anthropology,* 17, no. 3 (1969): 256–72; Mary Hollnsteiner, "Reciprocity in the Lowland Philippines," in *Four Readings in Filipino Values,* ed. Frank Lynch, S.J., and Alfonso de Guzman III (Quezon City: Institute of Philippine Culture, 1979), 69–92.

15. Reynaldo Ileto, *Pasyon and Revolution: Popular Movements in the Philippines, 1840–1940* (Quezon City: Ateneo de Manila University Press, 1979), 11–28.

16. Ileto, *Pasyon,* 331.

17. Pedro Serrano-Laktaw, *Diccionario tagalog-hispano,* pt. 2 (Manila: Imprenta de Santos y Bernal, 1914).

18. Serrano-Laktaw, *Diccionario,* 333.

19. We read, for example, the following exhortation to the native convert in Totanes's *Manual:*

S/he must straighten his/her sentences, open his/her *loob,* arrange his/her words, relate all of his/her sins, their number, their extent, their gravity; and if it were to be compared to walking [the telling of sins] should take to the middle road rather than fork out in various directions; tell and relate everything so that the Lord God might know what is in your *loob.* (82)

20. Hollnsteiner, "Reciprocity," 75–76; Kaut, "*Utang na Loob,*" 262.

21. Hollnsteiner, "Reciprocity," 76.

22. Hollnsteiner, "Reciprocity," 74.

23. This would not be surprising given the nature of Tagalog sociopolitical structure on the eve of Spanish colonization. Living in coastal village settlements called *barangays,* the Tagalogs did not have anything approaching a centralized state apparatus. Instead, they were led by village chieftains called *datu;* the chieftain's position was the result of a series of reciprocal ties that he (only men could be *datu*) could cultivate among the people in the village rather than of the sanction of any outside realm. As such, no institution of kingship, supravillage confederation, elaborate legal code, or organized system of worship adhered to the Tagalogs prior to the arrival of Spain in the Philippines. See William Henry Scott's brilliant essay, "Filipino Class Structure in the Sixteenth Century," in his *Cracks in the Parchment Curtain and Other Essays in Philippine History* (Quezon City: New Day Publishers, 1982), 96–126.

24. Hollnsteiner, "Reciprocity," 78.

25. Murillo Velarde, "Jesuit Missions," in *Philippine Islands,* ed. Blair and Robertson, 44:30.

26. Blancas de San José, *Librong,* 242–43.

27. Bienvenido Lumbera, "Poetry of the Early Tagalogs," *Philippine Studies* 16 (1968):223–30, has an extended discussion of the prosodic features of the Tagalog *bogtong.*

28. Blancas de San José, *Librong,* 245–47.

29. Blancas de San José, *Librong,* 251.

From Avoidance to Confrontation: Peasant Protest in Precolonial and Colonial Southeast Asia

Michael Adas

Although there has been a dramatic broadening of the definition of social protest in recent years to include collective behavior that was once dismissed as criminal, irrational, or insignificant, our attention has continued to be focused on movements involving direct, often violent, confrontations between the wielders of power and dissident groups. Avoidance protest, by which dissatisfied groups seek to attenuate their hardships and express their discontent through flight, sectarian withdrawal, or other activities that minimize challenges to or clashes with those whom they view as their oppressors, has at best remained a secondary concern of students of social protest. Although specific forms of avoidance protest, such as the flight of slaves in the plantation zones of the Americas or the migration of serfs to the towns of medieval Europe and peasants to the frontiers of Tsarist Russia, have merited a prominent place in the historical literature on some societies and time periods,[1] avoidance protest has rarely been systematically analyzed as a phenomenon in itself. There have been few detailed studies of the diverse forms that avoidance protest may take and the ways in which these are shaped by the sociopolitical contexts in which they develop. This neglect is serious because, in many societies and time periods (perhaps in most in the preindustrial era), modes of protest oriented to avoidance rather than confrontation have been the preferred and most frequently adopted means of resisting oppression and expressing dissatisfaction. Thus, rather than being treated as isolated episodes or indicators of social unrest that culminated in "major" forms of protest, such as riots or rebellions, as has been the case in the work of most scholars (including my own),[2] the various forms of avoidance protest ought to be examined in their own right.

This article will focus on several related forms of avoidance protest found in many Asian and African societies. Although, in illustrating the different patterns of avoidance protest and examining the sociopolitical contexts that gave rise to these forms of resistance, I will rely mainly upon evidence from Burma and Java, where most of my own research has been concentrated, I will also make use of examples from Africa, South Asia, and other areas in Southeast Asia. These supplemental examples, for which parallels can be found in works on China, Europe, and Latin America, are used to indicate the widespread distribution and importance of avoidance protest and, with significant variations, the prevalence of the type of political economy found in precolonial Burma and Java that I characterize as the "contest state." A wide variety of preindustrial political systems, ranging from the warrier-dominated kingdoms of medieval Europe or Japan, at one pole of a hypothetical continuum, to relatively highly centralized empires like the Mughal in India or the Asante in Ghana, at the other, can be grouped under the general type of the contest state. Central to this form of political organization is rule by a king or emperor who claims a monopoly of power and authority in a given society but whose effective control is, in reality, severely restricted by rival power centers among the elite, by weaknesses in administrative organization and institutional commitment on the part of state officials, by poor communications, and by a low population-to-land ratio that places a premium on manpower retention and regulation. These conditions gave rise to polities in which there was a constant struggle between the ruler and the nobility, between factions of the elite at various levels, and between supravillage elite groups and village notables and peasants for the control of labor and the agricultural production that formed the basis of these predominantly agrarian states. Although the fortunes of the contending parties fluctuated greatly over time, their continuing struggle over revenue control and the inability of any one of the parties to dominate the others decisively on a sustained basis suggest the concept of the contest state as a useful way to characterize this form of political organization.

One of the central purposes of this article is to examine the ways in which the coming of colonial rule transformed contest states into much more centralized, bureaucratic systems and to consider the effects of this transformation on the modes of protest adopted by peasant groups. One of the cruelest contradictions of the era of colonization arose from situations in which population growth and political centralization forced the peasantry of Africa and Asia to adopt methods of protest involving confrontation with incumbent regimes, rather than relying on resistance through avoidance, at a time when vastly improved military organization and weapons technology rendered such clashes lethal exercises in futility.

In societies similar to those found in Burma and Java before the advent of European colonial rule, various modes of avoidance protest were closely related to, and in many instances merely extensions of, longstanding defense mechanisms developed by peasant communities to buffer elite demands on village production and manpower. These defenses were, in turn, rooted in demographic and geographic conditions and in the nature of the political economies of the societies in which they emerged. As a result, it is often difficult to distinguish between defense mechanisms and expressions of protest, and it is also impossible to understand either of these in isolation from the political and social systems in which they arose. Peasant migration from the lands of an unpopular lord, for example, was both a means by which the group in flight protected itself from what it felt to be excessive exactions and a dramatic way of protesting and drawing attention to the maladministration of the noble or official in question. The option of flight was, in turn, dependent upon a low population density, the availability of refuge zones or unoccupied lands in which the runaways could settle, and a relatively low level of administrative control and coercive capacity.

These examples indicate the importance of beginning the analysis of avoidance protest with an overview of the state systems of precolonial Java and Burma, the nature of elite-peasant interaction in these societies, and the ways in which these institutions and exchanges shaped the persistent defense mechanisms employed by peasant communities in each area. I will then consider the conditions under which these defenses were violated or judged insufficient to provide adequate protection and were thus superseded by various forms of collective protest. Though the focus will be on modes of avoidance protest, I will also examine the relationship between these forms of collective behavior and the kinds of resistance aimed at confrontations with, and at times fundamental challenges to, those whom the peasants viewed as their oppressors. The remaining portions of the essay will be devoted to a discussion of the political, economic, and social changes that occurred in Burma and Java as a result of European colonization, and the impact of these transformations of the modes of protest adopted by dissident groups.

In precolonial Java and Burma, as in kingdoms throughout most of Southeast and South Asia and over much of Africa, administrative and military weaknesses and poor communications provided the main checks against excessive demands by elite groups on their peasant subjects. Although abstract ethical considerations set forth in religious texts or in political discourses on the attributes of a just ruler may have deeply influenced some monarchs and state officials,[3] elite rivalries, personalist patron-client ties, and poorly integrated (both vertically and horizontally) administrative systems were far more constant and secure sources of peasant protection. In the kingdoms of precolonial Burma and Java, control of political positions was determined primarily by inheritance and lineage patterns associated with Max Weber's ideal type of patrimonial domain.[4] This mode of allocating authority resulted in deep divisions among the elite and in incessant, often violent, struggles by groups allied to lineages at various levels from the court center to the local district as they vied for control of the limited resources of the state that emanated largely from the labors of the cultivating classes at the bottom of the sociopolitical hierarchy. These chronic and pervasive struggles greatly inhibited the rulers' and administrators' ability to control the village communities where the great majority of their subjects lived. The rivalries also made it possible for the peasant inhabitants of these communities to develop a wide range of techniques designed to defend their interests in the ongoing contest through the circumvention or reduction of elite demands.

Like the kingdoms and empires in the Middle East and South Asia upon which they modeled their political institutions and ideologies, the societies of Java and Burma were periodically ravaged by bloody strife that resulted from a fundamental contradiction in the sociopolitical order. In situations where monarchs were expected to, and normally did, have large numbers of wives, concubines, and children, the process of royal succession was not clearly defined or regulated. Because the royal blood line included the ruler's siblings and extended over several generations, there were usually many potential claimants to the throne of a given kingdom. Though only a few of these were likely to possess sufficient ambition and backing to attempt to seize the throne of a reigning monarch, the constant threat that his relatives, as well as members of powerful families among the nobility, posed for the ruler forced him to devote considerable time and resources to surveillance and Machiavellian maneuvers designed to prevent strong support from coalescing around promising rivals or to crush attempts at open rebellion.[5]

The rivals themselves and their supporters, which usually included many of the monarch's chief ministers and the most important nobles of the realm, were also deeply immersed in efforts to build the power of their own factions and to deprive competing groups of manpower and sources of revenue. If a ruler fell ill, suffered serious losses in wars with neighboring states or advancing European colonizers, or died, the rival claimants and their preexisting factions entered into intense, often bloody, contests for control of the throne. Though the winners of these struggles frequently conducted brutal purges to destroy rival power centers, new claimants and competing factions invariably emerged, even in the reigns of the strongest rulers.

Rivalries centered at the court and capital city were paralleled by tensions between the monarch and the regional lords. Although regional administrators were the appointees and nominally the representatives of the ruler, even the most powerful monarchs were unable to maintain effective control over more than just the capital city and the heartland areas of the kingdom that surrounded it.[6] As one moved away from the core areas of a state, the power of the ruler diminished perceptibly and that of the regional lords became increasingly evident. Regional administrators, whether they be members of the royal family, personal retainers of the sovereign, or local lords, used their positions to build up their own power bases and amass personal fortunes. In most instances, they ruled their provinces as autonomous and self-sufficient units and posed a constant threat to the rulers of Javanese and Burmese kingdoms—a threat that was often translated into plots or rebellions aimed at seizing the throne.

Regional administrators not only vied with the ruler in their attempts to build their own bases of power and wealth, they competed with other nobles and administrators for the loyalty of client-retainers and control over peasant producers. These lords were also locked in a ceaseless contest with their own retainers and subordinates as each strove to maximize the share of the collected revenue that he retained as the tribute passed upward through a complex hierarchy of administrators and tax collectors.[7] The fact that administrators at all levels were given a cut of the taxes collected, rather than a regular salary, made this contest inevitable. Institutionalized corruption in the forms of underreporting and embezzlement was rampant in precolonial Southeast Asian polities. Within certain informally prescribed limits, these practices were essential to the functioning of the administrative system because they compensated for the inadequacy of the formal remuneration of state officials. The withholding of up to 10 percent of the taxes collected appears to have been widespread and accepted. At times, however, even in periods of strong dynastic control, the amount held back illegally reached as high as 40 percent of the revenue that passed through the hands of administrators at different levels.[8]

Another key weakness of precolonial polities in Burma and Java that made it possible for cultivators to develop defenses against excessive elite demands was the failure of the administrative system to penetrate to the village level. Although village headmen had to be approved by regional officials and, in times of dynastic strength, by ministers in the capital, the local leaders gained and maintained their positions primarily through local influence and support. The village headmen of Java and Burma, who were generally drawn from the regional gentry families of these societies, were the most secure and best informed persons who exercised political authority in the precolonial era. Their control over local affairs rested on the extent of their holdings, the number of laborers and artisans dependent on the use of their land and their patronage, the wisdom they demonstrated in village councils, and their ability to defend the interests of their communities in dealings with supravillage officials and their agents. In contrast to the often short-lived careers of courtiers and tax farmers, the village gentry families frequently controlled local offices for generations and, in some cases, centuries. Village headmen and the local gentry from which they came, then, were pivotal intermediaries between the state and the mass of the peasantry. Without their cooperation, it would have been difficult, if not impossible, for transient tax farmers and even local men appointed to administrative posts to draw revenue and manpower from village communities on a regular basis.[9]

Underlying the weak political integration of precolonial states in Java and Burma were low population densities, poor communications, and a low level of achievement in military organization and technology. In Burma and Java, as in most Asian and African kingdoms, control of manpower, and not of land, was the state's chief concern. Even in regions that were fairly densely populated, such as central and eastern Java or the Dry Zone of Upper Burma, substantial amounts of unclaimed arable land were available, and large tracts of scantily populated forest wilderness beckoned to disgruntled cultivators. Except in riverine or coastal areas, movement of large military forces or bulk goods was ponderous and costly. Aside from cavalry regiments manned by the nobility or special service corps and small contingents of professional soldiers stationed in the capital, the armies of precolonial rulers were primarily made up of forcibly conscripted peasants who were poorly equipped and trained. These conditions greatly restricted the ruler's capacity to control regional lords and made it virtually impossible for him to forcibly collect taxes or mobilize labor on a sustained basis.[10]

Thus, precolonial rulers were compelled to rely mainly upon adherence to state cults centering on the ruler's powers to protect and to grant fertility, on chains of patron-client clusters extending from the court to local notables, and on the cooperation of village leaders, rather than on military clout, to ensure that taxes were collected and order maintained. Though the selective use of force and, more critical, the potential to apply force were essential to political survival, effective rulers relied heavily on bribes, diplomacy, bluffs, and intrigue to control fractious nobles and contain social unrest. In fact, a ruler's repeated use of force for internal control was normally a sign that the ruling house was in decline.[11]

The combination of low population-to-land ratios, poor communications, weakly integrated administrative systems, and elite rivalries that characterized the contest states of precolonial Java and Burma provided numerous opportunities for peasants to defend themselves from excessive exactions by their overlords. Incessant struggles between elite factions consumed a good deal of time and material resources that might otherwise have been devoted to improved record keeping, better bureaucratic and military organization, and the establishment of firmer controls over the village population. Elite rivalries also forced uneasy monarchs to develop elaborate devices to prevent strong coalitions of hostile nobles from forming and to limit the opportunities for regional officials or appanage holders to build up independent power bases.[12] These devices included the fragmentation of appanage holdings granted to the members of the royal family or nobility; the periodic rotation of officials appointed to high-level posts;[13] marriage alliances with powerful noble families and the requirement that members of these families reside in the capital city; periodic journeys by regional lords to the court to offer homage to the ruler or, especially in India and Africa,[14] royal tours of the provinces of the realm; and the maintenance of extensive networks of royal spies and informants.[15]

Although these devices were essential to the maintenance of a ruler's position vis-à-vis elite groups at different levels, they diminished the control that he could exert over the peasant base of the society. Appanage holders spent little or no time in the areas allotted for their support. Their residence at court, which most preferred in any case because of the vastly superior social and cultural amenities and political excitement in the capital, meant that day-to-day administration was left in the hands of subordinates. Even officials who governed in their home districts knew little about village conditions and were dependent on poorly trained and self-serving subordinates and village notables for the actual administration of the peasant population under their control. Because the time officials spent in particular posts was often limited, it was rare for them to develop a sense of identity with or responsibility toward those whom they governed. In fact, the reverse was the case. Rotation in office, in the absence of a firm commitment to an accepted code of bureaucratic ethics, meant that most officeholders were out to get all the material advantages they could before their tenure in a particular post ended. Periodic trips to the capital exacerbated these tendencies by orienting the ruling classes to events at court rather than to the concerns of their subjects.[16]

The staffing of the lower levels of the administrative hierarchy with a motley horde of transient tax farmers who had little commitment to the ruler, or to the political system per se, further reduced the possibility of effective control over the peasant producers. Because these functionaries, like the lords who appointed them, routinely underreported the taxes they collected in order to retain as much as possible for themselves, the revenue records of precolonial regimes reflected, at best, rough estimates of the population and productivity of a given region. As Soermasaid Moertono has observed with reference to the kingdom of Mataram in Java, court registers recorded only "the amount of tax that the ruler expected to draw from a territory given in appanage" rather than the actual resources of the area, which normally far exceeded those that were taxed.[17]

The sorry state of precolonial record keeping left many openings for concealment and evasion. For the cultivating classes, those openings exploited by the village headmen were the most critical. Like all of the administrators and tax collectors above them, the village headmen regularly underassessed the population and cultivated acreage from which they derived revenue payments and recruited manpower for services to the state. Because taxes were paid, though not always assessed, and labor recruited on a village basis, the efforts of the headmen to minimize payments to supravillage elite groups benefitted and were supported by all members of the community. Collusion between village notables and the state's revenue collectors and the employment of a wide range of time-tested evasion techniques were the most effective ways in which cultivators were able to defend themselves against excessive elite demands on a sustained basis. Beyond the inaccuracies that abounded in original tax inquest and census statistics, any new lands brought into production or increased yields on previously assessed lands often went unreported. Portions of harvested crops were buried or hidden away outside the village. A part of the village population would settle temporarily in a nearby forest in periods of military campaigns or during labor recruitment for public works or a monarch's indulgence in monumental construction. Villages were subdivided and records compiled in ways that were sure to bewilder even the most vigilant tax collector. Bribes were usually sufficient to win the silence, and often the cooperation, of revenue officials who ought to have exposed these irregularities and demanded the ruler's full due. If a ruler appointed special revenue supervisors or ordered surveys to revise revenue estimates, their effectiveness could usually be minimized by additional bribes and more elaborate measures for concealment.[18]

Although local notables paid village taxes in lump sums and strove to maximize the resources retained by the peasants themselves, the rewards garnered by collusion and evasion were not equally distributed. Precolonial villages in Burma and Java were not, as has often been claimed, egalitarian havens of communal harmony and cooperation. Village populations were divided into several socioeconomic strata, and village affairs were dominated by a small minority of large landholding families that often headed hostile factions. In central Java, for example, power and status in the village sphere as late as the first decades of the nineteenth century were monopolized by landowning families called *sikeps* that usually claimed to be descended from the founding families of the village. Most of the remaining families in the village were attached as clients, with varying degrees of dependence, to one of the *sikep* households. The clients, or *numpangs,* worked the *sikeps*'s fields for a customary share of the harvest yield, performed domestic and artisanal services, and in some cases actually lived in dwellings provided by their patrons.[19] Although the *sikeps* clearly derived greater advantages from the various devices by which the village community sought to reduce the exactions of supravillage elite groups, the *numpangs,* through their patron-client links to village notables, also benefitted, usually in proportion to their families' socioeconomic standing in the village. The great majority of cultivators in precolonial Asian and African societies relied primarily upon similar patron-client ties and on the guile of local leaders and their collusion with lower-level officials as their primary defenses against oppression.

In situations where the regular village defense mechanisms failed, the peasants were forced to resort to more extreme measures to protect their interests. Despite the fact that, in the literature on protest, there is an emphasis on riots and rebellion, these additional measures were actually more likely to involve passive withdrawal or a search for alternative sources of patron protection than they were to foster conflict with those responsible for the cultivators' discontent. Although the quality of the source materials relating to peasant groups in most of precolonial Asia and Africa makes it impossible to determine the incidence of different forms of agrarian protest with precision, violent upheavals growing out of the grievances of the cultivators themselves appear to have been rare relative to other forms of protest expression. A careful scrutiny of many of the rebellions that have been attributed to peasant unrest or labeled as agrarian risings often leads to the conclusion that these conflicts were, in fact, interelite feuds or dynastic struggles in which peasant conscripts and peasant communities became unwillingly involved.[20] This conclusion arises not from the fact that these movements were led by men who were not from peasant origins, for, as Gil Carl Alroy and others have correctly argued, in sustained protest movements peasants have almost always borrowed their leaders from the rural gentry, the military, or urban-based elite groups.[21] It rests, rather, upon an examination of the issues that gave rise to the rebellions on which we have information and the goals of the dissidents in these movements. With important exceptions of risings in which the peasantry rallied to messianic figures or charismatic leaders struggling to overthrow inept or tyrannical rulers,[22] the origins and outcomes of these struggles had little or nothing to do with the peasant concerns or the condition of the cultivating classes. The peasants themselves understood that they had little to gain and very often much to lose— including their homes, crops, livestock, and lives—in these elite squabbles. It is not surprising then that the peasants' usual response to civil disturbances was flight en masse from the affected areas and a refusal to return until the conflict had been abated.[23]

Rather than riot or rebellion, the admittedly scanty and largely elite-authored evidence we have for the precolonial era suggests that peasants preferred a wide variety of alternative modes of protest that minimized direct confrontations with those viewed as oppressors. The fact that we must interpret peasant responses indirectly, through sources provided either by the very elite groups to whom they were reacting or by alien European observers, is particularly troublesome in dealing with avoidance protest because such a filter often makes it difficult to distinguish clearly between the various forms of this sort of behavior and other modes of peasant adaptation. Peasants migrated or shifted patrons not only to protest elite excesses, but also to better their economic situations or to take up new occupations. There were numerous instances, however, when migrations, shifts to new patrons, or related activities were explicitly linked to peasant grievances. In most instances, it is elite reactions, rather than peasant proclamations—which were rare—that allow us to distinguish between avoidance protest and other forms of peasant response in the precolonial era. In court chronicles, legal codes, and royal decrees, instances of peasant migration, transfer of services to new lords, and flight to the refuge of temple estates or cult centers are identified as acts of protest designed to draw attention to elite misrule and to force reductions in tribute demands or the dismissal of overly rapacious officials from office. Evidence of a direct link between these peasant responses and the expression of peasant greivances and demands is essential to the identification of examples of the type of dissidence that I have labeled avoidance protest. Groups or individuals resorted to acts of evasion, rather than to spontaneous outbursts of violence or organizations for confrontation, as a means of expressing their discontent.

The peasants' preference for modes of protest other than open rebellion was partially shaped by their vertical orientation to men of power and influence in patron-client networks. This orientation, which existed at even the subvillage level and was paralleled by the patron-client ties that linked the members of other social groups such as cult communities and merchant associations, meant that horizontal links between different peasant groups tended to be weak. Thus, though the distinctions between the ruling and cultivating classes were clearly demarcated and readily apparent in different styles of dress, housing, behavior, and, in Java, even different language forms employed at each level, there was very little sense of class consciousness or peasant identity in societies such as Java and Burma that were organized along the lines of the contest state. Peasants responded as members of a particular community and, especially, as the clients of particular landlords, local officials, or royal appanage holders. If and when cultivators rose in rebellion, they normally did so in support of these patrons or, alternatively, as the devoted followers of a holy man–prophet. They rose up not to effect fundamental changes in a sociopolitical order, which they accepted as legitimate and divinely ordained, but to back a lord or faction against rivals, to express displeasure with the excessive demands of a particular lord, or, in times of dynastic collapse, to influence the outcome of contests that would determine which family and factions of the nobility would control the throne. Their vertical organization and local orientation made it difficult to mobilize widespread peasant support and rendered most peasant risings small and ephemeral affairs. The structure and organizational patterns associated with the contest state not only reduced the level of elite efficiency and control over the peasantry but, by blocking the emergence of a strong class identification on the part of the peasantry, they reduced the possibility of mobilizing and organizing peasant protest on a scale sufficient to make modes involving confrontation effective.

Very often the first act of protest employed by dissident peasants was one that was sanctioned both by longstanding custom and official approval. In both Burma and Java, peasants who felt that their taxes were too high or that they were being mistreated by a local lord could petition a higher official or the monarch himself for redress of their grievances. In Java, disgruntled villagers—at times led by their headmen or, in other instances, in opposition to them—organized processions to the residence of the most powerful lord in the region, which, in the vicinity of the capital, meant the royal palace. The participants often concluded their march with a sit-in on the *alun-alun,* or great square, in view of the royal audience hall. They remained there until the ruler or one of his advisers heard their complaints and assured them that measures would be taken to reduce their burdens and punish the offending officials.[24] It was also possible for peasants to petition local officials for reduction in tax or *corvée* labor demands, and there were severe penalties for administrators who were found dismissing village headmen unjustly. The fragmentary evidence that we have suggests that when these petitions failed to produce results, dissident villages turned to other, more radical means of resistance.[25] Given the fragmentation of power and responsibility in the precolonial Burman and Javanese state systems and the great potential for official evasion, one suspects that petitions and protest processions rarely brought effective redress to aggrieved cultivators. But the very existence of these legal or quasi-legal channels of protest must have given some pause to even the most tyrannical officials.

Perhaps the most common and least risky mode of peasant defense and protest in the precolonial era involved the cultivators' transfer of their allegiance and services from lords whose demands were felt to be exorbitant to other patrons from whom they hoped to receive better treatment. The reciprocal patron-client bonds that formed the organizational backbone of the village community extended, in most precolonial African and Asian societies, to all levels of the sociopolitical hierarchy.[26] Like that of a village notable, the power and status of a lord depended to a large degree on the number of his clients, who themselves sought to attract retainers of their own. Conversely, an individual's career and the well-being of his family—including their physical safety in societies where "soft" states offered little protection from violent assault— depended heavily on his ability to attach himself to a prosperous, powerful, and successful patron. In states where the demand for manpower exceeded the supply and where there was a constant rivalry between nobles and officials at all levels, client-retainers enjoyed considerable bargaining power. Ambitious men, hoping to make their way up the chain of patron-client clusters and establish the position of their families for succeeding generations, were expected to transfer their loyalties away from patrons whose power was on the wane to those with more promising prospects for the future. Those making their way up the social hierarchy relied on their connections with powerful patrons to gain even higher and more lucrative administrative posts. If successful, they would also attract growing numbers of client-dependents and, in some instances, supplant the very men who had made their rise to power possible.[27]

A similar relationship existed between peasant clients and their patrons within the village and beyond. In Java, peasant tenants or laborers who felt that the share of the harvest demanded by their landlords was too great or that they were not effectively shielded from state demands for labor and produce, could exercise the right, sanctioned by the *adat,* or customary law, to transfer their services to another landowner. Tradition obliged them to give the landlord whose fields they were leaving a chicken and a basket of rice, after which they were free to attach themselves to another notable either within the same village or in another community. Instances were recorded in which a majority of the cultivators of the villages in an entire district exercised this option. There were also cases in which discontented cultivators returned to their original villages to work the lands of their former patrons when the demands of such land-lords or those of the tax collector in that locality decreased.[28] The periodic visits of Javanese appanage holders and other officials to the court were apparently especially opportune times for disgruntled cultivators to attach themselves to new patrons. If the peasants who accompanied the lord felt that the demands—including the services they were expected to render during the period of residence at the court—made upon them by their present lords were too great, they could, through gossip and contacts with the retainers of other notables who were gathered in the capital, find new patrons who promised better terms of service.[29]

In Burma, the *myothugyis,* or township heads, also competed for peasants to reside in their villages and work their lands. In Lower Burma in particular, the low man-to-land ratio and the highly mobile nature of the peasant household forced the *myothugyis* to temper their revenue demands and foster the well-being of their peasant subjects or risk losing these to neighboring townships where taxes were lighter and the head-men's demands more reasonable.[30] Transfers of peasants also occurred, on a much larger scale, from the lands of one appanage holder or regional official to another. In some periods, peasants sold themselves as debt slaves to powerful ministers or rich merchants to escape the harsh con-ditions of service under a member of the nobility or the monarch himself. The loss of manpower from the royal domains was of special importance in Burmese history because such defections constituted one of the major causes of dynastic decline. In the more closely administered core areas of Burman kingdoms, there was a recurrent pattern of steadily increasing exactions as the needs of the royal household grew in proportion to the increase in the number of its retainers and servants and the spiraling costs of military campaigns required to hold the kingdom together. These demands resulted in a loss of manpower as peasants left the royal domains to enter the less rigorous service of princes, nobles, and powerful ministers. These defections forced even greater exactions from the population remaining on royal lands and thus further exacerbated the abuses that had led to client transfers from the ruler's domains.[31]

The intense competition between princely factions, regional lords, and members of the local gentry for client-retainers rendered the possibility of transferring one's loyalty and services an especially effective deferrent to excessive elite demands. In states where rulers went to war, in part for the captives they hoped to carry home from defeated kingdoms, and where local regional lords were not above resorting to open warfare with rivals over contested villages and retainers,[32] the peasants' chances of finding a new patron who offered, at least in the short term, better conditions of service were good. The possibility that absconding peasants would be returned because of the demand of their original lord was remote, unless that lord was willing to buy them back or risk an armed encounter with the new patron. The monarch found it difficult enough to keep his own cultivators in place; he had little inclination—and less means—to control population transfers between the territories allotted to his relatives or the nobility.

Shifting to a new patron was both an effective peasant defense and a potent means of protest, for the act of severing a patron-client link in itself drew attention to the shortcomings or misdeeds that the defecting cultivators claimed had spurred their search for a new patron. It also represented a blow to the status and esteem and a real reduction in the power of the original lord.

A form of peasant defense and protest that was closely related to the act of changing patrons, but a good deal more disruptive of the peasants' lives and potentially more risky, was flight. Flight was, of course, one of a cultivator's principal means of defending himself and his family from the ravages of war, the depredations of marauding bandits, starvation in times of drought, and the other malevolent forces that periodically intensified his already difficult struggle to survive.[33] Although there is no direct evidence relating to the process by which peasants decided to migrate, it is reasonable to infer that they opted for flight and the search for new lands to settle only in situations where transfer to the service of other lords either was not possible or appeared unlikely to redress their grievances. It was not a step that was taken lightly, but an act that arose out of a "really desperate situation."[34] This was particularly true in areas of wet-rice cultivation where peasant households had a large investment extending over many generations in painstakingly cleared and cultivated paddy fields and intricate irrigation works. In these areas, peasant dwellings were substantial and, in many cultures, villagers developed deep attachments to village shrines and deities and the gravesites of their ancestors.

Although the populations of areas cultivated on a dry crop or shifting basis appear to have been considerably more mobile and thus more prone to migrate if the demands of their overlords became too great,[35] numerous examples of mass protest migrations on the part of wet-rice agriculturists can be found in the sources relating to Southeast Asia, India, and other areas. Peasant families and whole villages fled to escape *corvée* labor or military conscription. They migrated to avoid and to protest against what they viewed as harsh treatment or unreasonable exactions by the nobles or officials who were given jurisdiction over them.[36] In some cases, they fled from the domains of one ruler into a rival kingdom.[37] More commonly, they migrated into sparsely settled frontier areas that bordered on or, in cases such as Java, were interspersed with the densely populated heartlands of precolonial kingdoms. In Burma, peasants moved into the hills and forests surrounding the Dry Zone or traveled south into the vast wilderness of the Irrawaddy delta where they struggled to found new settlements in defiance of wild animals, disease, floods, and hostile non-Burman inhabitants. In Java, disgruntled peasants found refuge in the forest and hill terrain that fringed the volcanic peaks of the heavily populated eastern and central portions of the island. In some societies, peasant migrants gathered in fortified settlements and openly defied the leaders whose authority they had rejected.[38]

In times of scarcity or man-made hardship, large numbers of villagers simply took to the roads that linked the major towns in precolonial kingdoms. Some became porters on the routes between the capital and other centers where merchants and nobles were concentrated. Others joined wandering theatrical troupes or settled in the towns as servants of courtiers or rich merchants—though the later option appears to have been less common in Southeast Asia or Africa than in more highly urbanized European kingdoms in the late Middle Ages. More adventurous peasant migrants joined bands of vagabonds or bandit gangs—a phenomenon that will be discussed in detail.[39]

Although the sacrifices and risks for uprooted peasants were considerable, flight was a potent means of defense and protest. Military service could be avoided and tax and *corvée* burdens evaded—though usually only until the state's agents also moved into areas newly settled by disaffected cultivators. Some peasant migrants gained a chance to take up other, and at times more rewarding, occupations. The importance of the threat of peasant protest migration as a check on official abuses is reflected in the numerous royal edicts in which state officials are warned to look to the welfare of their subjects or the latter would flee and their lands revert to wilderness. Lords from whose domains there were large-scale migrations not only suffered the loss of the manpower upon which they depended to meet revenue quotas and provide for their own sustenance; they also faced the danger of being accused by rival officials or the monarch's ministers of misrule and incompetence. In Thailand, the flight of large numbers of peasants was considered a key indicator of an administrator's incapacity and often led to demotion or dismissal from royal service. In Burma in the reign of King Tha-lun, officials considered responsible for peasant migration were liable to be executed.[40] The flight of the peasantry came to be seen in most African and Asian cultures as a sign of dynastic weakness and socioeconomic decline. Cruel and incompetent rulers were abandoned by their subjects and millenarian prophecies spoke of eras of chaos and confusion in which hordes of villagers wandered aimlessly on the roads.[41]

Cult movements and entry into monastic orders or religious schools represented important variants of another major form of peasant protest that involved transfer to a new patron-protector and often travel to distant regions. Though many peasants became the devotees of mystics and holy men for religious reasons that had nothing to do with social protest, and though numerous cult movements stressed spiritual enrichment rather than changes in the terrestrial realm, religious institutions and leaders also provided important outlets for peasant dissent in the precolonial era. In mainland Southeast Asia, the Buddhist Sangha and extensive monastic estates served as places of refuge for disgraced ministers, thwarted princely claimants to the throne, and overburdened peasants alike. Evidence relating to Burman dynasties separated by several centuries indicates that the large-scale migration of peasants onto monastic lands and the entry of young men into the Buddhist monkhood to escape taxes, *corvée* labor, or military conscription posed major problems for the rulers and nobles whose fields they abandoned and for the recruiters who consequently failed to meet their manpower quotas. Some rulers, like the seventeenth-century Taung-ngu monarch, Tha-lun, issued edicts forbidding marriages with pagoda slaves and prohibiting young men from entering the Sangha to escape taxes and labor services. From the time of the Pagan Dynasty (1044–1287) to the nineteenth century, the drain of manpower from state to monastic lands was a major factor in the decline of successive Burman dynasties. Thus, disgruntled peasants, protesting the increasing demands of princes and nobles or seeking improved terms of servitude on monastic estates, played a major political role in precolonial Burma.[42]

In Java, where there was no institutionalized religious establishment in the Islamic period comparable to the Sangha in mainland Southeast Asia, defections to religious sanctuaries proved less of a threat to the manpower reserves of the ruling classes. In both the Hindu-Buddhist and Muslim periods, however, there were religious schools and shrines that Javanese rulers endowed with a village or villages for their support. These centers of learning and worship, as well as the gravesites of renowned holy men and rulers that were often the foci of pilgrimages and popular veneration, were declared *perdikan* villages. This status, which was often retained for many generations and was usually honored by the Dutch colonizers, freed the villagers from regular tax and *corvée* obligations in return for their support of religious teachers or upkeep of graves and shrines. Although little has been written about conditions within these villages in the precolonial era, Dutch writers reported that *perdikan* villages were among the most prosperous in central Java in the early nineteenth century and that the sons of poor peasants were included among the students and devotees of Muslim teachers and holy men.[43] It is impossible to know the degree to which *perdikan* villages served as places of refuge for dissident cultivators in the precolonial period. It is not unreasonable to surmise, however, that *perdikan* centers may have performed a role in Javanese society analogous to that which Louis Dumont has assigned to renunciation in Indian society.[44] By attracting the more aware and articulate individuals, and by providing for them meaningful career alternatives and outlets for expression, these centers may have served as important antidotes to the buildup of discontent among both the peasants and the ruling social strata. In this way, they may have greatly reduced movements of protest arising out of the tensions and constructions inherent in the highly stratified Javanese sociocultural order.

In both Java and Burma, cult movements that coalesced around mystics, holy men, and religious seers also provided important outlets for peasant protest expression. The size and character of these movements and the nature of their leaders varied widely, but a number of general patterns can be discerned. Most leaders claimed, and their followers believed, that they possessed magical powers that usually included protective and healing abilities. Many propagated ideologies built around divine revelations or millenarian prophecies that sometimes posed direct challenges to the legitimacy of reigning dynasties. The majority of the adherents of these movements were illiterate peasants who were normally required to undergo rather elaborate rituals of initiation, provide material support for the holy man–leader, and swear oaths of unswerving allegiance to the leader and the cult rules. In some movements, ecstatic dancing, mesmerism, and drugs provided important sources of release for discontented peasants. In times of political strife and social breakdown, the number of these cults proliferated and the size of their followings increased dramatically. Some movements became openly hostile to local officials or the reigning monarch and ended in bloody but futile outbursts of violence. Most, however, stressed passive withdrawal and avoidance of contacts with state officials or nonbelievers. In some instances, local officials and even kings gave special honors and positions of authority to cult leaders in order to win their cooperation and support. The communities that formed around the hadjis (Muslims who had made the pilgrimage to Mecca) and *kyais* (Muslim religious teachers) in Java or the *sayas* (necromancers) and *gaing* (sect) leaders in Burma provided temporal relief for dissident peasants. The eschatological revelations of these cult leaders promised eternal salvation in the age of bliss that was to come.[45]

Burmese and Javanese theatrical entertainments also provided a form of protest that paralleled cult formation in its mystical and magical orientation and in its attempt to create, in a very different fashion, fantasy worlds in which the peasantry could find release from their afflictions. As Moertono has observed, the *wayang kulit* (puppit shadow plays) and *wayang wong* (plays staged by actors) were "weathervane[s] of public opinion" in Javanese society. The able *dalang* (puppeteer) cleverly wove commentary on current conditions and political satire into his dramatic narration of the great Indian epics that the Javanese have so brilliantly employed in their plastic arts and theatrical entertainments. The *dalang*, who, like the clowns in the *garabeg* (court festival) processions, was considered immune from punishment, was able to give voice to peasant complaints and to transmit them from one region to another. In Burma, as in Java, peasant grievances and frustrations also found expression in folk songs and popular stories that often criticized elite failings and excesses and contained thinly veiled ridicule of prominent political figures.[46]

Another form of peasant protest that involved both flight and attachment to a new leader was banditry. Given the paucity of reliable sources on bandit organization and aims in precolonial Java and Burma, it is difficult to determine whether, and to what degree, brigandage was a genuine vehicle of popular protest or was simply an organized form of criminal behavior. This dearth of information compounds the already considerable degree of ambiguity and the problems of interpretation identified by investigators studying bandit groups in Europe or China, where relevant evidence is far more abundant. The extent, for example, to which the images projected in folk legends about the heroic deeds of the Javanese *rampoks* (bandits)—such as Ken Angrok, who went on to found the Majapahit dynasty—or the *Bohs* of Burma correspond to the actual behavior of these men is impossible to determine. Information compiled in police reports in the colonial period is helpful, but it is heavily biased and rarely focused on questions relating to group composition and motivation that need to be answered in order to determine whether or not a particular gang or individual was truly an exponent of popular protest—a "social bandit" in Eric Hobsbawm's usage.[47]

The sources we do possess on banditry in precolonial Java and Burma indicate that it was widespread and that in certain periods, particularly those of civil conflict or dynastic decline, brigand gangs played important political roles. Banditry was popularly regarded as a regular occupation—however disreputable—in both of these societies. Bandit leaders were stereotyped as men of great physical courage, as evidenced by the attributes of the *jago* (literally, 'fighting cock') personality usually associated with brigands in Javanese society. Some bandit gangs were large enough to form their own communities that often controlled the villages in surrounding areas. Bandit leaders assumed official-sounding titles, like that of *Boh* or lieutenant-colonel commonly adopted by brigand chiefs in Burma, and they staked out territorial claims and divided their zones of operation among their subordinates in the manner of a feudal lord. Though many bandits were professional criminals, some of whom inherited their way of life from their fathers as one would a trade, others became brigands to escape the hardships of peasant life. The numbers of the latter swelled in periods of political strife, when many agriculturists' households found mere survival difficult. In Java and Burma, as in China and Vietnam, the growth of banditry beyond its normal endemic proportions was one of the key signs of dynastic decline. Peasant refugees from drought, famine, and excessive taxation often joined established bandit gangs. In these, they became members of new patron-client hierarchies extending downward from the bandit chief and his inner circle of followers.[48]

With the few exceptions of the runaway slaves or peasants who took up banditry and eventually emerged as major political figures or popular heros in the Robin Hood tradition,[49] it is not possible to follow the careers of peasants who became bandits, and therefore no determination can be made about whether or not they acted to avenge the wrongs they had suffered or to assist peasant communities in their struggles with the state. The initial flight, however, and the decision to join brigand gangs were acts of protest. It is important to note that these were responses oriented to evasion or avoidance of the sources of their suffering rather than confrontation with them. Though some bandits may have struck back at the tax collectors or landlords who were responsible for their decisions to become criminals, most appear to have been indiscriminate in their choices of targets. Merchants, who usually had few links to village communities in the precolonial era, were favorite targets, but the peasants themselves were often the prey. Rather than challenging the state and its agents, brigands very often cooperated with local officials or were persuaded to assume quasi-administrative roles that their fame and influence in a particular locality well suited them to fill. In Java, successful bandit leaders rose to high rank, and the greatest of all founded a dynasty. In Burma, brigand gangs played important roles in succession struggles and in resistance campaigns against foreign invaders. Thus, though banditry was very often a career chosen by local bullies and ne'er-do-wells and constituted a source of peasant oppression, it was also a means through which peasants could escape intolerable elite demands and, if they were competent and fortunate, rise to positions of wealth and influence.

In addition to banditry, other, less well-organized activities that were also considered crimes by those in power provided more sporadic and transitory ways in which peasants could react to excessive demands. The burning of standing crops or, in Java, of the toll stations that made travel in the interior so costly and unpleasant was a mode of peasant reprisal for which we have good documentation from the early colonial period. It is probable that peasants had also resorted to these measures in much earlier time periods. In periods of extreme political and social dislocation, rebellious villagers were known to join the burning and pillage of the residences of the nobility and, on at least one occasion in Burma, the royal palace itself.[50] Excepting hit-and-run arson incidents, these acts were likely to lead to direct confrontations with those whom the peasants saw as their oppressors, rather than to the evasion that I have argued was the preferred orientation of peasant dissent in the precolonial era. They indicate the danger of overstating the case for avoidance protest. Although village riots and peasant risings were usually localized and short-lived affairs, they did occur. When linked to the campaigns of ambitious and able nobles or princes seeking to carve out their own kingdoms or usurp power in existing ones, peasant rebellions could and did have considerable political impact. Nonetheless, the paucity of references in the precolonial sources to jacqueries or peasant riots, and the availability of a wide range of defense techniques and less hazardous modes of resistance stressing evasion rather than confrontation, suggest that peasants resorted to violent resistance only out of sheer desperation in situations where severe dislocations undermined the effectiveness of village defenses and rendered avoidance protest an insufficient response to excessive elite demands.

The coming of colonial rule to Java and Burma did not bring a sudden end to village defense mechanisms and peasant protest oriented to avoidance. Collusion and concealment, flight, banditry, and sectarian withdrawal persisted as modes of peasant resistance and protest throughout the colonial period and, in many cases, into the era of independence. In Burma, for example, bandit groups spearheaded postconquest resistance to the advance of British colonial control throughout the nineteenth century. Large bandit gangs continued to operate, in some regions with impunity, until well into the twentieth century. Guerilla resistance by dacoit bands proved the most difficult aspect of the agrarian rebellions of the 1930s for the British to suppress. Large-scale bandit activities and, in coastal regions, pirate raids were reported in Java in areas such as Banten throughout the nineteenth century, and bandit leaders assumed lofty titles and set up petty chiefdoms as late as the 1940s.[51] In colonial Burma, peasants seeking to escape obligations to moneylenders, or the chance to work their own holdings free from the control of large landowners, migrated by the hundreds of thousands into the fertile but undeveloped expanses of the Irrawaddy delta where the booming rice-export economy was centered. In Java, peasants migrated from areas controlled directly by the Dutch to those that remained under Javanese rule or vice versa, depending on where tax demands were lower. They also fled to escape Dutch census inquests, which they rightly suspected were linked to Dutch efforts to increase tax revenues and *corvée* labor quotas.[52]

In both societies, there was a great proliferation of sectarian movements and local cults. Many of these movements stressed withdrawal from, rather than challenges to, the colonial system, but often they ended in police repression or bloody clashes with the colonial authorities.[53] Particularly in the early decades of colonial control, peasants also relied on evasion techniques and on collusion between village leaders and local officials to buffer European demands for cash revenue and produce.[54] The persistence of these modes of defense and protest underscores the need for caution against drawing too sharp a distinction between the precolonial and colonial periods. European conquest in both Java and Burma was gradual and advanced by stages, spread over nearly two centuries in the former and several decades in the latter area. The extension of effective control over local areas and the village populace came only decades after formal annexations in most regions, and in some areas it scarcely came at all. As late as the 1880s, Sir Charles Crosthwaite could write that large areas in the vicinity of the colonial capital of Burma at Rangoon were controlled by bandit gangs or local leaders rather than by the British.[55]

In the contested transition period between the defeat of indigenous states and the advance, but not yet full establishment, of colonial authority, many of the conditions—poor political integration, weak military control, and low population-to-land ratios—that had made avoidance protest possible still persisted. As a result, underreporting, flight, and brigandage remained viable and often the preferred modes of protest for peasant dissidents in this period. However, as precolonial contest states were gradually transformed into highly centralized bureaucracies that increasingly impinged on local and village affairs, the usual peasant defense mechanisms were greatly reduced in effectiveness or rendered completely impotent. Fundamental transformations of the political economies of Burma and Java and major demographic and social changes in these and other colonies also altered the conditions that had been essential to peasant reliance on avoidance protest. Though some forms remained viable, particularly in inaccessible frontier areas,[56] for the great majority of colonized peoples, stratagems of flight, banditry, and sectarian withdrawal were no longer effective responses to excessive elite demands. In these circumstances, peasant unrest, which rose sharply in the colonial period in response to the profound dislocations that accompanied far-reaching political and socioeconomic change, was increasingly channeled into collective protest expression that involved confrontations, and often violent clashes, with the European colonizers and their allies.

As the limited control exercised by indigenous lords over the peasant population gave way to colonial bureaucracies that penetrated to the village level, collusion and evasion, which had formed the first line of defense for the precolonial peasant community, were eliminated or took on new forms that served the interests of village leaders and large landholders and not those of the community as a whole.[57] In many areas, peasant settlements were reorganized in ways that were often arbitrary. In all cases, they were gradually integrated into a bureaucratic hierarchy that was geared primarily to the efficient collection of revenue and the mobilization of labor, the maintenance of law and order, and the promotion of commercial expansion. Though the colonizers' priorities varied somewhat by region and time period, far less effort was expended on community development and peasant welfare than on tax collection or keeping the peace. Village leaders, even though they were still chosen by the peasants themselves in some areas, were transformed into agents of the state. The frequency with which village headmen were the targets of peasant risings in the colonial period indicates the degree to which they became alienated from the village population as a whole and to which they came to be perceived, usually quite justifiably, as tools of the European colonizers.

Costly and time-consuming cadastral surveys, special training for revenue assessors, more sophisticated methods of record keeping, and more effective administrative surveillance greatly reduced opportunities for tax evasion or bribery of revenue officials. Even though colonial officials argued that they took a smaller share of the cultivators' harvest than had the indigenous rulers who preceded them, the reality was often very different. The Europeans had far more accurate assessments of what and how much was actually produced than did the precolonial lords, and the Europeans also had the capacity actually to collect a far larger proportion of what they claimed as their due. Precolonial rulers, by contrast, demanded a greater share of the peasants' production, but lacked the means of accurately determining the output on which their claims were based and of ensuring that the revenue that was collected actually reached the royal coffers.[58] Of course, embezzlement and bribery at the village level continued in the colonial era, but on a much reduced scale and for the benefit of individuals—mainly petty officials—and not peasant communities as a whole.

Not only were village defenses eroded in the colonial period, but peasant communities were exposed to new influences that often had adverse effects on the majority of their households. The uneven, but greatly intensified, involvement of the peasantry in many regions of Java and Burma in production for the market sharpened competition and exacerbated existing divisions within the village. Local notables became increasingly involved in financial enterprises that transcended or had little to do with production in their home villages. They were also captivated by the more exciting social life that came with residence in the towns that grew up in response to bureaucratic and commercial expansion. These shifts, and the growing reliance of the landed classes on the state for political backing, dissolved or greatly distorted the patron-client bonds that had once been a key source of peasant protection.[59]

Merchants and moneylenders came to play major roles in all but the most remote village communities, and many peasant households were reduced to debt servitude to these outsiders, against whom they had little bargaining power. Though Samuel Popkin is correct in arguing that the peasants responded to these altered circumstances by establishing new links to landlords, merchants, and government officials,[60] the advantage in the new networks of dependence rested overwhelmingly with landed and mercantile groups. Landlords and moneylenders controlled the resources and market outlets essential to peasant production and economic well-being. They were also tied into financial networks and became members of political associations that gave them financial and legal support should disputes arise with their tenants or laborers. These associations exerted, in many cases, considerable influence over colonial administrators and policy decisions regarding agrarian affairs. The wealth of landed and mercantile groups and their connections with members of Western-educated, professional families—particularly lawyers and judges—made it possible for them to exploit fully the openings that the property-oriented courts and legal codes of the European colonizers provided for them. Thus, they were able to beat back the challenges of tenants or laborers and strengthen their hold over the cultivating classes.[61]

Paralleling the decline of defense mechanisms centered on the village were a number of developments that greatly reduced the efficacy of various forms of avoidance protest. The more effective horizontal integration of the colonial bureaucracy rendered peasant transfers from one patron-official to another difficult, if not impossible. Greater uniformity of tax demands from one administrative division to another meant that there was little relief to be found in attaching oneself to another official, because the new patron was obliged to follow the same rules and enforce the same policies as the one whose jurisdiction was abandoned.

The decrease in effectiveness of patron transfers also resulted from fundamental demographic changes that eliminated the option of protest through flight in many areas. For a number of reasons, some of which remain in dispute, European colonization brought first gradual and then increasingly rapid population growth in Java and Burma, as in many areas of Africa and Asia. As early as the first decades of the nineteenth century in some parts of central and eastern Java, and by the last decade of the same century on the Lower Burma rice frontier,[62] unclaimed cultivable lands were no longer available. The loss of frontier regions as areas of refuge was accelerated by a penchant on the part of European officials for closing off vast forest reserves from peasant occupancy and use. This policy not only further reduced the number of areas to which peasants might migrate, it deprived them of the firewood, materials for housing and tools, and supplementary foods that they had once gathered free in the forest. These measures increased peasant reliance for household necessities on market exchanges, which was usually one of the effects that their colonial overlords intended. The closing of forest regions often contributed to peasant protests that ended in violent clashes with forestry officials and the police or led to movements that rejected the colonizers' restrictions and advocated the founding of settlements in the frontier wilderness.[63]

Unless peasant groups were located in border regions from which they could migrate into other colonial territories,[64] the possibility of using flight as an effective response to excessive tax or debt burdens was also limited by the greatly increased bureaucratic and military reach of the colonial state. Only those dissidents who fled into the most inaccessible, and therefore most inhospitable, areas were likely to find relief from oppression.

The greatly enhanced military power and communications technology of colonial regimes rendered banditry a much more hazardous, and usually less rewarding, outlet for peasant protest than it had been in the precolonial era. The activities of brigand gangs clashed sharply with the

maintenance of law and order—or the passive acceptance of alien rule—
that was so cherished by colonial administrators. European officials were
less apt than their predecessors to look the other way when merchants
or moneylenders were robbed, landlords' estate houses sacked, or villages
raided. Considerable resources—including machine guns and, by the
1920s, airplanes—were mobilized to eradicate the bandit gangs that were
endemic to most colonial areas. Given the bias of the colonial observers
who have provided virtually all the information we possess on these
campaigns and the Europeans' habit of indiscriminately labeling anyone
who resisted colonial rule as a bandit or dacoit, it is very difficult to
determine the extent to which different bandit groups were the exponents
of popular resistance or were merely common criminals. The widespread
support provided for many brigand gangs by peasant communities in
Burma, Java, and other colonial areas suggests, however, that, like the
social bandits studied by Hobsbawm, these men were viewed by large
numbers of the colonized peasantry as allies and proponents of the
precolonial order.[65] Though some bandits enjoyed fairly long and lucrative careers and others even managed to work their way into the colonial
administrative systems,[66] most peasants found brigandage a high-risk,
short-lived occupation that very often ended with imprisonment or violent death. Banditry continued, but the coming of the colonial order
had vitiated its potential as a vehicle of avoidance protest and transformed it into a pursuit that was sure to force direct and often violent
confrontations with the European overlords and their allies.

As a career as a full-fledged bandit became less attractive, it is likely
that aggrieved peasants increasingly resorted instead to arson, vandalism,
and other more spontaneous criminal acts to strike back at onerous
landlords, moneylenders, and officials. Because the information on such
forms of protest in the precolonial era is extremely limited, it is difficult
to know if peasant reliance on them increased in the colonial period,
but many incidents were reported and it is probable that there were many
more than the official records indicate. Favorite targets were telegraph
and railway lines, standing crops in the fields of large landowners, and
the homes and offices of moneylenders, tax and toll collectors, and
headmen who collaborated with the colonial authorities. In some cases,
acts of vandalism, such as the uprooting of crops grown for export by
forced labor or the severing of communication links between colonial
administrative centers, were the signals for widespread agrarian rebellions. In these instances, the mode of protest shifted from avoidance to

direct confrontation, and frequently to violent clashes with the colonial authorities.[67]

Like banditry, sectarian protest became much more likely to provoke forcible repression in the colonial era than it had in the precolonial period. Cult groups, whose leaders initially stressed withdrawal from, rather than clashes with, the colonial authorities, were very often eventually drawn into direct and bloody conflict with the police and local officials. In part, these clashes were inevitable in a situation where passive withdrawal meant, among other things, the nonpayment of taxes and a refusal to give deference to colonial administrators, behavior that the latter found an intolerable affront to their authority. Equally critical was the intense suspicion, often verging on paranoia, that colonial officials felt toward specific cult movements and the more devout followers of the indigenous religions in general. Religious teachers, holy men, or monks who gained large numbers of adherents among the peasantry quickly came under police surveillance. Administrators viewed even the most innocuous cult groups as seedbeds of sedition and as conspiracies to overthrow the colonial regime. Colonial investigators into civil disturbances tended to stress the roles of "fanatical" hadjis or "perfidious" monks in fomenting every outburst of protest.[68] These attitudes and the persistent overreaction on the part of colonial administrators to cult movements were not completely without foundation. Before the emergence of nationalism in Burma and Java, the monks, holy men, and religious teachers were, in fact, the main catalysts of popular resistance to colonial rule. Their teachings implicitly, if not openly, posed direct challenges to the legitimacy of the rule of European colonizers, who were branded as infidels and aliens. Thus, even sectarian movements that stressed passive withdrawal and refuge in the community of believers presented major political challenges that similar groups did not in the precolonial era. Consequently, colonial officials believed that they had to curb or crush movements that the indigenous rulers and officials had been able either to ignore or to enlist in actual support for their efforts to control the peasant masses. Tragically, for the peasants of Java and Burma, yet another major mode of avoidance protest had been transformed into a likely cause for forcible repression and violent conflict.

Given the limited acquaintance of most colonial officials with the languages of the peoples they ruled and their disinterest, or contempt, toward the cultural expression of colonized peoples, it is not surprising that the tradition of peasant protest through theatrical satire and other vehicles of ridicule flourished in the colonial era. Gestures of contempt and mockery that were incomprehensible to or passed unnoticed by the Europeans were also added to the peasant arsenal of impromptu protest. Messianic and nationalist leaders exploited the colonizers' lack of familiarity with the local culture; they worked double entendres into speeches to peasant gatherings and made references to legendary heroes and stirring events from the past that had great emotional impact on their audiences but meant little to police observers. Peasant grievances were also articulated in literary form by members of the emerging bourgeois intelligentsia, who penned novels and plays that drew attention to the miserable condition of the majority of the cultivating classes under colonial rule. Pamphlets, vernacular newspapers, and satirical cartoons (which were the most accessible of these forms to the illiterate or semiliterate peasantry) were additional means by which peasant awareness was aroused and the problems of the rural masses brought to the attention of the emerging nationalist elite.[69]

The proliferation of new literary and cultural vehicles to express dissent was symptomatic of a wider search for effective modes of protest to sustain peasant groups in their increasingly unequal struggle with the European colonizers and their non-European allies, both immigrant and indigenous. As village defenses disintegrated and community autonomy gave way to bureaucratic interference and control, peasant reliance on evasion, patron protection, and avoidance shifted to forms of protest expression that involved more direct challenges to and clashes with the wielders of power. The adoption of modes of protest involving confrontation was also influenced by a gradual, but definite, shift in the locus of peasant identity and orientation from the landlord or noble patron to their fellow cultivators. As vertical patron-client ties were transformed in ways that worked increasingly against the cultivators' interests, and new patterns of property ownership and market demands turned large numbers of village dwellers into migrant laborers and tenants without land or strong community roots, horizontal links and a sense of class consciousness began to emerge. At the same time, the European colonizers failed to surround themselves with the symbols and roles that had given legitimacy to the precolonial rulers. Fertility ceremonies were no longer performed; sacred shrines and palace centers were neglected or turned into museums or European social clubs; religious or customary strictures regarding the behavior of the ruling classes had no influence on the policies of alien and infidel European overlords.

These changes not only gave rise to ideologies of rebellion that were more radical than those associated with precolonial peasant dissidents, they made it more possible to mobilize and organize large numbers of peasants over wide areas. The awesome organizational and technological superiority that the colonizers could bring to bear in the confrontations that often resulted and the heavy casualties these clashes inflicted forced peasant dissidents to seek new allies and new ways of redressing their grievances. Although protective magic and millenarian solutions proved capable of mobilizing large numbers of peasant supporters for anticolonial resistance movements in many areas, numbers alone were no match for European howitzers and machine guns. In some colonies, such as India and Ghana, peasants became deeply involved in constitutional agitation and passive resistance campaigns that sought to challenge the colonizers without provoking violent repression. In other areas, such as Algeria and Vietnam, those who sought to arouse the peasantry turned to ancient traditions of guerilla warfare. When combined with tactics modified for postindustrial military technology, well-articulated revolutionary ideologies, the discipline of cadre organization, and broad military strategies, guerilla warfare proved capable of offsetting the advantages of superior firepower and mechanization enjoyed by the conventional colonial armies. Though guerilla resistance failed in many colonies, and for reasons that often differed widely, victories in China, Vietnam, and other areas have elevated guerilla tactics to the position of the preferred mode of peasant protest and resistance in the twentieth century. Avoidance and selective confrontation have been combined to erase many of the advantages that industrialization had given to colonial elite groups in their incessant contest with the cultivating classes.

NOTES

I would like to thank Peter Carey, Victor Lieberman, William Koenig, and the members of the Social History Group of Rutgers University for their contributions to the original draft of this article. I would also like to thank the participants in the Symposium of Peasant Rebellions at Johns Hopkins University and the members of the Ethnohistory Program at the University of Pennsylvania for their valuable comments and critiques.

1. For sample discussions of avoidance protest in each of these situations, see, respectively, Eugene D. Genovese, *Roll, Jordan, Roll* (New York, 1972), esp. 648–57, and Gerald Mullin, *Flight and Rebellion: Slave Resistance in Eighteenth-*

Century Virginia (New York, 1972); Rodney Hilton, *Bond Men Made Free* (New York, 1973), esp. chap. 2, and H. S. Bennett, *Life on the English Manor* (Cambridge, 1937), chap. 11; Jerome Blum, *Lord and Peasant in Russia* (Princeton, 1961), esp. chap. 14.

2. Notable recent exceptions to this trend include the work of James Fernandez, especially his article "The Affirmation of Things Past: Alar Ayong and Bwiti as Movements of Protest in Central and Northern Gabon," in *Protest and Power in Black Africa,* ed. Robert Rotberg and Ali Mazrui (Oxford, 1970), 427–57; A. I. Asiwaju's article "Migrations as Revolt: The Example of the Ivory Coast and the Upper Volta before 1945," *Journal of African History* 17, no. 4 (1976): 577–94; Allen Isaacman, *The Tradition of Resistance in Mozambique* (Berkeley, 1976), chap. 5.

3. For examples, see Soermarsaid Moertono, *State and Statecraft in Old Java* (Ithaca, N. Y., 1968), 35ff.; Thaung, "Burmese Kingship in Theory and Practice under the Reign of King Mindon," *Journal of the Burma Research Society* (hereafter cited as *JBRS*) 42 (1959): 178–83; John W. Spellman, *Political Theory of Ancient India* (Oxford, 1964), chap. 8; Max Gluckman, "The Kingdom of the Zulu in South Africa," in *African Political Systems,* ed. M. Fortes and E. E. Evans-Pritchard (London, 1940), esp. 28–34.

4. Max Weber, *Economy and Society: An Outline of Interpretive Sociology,* ed. G. Roth and C. Wittich (New York, 1968), 3, chap. 12. To a lesser degree than empires in the Islamic heartland or Mughal India, Javanese and Burmese administrative systems also contained prebendal elements.

5. Court intrigues and succession disputes received much attention in earlier historical works on Burma and Java, as the writings of G. E. Harvey, Arthur Phayre, M. L. van Deventer, and H. J. de Graaf amply illustrate. For more recent studies that attempt to relate these phenomena to broader political analyses, see William Koenig, "The Early Kòn-baung Polity, 1752–1819" (Ph.D. diss., University of London, 1978), chap. 6; Victor Lieberman, "The Burmese Dynastic Pattern, circa 1590–1760" (Ph.D. diss., University of London, 1976); Peter Carey, "Pangeran Dipanagara and Origins of the Java War, 1825–1830," in *Verhandelingen van het Koninklijk Instituut* (Leiden, forthcoming), chap. 2. For Indian examples, see the writings of Satish Chandra or Athar Ali on the Mughal court and nobility; for Africa, see Ivor Wilks, *Asante in the Nineteenth Century* (Cambridge, 1975), esp. chap. 12; Max Gluckman, *Custom and Conflict in Africa* (Glencoe, Ill., 1959), 39, 43, 45–46, et passim.

6. For discussion of regional autonomy, see Moertono, *State and Statecraft,* 88ff., 104–5, 107, 134; H. J. de Graaf, *De Regering van Sultan Agung, Vorst van Mararam, 1613–1645* (The Hague, 1958), 118–21; Koenig, "Early Kòn-baung Polity," 34–36, 41ff.; Lieberman, "Burmese Dynastic Pattern," 36, 39–40, 45, 120ff., 227ff. For a superb study of this pattern in India, see Richard G. Fox, *Kin, Clan, Raja, and Rule* (Berkeley, 1971). For African examples, see Gluckman, *Custom*

and Conflict, 34–35, 37–44; R. E. Bradbury, "The Kingdom of Benin," in *West African Kingdoms in the Nineteenth Century,* ed. D. Forde and P. M. Kaberry (Oxford, 1967), 5–6, 9, 27; Jan Vansina, "A Comparison of African Kingdoms," *Africa* 32 (1963): 329–30.

7. De Graaf, *De Regering,* 119; Peter Carey, "Origins of the Java War," manuscript, 8–11; Onghokham, "The Residency of Madiun Pryayi and Peasant in the Nineteenth Century" (Ph.D. diss., Yale University, 1975), 44ff., 60–61, 84; W. A. J. van Davelaar, "Middenpersonen tusschen de districts-beambten en desahoofden op Java," *Tijdschrift voor Indische Taal, Land, en Volkenkunde* (hereinafter cited as *TGB*) 34 (1891): 365–72; Koenig, "Early Kòn-baung Polity," 273ff., esp. 295–96, 303–7; Kennon Breazeale, "Thai Provincial Minority Elites" (Paper read at the Seventh Conference of the International Historians of Asia, Bangkok, 1977), 3–4, 11–12; S. N. Hasan, "Zamindars under the Mughals," in *Land Control and Social Structure in Indian History,* ed. R. E. Frykenberg (Madison, Wis., 1969), 17–32.

8. Koenig, "Early Kòn-baung Polity," 245–46, 311–12; Daw Mya Sein, *Sir Charles Crosthwaite and the Administration of British Burma* (Rangoon, 1938), 63–64, 67–68.

9. Mya Sein, *Crosthwaite,* 47, 67, 69, 72; J. S. Furnivall, "Notes on the History of Hanthawaddy," *JBRS* 4, no. 4 (1914): 209; Mya Kyan, "Village Administration in Upper Burma," *JBRS* 52 (1969): 68; Onghokham, "Residency," 63–68; Thomas Raffles, *The History of Java* (London, 1817), 1:145, 284–86; John Beattie, *The Nyoro State* (Oxford, 1971), 132ff.; Gluckman, *Custom and Conflict,* 35–41, 51–52; Jacques Berque, *Egypt: Imperialism and Revolution* (New York, 1972), esp. 51–57.

10. For detailed discussions of transport and communication difficulties in central Java and the Javanese military system, see Pieter Louw and E. S. de Klerck, *De Java-Oorlog van 1825–1830* (The Hague-Batavia, 1894–1909), 1:23–50, 203–8. For a discussion of the population of Java in the late eighteenth and early nineteenth centuries, see Bram Peper, *Grootte en Groei van Java's Inheemse Bevolking in de Negentiende Eeuw* (Amsterdam, 1967). For Burma, see James G. Scott [Shway Yoe], *The Burman: His Life and Notions* (New York, 1963), chap. 54; Henry Burney, "On the Population of the Burman Empire," *Journal of the Royal Statistical Society of London* 4, no. 4 (1842): 335–47.

11. For an incisive discussion of these patterns, see Merle Ricklefs, *Jogjakarta under Sultan Mangkubumi, 1749–1792* (Oxford, 1974), chap. 1.

12. Max Weber has analyzed these control devices in general terms. See *Economy and Society,* 3:1042–44. For Java, see Onghokham, "Residency," 15, 35–36, 40–43, 61ff.; G. P. Rouffaer, "Vorstenlanden," *Encyclopedia van Nederlandsch-Indie* (The Hague, 1905), 4:588–90, 624–25. For Burma, see Koenig, "Early Kòn-baung Polity," 40, 249ff., 312–20; Lieberman, "Burmese Dynastic Pattern," 88, 129ff. For African examples, see S. R. Karugire, *A History of the Kingdom of*

Nkore in Western Uganda to 1896 (Oxford, 1971), 64ff.; Beattie, *Nyoro State,* 137-39.

13. In the more highly developed bureaucratic system found in China, officials were prohibited, at least in times of dynastic strength, from serving in their home districts. This was not the case in Java or Burma.

14. Beattie, *Nyoro State,* 138ff.; John F. Richards, ed., *Kingship and Authority in South Asia* (Madison, Wis., 1978), iii, v.

15. Koenig, "Early Kòn-baung Polity," 35, 40-41 et passim; Lieberman, "Burmese Dynastic Pattern," 124. The most graphic account of the use of spies and subterfuge in this sort of polity remains Vishakadatta's play, *The Signet Ring of Rakshasa.* See P. Lal, *Great Sanskrit Plays* (New York, 1957).

16. Carey, "Origins of the Java War," 6-10; J. L. V., "Bijdrage tot de kennis der residentie Madioen," *Tijdschrift voor Nederlandsch Indië* (hereafter cited as *TNI*) 17, no. 2 (1855): 2-3, 7-8; "De toestand van Bagelen in 1830," *TNI* 20, no. 2 (1858): 30; Koenig, "Early Kòn-baung Polity," esp. 308-12; and Lieberman, "Burmese Dynastic Pattern," 186.

17. Moertono, *State and Statecraft,* 139-40, 143-44. See also Onghokham, "Residency," 95-96; James G. Scott and John P. Hardiman, *Gazetteer of Upper Burma and the Shan States* (Rangoon, 1900), 1:413, 416-18; Koenig, "Early Kòn-baung Polity," 95, 312, 315-16.

18. Onghokham, "Residency," 167-76, 199-200; Carey, "Origins of the Java War," 6, 8-9, 37-38, 40-42, 50; J. L. V., "Kennis der Madioen," 5-6, 9; Mya Sein, Crosthwaite 40-41, 52, 65, 67-69; Scott and Hardiman, *Gazetteer,* 415-16.

19. M. J. H. Kollman, "Bagelen onder het bestuur van Soerkarta en Djokjokarta," *TGB* 14 (1864): 362-64, 368. For greater detail and regional variations, see W. Bergsma, comp., *Eindresume . . . de rechten van den inlander op de grond op Java en Madoera,* 3 vols. (Batavia, 1876, 1880, 1896). Insofar as I am aware, information of comparable quality on precolonial conditions in village Burma is not available.

20. For examples, see Jean Chesneaux, *Contributions à l'histoire de la nation Vietnamienne* (Paris, 1955), 91ff.; Gluckman, *Custom and Conflict,* 39, 43, 45; Jan Myrdal and Gun Kessel, *Angkor: An Essay on Art and Imperialism* (New York, 1970). For a discussion of the low incidence of peasant rebellion in precolonial Java, see Moertono, *State and Statecraft,* 5, 75.

21. Gil Carl Alroy, *The Involvement of Peasants in Internal Wars* (Princeton, 1966), esp. 12, 18-20.

22. See, for examples, Koenig, "Early Kòn-baung Polity," 91-92; Gluckman, "Kingdom of the Zulu," 43-44; Lê Thanh Khôi, *Le Viêtnam: histoire et civilisation* (Paris, 1955), 296-310.

23. Moertono, *State and Statecraft,* 5-6; Gustaaf W. van Imhoff, "Reis van den Gouverneur-General van Imhoff in het Jaar 1746," *Bijdragen tot Taal-Land-, en Volkenkunde* (hereafter cited as *BKI*) 1, no. 3 (1853): 361-62, 409.

24. Moertono, *State and Statecraft,* 76–77; H. J. de Graaf, *Geschiedenis van Indonesië* (The Hague, 1949), 428–29. For Burma, see Scott and Hardiman, *Gazetteer,* 1:432; Mya Sein, *Crosthwaite,* 67. For a form of protest similar to the sit-in on the *alun-alun,* see Howard Spodek, "On the Origins of Gandhi's Political Methodology: The Heritage of Kathiawad and Gujarat," *Journal of Asian Studies* 30, no. 2 (1971): 361–72.

25. Carey, "Origins of the Java War," 10; "De toestand van Bagelen," 81; Rouffaer, "Vorstenlanden," 624; Raffles, *History of Java,* 284.

26. Koenig, "Early Kòn-baung Polity," esp. 128–30; Moertono, *State and Statecraft,* 104ff.; Akin Rabibhadana, *The Organization of Thai Society in the Early Bangkok Period* (Ithaca, N.Y., 1969), esp. 82–89; Beattie, *Nyoro State,* 132–33, 137, et passim.

27. For a brilliant analysis of these patterns, see Lucien M. Hanks, "Merit and Power in Thai Social Order," *American Anthropologist* 64, no. 6 (1962): 1247–62.

28. Carey, "Origins of the Java War," 19; Moertono, *State and Statecraft,* 76; Akin Rabibhadana, *Thai Society,* 87. For an African parallel, see Karugire, *Kingdom of Nkore,* 105–6.

29. Onghokham, "Residency," 44; Akin Rabibhadana, *Thai Society,* 181–82.

30. Mya Sein, *Crosthwaite,* 67; Charles Crosthwaite, *The Pacification of Burma* (London, 1912), 5–6.

31. Lieberman, "Burmese Dynastic Pattern," 45, 165, 189, 190, 196ff., 205–6, 221–22. For other areas, see Beattie, *Nyoro State,* 137; Irfan Habib, *The Agrarian System of Mughal India* (Bombay, 1963), 116–17, 334ff.; Vansina, "African Kingdoms," 326.

32. Koenig, "Early Kòn-baung Polity," 304–5, 321–22; Lieberman, "Burmese Dynastic Pattern," 102; Rouffaer, "Vorstenlanden," 624; Carey, "Origins of the Java War," 9–10; Breazeale, "Thai Elites," 3–4; Vansina, "African Kingdoms," 326.

33. M. L. van Deventer, *Geschiedenis der Nederlanders op Java* (Haarlem, 1886–87), 1:127, 158, 230, 255, 301, 313; Elizabeth Hopkins, "The Nyabingi Cult of Southwest Uganda," in *Protest and Power,* ed. Rotberg and Mazrui, 283.

34. Moertono, *State and Statecraft,* 76.

35. Crosthwaite, *Pacification,* 5–7; Gustaaf W. van Imhoff, "Reis van den Gouverneur-General Gustaaf Willem Baron van Imhoff in en door je Jakatrasche Bovenlanden in 1744," *BKI* 7 (1863): 234, 237, 244, 247. For another social pattern that also provided a high degree of mobility and potential for avoidance migration, see Alexander Woodside's discussion of the boat people of Cochin China in *Vietnam and the Chinese Model* (Cambridge, Mass., 1971), 141.

36. For examples, see Moertono, *State and Statecraft,* 75–76, 145ff.; Raffles,

History of Java, 1:273; Carey, "Origins of the Java War," 11, 42–43; Koenig, "Early Kòn-baung Polity," 88–92, 130, 144.

37. van Deventer, *Geschiedenis,* 1:155, 199; Kollman, "Bagelen," 354; Lieberman, "Burmese Dynastic Pattern," 45; Gluckman, "Kingdom of the Zulus," 42.

38. B. Schrieke, *Indonesian Sociological Studies* (The Hague, 1957), 300–301; Moertono, *State and Statecraft,* 5–6, 75; Onghokham, "Residency," 154, 175, 188, 224; Lieberman, "Burmese Dynastic Pattern," 45, 52; Akin Rabibhadana, *Thai Society,* 73, 87–88; Robert Tignor, *The Colonial Transformation of Kenya* (Princeton, 1976), 66. For the fortress-defiance pattern, see I. N. Kamambo, "Mbiru, Popular Protest in Colonial Tanzania, 1944–47," in *War and Society in Africa,* ed. B. A. Ogot (London, 1972), 242.

39. Carey, "Origins of the Java War," 14–15; Louw and de Klerck, *Java-Oorlog,* 1:25–26; Th. Pigeaud, *Javaanse Volksvertoningen* (Batavia, 1938), 35–36; Koenig, "Early Kòn-baung Polity," 90; Lieberman, "Burmese Dynastic Pattern," 45; Chesneaux, *Contributions,* 40; Berque, *Egypt,* 130.

40. Than Tun, "Administration under King Thalun (1629–48)," *JBRS* 51, no. 2 (1968): 177–80; Lieberman, "Burmese Dynastic Pattern," 120; Akin Rabibhadana, *Thai Society,* 73–74; Onghokham, "Residency," 37.

41. Pe Maung Tin and G. H. Luce, *The Glass Palace Chronicle of the Kings of Burma* (Oxford, 1923), 177; J. A. B. Wiselius, "Djaja Baja, zijn leven en profetieën," *BKI* 7 (1872): 185.

42. Than Tun, "Administration," 181, 186–87; Lieberman, "Burmese Dynastic Pattern," 45, 161, 203–4, 217; Michael Aung Thwin, "Kingship, the *Sangha* and Society in Pagan," in *Explorations in Early Southeast Asian History: Origins of Statecraft,* ed. K. Hall and J. Whitmore (Ann Arbor, 1976), 205–56; Akin Rabibhadana, *Thai Society*, 87. Victor Lieberman argues in a recent article that Aung Thwin has overestimated the importance of this pattern in the post-Pagan period. See "The Political Significance of Religious Wealth in Burmese History: Some Further Thoughts," *Journal of Asian Studies* 39, no. 4 (1980): 753–69.

43. F. Fokkens, "Vrije Desa's op Java en Madoera," *TGB* 31 (1886): 477–517; J. L. V., "Kennis der Madioen," 10–11; Onghokham, "Residency," 46. For a somewhat different view of *perdikan* conditions late in the nineteenth century, see K. W. van Gorkom, "Over het desabestuur op Java," *Indische Gids* (hereafter cited as *IG*) 27, no. 2 (1905): 1028–29.

44. Louis Dumont, *Homo Hierarchius* (London, 1970), 230–33.

45. On the traditions of cult and eschatological protest in Java and Burma respectively, see Michael Adas, *Prophets of Rebellion: Millenarian Protest against the European Colonial Order* (Chapel Hill, N.C., 1979), 97–99, 101–2.

46. Moertono, *State and Statecraft,* 77–79; Margaret J. Kartoni, "Performance, Music, and Meaning of Réyog Ponorogo," *Indonesia* 22 (1976): 114–15;

Benedict R. O'G. Anderson, *Mythology and the Tolerance of the Javanese* (Ithaca, N.Y., 1965), 28; Maung Htin Aung, *Burmese Law Tales* (London, 1962), esp. 68–71, 94–95, 103–4, 120–21, 146–47; Aung, *Epistles Written on the Eve of the Anglo-Burmese War* (The Hague, 1968), 27; Aung, *Burmese Drama* (Oxford, 1937), 19–20, 50–51, 74, 77, 86–87, 107–8.

47. For the original formulation of this concept, see Eric Hobsbawm, *Primitive Rebels* (New York, 1959), chap. 2. For a later elaboration, see Hobsbawm, *Bandits* (New York, 1969), and the incisive critique by Anton Blok, "The Peasant and the Brigand: Social Banditry Reconsidered," *Comparative Studies in Society and History* 14 (1972): 494–503.

48. On banditry in precolonial Java and Burma, see Moertono, *State and Statecraft,* 85–86, 185; Onghokham, "Residency," 16–17, 65–69, 86; de Graaf, *Geschiedenis,* 102, 205; Lieberman, "Burmese Dynastic Pattern," 223–28; Koenig, "Early Kòn-buang Polity," 15, 88–90, 132, 166; Crosthwaite, *Pacification,* 6–7; Mya Sein, *Crosthwaite,* 88; Scott and Hardiman, *Gazetteer,* 1:512. For parallels in other areas, see Lê Thanh Khôi, *Le Viêtnam,* 259, 261–62; Berque, *Egypt,* 130ff.; Wolfgang Franke, *A Century of Chinese Revolution, 1851–1949* (New York, 1971), esp. 6–12.

49. Van Deventer, *Geschiedenis,* 2:6–8; E. Sarkisyanz, *Buddhist Backgrounds of the Burmese Revolution* (The Hague, 1965), 70.

50. Koenig, "Early Kòn-baung Polity," 90–91.

51. Crosthwaite, *Pacification,* 14, 17, 23, 27, 31ff.; Grattan Geary, *Burma after the Conquest* (London, 1886), 46–47, 71, 232, 276, 292–93; Government of Burma, *Report[s] on the Police Administration in Burma* (Rangoon, 1888–1913), esp. those for 1888, 1894, 1902, 1909, 1910, 1912, 1913; Sartono Kartodirdjo, *The Peasants' Revolt of Banten in 1888* (The Hague, 1966), esp. 24, 110–16; "Binnenlandsche onlusten op Java," *TNI* (1861): 288–300; D. H. Meijer, "Over het bendwezen op Java," *Indonesië* 3 (1949–50): 178–84.

52. Michael Adas, *The Burma Delta: Economic Development and Social Change on an Asian Rice Frontier, 1852–1941* (Madison, Wis., 1974), chaps. 2, 3, 6; J. L. V., "Kennis der Madioen," 6; Onghokham, "Residency," 194, 215–18, 222; van Imhoff, "Reis van 1774," 230. For African parallels, see Hopkins, "Nyabingi Cult," and J. M. Lonsdale, "Political Associations in Western Kenya," in *Protest and Power,* ed. Rotberg and Mazrui, 283 and 592, respectively.

53. For examples, see Adas, *Prophets,* esp. chap. 5.

54. Adelante, "De ontwikkeling van de inlandsche hoofden op Java," *IG* 14 (1892): 683–84; Government of Burma, *Report on the Settlement Operations in the Bassein and Thongwa Districts, 1888–89* (Rangoon, 1890), 23. For Africa, see Isaacman, *Tradition,* 103–5.

55. Crosthwaite, *Pacification,* 23.

56. For examples, see Allen Isaacman, "Social Banditry in Zimbabwe

(Rhodesia) and Mozambique, 1894–1907: An Expression of Early Peasant Protest, *Journal of Southern African Studies* 4, no. 1 (1977): 1–30; David Sturtevant, *Popular Uprisings in the Philippines 1840–1940* (Ithaca, N.Y., 1976), 94–95, 127ff.

57. The discussion of integration of peasant villages into the colonial systems of Java and Burma is based primarily upon J. S. Furnivall, *Colonial Policy and Practice* (New York, 1956), 71–77, 241–43; Mya Sein, *Crosthwaite,* 81–115, 157, 161, 165–75; D. H. Burger, "Structuurveranderingen in de Javaanse samenleving," pt. 1, *Indonesië* 2 (1948–49): 381–94. For sample parallels in sub-Saharan Africa, see Lonsdale, "Political Associations in Western Kenya," and Rene Lemarchand, "The Coup in Rwanda," in *Protest and Power,* ed. Rotberg and Mazrui, 589–96 and 889–90, respectively. In some areas, the reach of the colonial bureaucracy was more limited until well into the twentieth century. See D. A. Washbrook, *The Emergence of Provincial Politics: The Madras Presidency, 1870–1920* (Cambridge, 1976).

58. Scott and Hardiman, *Gazetteer,* 1:416; Government of Burma, *Report on Settlement Operations in the Mandalay District, 1892–93* (Rangoon, 1894), 24; Onghokham, "Residency," 416ff.

59. For a comparative discussion of this process, see James C. Scott, "The Erosion of Patron-Client Bonds and Social Change in Southeast Asia," *Journal of Asian Studies* 33 (1972): 5–37.

60. Samuel Popkin, *The Rational Peasant: The Political Economy of Rural Society in Vietnam* (Berkeley, 1979), 61–66, 71–72, 76, 80–82, et passim.

61. Adas, *Prophets,* esp. chap. 3.

62. Carey, "Origins of the Java War," 15; Adas, *Burma Delta,* chap. 6.

63. Harry Benda and Lance Castles, "The Samin Movement," *BKI* 125, no. 2 (1965): 222–23; Government of Burma, *The Origin and Causes of the Burma Rebellion 1930–1932* (Rangoon, 1934), 33–34.

64. Isaacman, *Tradition,* 98ff., 101, 105–6; Asiwaju, "Migrations," passim; Lonsdale, "Political Associations," 592.

65. See Government of Burma, *Reports on Police Administration;* Sartono, *Peasants' Revolt.* For other areas, see Isaacman, "Social Banditry," 15–16, 19, 23; Sturtevant, *Popular Uprisings,* 121ff., 135–36.

66. Sartono, *Peasants' Revolt,* 135–36; Berque, *Egypt,* 134ff.

67. Onghokham, "Residency," 226, 230; Louw and de Klerck, *Java-Oorlog,* 1:267, 269, 273; Adas, *Burma Delta,* 149–50, 203–4; Isaacman, "Social Banditry," 23; Isaacman, *Tradition,* 100–101, 107, 115–16; John Iliffe, "Organization of the Maji Maji Rebellion," *Journal of African History* 8 (1967): 499.

68. For a superb illustration of these fears applied to several colonized areas, see W. J. Schoemaker, "Het Mohammedaansche fanatisme," *IG* 20, no. 2 (1896): 1517–37. For discussions of actual government overreactions, see G. W. J. Drewes, *Drie Javaansche Goeroe's: Hun Leven, Onderricht en Messiasprediking* (Leiden,

1925), esp. 39–40, 49; E. Michael Mendelson, *State and Sangha in Burma* (Ithaca, N.Y., 1975), 173–79; Berque, *Egypt,* 233, 262.

69. For examples of these forms of protest see, respectively, Raden Adjeng Kartini, *Letters of a Javanese Princess* (New York, 1964), 60; James R. Brandon, *Theatre in Southeast Asia* (Cambridge, Mass., 1964), 259, 284–88; James L. Peacock, "Anti-Dutch, Anti-Muslim Drama among Surabaja Proletarians: A Description of Performances and Responses," *Indonesia* 4 (1967): 44–73; Kartomi, "Performance, Music, and Meaning," 115–16; Bernhard Dahm, *Sukarno and the Struggle for Indonesian Independence* (Ithaca, N.Y., 1969), esp. 102–5; Thein Pe Myint, "Her Husband or Her Money," "Oil," "Bittersweet," and "A Song to Make One Weep," in *Selected Short Stories of Thein Pe Myint,* trans. P. M. Milne (Ithaca, N.Y., 1973); Ngo Vinh Long, *Before the Revolution: The Vietnamese Peasants under the French* (Cambridge, Mass., 1973); Adas, *Burma Delta,* 193–96; Mendelson, *State and Sangha,* 214–21.

Comment

Michael Adas

The attention given in recent years to "everyday resistance" and "avoidance protest" has developed into a fundamental reassessment of the
approach to peasant societies and rural protest that dominated the work
of social scientists through much of the 1960s and 1970s. The then-
prevailing view of the peasantry was very much a product of a post-
World War II era that had seen rural revolutionary movements, both
successful and failed, throughout much of the Third World. A somewhat
romanticized vision—the/peasantry as a class prone to confrontational
protest and highly susceptible to mobilization in the revolutionary movements that resulted—overcorrected for an earlier consensus that peasants
were passive, hopelessly divided by "amoral familialism," and resigned
to oppression due to their acceptance of a "limited good" view of the
world. Emphasis on nonconfrontational and quotidian modes of peasant
response has provided an important middle ground between the passive
and revolutionary extremes of conceptualizing peasant societies and
responses. It also offers a way around the stalemate that had developed
in the late 1970s as a result of the often heated debate over the false
dichotomy between the peasant as a "moral"—primarily ideological—
or a "rational"—overwhelmingly pragmatic—actor. The everyday or
avoidance approach redirects our attention to the larger context in which
peasant communities operate and to their ongoing struggle to scale back
the demands of the state and elite groups and, thereby, retain enough
of what they produce to build decent lives for themselves. It also results
in an understanding of confrontational protest that is very different than
that of the protest as an aberration or abnormality that prevailed before
and just after the war, and different than the "building to the big event"
(peasant riots or rebellion) approach that dominated work on agrarian
protest, including my own, in the 1960s and 1970s.

Like all reassessments, the reorientation of our approaches to peasant societies suggested by the literature on everyday and avoidance protest creates new problems in methodology and conceptualization and resurrects issues that were never fully resolved in earlier debates. A major source of the former has resulted from the tendency to conflate modes of avoidance protest, which was the focus of the 1981 *CSSH* essay reprinted here, with forms of everyday resistance like foot-dragging, pilfering, and grousing behind the back of the local landlord. As I argue implicitly in this article and have done so explicitly elsewhere, the two are quite different phenomena in a number of important respects.[1] To begin with, everyday forms of peasant response are much more limited in time span and the numbers involved *in any given occurrence,* as well as in the degree to which they challenge or disrupt the existing order. The fact that everyday protest involves acts that are meant to be hidden— in fact, must be hidden if they are to be successful—from the dominant groups at whom they are directed, means that a record of them is unlikely to be preserved in the sorts of sources used by historians. As studies such as James Scott's *Weapons of the Weak* have so ably shown, the members of peasant communities at all class levels are well aware that subordinate groups are engaging in these defensive and retributive activities.[2] But the sorts of oral documentation for these responses that Scott and others have painstakingly recorded and insightfully analyzed in recent years rarely, if ever, exist for the precolonial or colonial periods, which are the subject of my *CSSH* essay. Official sources and written memoirs rarely, if ever, tell us much about everyday resistance in times past. In contrast, protest migrations, the spread of banditry, sectarian withdrawal, and other forms of avoidance protest are often treated in official sources, both those of central administrations and local functionaries, though rarely in the detail that the historian would like.

By interpolation from contemporary studies, we may surmise that, in former times, peasant groups widely resorted to everyday forms of resistance—perhaps even more commonly than today, given the more modest means at the disposal of the state and landed groups to control them. But the clandestine nature of everyday responses meant that they were unlikely to be recorded in village records, much less the reports of princely or colonial officials. A major exception to this general rule involved practices such as the concealment of produce and able-bodied laborers and the collusion of villagers with local officials to underreport crop yields or *corvée* labor quotas. These tactics, which are treated as peasant defenses rather than protest in the 1981 essay, can, I think, be included among everyday forms of peasant resistance. Interestingly, they were recorded because they were forms of everyday resistance that were primarily aimed at the state. On the whole, however, modes of everyday resistance tend to be employed to redress imbalances in the terms of exchange with landlords, moneylenders, and other local power brokers or in efforts to defame these individuals for their perceived injustices. The primacy of the local arena in the quotidian contests between the peasant underclasses and those who dominate them, contrasts with the centrality of the state's role in most occurrences of avoidance protest. As I try to show in this essay, the latter cannot be understood apart from the context provided by the state. On the other hand, the relatively minor presence of the state, aside from discussions of efforts to cheat on the *zakat* or religious tithe, in Scott's description in *Weapons of the Weak* of everyday resistance in a Malaysian village suggests the rather different targets typically associated with each type of nonconfrontational protest.

The existence of written documents dealing with various modes of avoidance protest in both the precolonial and colonial periods makes it possible to explore the significant continuities between systems of dominance and dependence and peasant responses in the two eras, as well as to assess the major shifts that occurred in each. The arguments advanced in the *CSSH* essay were intended to call into question the extent to which European conquest marked a significant break with the precolonial past for the majority of the peoples who came under colonial rule. For this reason, I have much regretted titling and organizing the essay in such a way that many have seen the precolonial/colonial division as central to shifts in the patterns of peasant response I have tried to identify. As I have argued here and elsewhere, the assumption of political power by the European colonizers often had little immediate effect on peasants and other subordinate groups.[3] In most instances, the continuities between political economies existing under indigenous rulers and those that emerged under colonial rule were far more striking than the changes under way. Though the incidence of confrontation in the early stages of European rule was often increased by the colonizers' suspicion, at times bordering on paranoia, of indigenous sectarian movements, whenever possible the colonizers retained the indigenous lords and employed indigenous symbols and rituals (which were often religious in origin) of political authority. In most instances, it was decades after the

European takeover before the forces that reduced, or eliminated altogether, the effectiveness of longstanding modes of avoidance protest began to take hold.

Without question, the aims and policies pursued by the colonizers and their new military and communications technology unleashed these forces. But the shift from avoidance protest techniques to increasingly confrontational forms of agitation was a gradual and uneven process that differed considerably from one colony—or even from one district—to the next. The extent to which it occurred depended on the mix of forces found in a particular area. Among other factors, the viability of different modes of avoidance protest tended to be undermined by the spread of the market economy and the consequent erosion of patron-client ties and community cohesion; demographic shifts, which altered population-to-land ratios and eliminated remaining frontier areas; and the communications revolution, which greatly increased the reach of the ruling elites. Virtually all peasant groups continued to rely on modes of avoidance protest well into the colonial era, and often this attachment continued long after they had ceased to be effective. It is also fair to assume that everyday forms of protest that are so prevalent in the present day have been inherited from the distant past. Indeed, if one can generalize from the evidence provided by Scott, this type of peasant resistance has fared better than most forms of avoidance response in the late- and postcolonial eras. On the other hand, as Gandhi's nonviolent approach to mass nationalist agitation or even revolutionary guerrilla warfare demonstrate, the principles of avoidance protest, and in some cases specific modes of avoidance response like flight and sabotage, have exerted considerable influence on movements designed to promote confrontations with, and eventually overthrow, the existing political order.

In contrast to clandestine acts of everyday retribution, avoidance protest involves open challenges to dominant elite groups and, at times, to the state itself. Because modes of avoidance protest are likely to be more open, more collective, and more threatening (while minimizing direct confrontation) to those in power, they also involve far greater risk for those who resort to them. In fact, challenge and risk are key attributes of the protest dimension of this type of response on the part of peasants and other subordinate groups. Transferring one's loyalties and services from one patron to another, for which, in societies such as in central Java, there was an accepted procedure to be observed, involved the explicit expression of the client's dissatisfaction with the patron he was abandoning. Mass migrations of village communities or a considerable portion of the population of entire districts was a potent way for peasants to draw attention to the oppression of local notables or the maladministration of state officials in their region. There are numerous instances of the dismissal and punishment of officials whose misdeeds were publicized in this manner. At times, the movement of populations across territorial boundaries or into unsettled frontier areas was so extensive that the continued viability of the state itself was put at risk. In fact, the spread of vagabondage and retributive forms of avoidance protest, such as banditry, have traditionally been associated in many societies with the decline of dynastic houses.

The indirect and nonviolent, but very real and well recognized, challenges that avoidance protest poses for the existing order contrast with the hidden, nondisruptive occurrence of everyday resistance. Although Scott argues that the cumulative effect of everyday protest actions on the part of the peasant classes of a given polity over a period of time can undermine the polity's viability, this is a proposition that has yet to be tested.[4] In fact, the evidence we have to date suggests that the reverse is the case, that as rulers begin to lose control and state systems go into decline, the need and opportunities for both everyday and avoidance types of protest increase dramatically. On the face of it, mass migrations and banditry are more likely to play major roles in a state's continuing decline and collapse than shoddy work, illegally gleaning the spilled seeds in the local headman's fields, and "accidents" that damage a landlord's equipment or disable his or her livestock.

It is also important to keep in mind that neither everyday nor avoidance protest responses are intended to destroy, or even radically alter, the political system or the social structure in which peasants or other subordinate groups operate. They have developed both types of response to defend themselves against the excessive demands of dominant groups in the first instance, and, when the defenses fail, to provide ways of protesting their exploitation without directly confronting their oppressors. In terms of the latter, modes of the avoidance type tend to be a good deal more effective than the everyday tactics that are the focus of much recent work. But both types of response are designed to work within the existing system. As the terms *everyday* and *avoidance* suggest, these modes of response to oppression by subordinate groups are built into the ongoing interaction between dominant and subordinate classes. Many forms of everyday resistance are, in effect, routinized. Though more sporadic, avoidance responses become predictable in particular circumstances—the peasantry will fall back on them; their overlords must anticipate them and find ways of containing or fending them off. When peasants or other subordinate groups turn to responses that involve open confrontation with those whom they identify as the source of their suffering, they do so because everyday and avoidance tactics are ineffective. Riots and rebellions signal the breakdown of the uneasy and ever-shifting networks of dominance and dependency that provide the essential contexts for everyday and avoidance protest.

Both everyday resistance and avoidance protest give a degree of agency and voice to peasants and other subordinate groups, but we should be cautious about overestimating either the extent of the autonomy or the level of ideological sophistication that underclass groups can attain by employing them. Both are responsive: they are aimed at winning relief or some degree of retribution within a system that is taken as a given. The very modes of expression associated with either type of protest are dependent on the existing order, as recent studies of ritual protest through role reversals at carnival time and in other sorts of religious festivals dramatically illustrate.[5] Social roles are symbolically—and temporarily—exchanged, and members of the underclass are permitted to act in ways normally prohibited. But the reversals and outrageous behavior of the subordinate take the established order and elite classes as their referents. When carnival rowdiness leads to rioting or role reversals are proclaimed by millennarian rebels who hold out the promise of a world turned upside down, we have moved to a different type of protest response on the part of subordinate groups.

This is not to deny that subordinate groups play far more active roles than many writers have allowed in the making of the existing order, and that, through devices such as everyday resistance and avoidance protest, they are able to bring pressure on dominant groups to reformulate aspects of that order. But, despite small and usually temporary victories, they continue to accept their subordination; they remain victims of political economies designed to further the interests of elites, whether they be local landlords or the functionaries of princely or colonial regimes. In fact, both types of peasant response reinforce the existing order in a number of ways. If effective, they render the hard lot of the cultivators who resort to them bearable by ameliorating the oppressive demands of state and landlord. At the same time, they force necessary, but often temporary, concessions from dominant groups. Though varying in importance, the cumulative effect of these adjustments may well have proved critical to the persistence of systems based on exploitation and injustice. In addition, everyday resistance and avoidance protest provide outlets for peasants and other subordinate groups to vent their anger and, in a limited way, to strike back against those who use and humiliate them. Though we lack the evidence to determine this sort of thing with any precision, it is possible that activities like flight to the frontier, banditry, and sectarian retreat draw off the boldest, most politically conscious members of peasant communities and other subordinate groups. If this is the case, they cannot help but weaken whatever impetus there is for fundamentally restructuring the existing order, either through lasting reforms or revolutionary action.

The stress in my *CSSH* essay on the limits of both types of protest should not be taken as an implicit argument that members of subordinate social groups are incapable of doubting, indeed rejecting, the hegemonic ideas and structures designed to keep them in their place. Skillfully using oral testimony of a sort rarely available to the historian, Scott demonstrates just how pervasive and sophisticated this sort of demystification can be. The alternative "transcript" that he uncovers by listening to villagers from the underclasses leads him to doubt the utility of the concept of hegemony itself, at least as it was intended by Gramsci and has been frequently applied by social scientists in recent years. If the concept is used in the elite-centric, uncontested, and static formulation found in Gramsci's admittedly fragmentary writings on the subject, and so effectively demolished by Scott, it is indeed of questionable utility. But Scott's comparisons of the current situation of disarray with an apparently effective hegemonic system that existed in the Malaysian villagers' past and his admission that the peasants with whom he worked had just experienced a decade of unprecedented change, both point to the need to revise rather than outright reject Gramsci's formulation of hegemony. If hegemony is viewed as ideological and institutional dominance that is continually being tested and challenged (both openly and behind the scenes) by subordinate groups at a variety of levels and being reworked by elite groups to respond to these challenges and changing conditions more generally,[6] it becomes a far more useful analytical tool.

A dyachronic approach, which assumes that dominant and subordinate social groups are locked in an ongoing contest over the terms by which hegemony is imposed and accepted, gives the peasantry agency without attributing to them a capacity, which they have rarely possessed, to master fully the intricacies of the political or social systems in which they live and to act collectively to right the injustices they perceive in those arrangements. Both tactics of everyday resistance and modes of avoidance protest are key ways by which peasants and other subordinate groups test and challenge, and sometimes force changes in, hegemonic systems. But the limitations of these responses and the draconian repression they have frequently brought upon those who resort to them caution against a new sort of romanticization of peasant consciousness and overestimating the capacity of subordinate groups in rural or urban settings to right the wrongs inflicted upon them by those who monopolize power and control the resources of the societies in which they live.

NOTES

1. See Michael Adas, "From Foot-dragging to Flight: The Evasive History of Peasant Avoidance Protest in South and Southeast Asia," *Journal of Peasant Studies* 13, no. 2 (1986): 64–86.

2. James Scott, *Weapons of the Weak* (New Haven: Yale University Press, 1985), esp. chaps. 5 and 6. See also the essays in James Scott and Benedict J. Tria Kerkvliet, eds., *Everyday Forms of Peasant Resistance in Southeast Asia* (London: Frank Cass, 1986); and the contributions to *Contesting Power: Everyday Resistance in South Asian Society and History,* ed. Douglas Haynes and Gyan Prakash (Delhi: Oxford University Press, 1991).

3. See Michael Adas, "Bandits, Monks, and Pretender Kings: Patterns of Peasant Resistance and Protest in Colonial Burma, 1826–1941," in *Power and Protest in the Countryside,* ed. Robert P. Weller and Scott E. Guggenheim (Durham, N.C.: Duke University Press, 1982), 75–105.

4. See Scott, *Weapons,* 35–37, 348–50.

5. Perhaps the fullest exploration of these patterns can be found in Emmanuel LeRoy Ladurie, *Carnival in Romans* (New York: Braziller, 1979). For further examples in a variety of contexts, see Peter Burke, *Popular Culture in Early Modern Europe* (New York: Harper and Row, 1978); Barbara A. Babcock, ed., *The Reversible World: Symbolic Inversion in Art and Society* (Ithaca, N.Y.: Cornell University Press, 1978).

6. As Williams argued (over a decade ago) that it must be. See Raymond Williams, *Marxism and Literature* (London: Oxford University Press, 1977), esp. 111–14.

Culture of Terror—Space of Death: Roger Casement's Putumayo Report and the Explanation of Torture

Michael Taussig

This article is about torture and the culture of terror, which for most of us, including myself, are known only through the words of others. Thus my concern is with the mediation of the culture of terror through narration—and with the problems of writing effectively against terror.

Jacobo Timerman ends his recent book, *Prisoner without a Name, Cell without a Number,* with the imprint of the gaze of hope in the space of death.

> Have any of you looked into the eyes of another person, on the floor of a cell, who knows that he's about to die though no one has told him so? He knows that he's about to die but clings to his biological desire to live, as a single hope, since no one has told him he's to be executed.
>
> I have many such gazes imprinted upon me. . . .
>
> Those gazes which I encountered in the clandestine prisons of Argentina and which I've retained one by one, were the culminating point, the purest moment of my tragedy.
>
> They are here with me today. And although I might wish to do so, I could not and would not know how to share them with you.[1]

The space of death is crucial to the creation of meaning and consciousness, nowhere more so than in societies where torture is endemic and where the culture of terror flourishes. We may think of the space of death as a threshold, yet it is a wide space whose breadth offers positions of advance as well as of extinction. Sometimes a person goes

135

through it and returns to us to tell the tale, like Timerman, who entered it, he says, because he believed the battle against military dictatorship had to be fought.[2]

Timerman fought with words, with his newspaper *La Opinion,* in and against the silence imposed by the arbiters of discourse who beat out a new reality in the prison cells where the torturers and the tortured came together. "We victims and victimizers, we're part of the same humanity, colleagues in the same endeavor to prove the existence of ideologies, feelings, heroic deeds, religions, obsessions. And the rest of humanity, what are they engaged in?"[3]

The construction of colonial reality that occurred in the New World has been and will remain a topic of immense curiosity and study—the New World where the Indian and the African became subject to an initially far smaller number of Christians. Whatever conclusions we draw about how that hegemony was so speedily effected, we would be most unwise to overlook or underestimate the role of terror. And by this I mean us to think through terror, which as well as being a physiological state is also a social fact and a cultural construction whose baroque dimensions allow it to serve as the mediator par excellence of colonial hegemony. The space of death is one of the crucial spaces where Indian, African, and white gave birth to the New World.

This space of death has a long and rich culture. It is where the social imagination has populated its metamorphosing images of evil and the underworld: in the Western tradition, Homer, Virgil, the Bible, Dante, Bosch, the Inquisition, Baudelaire, Rimbaud, *Heart of Darkness;* in Northwest Amazonian tradition, zones of visions, communication between terrestrial and supernatural beings, putrefaction, death, rebirth, and genesis, perhaps in the rivers and land of maternal milk bathed eternally in the subtle green light of coca leaves.[4] With European conquest and colonization, these spaces of death blend as a common pool of key signifiers or caption points binding the culture of the conqueror with that of the conquered. The space of death is preeminently a space of transformation: through the experience of death, life; through fear, loss of self and conformity to a new reality; or through evil, good. Lost in the dark woods, then journeying through the underworld with his guide, Dante achieves paradise only after he has mounted Satan's back. Timerman can be a guide for us, analogous to the ways Putumayo shamans I know are guides to those lost in the space of death.

An old Ingano Indian from the Putumayo once told me of this space.

> With the fever I was aware of everything. But after eight days I became unconscious. I knew not where I was. Like a madman I wandered, consumed by fever. They had to cover me up where I fell, mouth down. Thus after eight days I was aware of nothing. I was unconscious. Of what people were saying, I remembered nothing. Of the pain of the fever, I remembered nothing; only the space of death— walking in the space of death. Thus, after the noises that spoke, I remained unconscious. Now the world remained behind. Now the world was removed. Well, then I understood. Now the pains were speaking. I knew that I would live no longer. Now I was dead. My sight had gone. Of the world I knew nothing, nor the sound of my ears. Of speech, nothing. Silence. And one knows the space of death, there. . . . And this is death—the space that I saw. I was in its center, standing. Then I went to the heights. From the heights a star-point seemed my due. I was standing. Then I came down. There I was searching for the five continents of the world, to remain, to find me a place in the five continents of the world—in the space in which I was wandering. But I was not able.

We might ask, what place in the five continents of the world will the wanderer in the space of death find himself? And by extension, where will a whole society find itself? The old man fears the evil of sorcery, the struggle for his soul. Between himself, the sorcerer, and the curing shaman, the five continents are sought and fought for. Yet here there is laughter too, puncturing the fear of the mystery, reminding us of Walter Benjamin's comment on the way in which romanticism may perniciously misunderstand the nature of intoxication. "Any serious exploration of occult, surrealistic, phantasmagoric gifts and phenomena," he writes,

> presupposes a dialectical intertwinement to which a romantic turn of mind is impervious. For histrionic or fanatical stress on the mysterious side of the mysterious takes us no further; we penetrate the mystery only to the degree that we recognize it in the everyday world, by virtue of a dialectical optic that perceives the everyday as impenetrable, the impenetrable as everyday.[5]

From Timerman's chronicle and texts like Miguel Angel Asturias's *El señor presidente* it is abundantly clear that cultures of terror are based on and nourished by silence and myth in which the fanatical stress on the mysterious side of the mysterious flourishes by means of rumor and fantasy woven in a dense web of magical realism. It is also clear that the victimizer needs the victim for the purpose of making truth, objectifying the victimizer's fantasies in the discourse of the other. To be sure, the torturer's desire is also prosaic: to acquire information, to act in concert with large-scale economic strategies elaborated by the masters and exigencies of production. Yet equally, if not more, important is the need to control massive populations through the cultural elaboration of fear.

That is why silence is imposed, why Timerman, the publisher, was so important, why he knew when to be silent and close off reality in the torture chamber. "Such silence," he tells us,

> begins in the channels of communication. Certain political leaders, institutions, and priests attempt to denounce what is happening, but are unable to establish contact with the population. The silence begins with a strong odor. People sniff the suicides, but it eludes them. Then silence finds another ally: solitude. People fear suicides as they fear madmen. And the person who wants to fight senses his solitude and is frightened.[6]

Hence, there is the need for us to fight that solitude, fear, and silence, to examine these conditions of truth making and culture making, to follow Michel Foucault in "seeing historically how effects of truth are produced within discourses which are in themselves neither true nor false."[7] At the same time we not only have to see, we also have to see anew through the creation of counterdiscourses.

If effects of truth are power, then the question is raised not only concerning the power to speak and write, but about what form shall that counterdiscourse take. This issue of form has lately been of much concern to those involved in writing histories and ethnographies. But faced with the endemicity of torture, terror, and the growth of armies, we in the New World are today assailed with a new urgency. There is the effort to understand terror, in order to make *others* understand. Yet the reality at stake here makes a mockery of understanding and derides rationality, as when the young Jacobo Timerman asks his mother, "Why do they hate us?" And she replies, "Because they do not understand." And after his ordeal, the old Timerman writes of the need for a hated object and the simultaneous fear of that object—the almost magical inevitability of hatred. "No," he concludes, "there can be no doubt my mother was the one who was mistaken. It is not the anti-Semites who must be made to understand. It is we Jews."[8]

Hated and feared, objects to be despised, yet also of awe, the reified essence of evil in the very being of their bodies, these figures of the Jew, the black, the Indian, and woman herself, are clearly objects of cultural construction, the leaden keel of evil and of mystery stabilizing the ship and course that is Western history. With the cold war we add the communist. With the time bomb ticking inside the nuclear family, we had the feminists and the gays. The military and the New Right, like the conquerors of old, discover the evil they have imputed to these aliens, and mimic the savagery they have imputed.

What sort of understanding—what sort of speech, writing, and construction of meaning by any mode—can deal with and subvert that?

On one thing Timerman is clear. To couterpose the eroticization and romanticization of violence by the same means or by forms equally mystical is a dead end. Yet to offer one or all of the standard rational explanations of the culture of terror is similarly pointless. For behind the search for profits, the need to control labor, the need to assuage frustration, and so on, lie intricately construed, long-standing cultural logics of meaning—structures of feeling—whose basis lies in a symbolic world and not in one of rationalism. Ultimately there are two features; the crudest of empirical facts such as the electrodes and the mutilated body, and the experience of going through torture. In his text, Timerman creates a powerful counterdiscourse, precisely because, like torture itself, it moves us through that space of death where reality is up for grabs, to confront the hallucination of the military. His text of madness and evil finds its counterweight and sanity in what I take to be the most difficult of political positions marked out by a contradictory space between socialism and anarchism. He is to Victor Serge as V. S. Naipaul is to Arthur Koestler and Joseph Conrad.

Conrad's way of dealing with the terror of the rubber boom in the Congo was *Heart of Darkness*. There were three realities there, comments Frederick Karl: King Leopold's, made out of intricate disguises and deceptions; Roger Casement's studied realism; and Conrad's, which, to quote Karl, "fell midway between the other two, as he attempted to penetrate the veil and yet was anxious to retain its hallucinatory quality."[9]

This formularization is sharp and important: *to penetrate the veil while retaining its hallucinatory quality.* It evokes Paul Ricoeur's two hermeneutics in his major discussion of Freud: that of suspicion (or reduction) and that of revelation.[10] As to the political effect of *Heart of Darkness,* while Ian Watt regards it as the enduring and most powerful literary indictment of imperialism,[11] I am not so sure that its strikingly literary quality and hallucinatory filminess do not finally blind and stun the reader into a trance, drowning in a sea storm of imagery. The danger here lies with aestheticizing horror, and while Conrad manages to stop short of doing that, we must realize that just to the side lurks the seductive tropes of fascism and the imaginative source of terror and torture embedded deep within us all. The political and artistic problem is to engage with that, to maintain that hallucinatory quality, while effectively turning it against itself. That would be the true catharsis, the great counterdiscourse we must ponder in the political terrain urgently exposed today; the form wherein all that appeals and seduces in the iconography and sensuality of the underworld becomes its own force for self-subversion. Foucault's concept of discourse eludes this aspiration and concept of dialectically engaged subversion. But it is with this poetics that we must develop the cultural politics appropriate to our times.

Casement offers a useful and startling contrast to Conrad, all the more vivid because of the ways their paths crossed in the Congo in 1890, because of the features common to their political backgrounds as exiles or quasi exiles from imperialized European societies, Poland and Ireland, and because of an indefinable if only superficial similarity in their temperaments and love of literature. Yet it was Casement who resorted to militant action on behalf of his native land, organizing gun running from Germany to the rebels at Dublin for Easter Sunday 1916, and was hung for treason, while Conrad resolutely stuck to his task as an artist, bathed in nostalgia and guilt for Poland, lending his name but otherwise refusing to assist Casement in the Congo Reform Society, claiming he was but a "wretched novelist." The key text for our purposes is Conrad's letter to his beloved friend and socialist, the aristocrat don Roberto, otherwise known as R. B. Cunninghame Graham (whom

Jorge Luis Borges regards together with that other great English romantic, W. H. Hudson, as providing the most accurate sketches and literary
works of nineteenth-century Pampa society). In this letter, dated
December 26, 1903, Conrad salutes don Roberto on the excellence of
his book on the great Spanish conquistador, Hernando de Soto, and
especially for the sympathetic insight into the souls of the conquistadores—the glamour, pathos, and romance of those times—which functions as an anodyne inducing one to forget the modern conquistadores
such as Leopold and the lack of romance and vision in nineteenth- and
early twentieth-century bourgeois imperialism. Conrad then goes on to
inform don Roberto about "a man called Casement" and his plans for
a Congo reform society to stop the terror associated with the rubber
industry there, the same terror that inspired Conrad's novella. Conrad
likens Casement to a conquistador, and indulges in a hopelessly romanticized image of him—curtly corrected by Brian Inglis, one of Casement's biographers, seventy years later.[12] What is so galling and
instructive about this sort of indulgence, which stems from and informs
Conrad's theory of art as formulated in the introduction to *The Nigger
of the Narcissus* (see page 150 of this essay), is that at the time of
Casement's trial for treason and villification as a homosexual in 1916,
Conrad displayed a permutation of the romanticism that had led him
almost to deify the Casement he first met in the Congo in 1890. Writing
to John Quinn, Conrad reimages his first acquaintance with Casement,
now pigeonholing him not as in the *Congo Diary,* as a man who
"thinks, speaks well, [is] most intelligent and very sympathetic," but
as a labor recruiter. He goes on to disparage Casement as a romantic
opportunist and adds:

> He was a good companion, but already in Africa I judged that he was
> a man, properly speaking, of no mind at all. I don't mean stupid. I
> mean he was all emotion. By emotional force (Congo report,
> Putumayo—etc) he made his way, and sheer emotionalism has undone
> him. A creature of sheer temperament—a truly tragic personality: all
> but the greatness of which he had not a trace. Only vanity. But in the
> Congo it was not visible yet.[13]

Yet it remains a fact that Casement's reports on the Congo and the
Putumayo did much to stop the pervasive brutality there and, in Edmund
Morel's opinion, "innoculated the diplomacy of this country [Britain]

with a moral toxin" such that "historians will cherish these occasions as the only two in which British diplomacy rose above the commonplace."[14]

In addition to the coincidences of imperialist history, what brings Casement and Conrad together is the problem they jointly create concerning the rhetorical power and political effect of social realism and mythic realism. Between the emotional consul-general who wrote effectively on the side of the colonized as a realist and a rationalist, and the great artist who did not, lie many of the crucial problems concerning the domination of culture and cultures of domination.

The Putumayo Report

At this point it is instructive to briefly analyze Casement's Putumayo report, which was submitted to Sir Edward Grey, head of the British Foreign Service, and published by the House of Commons on July 13, 1913, when Casement was forty-nine years old.

At the outset it should be noted that Casement's attachment to the cause of Irish home rule and his anger at British imperialism made his almost lifelong work as a British consul extremely fraught with contradiction; in addition, he felt his experiences in Africa and South America increased his understanding of the effects of colonialism in Ireland, which in turn stimulated his ethnographic and political sensibilities regarding conditions south of the equator. He claimed, for example, that it was his knowledge of Irish history that allowed him to understand the Congo atrocities, whereas the Foreign Office could not because the empirical evidence made no sense to them. In a letter to his close friend, Alice Green, he noted:

> I knew the Foreign Office would not understand the thing, for I realized that I was looking at this tragedy with the eyes of another race of people once hunted themselves, whose hearts were based on affection as the root principle of contact with their fellow men, and whose estimate of life was not something eternally to be appraised at its market price.[15]

In the article he wrote for the respected *Contemporary Review* in 1912, he argued that the Putumayo Indians were more highly developed, morally speaking, than their white oppressors. The Indian lacked a competitive streak; he was "a socialist by temperament, habit, and possibly, age-long memory of Inca and pre-Inca precept." In conclusion, Casement asked, "Is it too late to hope that by means of the same humane and brotherly agency, something of the goodwill and kindness of Christian life may be imparted to the remote, friendless, and lost children of the forest?"[16] He later referred to the peasants of Connemara in Ireland as "white Indians."[17]

The essence of his 136-page Putumayo report, based on seven weeks of travel in 1910 through the rubber-gathering areas of the jungles of the Caraparaná and Igaraparaná affluents of the middle reaches of the Putumayo River, and on some six months in the Amazon basin, lay in its detail of the terror and tortures together with Casement's explanation of causes and his estimate of the toll in human life. Putumayo rubber would be unprofitable were it not for the forced labor of local Indians, principally those called Huitotos. For the twelve years from 1900, the Putumayo output of some 4,000 tons of rubber cost thousands of Indians their lives. Deaths from torture, disease, and possibly flight had decreased the population of the area by around 30,000 during that time.[18]

The British government felt obliged to send Casement as its consular representative to the Putumayo because of the public outcry aroused in 1909 by a series of articles in the London magazine, *Truth*; the series depicted the brutality of the rubber company, which since 1907 had been a consortium of Peruvian and British interests in the region. Entitled "The Devil's Paradise: A British Owned Congo," these articles were the work of a young "engineer" and adventurer from the United States named Walter Hardenburg, who, with a companion, had entered the remote corner of the Amazon basin from the Colombian Andes in 1907 and had been taken prisoner by the Peruvian Rubber Company (founded by Julio César Arana in 1903). Hardenburg's chronicle is, to an important extent, an elaboration on a text basic to the Putumayo saga, an article published in the Iquitos newspaper *La Sanción* shortly before its publication was suspended by the Peruvian government and Arana.

Asserting that the rubber trees are in rapid decline and will be exhausted in four years' time because of the rapacity of the production system, the article continues by declaring that the peaceful Indians work night and day collecting rubber without the slightest remuneration. They are given nothing to eat or wear. Their crops, together with the women and children, are taken for the pleasure of the whites. They are inhumanly flogged until their bones are visible. Given no medical treatment, they are left to die after torture, eaten by the company's dogs. They are castrated, and their ears, fingers, arms, and legs are cut off. They are also tortured by means of fire, water, and crucifixion tied head-down. The whites cut them to pieces with machetes and dash out the brains of small children by hurling them against trees and walls. The elderly are killed when they can no longer work. To amuse themselves, company officials practice shooting, using Indians as targets, and on special occasions such as Easter Saturday—Saturday of Glory—shoot them down in groups, or, in preference, douse them in kerosene and set them on fire to enjoy their agony.[19]

In a letter written to Hardenburg by an employee of the company, we read how a "commission" was sent out by a rubber-station manager to exterminate a group of Indians for not bringing in sufficient rubber. The commission returned in four days with fingers, ears, and several heads of Indians to prove the orders had been carried out.[20] On another occasion, the manager called in hundreds of Indians to assemble at the station.

> He grasped his carbine and machete and began the slaughter of these defenseless Indians, leaving the ground covered with over 150 corpses, among them men, women, and children. Bathed in blood and appealing for mercy, the survivors were heaped with the dead and burned to death, while the manager shouted, "I want to exterminate all the Indians who do not obey my orders about the rubber that I require them to bring in."

"When they get drunk," adds the correspondent, "the upper-level employees of the company toast with champagne the man who can boast of the greatest number of murders."[21]

The drama perhaps most central to the Putumayo terror, quoted from an Iquitos newspaper article in 1908, and affirmed as fact by both Casement and Hardenburg, concerns the weighing of rubber brought by the Indians from the forest.

> The Indian is so humble that as soon as he sees that the needle of the scale does not mark the ten kilos, he himself stretches out his hands and throws himself on the ground to receive the punishment. Then the chief [of the rubber station] or a subordinate advances, bends down, takes the Indian by the hair, strikes him, raises his head, drops it face downwards on the ground, and after the face is beaten

and kicked and covered with blood, the Indian is scourged. This is
when they are treated best, for often they cut them to pieces with
machetes.[22]

In the rubber station of Matanzas, continues the writer, "I have seen
Indians tied to a tree, their feet about half a yard above the ground.
Fuel is then placed below, and they are burnt alive. This is done to pass
the time."

Casement's report to the House of Commons is staid and sober, somewhat like a lawyer arguing a case and in marked contrast to his diary
covering the same experience. He piles fact on brutal fact, suggests an
overall analysis, and makes his recommendations. His material comes
from three sources: what he personally witnessed; testimony of 30 Barbados blacks who, with 166 others, were contracted by the company
during 1903-4 to serve as overseers, and whose statements occupy eighty-
five published foolscap pages; and, interspersed with Casement's direct
observations, numerous stories from local residents and company
employees.

Early on in the report, in a vivid throwaway line, he evokes the
banality of the cruelty. "The employees at all stations passed the time
when not hunting Indians, either lying in their hammocks or in gam-
bling."[23] The unreal atmosphere of ordinariness, of the ordinariness of
the extraordinary, can be startling. "At some of the stations the principal
flogger was the station cook—two such men were directly named to me,
and I ate the food they prepared, while many of their victims carried
my baggage from station to station, and showed often terrible scars on
their limbs inflicted at the hands of these men."[24]

From the evidence of scarring, Casement found that the "great majority" (perhaps up to 90 percent) of the more than 1,600 Indians he saw
had been badly beaten.[25] Some of the worst affected were small boys,
and deaths due to flogging were frequent, either under the lash, or more
frequently, a few days later when the wounds became maggot infested.[26]
Floggings occurred when an Indian brought in insufficient rubber and
were most sadistic for those who dared to flee. Flogging was mixed with
other tortures such as near drowning, "designed," as Casement points
out, "to just stop short of taking life while inspiring the acute mental
fear and inflicting much of the physical agony of death."[27] Casement
was informed by a man who had himself often flogged Indians that he

had seen mothers flogged because their little sons had not brought in enough rubber. While the boy stood terrified and crying at the sight, his mother would be beaten "just a few strokes" to make him a better worker.[28]

Deliberate starvation was resorted to repeatedly, sometimes to frighten, more often to kill. Men and women were kept in the stocks until they died of hunger. One Barbadian related how he had seen Indians in this situation "scraping up the dirt with their fingers and eating it." Another declared he had seen them eating the maggots in their wounds.[29]

The stocks were sometimes placed on the upper verandah or residential part of the main dwelling house of the rubber stations, in direct view of the manager and his employees. Children, men, and women might be confined in them for months, and some of the Barbados men said they had seen women raped while in the stocks.[30]

Much of the surveillance and punishment was carried out by the corps of Indian guards known as the *muchachos*. Members of this armed corps had been trained by the company from an early age, and were used to control *salvajes* other than those to whom they were kin. Casement thought them to be generally every bit as evil as their white masters.[31] When Barbados men were present, they were frequently assigned the task of flogging, but, Casement emphasizes, "no monopoly of flogging was enjoyed by any employee as a right. The chief of the section frequently himself took the lash, which, in turn, might be wielded by every member of the civilized or 'rational staff.'"[32]

"Such men," reports Casement, "had lost all sight or sense of rubber-gathering—they were simply beasts of prey who lived upon the Indians and delighted in shedding their blood." Moreover, the station managers from the areas where Casement got his most precise information were in debt (despite their handsome rates of commission), running their operations at a loss to the company that in some sections ran to many thousands of pounds sterling.[33]

It is necessary at this point to note that, although the Indians received the brunt of the terror, whites and blacks were also targets. Whether as competitors for Indian rubber gatherers, like the independent Colombian rubber traders who first conquered the Putumayo and were then dislodged by Arana's company in 1908, or as employees of the company, extremely few escaped the ever-present threat of degradation and torture. Asked by Casement if he did not know it to be wrong to torture Indians, one of the Barbados men replied that he was unable to refuse orders, "that a man might be a man down in Iquitos, but 'you couldn't be a man up there.'"[34] In addition, most of the company's white and black employees were themselves trapped in a debt-peonage system, but one quite different from the one the company used in controlling its Indians.

From the testimony of the Barbados men it is clear that dissension, hatred, and mistrust ran riot among all members of the company—to the degree that one has to consider seriously the hypothesis that only in their group ritualization of torturing Indians could such anomie and mistrust be held in check, thus guaranteeing to the company the solidarity required to sustain it as an effective social unit.

To read Casement's secondhand and Hardenburg's eyewitness accounts of the company attacks against independent white Colombian traders is to become further aware of the ritualistic features that assured the violence of the Putumayo rubber boom of its success as a culture of terror.

Casement's Analysis

Casement's main line of analysis lies with his argument that it was not rubber but labor that was scarce in the Putumayo, and that this scarcity was the basic cause of the use of terror. Putumayo rubber was of the lowest quality, the remoteness of its source made its transport expensive relative to rubber from other zones, and wages for free labor were very high. Hence, he reasons, the company resorted to the use of forced labor under a debt-peonage system and used torture to maintain labor discipline.

The problem with this argument, which assumes the purported rationality of business and the capital-logic of commodities (such as labor), is that it encounters certain contradictions and, while not exactly wrong, strikes me as giving insufficient weight to two fundamental considerations. The first consideration concerns the forms of labor and economic organization that local history and Indian society made available, or potentially available, to world capitalism in the jungles of the Putumayo. The second, put crudely, is that terror and torture do not derive only from market pressure (which we can regard here as a trigger), but also from the process of cultural construction of evil as well. "Market pressure" assumes the paradigm of scarcity essential to capitalist economism and capitalist socioeconomic theory. Leaving aside the question of how accurate a depiction of capitalist society results from this paradigm, it is highly dubious that it reveals much of the reality of the Putumayo rubber boom where the problem facing capitalist enterprise was precisely that there were no capitalist social institutions and no market for abstract labor into which capital could be fed and multiplied. Indeed, one could go further to develop an argument that begins with the premise that it was just this lack of commoditized social relationships, in interaction with commodity forces emanating from the world rubber market, that accounts for the production of torture and terror. We can say that the culture of terror was functional to the needs of the labor system, but that tells us little about the most significant contradictions to emerge from Casement's report, namely, that the slaughter of this precious labor was on a scale vast beyond belief, and that, as Casement himself states, not only were the station managers costing the company large sums of money but that "such men had lost all sight or sense of rubber-gathering—they were simply beasts of prey who lived upon the Indians and delighted in shedding their blood." To claim the rationality of business for this is to claim and sustain an illusory rationality, obscuring our understanding of the way business can transform the use of terror from the means into an end in itself.

The consideration of local history and economic organization requires far fuller treatment than can be attempted here. But it should be noted in passing that the "scarcity" of labor cannot refer to a scarcity of Indians, of whom there seems to have been an abundance, but rather to the fact that the Indians would not work in the regular and dependable manner necessary to a large-scale capitalist enterprise. Casement downplayed this phenomenon, now often referred to as "the backward sloping supply curve of labor," and did so even though, in the Congo, he had himself complained that the problem was that the natives would not work;[35] he felt sure that if paid with more goods, the Indians would work to the level required by the company without force. Many people with far longer experience in the Putumayo denied this naive assertion and pointed out, with logic as impeccable as Casement's, that the scarcity of labor and the ease with which the Indians could live off the forest obliged employers elsewhere in the Putumayo to treat them with consideration.[36] In either case, however, with or without the use of coercion, the labor productivity obtained fell far short of what employers desired.

The contradictions mount further on close examination of the debt-peonage system, which Casement regards as slavery. It was a pretext, he says, that the Indian in such a relation was in debt, for the Indian was bound by physical force to work for the company and could not escape.[37] One then must ask why the company persisted in this pretense, especially given the means of coercion at its disposal.

Accounts of advances paid in goods (such as machetes, cloth, and shotguns) were supposedly kept for each rubber gatherer; the advances were roughly equal to fivepence per pound weight of rubber, which was fetching three shillings tenpence on the London market in 1910. (In West Africa, natives were paid an equivalent of between two shillings and two shillings sixpence per pound of "Ibi Red niggers" rubber, equal in quality to the Putumayan.)[38] A station manager told Casement that the Indians never asked the price or value of rubber. Sometimes a single coin was given, and Casement met numbers of Indian women wearing necklaces made of coins.[39] Joaquin Rocha writes that the Indians of the Tres Esquinas rubber station valued money not as a means of exchange but as a precious object; they would beat coins into smooth and shining triangular shapes to use as nose rings or ear pendants.[40] Yet, it would be naive to suppose that the Indians lacked interest or understanding of the terms of trade and of what the whites got for rubber in the outside world. "You buy these with the rubber we produce," said an Indian chief as one entranced, looking through Casement's binoculars.[41] Casement was told that the station managers would fix the quantity of rubber due from each individual according to the goods that had been advanced, and in this connection Father Gridilla relates an episode of interest from when he traveled up the Caraparaná in 1912.

It was at a time when thousands of Indians came to the rubber station of La Occidente to deliver rubber. First there was a great dance lasting five days—the sort of event Joaquin Rocha a decade earlier likened to a harvest festival. Then the rubber was handed over and goods were advanced, Father Gridilla commenting "the savages don't know money, their needs are very limited, and they ask only for shotguns, ammunition, axes, machetes, mirrors, and occasionally hammocks." An Indian he described as a corpulent and ugly savage declined to accept anything and, on being pressed, replied, "I don't want anything. I've got everything." The whites insisted again and again that he must ask for something. Finally he retorted, "I want a black dog!" "And where am I going to find a black dog or even a white one if there aren't any in all of Putumayo?" responded the station manager. "You ask me for rubber," replied the savage, "and I bring rubber. If I ask for a black dog you have to give me one!"[42]

Relying on stories told him, Hardenburg wrote that the Indians received their advances with great pleasure, because if they did not, they were flogged to death.[43]

Pretext as it was, the debt that ensured peonage was nonetheless real, and as a pretense its magical realism was as essential to the labor organization of the Putumayo rubber boom as is the "commodity fiction" Karl Polanyi describes for a mature capitalist economy.[44] To analyze the construction of these fictional realities we need now to turn to some of their more obviously mythic features, enclosed as they are in the synergistic relation of savagery and business, cannibalism and capitalism. Interrogated by the British Parliamentary Select Committee on Putumayo in 1913, Julio César Arana, the driving force of the rubber company, was asked to clarify what he meant when he stated that the Indians had resisted the establishment of civilization in their districts, that they had been resisting for many years, and had practiced cannibalism. "What I mean by that," he replied, "is that they did not admit of exchange, or anybody to do business with them—Whites, for example."[45]

Jungle and Savagery

There is a problem that I have only hinted at in all of the accounts of the atrocities of the Putumayo rubber boom. While the immensity of the cruelty is beyond question, most of the evidence comes through stories. The meticulous historian would seize upon this fact as a challenge to winnow out truth from exaggeration or understatement. But the more basic implication, it seems to me, is that the narratives are in themselves *evidence* of the process whereby a culture of terror was created and sustained.

Two interlacing motifs stand out: the horrors of the jungle, and the horrors of savagery. All the facts are bent through the prism formed by these motifs, which, in keeping with Conrad's theory of art, mediate effective truth not so much through the dissemination of information as through the appeal of temperaments through sensory impressions. Here, the European and colonist image of the primeval jungle with its vines and rubber trees and domination of man's domination stands forth as the colonially apt metaphor of the great space of terror and deep cruelties. (Europe—late nineteenth century, penetrating the ancient forests of the tropics.) Carlos Fuentes asserts that Latin American literature is woven between the poles formed by nature and the dictator, in which the destructiveness of the former serves to reflect even more destructive social relations. A Colombian author, José Eustacio Rivera, writes in the 1920s as a debt-entrapped peon in the Putumayo:

> I have been a *cauchero* [rubber gatherer] and I will always be a *cauchero*. I live in the slimy mire in the solitude of the forests with my gang of malarial men, piercing the bark of trees whose blood runs white, like that of gods. . . . I have been and always will be a *cauchero*. And what my hand inflicts on the trees, it can also inflict on men.[46]

In *Heart of Darkness,* the narrator, Marlow, sits back, like a Buddha, introducing his yarn, prefiguring the late nineteenth-century colonial exploitation of the Congo by evoking a soldier of imperial Rome, moving through the marshes of the Thames.

> Land in a swamp, march through the woods, and in some inland post feel the savagery, the utter savagery, had closed around him,—all that mysterious life of the wilderness that stirs in the forest, in the jungles, in the hearts of wild men. There's no initiation either into such mysteries. He has to live in the midst of the incomprehensible, which is also detestable. And it has a fascination, too, that goes to work upon him. The fascination of the abomination—you know, imagine the growing regrets, the longing to escape, the powerless disgust, the surrender, the hate.

The Capuchin father, Gaspar de Pinell, who made a legendary *excursión apostólica* to the Huitotos and other savage tribes in the Putumayo forests in the late 1920s, records how his white guide, a man of much experience, sickened and sought cure from a Huitoto shaman (whom the padre calls a witch) rather than from the pharmacy of the whites. He died shortly thereafter, providing Father Pinell with the moral dilemma of the colonist: "This shows," he wrote, "that it is more likely that the civilized man will become a savage on mixing with Indians, than the Indians are likely to become civilized through the actions of the civilized."[47] And with a torrent of phenomenological virtuosity, his colleague, Father Francisco de Vilanova, addresses the same vexing problem, only here it is the Putumayo jungle that constitutes the great figure of savagery. In a book describing Capuchin endeavors among the Huitotos from the 1920s on, we read:

> It is almost something unbelievable to those who do not know the jungle. It is an irrational fact that enslaves those who go there. It is a whirlwind of savage passions that dominates the civilized person who has too much confidence in himself. It is a degeneration of the spirit in a drunkeness of improbable but real circumstances. The rational and civilized man loses respect for himself and his domestic place. He throws his heritage into the mire from where who knows when it will be retrieved. One's heart fills with morbidity and the sentiment of savagery. It becomes insensible to the most pure and great things of humanity. Even cultivated spirits, finely formed and well educated, have succumbed.[48]

But of course it is not the jungle but the sentiments men project into it that is decisive in filling their hearts with savagery. And what the jungle can accomplish, so much more can its native inhabitants, the wild Indians, like those tortured into gathering rubber. It must not be overlooked that the colonially constructed image of the wild Indian here at stake was a powerfully ambiguous image, a seesawing, bifocalized, and hazy composite of the animal and the human. In their human or human-like form, the wild Indians could all the better reflect back to the colonists the vast and baroque projections of human wildness that the colonists needed to establish their reality as civilized (not to mention businesslike) people. And it was only because the wild Indians were human that they were able to serve as labor—and as subjects of torture. For it is not the victim as animal that gratifies the torturer, but the fact that the victim is human, thus enabling the torturer to become the savage.

How Savage Were the Huitotos?

The savagery of the wild Indians occupied a key role in the propaganda of the rubber company. Hardenburg writes that the Huitotos "are hospitable to a marked degree," and that while the church improves their morals, in the company's domain, priests have been carefully excluded. "Indeed," he continues, "in order to frighten people and thus prevent them from entering the region, the company has circulated the most blood-curdling reports of the ferocity and cannibalism of these helpless

Indians, whom travellers such as myself have found to be timid, peaceful, mild, industrious, and humble."[49] Father Pinell published a document from Peru describing a film commissioned by Arana's company in 1917. Shown in the cinemas of Lima, it portrayed the civilizing effect of the company on "these savage regions that as recently as twenty-five years ago were peopled entirely by cannibals. Owing to the energy of this tireless struggler [Arana] they have been converted into useful elements of labor."[50]

Propaganda usually flowers only where the soil has been long and well prepared, and it seems to me that Arana's was no exception, since the mythology of savagery dates from times long before his. Yet, the passions unleashed by the rubber boom invigorated this mythology with a seductive power. Before probing further into the ways the rubber company acquired the savagery it imputed to the Indians, it is necessary to pause and examine the colonists' mythology and folklore concerning the Upper Amazon forest people.

Time and again Casement tells us that the Huitotos and all Upper Amazon Indians were gentle and docile. He downplays their cannibalism, says that they were thoughtless rather than cruel, and regards their docility as a *natural* and remarkable characteristic. This helps him to explain the ease with which they were conquered and forced to gather rubber.

An Indian would promise anything for a gun, or for some of the other tempting things offered as inducements to him to work rubber. Many Indians submitted to the alluring offer only to find that once in the "conquistadores'" books they had lost all liberty, and were reduced to unending demands for more rubber and varied tasks. A cacique or "capitán" might be bought over to dispose of the labor of his clan, and as the cacique's influence was very great and the natural docility of the Indian a remarkable characteristic of Upper Amazon tribes, the work of conquering a primitive people and reducing them to a continual strain of rubber finding was less difficult than might at first be supposed.[51]

Yet, on the other hand, such docility makes the violence of the whites even harder to understand.

Many points can be contested in Casement's rendering here, such as his assertion of the degree of chiefly power and the deceptive simplicity he evokes with regard to the issue of toughness and tenderness in a society so foreign to his own. It should also not be forgotten that the story he wanted to tell was one of innocent and gentle childlike Indians brutalized by the rubber company, and this controlling image gives his report considerable rhetorical power. In addition there was his tendency to equate the sufferings of the Irish with those of the Indians and see in both of their preimperialist histories a culture more humane that that of their civilizing overlords. (Conrad never indulged in that kind of transference.) Still another factor blended with the foregoing, and that was the innate tenderness of Casement's character and his ability to draw that quality out of others, as testified by numerous people. It is this aspect of his homosexuality, and not sexual lust, that should be dwelt on here, as shown, for example, in this note in his Putumayo diary.

> ... floggings and putting in guns and floggings with machetes across the back.... I bathed in the river, delightful, and Andokes [Indians] came down and caught butterflies for Barnes and I. Then a captain [Indian chief] embraced us laying his head down against our breasts. I never saw so touching a thing, poor soul, he felt we were their friends.[52]

Alfred Simson, an Englishman who traveled the Putumayo and Napo rivers in the 1880s and spent far more time there than Casement, conveys a picture quite different from Casement's. An example is his description of the Zaparos, who, like the Huitotos, were considered by the whites to be wild Indians. Noting that they raided other groups and abducted their children for sale to white traders, Simson goes on to state:

> When unprovoked they are, like really wild Indians, very shy and retiring, but are perfectly fearless, and will suffer no one, either whites or others, to employ force with them. They can only be managed by tact, good treatment, and sometimes simple reasoning: otherwise resenting ill treatment or an attempt to resort to blows, [they react] with the worst of violence.... At all times they are changeable and unreliable, betraying under different circumstances, and often apparently under the same, in common with so many of their class, all the most opposite traits of character, excepting perhaps servility—a true characteristic of the old world—and stinginess,

which I have never observed in them. The absence of servility is typical of all the independent Indians of Ecuador.[53]

And he observes that "they also gain great enjoyment from the destruction of life. They are always ready to kill animals or people, and they delight in it."[54]

Simson was employed on the first steam launch to ascend the Putumayo, that of Rafael Reyes, later a president of Colombia. Hence he witnessed the opening of the region to modern commerce, and was in a special position to observe the institutionalization of ideologies concerning race and class. Not only does he present a contrary and more complex estimate of Indian toughness than does Casement; he also provides the clue and ethnographic motif necessary to understand why such contrary images coexist and flourish, how Indian images of wildness come halfway, as it were, to meet and merge with white colonial images of savagery, and, finally, how such imagery functions in the creation of terror.

It is first necessary to observe that the inhabitants of the Putumayo were, according to Joaquin Rocha at the turn of the century, divided into two great classes of social types: whites and savage Indians. The category whites (also referred to as "rationals," Christians, and "civilized") included not only people phenotypically white, but also mestizos, negros, mulattos, Zambos, and Indians "of those groups incorporated into civilization since the time of the Spanish conquest."[55] Simson takes us further into this classification, and although his remarks here pertain to the *montaña* region at the headwaters of the rivers, they seem to me generally applicable to the middle reaches of the Putumayo as well, and are certainly relevant to the understanding of colonist culture.

Simson notes that what he calls the "pure Indians of the forest" are divided, by whites and Spanish-speaking Indians, into two classes; Indians (*Indios*) and heathens (*infieles*). The *Indios* are Quichua-speaking, salt-eating, semi-Christians, while the heathens, also known as *aucas,* speak distinct languages, eat salt rarely, and know nothing of baptism or of the Catholic Church.[56] In passing it should be observed that today, if not in times long past, the term *auca* also connotes cannibals who roam the forest naked, are without marriage rules, and practice incest.

Simson also states that the term *auca* as commonly understood bears "the full meaning it did anciently in Peru under the Incas. It includes the sense of infidel, traitor, barbarian, and is often applied in a malignant sense." In Peru it was used, he says, "to designate those who rebelled against their king and incarnation of their deity, the Inca."[57] Whether or not this assertion is historically accurate (as it certainly seems to be) is somewhat beside the point, for its importance lies in its character as a myth informing everyday life at the time of the rubber boom.

Simson's second major point about *aucas* concerns their animallike qualities, so pronounced, he says, that they partake of the occult and spiritual. With reference to the Zaparos, for example, he writes that their perceptions of eye and ear are perfectly marvellous, and surpass those of the non-*auca* Indians considerably. Their knowledge of the forest is so perfect that they often travel at night in unknown parts. They are great fighters, and can detect sounds and footmarks where white men perceive nothing. On the trail of an animal, they suddenly swerve, then change again as if following the scent of their prey. Their motions are catlike and they move unscathed through the entangled underwood and thorns. To communicate with each other, they generally imitate the whistle of the toucan or partridge—and all this is in marked contrast to non-*aucas* or civilized Indians, "who stand in fear and respect of them, but despise or affect to despise them as infidels behind their backs."[58]

I should add that the highland Indian shaman with whom I work in the Colombian Andes, which overlook the Putumayo jungles, regards the jungle shamans below as *aucas,* as animal/spirit hybrids possessing great magic. He singles out the Huitotos as a spiritual force with whom he makes a mystical pact in incantations and songs, with or without hallucinogens, to assure the success of his own magical battles with evil.

It is crucial to grasp the dialectic of sentiments involved here by the appelation *auca,* a dialectic enshrouded in magic and composed of both fear and contempt—identical to the mysticism, hatred, and awe projected onto the Zionist socialist Timerman in the torture chambers of the military. In the case of the *aucas,* this projection is inseparable from the imputation of their resistance to sacred imperial authority and the further imputation of magical power possessed by lowland forest dwellers as a class and by their oracles, seers, and healers—their shamans—in particular. Moreover, this indigenous, and what may well be a pre-Colombian, construction blends with the medieval European mythology of the Wild Man brought to the Andes and the Amazon by the Spaniards and Portuguese. Today, in the upper reaches of the Putumayo with which

I am acquainted, the mythology of *auca* and Wild Man underlies the resort to Indian shamans by white and black colonists who seek cures from sorcery and hard times, while these very same colonists despise Indians as savages.[59] In the rubber boom, with its desperate need for Indian labor, the same mythology nourished incalculable cruelty and paranoia on the part of the whites. It is to this mythic endowment inherited by world capitalism in the jungles of the Putumayo that we need to pay attention if we are to understand the irrational "excesses" of the terror and torture depicted by Casement.

Fear of Indian Rebellion

Casement mentions the possibility that, in addition to their drive for profit, the whites' fear of Indian rebellion impelled them toward viciousness. But in keeping with his stress on Indian docility, he gives four reasons why Indian rebellion was unlikely. Indian communities were disunited long before the advent of the rubber boom, while the whites were armed and well organized. The Indians were poorly armed and their blowpipes, bows, and lances had been confiscated. Most important, in his opinion, was the fact that the elders had been systematically murdered by the company for the crime of giving "bad advice."[60]

Rocha, who was in the area some seven years before Casement, thought differently. He claims that the whites feared the consequences of the Indians' hatred and that this fear was central to their policies and thought. "Life for the whites in the land of the Huitotos," he declares, "hangs by a thread." Small uprisings were common, and he provides an account of one of these.

In 1903, the Colombian Emilio Gutiérrez navigated up the Caquetá from Brazil searching for Indians to use to establish a rubber station. Reaching the area whose conquest he desired, he sent the bulk of his men back to carry in merchandise, and he and three others remained. While asleep, Gutiérrez and the companions were killed by wild Indians. Hearing the news, other whites prepared to retaliate when news reached them that thirty of Gutiérrez's civilized Indian work force had also been killed, all at the same time yet in different parts of the jungle. Indians working for whites were set in pursuit of the rebels; some were caught and killed outright, some were taken as prisoners for the whites, and the majority escaped. A few were captured and eaten by the Indian mercenaries—so the tale goes.[61]

In 1910, Casement heard the same episode from a Peruvian, who introduced his story by saying that the methods used by Colombian conquerors were very bad. In this version, the rebel Indians decapitated Gutiérrez together with an unstated number of other whites and exposed their skulls on the walls of their "drum house," keeping the limbless bodies in water for as long as possible to show them off to other Indians. Casement's informant said he had found the bodies of twelve others tied to stakes, assuring Casement that the reason they had not been eaten was that Indians "had a repugnance to eating white men, whom they hated too much." Terrible reprisals subsequently fell upon the Indians, notes Casement.[62]

Considered separately, and especially in relation to Rocha's version, this account of Casement's establishes the point that the white fear of Indian rebellion was not unjustified, but that, in addition, such rebellion was perceived in a mythic and colonially paranoid vision in which the image of dismemberment and cannibalism glowed vividly.

Fear of Cannibalism

Cannibalism acquired great ideological potency for the colonists from the beginning of the European conquest of the New World. The figure of the cannibal was elaborated and used for many sorts of ends, responding as it did to some of the most powerful symbolic forces known to humankind. It could be used to justify enslavement and, as such, was apparently important in the early economy of Brazil,[63] thereby affecting even the headwaters of the Amazon such as the Putumayo where cannibalism was kept luridly alive in the imagination of the whites down to the era of the rubber boom.

Rocha provides many examples. He signals his arrival at Huitoto territory writing of "this singular land of the cannibals, the land of the Huitotos conquered by a dozen valiant Colombians repeating the heroism of their Spanish ancestors."[64] The rubber traders, he emphatically asserts, have tried to stamp out cannibalism with severe punishments. Yet cannibalism is an addiction. The Huitotos think they can deceive the whites about this, but "they succumb to the satisfaction of their beastly appetites."[65] The most notorious of the modern conquistadores, the Colombian Crisóstomo Hernandez (a Colombian highlands mulatto who had fled the police and sought refuge in the jungle), had, so Rocha was told, killed all the children, women, and men of an Indian long house because they practiced cannibalism—a surprising story given the need for labor, yet typical of white folk tales in the Putumayo.[66]

Don Crisóstomo was the hero of another legendary story as well, one that makes the point that although Indian customs could conflict with those of whites, as, for example, in their "misunderstandings" over the value of money and of work, there were nevertheless ritual features of Indian culture that whites could harness to the needs of the rubber company. The practice of sometimes delivering rubber in conjunction with a great dance as a prelude to a sort of gift-giving exchange, as reported by Gridilla and Rocha, has been mentioned. Even more interesting is the rite the whites called *chupe del tabaco,* or tobacco sucking, by adult Indian men during most if not all ritual occasions, a rite that perhaps fascinated the whites even more than it did the Indians.

Seated in a circle, usually at night, with the women and children set back in their hammocks but within earshot, the men took turns placing a finger in a thick concoction of cooked tobacco juice and then sucked it. Hardenburg reports that this ceremony was indispensable to any fiesta or to solemnize any agreement or contract. These were times when the men in general, and the chief in particular, held forth with great oratory lasting perhaps the entire night. "This is the Huitoto's solemn oath," writes Hardenburg, "and is never said to be broken. Whenever the whites wish to enter into any important agreement with the Indians, they always insist upon this ceremony being performed."[67] Casement says the same, yet goes on to quote from a French explorer, Eugenio Robuchon, under whose name it was written that this rite was one "in which the Indians recall their lost liberty and their actual sufferings, and formulate terrible vows of vengeance against the whites."[68]

Rocha was told that Crisóstomo Hernandez was a marvellously skilled orator, taking his place as a *capitán* or *capitán general* among the circle of Indian men. Gathering with a large assembly of chiefs around the tobacco pot, don Crisóstomo would orate in Huitoto language and style from eight in the evening till four in the morning, with such power of seduction that the chiefs unanimously adopted his proposals. This, says Rocha, was before he reigned through terror and military might; his dominion came to rest on force of arms, yet it was through oratory that he initiated his conquest, "because for the Huitotos, he was their king and god."[69]

The story that most impressed Rocha was the one about the Huitoto rite of judicial murder, or capital punishment. One can easily imagine the chords of exotic terror it provoked among the colonists and employees of the rubber company listening to it in the chitchat of a jungle night.

All the individuals of the nation that has captured the prisoner retire to an area of the bush to which women are absolutely prohibited, except for one who acts a special role. Children are rigorously excluded also. In the center, a pot of cooked tobacco juice is placed for the pleasure of the men, and in a corner seated on a little bench and firmly bound is the captive.

Clasping each other's arms, the savages form a long line, and to the sound of drum beats advance dancing very close to the victim. They retreat and advance many times, with individuals separating to drink from the pot of tobacco. Then the drum stops for the dancing cannibals, and so that the unfortunate victim can see how much he is going to lose by dying, the most beautiful girl of the tribe enters, regally attired with the most varied and brilliant feathers of the birds of these woods. The drum starts again, and the beautiful girl dances alone in front of and almost touching him. She twists and advances, showering him with passionate looks and gestures of love, turning around and repeating this three or four times. She then leaves, terminating the second act of this solemn occasion. The third follows with the same men's dance as before, except that each time the line of dancers approaches the prisoner, one of the men detaches himself and declaims something like this: "Remember when your people killed Jatijiko, man of our nation whom you couldn't take prisoner because he knew how to die before allowing himself to be dragged in front of your people? We are going to take vengeance of his death in you, you coward, that doesn't know how to die in battle like he did." Or else: "Remember when you and your people surprised my sister Jifisino bathing, captured her and while alive made a party of her flesh and tormented her until her last breath? Do you remember? Now you god-cursed man we are going to devour you alive and you won't die until all traces of your bloody flesh have disappeared from around our mouths."

Following this is the fourth and last act of the terrifying tragedy. One by one the dancers come forward and with his knife each one cuts a slice of meat off the prisoner, which they eat half roasted to the sound of his death rattle. When he eventually dies, they finish cutting him up and continue roasting and cooking his flesh, eating him to the last little bit.[70]

Narrative Mediation: Epistemic Murk

It seems to me that stories like these were the groundwork indispensable to the formation and flowering of the colonial imagination during the Putumayo rubber boom. "Their imagination was diseased," wrote the Peruvian judge, Rómulo Paredes, in 1911, referring to the rubber station managers, "and they saw everywhere attacks by Indians, conspiracies, uprisings, treachery etc.; and in order to save themselves from these fancied perils . . . they killed, and killed without compassion."[71] Far from being trivial daydreams indulged in after work was over, these stories and the imagination they sustained were a potent political force without which the work of conquest and of supervising rubber gathering could not have been accomplished. What is essential to understand is the way in which these stories functioned to create a culture of terror dominating both whites and Indians.

The importance of this fabulous work extends beyond the epic and grotesque quality of its content. The truly crucial feature lies in creating an uncertain reality out of fiction, a nightmarish reality in which the unstable interplay of truth and illusion becomes a social force of horrendous and phantasmic dimensions. To an important extent, all societies live by fictions taken as reality. What distinguishes cultures of terror is that the epistemological, ontological, and otherwise purely philosophical problem of reality-and-illusion, certainty-and-doubt, becomes infinitely more than a "merely" philosophical problem. It becomes a high-powered tool for domination and a principal medium of political practice. And in the Putumayo rubber boom, this medium of epistemic and ontological murk was most keenly figured and objectified as the space of death.

In his report, Paredes tells us that the rubber station managers lived obsessed with death. They saw danger everywhere and thought solely of the fact that they were surrounded by vipers, tigers, and cannibals. It is these ideas of death, he writes, that constantly struck their imaginations, making them terrified and capable of any act. Like children who read the *Arabian Nights,* he goes on to say, they had nightmares of witches, evil spirits, death, treason, and blood. The only way they could live in such a terrifying world, he observes, was by inspiring terror themselves.[72]

Sociological and Mythic Mediation: The *Muchachos*

If it was the telling of tales that mediated inspiration of the terror, then it behooves us to inquire a little into the sociological agency that mediated this mediation, namely, the corps of Indian guards trained by the company and known as the *muchachos*. For, in Rómulo Paredes's words, they were "constantly devising executions and continually revealing meetings of Indians 'licking tobacco'—which meant an oath to kill white men—imaginary uprisings which never existed, and other similar crimes."[73]

Mediating as civilized or rational Indians between the savages of the forest and the whites of the rubber camps, the *muchachos* personified all the critical distinctions in the class and caste system of rubber production. Cut off from their own kind, whom they persecuted and betrayed and in whom they inspired envy and hatred, and now classifed as civilized yet dependent on whites for food, arms, and goods, the *muchachos* wrought to perfection all that was horrifying in the colonial mythology of savagery—because they occupied the perfect sociological and mythic space to do so. Not only did they create fictions stoking the fires of white paranoia, they embodied the brutality that the whites feared, created, and tried to harness to their own ends. In a very literal sense, the *muchachos* traded their identity as savages for their new social status as civilized Indians and guards. As Paredes notes, they placed at the disposal of the whites "their special instincts, such as sense of direction, scent, their sobriety, and their knowledge of the forest."[74] Just as they bought rubber from the wild Indians of the forest, so the whites also bought the *auca*-like savage instincts of the Indian *muchachos*.

Yet, unlike rubber, these savage instincts were manufactured largely in the imaginations of the whites. All the *muchachos* had to do in order to receive their rewards was to objectify and, through words, reflect back to the whites the phantoms that populated colonist culture. Given the centuries of colonial mythology concerning the *auca* and the Wild Man, and given the implosion of this mythology in the contradictory social being of the *muchachos,* the task was an easy one. The *muchachos'* stories were, in fact, stories within a much older story encompassing the *muchachos* as objects of a colonialist discourse rather than as its authors.

The trading system of debt-peonage established by the Putumayo rubber boom was thus more than a trade in white goods for rubber gathered by the Indians. It was also a trade in terrifying mythologies and fictional realities, pivoted on the mediation of the *muchachos,* whose storytelling bartered betrayal of Indian realities for the confirmation of colonial fantasies.

The Colonial Mirror

I began this article stating that my concern was with the mediation of the culture of terror through narration, and with the problems of writing against terror. In part, my concern stemmed from my problems in evaluating and interpreting the "facts" constituted in the various accounts of the Putumayo atrocities. This problem of interpretation grew ever larger, eventually bursting into the realization that that problem is precisely what is central to the culture of terror—not only making effective talking and writing against terror extremely difficult, but, even more to the point, making the terrible reality of the death squads, disappearances, and torture all the more effectively crippling of people's capacity to resist.

While much attention is given to "ideology" in the social sciences, virtually none as far as I know is given to the fact that people delineate their world, including its large- as well as microscale politics, in stories and storylike creations and very rarely, if ever, in ideologies (as customarily defined). Surely it is in the coils of rumor, gossip, story, and chitchat where ideology and ideas become emotionally powerful and enter into active social circulation and meaningful existence? So it was with the Putumayo terror, from the accounts of which it seems clear that the colonists and rubber company employees not only feared but also themselves created through narration fearful and confusing images of savagery— images that bound colonial society together through the epistemic murk of the space of death. The systems of torture they devised to secure rubber mirrored the horror of the savagery they so feared, condemned—and fictionalized. Moreover, when we consider the task of creating counterrepresentations and counterdiscourses, we must take stock of the way that most if not all the narratives reproduced by Hardenburg and Casement, referring to and critical of the atrocities, were similarly fictionalized, drawing upon the same historically molded source that men succumbed to when torturing Indians.

Torture and terror in the Putumayo were motivated by the need for cheap labor. But labor per se—labor as a commodity—did not exist in the jungles of the Caraparaná and Igaraparaná affluents of the Putumayo. What existed was not a market for labor but a society and culture of human beings whom the colonists called Indians, irrationals, and savages, with their very specific historical trajectory, form of life, and modes of exchange. In the blundering colonial attempt to forcibly dovetail the capitalist commodity structure to one or the other of the possibilities for rubber gathering offered by these modes of exchange, torture, as Casement alludes, took on a life of its own: "Just as the appetite comes in the eating so each crime led on to fresh crimes."[75] To this we should add that, step by step, terror and torture became *the* form of life for some fifteen years, an organized culture with its systematized rules, imagery, procedures, and meanings involved in spectacles and rituals that sustained the precarious solidarity of the rubber company employees as well as beating out through the body of the tortured some sort of canonical truth about civilization and business.

It was not commodity fetishism but debt fetishism drenched in the fictive reality of the debt-peonage institution, with its enforced "advances" and theaterlike farce of business exchanges, that exercised the decisive force in the creation of terror, transforming torture from the status of a means to that of the mode if not, finally, the very aim of production.

From the reports of both Timerman and Casement it is obvious that torture and institutionalized terror is like a ritual art form, and that far from being spontaneous, sui generis, and an abandonment of what are often called "the values of civilization," such rites have a deep history deriving power and meaning from those values. What demands further analysis here is the mimesis between the savagery attributed to the Indians by the colonists and the savagery perpetrated by the colonists in the name of what Julio César Arana called civilization.

This reciprocating yet distorted mimesis has been and continues to be of great importance in the construction of colonial culture—the *colonial mirror* that reflects back onto the colonists the barbarity of their own social relations, but as imputed to the savage or evil figures they wish to colonize. It is highlighted in the Putumayo in the colonist lore as related, for instance, through Joaquin Rocha's lurid tale of Huitoto cannibalism. And what is put into discourse through the artful storytelling of the colonists is the same as what they practiced on the bodies of the Indians.[76]

Tenaciously embedded in this artful practice is a vast and mystifying Western history and iconography of evil in the imagery of the inferno and the savage—wedded to and inseparable from paradise, utopia, and the good. It is to the subversion of that apocalyptic dialectic that all of us would be advised to bend our counterdiscursive efforts, in a quite different poetics of good-and-evil whose cathartic force lies not with cataclysmic resolution of contradictions but with their disruption.

Post-Enlightenment European culture makes it difficult, if not impossible, to penetrate the hallucinatory veil of the heart of darkness without either succumbing to its hallucinatory quality or losing that quality. Fascist poetics succeed where liberal rationalism self-destructs. But what might point a way out of this impasse is precisely what is so painfully absent from all the Putumayo accounts, namely, the narrative and narrative mode of the Indians, which desensationalizes terror so that the histrionic stress on the mysterious side of the mysterious (to adopt Benjamin's formula) is indeed denied by an optic that perceives the everyday as impenetrable, the impenetrable as everyday. At least this is the poetics of the sorcery and shamanism I know about in the upper reaches of the Putumayo, but that is another history for another time, not only of terror but of healing as well.

NOTES

I first visited the upper reaches of the Putumayo River in Colombia in 1972 and have returned many times since, engaged in writing a history of conquest and shamanism. The first version of this article was prepared for an informal seminar group of students and faculty from the Anthropology Department at the University of Sydney and MacQuarie University in Sydney, Australia. A similar version was read to the Department of Anthropology at the University of Michigan and the University of Chicago in April, 1982. I wish to acknowledge those participants, and especially Guillermo O'Donnell, by whom I was prodded into first thinking hard about what O'Donnell called "the culture of fear" in Argentina. I thank Raymond Grew and Ross Chambers of the University of Michigan for their advice and encouragement, and I also note that, without the fine sense of judgment exercised by Rachel Moore, it is unlikely that this article in its final form would have been completed.

1. Jacobo Timerman, *Prisoner without a Name, Cell without a Number* (New York: Vintage Books, 1982), 164.

2. Timerman, *Prisoner,* 28.

3. Timerman, *Prisoner,* 111.

4. Gerardo Reichel-Dolmatoff, *Amazonian Cosmos: The Sexual and Religious Symbolism of the Tukano Indians* (Chicago: University of Chicago Press, 1971).

5. Walter Benjamin, "Surrealism: The Last Snapshot of the European Intelligentsia," in *Reflections,* trans. Edmund Jephcott, ed. Peter Demetz (New York: Harcourt Brace Jovanovich, 1978), 189–90.

6. Timerman, *Prisoner,* 52.

7. Michel Foucault, "Truth and Power," in *Power/Knowledge,* ed. Colin Gordon (New York: Pantheon, 1980), 118.

8. Timerman, *Prisoner,* 62, 66.

9. Frederick R. Karl, *Joseph Conrad: The Three Lives* (New York: Farrar, Straus and Giroux, 1979), 286.

10. Paul Ricoeur, *Freud and Philosophy: An Essay on Interpretation* (New Haven: Yale University Press, 1970).

11. Ian Watt, *Conrad: In the Nineteenth Century* (Berkeley: University of California Press, 1979), 161.

12. Brian Inglis, *Roger Casement* (London: Hodder Paperbacks, 1974), 32. The text of Conrad's letter to Cunninghame Graham reads: "I can assure you that he [Casement] is a limpid personality. There is a touch of the conquistador in him too; for I've seen him start off into an unspeakable wilderness swinging a crook-handled stick for all weapons, with two bulldogs, Paddy (white) and Biddy (brindle) at his heels, and a Loanda boy carrying a bundle for all company. A few months afterwards it so happened that I saw him come out again, a little leaner, a little browner, with his stick, dogs, and Loanda boy, and quietly serene as though he had been for a stroll in a park." Inglis comments: "Time had embroidered Conrad's recollection. Casement himself described what the construction work entailed, in a letter to his young cousin [and] the countryside through which the railway was being constructed, he told her, consisted of grassy plains covered with scrub—inhospitable, but hardly unspeakable." The Jorge Borges reference is "About the Purple Land" in *Borges: A Reader,* ed. Emir Rodriguez Monegal and A. Reid (New York: Dutton, 1981), 136–39.

13. Karl, *Joseph Conrad,* 289n. The full text of Conrad's letter to Cunninghame Graham may be found in C. T. Watts, *Joseph Conrad's Letters to R. B. Cunninghame Graham* (Cambridge: Cambridge University Press, 1969), 148–52. Also see Zdizislaw Najder, ed., *Joseph Conrad: Congo Diary and Other Uncollected Pieces* (Garden City, N. Y.: Doubleday, 1978), 7.

14. Inglis, *Casement,* 46.

15. Inglis, *Casement,* 131.

16. Inglis, *Casement,* 214.

17. Inglis, *Casement,* 234.

18. Some authorities glean Casement's report and state the figure of 30,000 deaths from 1900 to 1912 as a fact, while others, who had some knowledge of the area and its history, either present different figures (a wide range) or state that it is impossible to give any figure because census taking was impossibly difficult. Furthermore, how much of the population decrease was due to disease (especially smallpox), and how much to torture or flight, is a very vexed question. Similarly, the number of Huitotos living in the Igaraparaná and Caraparaná region in the late nineteenth century is variously stated as around 50,000 all the way up to a quarter of a million, the latter estimate being that of Joaquin Rocha (*Memorandum de un viaje* [Bogotá: Editorial El Mercurio, 1905], 138). In any event, the number of Indians in the area seems to have been extremely large by Upper Amazon standards and an important cause for the establishment of rubber trading there. It is worth noting that Casement, in his report, was extremely cautious in presenting figures on population and population decrease. He gives details of the problem in his evidence presented to the British Parliamentary Select Committee on Putumayo (*House of Commons Sessional Papers*, 1913, 14:30, no. 707). Father Gaspar de Pinell, *Un viaje por el Putumayo el Amazonas* (Bogotá: Imprenta Nacional, 1924), 38–39, presents an excellent discussion, as does his *Excursión apostólica por los ríos Putumayo, San Miguel de Sucumbios, Cuyabueno, Caquetá, y Caguán* (Bogotá: Imprenta Nacional, 1929 [also dated 1928]), 227–35.

19. Walter Hardenburg, *The Putumayo: The Devil's Paradise. Travels in the Peruvian Amazon Region and an Account of the Atrocities Committed upon the Indians Therein* (London: T. Fisher Unwin, 1912), 214. The first publication of Hardenburg's revelations, in the magazine *Truth* in 1909, began with this article from the Iquitos newspaper, *La Sanción*. These articles, and probably the later book, were possibly ghostwritten by Sidney Paternoster, assistant editor of *Truth*.

20. Hardenburg, *Putumayo*, 258.

21. Hardenburg, *Putumayo*, 260, 259.

22. Hardenburg, *Putumayo*, 236. Also cited by Casement in his Putumayo report to Sir Edward Grey. There, Casement declares that this description was repeated to him "again and again . . . by men who had been employed in this work" (Roger Casement, "Correspondence Respecting the Treatment of British Colonial Subjects and Native Indians Employed in the Collection of Rubber in the Putumayo District," *House of Commons Sessional Papers*, 14 February 1912 to 7 March 1913, 68:35; [hereafter cited as Casement, *Putumayo Report*].

23. Casement, *Putumayo Report*, 17.

24. Casement, *Putumayo Report*, 34.

25. Casement, *Putumayo Report*, 33, 34.

26. Casement, *Putumayo Report*, 37.

27. Casement, *Putumayo Report*, 39.

28. Casement, *Putumayo Report,* 37.

29. Casement, *Putumayo Report,* 39.

30. Casement, *Putumayo Report,* 42.

31. Casement, *Putumayo Report,* 31. From various estimates it appears that the ratio of armed supervisors to wild Indians gathering rubber was somewhere between 1:16 and 1:50. Of these armed supervisors, the *muchachos* outnumbered the whites by around 2:1. See Howard Wolf and Ralph Wolf, *Rubber: A Story of Glory and Greed* (New York: Covici, Friede, 1936), 88; U.S. Consul Charles C. Eberhardt, *Slavery in Peru,* report prepared for U.S. House of Representatives, 62d Cong., 3d Sess., 1912, H. Doc. 1366, 112; Roger Casement, British Parliamentary Select Committee on Putumayo, *House of Commons Sessional Papers,* 1913, 14:xi; Casement, *Putumayo Report,* 33.

32. Casement, *Putumayo Report,* 33.

33. Casement, *Putumayo Report,* 44–45.

34. Casement, *Putumayo Report,* 55.

35. Inglis, *Casement,* 29.

36. Rocha, *Memorandum,* 123–24, asserts that because the Indians are "naturally loafers" they postpone paying off their advances from the rubber traders, thus compelling the traders to use physical violence. Eberhardt (*Slavery,* 110) writes that "the Indian enters the employ of some rubber gatherer, often willingly, though not infrequently by force, and immediately becomes indebted to him for food, etc.... However, the scarcity of labor and the ease with which the Indians can usually escape and live on the natural products of the forest oblige the owners to treat them with some consideration. The Indians realize this and their work is not at all satisfactory, judging from our standards. This was particularly noticeable during a recent visit I made to a mill where "cachassa" or aguadiente is extracted from cane. The men seemed to work when and how they chose, requiring a liberal amount of the liquor each day (of which they are all particularly fond), and if this is not forthcoming or they are treated harshly in any way they run to the forests. The employer has the law on his side, and if he can find the runaway he is at liberty to bring him back; but the time lost and the almost useless task of trying to track the Indian through the dense forests and small streams makes it far more practical that the servant be treated with consideration in the first place."

37. Casement, British Parliamentary Select Committee on Putumayo, *House of Commons Sessional Papers,* 1913, 14:113, no. 2809.

38. E. D. Morel, British Parliamentary Select Committee on Putumayo, *House of Commons Sessional Papers,* 1913, 14:553, 556. Also see, in the same papers, the evidence of the British accountant, H. Parr, of the Peruvian Amazon Company, in 1909–10, at the La Chorrera station (336–48).

39. Casement, *Putumayo Report,* 50.

40. Rocha, *Memorandum,* 75.

41. Peter Singleton-Gates and Maurice Girodias, *The Black Diaries* (New York: Grove Press, 1959), 261.

42. P. Alberto Gridilla, *Un año en el Putumayo* (Lima: Colección Descalzos, 1943), 29. Rocha's description is of a Colombian rubber trading post, and not one of Arana's (Rocha, *Memorandum,* 119–20).

43. Hardenburg, *Putumayo,* 218.

44. Karl Polanyi, *The Great Transformation* (Boston: Beacon Press, 1957), 72. Cf. Michael Taussig, *The Devil and Commodity Fetishism in South America* (Chapel Hill: University of North Carolina Press, 1980).

45. Julio César Arana, Evidence to the British Parliamentary Select Committee on Putumayo, *House of Commons Sessional Papers,* 1913, 14:488, no. 12,222.

46. See Carlos Fuentes, *La nueva novela hispanoamericana* (Mexico, D.F.: Editorial Joaquin Mortiz, 1969), 10–11; José Eustasio Rivera, *La vorágine* (Bogotá: Editorial Pax, 1974), 277, 279.

47. Pinell, *Excursión apostólica,* 156.

48. P. Francisco de Vilanova, introduction to P. Francisco de Igualada, *Indios Amazonicas: Colección Misiones Capuchinas,* vol. VI (Barcelona: Imprenta Myria, 1948).

49. Hardenburg, *Putumayo,* 163.

50. Pinell, *Excursión apostólica,* 196.

51. Casement, *Putumayo Report,* 27–28.

52. Singleton-Gates and Girodias, *Black Diaries,* 251.

53. Alfred Simson, *Travels in the Wilds of Ecuador and the Exploration of the Putumayo River* (London: Samson Low, 1886), 170.

54. Simson, *Travels,* 170–71.

55. Rocha, *Memorandum,* 64.

56. Simson, *Travels,* 58. It is worth noting that, during the seventeenth or eighteenth century, missionaries worked among at least some of the Indian groups Simson designates as *auca,* and thus it is not true that they (to quote Simson), "know nothing of the Catholic Church." See P. José Chantre y Herrera, *Historia de las misiones de la Companía de Jesus en el Marañon español, 1637–1767* (Madrid: Imprenta de A. Avrial, 1901), 283, 321–28, 365–69.

57. Simson, *Travels,* 58. This meaning of rebel against the Inca is sustained, referring to the Auracanians of Chile, in John M. Cooper, "The Auracanians," in *The Handbook of South American Indians,* ed. Julian H. Steward (New York: Cooper Square, 1963), 2:690. For the eastern montaña of the northern Andes, the term *auca* means pagan as against Christian Indians, according to Steward and Alfred Metraux, "Tribes of the Ecuadorian and Peruvian Montaña," in *Handbook,* 3:535–656, esp. 629 (Zaparos), 637 (Canelos/Napos),

653 (Quijos). Unlike Simson, the mere traveler, these anthropologists of the *Handbook* fail dismally to indicate the magical and mythic connotations of the term *auca*.

58. Simson, *Travels*, 166, 168.

59. Michael Taussig, "Folk Healing and the Structure of Conquest," *Journal of Latin American Lore* 6:2 (1980): 217–78.

60. Casement, *Putumayo Report*, 45.

61. Rocha, *Memorandum*, 126.

62. Casement, *Putumayo Report*, 30. Father Pinell was told of a large uprising by rubber-working and other Indians along the Igaraparaná in 1917; the use of Peruvian troops was required to put it down (Pinell, *Un viaje*, 39–40).

63. An excellent discussion of this is to be found in David Sweet, "A Rich Realm of Nature Destroyed: The Middle Amazon Valley, 1640–1750" (Ph.D. diss., University of Wisconsin, 1975), 1:113–14, 116, 120, 126, 130–31, 141, 347.

64. Rocha, *Memorandum*, 92–93.

65. Rocha, *Memorandum*, 118.

66. Rocha, *Memorandum*, 106–7.

67. Hardenburg, *Putumayo*, 115. For use of coca in the *chupe del tabaco*, see Joseph F. Woodroffe, *The Upper Reaches of the Amazon* (London: Methuen, 1914), 151–55. With regard to the reliability and sources of Hardenburg's statements, it is perhaps of use to cite some of the evidence he gave to the British Parliamentary Select Committee on Putumayo (*House of Commons Sessional Papers*, 1913, vol. 14). Asked what he saw himself of actual cruelties to the Indians, Hardenburg replied, "Of actual crimes being committed I did not see anything, practically; all I saw was that the Indians in [the rubber station of] El Encanto were nearly naked and very thin and cadaverous looking; I saw several scores of them, and I saw what they were being fed on" (510, no. 12,848). His information came through accounts from other people: "In fact, I think I might say that most of the people came through others. They would say, 'I know another man who could state this and that,' and they would bring them" (511, no. 12,881). Asked if he questioned these people in detail about their statements, Hardenburg replied, "I cannot say I did much of that" (511, no. 12,882). It was, said Hardenburg, general knowledge that the atrocities were occurring. This "general knowledge" is precisely what I have been at pains to track down, not because I believe that the atrocities were less than described by the several authors upon whom I draw, but because it is this general knowledge in the shape of mythic narratives that acts as a screen and as a network of signifiers without which "the facts" would not exist. More specifically, the function of this screen of signifiers is to heighten dread and hence the controlling function of the culture of terror. Casement's evidence is altogether of another category, being more carefully gathered, cross-checked, etc. and as a result of it we can affirm reports, such as Hardenburg's, that are less well substantiated. Nevertheless, Casement's evidence serves not to puncture the mythic character so much as indicate its terrific reality.

68. Casement, *Putumayo Report,* 48. Robuchon's text appeared as a book ("Official Edition"), printed in Lima in 1907 and entitled *En el Putumayo y sus afluentes.* It was edited by Carlos Rey de Castro, a lackey of Julio César Arana's and one-time Peruvian consul in Brazil, from Robuchon's papers after his mysterious death in the Putumayo rain forest. Judging from Rey de Castro's book on the Putumayo, *Los pobladores del Putumayo* (Barcelona: Imp. Vda de Luis Tasso, 1917), and his relation to Arana, one can surmise that it would be unwise to read the Robuchon text as though it were really Robuchon's unadulterated work. The chances are that it was edited with a view to presenting a case favorable to Arana. The importance of prehistory, "ethnohistory," and Indian history in the ideological war for world opinion is well brought out by Rey de Castro's bold stroke in his *Los pobladores del Putumayo,* in which he sets out to prove that the Huitotos and adjacent Indian groups are in reality descendant from the *orejones* of Cuzco in the highlands of Peru—thus supposedly strengthening the Peruvian claims over the Putumayo rubber zone and its indigenous inhabitants.

69. Rocha, *Memorandum,* 111.

70. Rocha, *Memorandum,* 116, 117.

71. Rómulo Paredes, "Confidential Report to the Ministry of Foreign Relations, Peru," September, 1911, translated in Eberhardt, *Slavery,* 146. Paredes's work is explained and put into context in a mass of testimony in Carlos A. Valcarcel, *El proceso del Putumayo* (Lima: Imp. Comercial de Horacio La Rosa, 1915).

72. Paredes, "Confidential Report," in Eberhardt, *Slavery,* 158.

73. Paredes, "Confidential Report," in Eberhardt, *Slavery,* 147. I am grateful to Fred Chin and Judy Farquhar of the Department of Anthropology at the University of Chicago for impressing upon me the importance of the *muchachos* as a mediating force. Then, of course, one should not omit the role of the blacks recruited in Barbados, mediating between the whites and the Indians. In much the same way as the British army from the mid-nineteenth century on deployed different colonial and ethnic groups to maximize reputations for ferocity and check one against the other, the British and Peruvian rubber companies used their "ethnic soldiers" in the Putumayo.

74. Paredes, "Confidential Report," in Eberhardt, *Slavery,* 147.

75. Casement, *Putumayo Report,* 44.

76. Illustrations of the way in which this following of the letter of the tale was enacted in the torture of Indians can be found in the rare instances of dialogue that Casement allows his witnesses in the section of his report given over to testimony by men recruited in Barbados, as, for example:

"And you say you saw the Indians burnt?" Consul-General Casement asked Augustus Walcott, born in the Caribbean island of Antigua but twenty-three years before.
"Yes."

"Burnt alive?"

"Alive."

"How do you mean? Describe this."

"Only one I see burnt alive."

"Well, tell me about that one?"

"He had not work 'caucho,' he ran away and he kill a 'muchacho,' a boy, and they cut off his two arms and legs by the knee and they burn his body. . . ."

"Are you sure he was still alive—not dead when they threw him on the fire?"

"Yes, he did alive, I'm sure of it—I see him move—open his eyes, he screamed out. . . ."

"Was Aurelio Rodriguez [the rubber station manager] looking on—all the time?"

"Yes, all the time."

"Giving directions?"

"Yes, Sir."

"He told them to cut off the legs and arms?"

"Yes."

There was something else the Consul-General could not understand and he called Walcott back to explain what he meant by saying, "because he told the Indians that we was Indians too, and eat those—." What he meant, Casement summarized, was that the station manager, Señor Normand, in order "to frighten the Indians told them that the Negroes were cannibals, and a fierce tribe of cannibals who eat people, and that if they did not bring in rubber these black men would be sent to kill and eat them" (Casement, *Putumayo Report,* 115, 118).

Another, more complicated, example follows.

"Have you ever seen Aguero kill Indians?" the Consul-General asked Evelyn Bateson, aged twenty-five, born in Barbados, and working in the rubber depot of La Chorrera.

"No, Sir; I haven't seen him kill Indians—but I have seen him send 'muchachos' to kill Indians. He has taken an Indian man and given him to the 'muchachos' to eat, and they have a dance of it. . . ."

"You saw the man killed?"

"Yes, Sir. They tied him to a stake and they shot him, and they cut off his head after he was shot and his feet and hands, and they carried them about the section—in the yard and they carries them up and down and singing, and they carries them to their house and dances. . . ."

"How do you know they ate them?"

"I heard they eat them. I have not witnessed it, Sir, but I heard the manager Señor Aguero tell that they eat this man."

"The manager said all this?"

"Yes, Sir, he did" (Casement, *Putumayo Report,* 103).

This sort of stimulation if not creation of cannibalism by colonial pressure is also recorded in missionaries' letters concerning King Leopold's Congo Free State and the gathering of rubber there. See, for example, the account of Mr. John Harris in the work by Edmund Morel, *King Leopold's Rule in Africa* (New York: Funk and Wagnalls, 1905), 437–41.

From Little King to Landlord: Colonial Discourse and Colonial Rule

Nicholas B. Dirks

In the last few years, colonial discourse has come to stand for a field of studies in which the writings of colonial officers and agents portray vivid examples of domination.[1] Colonial texts are read to reveal the ways in which language inscribes, both in its fundamental categories and its florid expressions, the topoi of worlds made up of masters and slaves, colonizers and colonized. So powerful are these texts and their retellings that colonialism has come to occupy a paradigmatic position in the tropics of discursive power; it is clear we have much to learn about the way domination works through the quotidian categories of race, gender, ethnicity, and nationality when we look back on the history of colonialism.

But if colonial texts can be read to tell stories about the power of language to naturalize the structures of domination in worlds that are relevant to contemporary politics, it is all too often the case that the historical experience of colonialism—along with the contemporary politics of postcolonialism—gets lost in the elegant new textualism of colonial discourse studies. While our readings of colonial texts have been reanimated by the recent efflorescence of interest in colonialism, we must realize that the contexts for interrogating these texts are multiple and, necessarily, historical. I will not assert here that historical study will reveal the one true context for understanding past utterances of colonial power; I will, however, suggest that serious attention to context (reading contexts as texts) demonstrates how colonial texts did not always mean what they seemed, that colonial discourse was most powerful and most effective for reasons that had to do with the specific, contingent, heterogeneous, circuitous, incomplete, and often contradictory character of

175

colonial forces. Colonial discourse was so powerful because texts and contexts were indistinguishable.

Colonial discourse was shaped by colonial rule, even as colonial rule was continuously shaped by discursive conventions, regimes, and imperatives. However, as much as colonial knowledge was both facilitated and certified by colonial power, there were always serious limits to what colonial powers could know. Colonial knowledge was frequently based on misunderstandings that led to an uneasy relationship between knowledge and power. It was often the uneasiness of this relationship that made colonial knowledge, in the end, so effective. In this article, I engage in the historical anthropology of colonial discourse in British India, tracing out the genealogies of discursive constructions, excavating the logic of colonial conquest, following the successes and failures of colonial projects, disclosing the contradictions of colonial domination. And I will show that discourse did not do it alone, but, rather, achieved its full power because of its historical activation in the institutional context of colonial rule. In this endeavor, the question of continuity and change under the colonial regime in India becomes central, for the historical evaluation of change and the colonial representation of change constantly bleed into each other. The more one looks, the more continuity and change seem like mirror images of each other.

I examine the question of change and continuity under the colonial regime in South India in light of two of the most conspicuous events under colonialism, namely, the transformation of the structure of landholding and property rights and the introduction of a legal system to frame and legislate this new structure. While these changes were major, they did not eradicate significant continuities for two important, and interrelated, reasons. First, the strong and persistent role of precolonial formations made them unfamiliar and often unpalatable. Second, the peculiar nature and paradoxical impact of colonial understandings and institutions rendered the continuation of certain cultural values not only possible but, strangely, meaningful, particularly when the social context was as little altered as in the permanently settled zamindari estate. While far different in many ways from the old regime, the colonial regime changed things far less than its discursive self-representations would lead one to believe. At the same time, the language of colonialism was itself fundamental to the success of the regime as well as to the complex interrelation of change and continuity under colonialism. Colonial change was both limited and delayed by colonial understandings that, as much as they involved the fundamental reordering of epistemic constructions of social reality, also led to the paradoxical but largely successful attempt to freeze the wolf in sheep's clothing.

The deployment of colonial discourse within the specific institutional framework of colonial law was, I argue here, an important key to this paradox. Law was an arena in which discourse could be seen immediately to have powerful effects; there were enormously important consequences to success or failure in legal courts, where titles, land, authority, and wealth were transacted and redistributed according to the new and rational principles of legal practice. The categories of the law framed the way stories were told and truth was judged, changing the character of political relations and everyday life even when sacrosanct elements of tradition appeared to be upheld. Under the British in India, law became the most effective and the most valued domain for the dispensation of the new truths of colonial rule.

Land and Polity in the Old Regime

The meaning of land, as something that was "owned," "possessed," or even "controlled," became something very different after the British arrived on Indian soil and set out to determine property "rights" in order to assess and collect revenue.[2] Nonetheless, much discussion about the nature of pre-British property continues to be shaped by the colonial sociology that was constructed with the land systems of British India. The British were concerned about property partly because they perceived it as the fundamental means for ordering Indian agrarian society and also because they wanted to establish an ideologically coherent and functionally systematic basis for revenue collection. Similarly, in our historiography, the collection of revenue has been seen both as the principal modality of agrarian relations within villages and as the basic function, and agrarian concern, of the state.

The problem with this preoccupation with revenue, let alone with the more traditional obsession with the question of who owned the land, is that property in India existed not as some independent entity but rather in the context of social and political relations. At the risk of some oversimplification, I will propose here that the two terms used for property in Tamil—*panku* and *kani*—suggest the different but interdependent natures of these social and political relations.[3] *Panku* means "share" and was often used to characterize the shares of rights to the usufruct as well as hereditability of land. It is fundamentally a horizontal term. Shares of land were shares among a group of family or lineage members, and sometimes among the dominant caste (or castes) of an entire village (or locality). These *pankus* were sometimes related to particular plots of land and sometimes to a particular proportion of a larger unit of land, proportions that would be redistributed and reallocated periodically.[4] *Pankus* in land were related to *pankus* in a variety of other contexts: shares in local temple festivals and shares in kinship units (in which, for example, members of the same lineage were called *pankalis*).

The complementary term, *kani,* means a heritable right, and as such implies a vertical relation, since entitlement to a share was usually seen to have been granted by a superior agent. This agent was ideally a king, or the agent of a king, although in certain cases it could have been the chief of a previously resident dominant caste group. To have this entitlement, or *kani,* was to have *kaniyatci,* which was related both to control over land and to participation in the village/lineage assembly and also, as with *panku,* to rights to a share in the local temple, which in turn entailed rights to receive honors and responsibilities to invest in the temple. Indeed, the *pankus* were themselves shares in this *kaniyatci,* or general entitlement. The group of *kaniyatcikarars* in any given village or locality made up a corporate group that, in the drier areas of the south—not yet brought under patrimonial forms of rule and revenue collection—was hierarchically situated within a larger structure of sub-caste and caste dominance at the level of the little kingdom.

There is one more concept of importance in this brief discussion of property in pre-British India. The king who gives land is the overlord of all the land in his kingdom. The term that suggests the nature of the king's mastery over land perhaps better than any other is *ksatra.* According-ing to Robert Lingat, "*Ksatra* . . . is power of a territorial character, exercised within a given territory and stopping at the frontier of the realm. . . . Of the same nature as property, it implies a direct power over the soil."[5] That is why the king is also called *svamin,* a word that can be applied equally to a proprietor or to a husband or a chief, and denotes an immediate power over a thing or over a person.

The king's mastery of the land, far from being opposed to the *panku* and *kani* rights in land held by peasant cultivators, complemented, indeed made possible, those rights, for, as we have seen, entitlement to land was usually conferred by a higher agency, preferably a king. The British, with a very different view of property rights, misunderstood all this.

When they attempted to sort out who owned the land, they assumed opposition, not complementarity; the owner, they thought, must be either the cultivator or the king, thus creating many of the classificatory problems of the land systems debates in the late eighteenth centuries.

In precolonial South India, most land rights were seen as having been granted in one form or another by a king. *Kaniyatci* rights and lands were granted by kings to local lineage heads, called *nattampalams*—heads (*ampalams*) of localities (*natus*)—or *nattanmaikarars,* and later dubbed *miracidars* under the influence of eighteenth-century Persian terminology. Other land rights and privileges were granted to military chiefs, retainers, temples, Brahmans, village officers, priests, servants, and artisans. Rights to land were granted along with other types of rights, for landholding was not an isolated economic fact. Landholding, rather, was one element in a whole system of privileges in which rights to exercise local authority, to use certain titles, to carry certain emblems, and to receive temple honors (from temples that ritually symbolized local territorial and social units) were part of the same package of rights as the right to "enjoy" land. Landholding also indicated a great deal about one's participation in local communities, as has been generally acknowledged by historians, who have noted that even when a "free" market in land existed in the colonial period, such land was often not, or at least not readily, purchasable by people from outside the local community.[6] Thus, to understand the meaning of land in precolonial India, we must not only see it in the context of such other things as emblems and honors, but also realize that it was constituted in relational terms, of both a horizontal and vertical nature.

Gifts of rights to land, titles, emblems, and honors by kings to their subjects became, in cultural terms, the dynamic medium for the constitution of political relations.[7] These gifts linked individuals, and also corporations, symbolically, morally, and politically with the sovereignty of the king and created both a moral unity and a political hierarchy. There ritual gifts were not mere tokens, nor were they signs of political weakness. In many of the smaller states in Tamil Nadu in the eighteenth century, 60–80 percent of all cultivable land was given away under the category of *inam* ('tax-exempt land') to the persons and institutions of the types mentioned previously. Overall, these *inam* lands were given away in both central and peripheral areas of the state, although military grants did tend to correspond with strategic borders. When insufficient cultivable land was available for such grants, the king would give grants of forest land to be brought under cultivation, or he would embark upon predatory warfare with the aim of securing honor, fame, booty, and new lands over which to rule and could then grant to his supporters. Furthermore, old grants were continually renewed on the occasion of generational succession, since only lands granted to Brahmans and temples were granted in absolute perpetuity.

The acceptance of gifts, which to a very large extent reflected a complicated set of categorizations and gradations of kinship relations, entailed loyalty and service. It is common sense that, in the dry regions of southern India in the eighteenth century, where vast portions of scrub jungle lay still uncultivated, control over people was more important than control over land, since control over people was in effect control over land. But it would be a mistake to think too exclusively in functionalist terms about the grants because such analysis depends solely on Western notions of what is and what is not functional. The chief point here is simply that the king ruled by making gifts, not by administering a land system in which land derived its chief value from the revenue he could systematically extract from it. These gifts were the fundamental signs of sovereignty, which, as long as it emanated from the center, was distributed and displayed at every level within the kingdom. Without the continuance of gifts, therefore, there could be no sovereignty. And it was sovereignty, above all, that the little kings, when converted into zamindars and princes, continued to seek.

The Permanent Settlement

The transformation from little king, or *palaiyakkarar*, to permanently settled rural landholder, or zamindar, did not happen overnight. Indeed, in 1801, the British concluded what had been half a century of intermittent warfare against the *palaiyakkarars* of southern India.[8] The principal objective of all this warfare had been revenue. While the early expeditions were largely without result, the proportion of years when collections of "poligar peshkash" were made rose more or less steadily after 1761, the decade before which they were made only 40 percent of the time. In the 1780s, the figure rose to 80 percent, and, in the 1790s, collections were made 90 percent of the time, with the yearly average collection rising from 2,560 *chakrams* for the 1780s all the way up to 5,300 *chakrams* for the subsequent decade.[9] In 1799 the last major rebel chief was captured, and in 1801 the *palaiyakkarar* rebellion was finally put to rest. The traditional historiographic interpretation of Britain's conquest of India as virtually absentminded must therefore not obscure the actual military record of those years. The respect with which the British East India Company regarded the *palaiyakkarars,* if not for their moral character, indubitably for their capacity of military resistance—a capacity based not on technological superiority but on guerilla techniques of resistance, command of deep-rooted local loyalties, as well as their potential for collaboration with more powerful foes, from the French to the Mysoreans—was very real indeed. The extension of the Permanent Settlement into Madras Presidency must thus be seen against the backdrop of years of protracted warfare, and as testimony to the fact that there were still major areas where local kings continued to rule with power and authority through the late eighteenth century.

When the British consolidated their position in South India in the late eighteenth century, they immediately began to introduce a political economy in which both relations among Indians themselves and between the Indians and the colonial government would be regulated according to law and new forms of property. Most of the little kings who had survived the eighteenth century and who were not deemed subversive by the British were "permanently" settled as zamindars, the Persian term for landlord, on proprietary estates. Political relations were rechanneled into the new domain of proprietary law. If the zamindar defaulted on his fixed yearly payment to the government, the estate would be put up for auction. However, as long as the terms of the property right were upheld, the zamindar's position was secure. Whoever held the title— whether by inheritance, purchase, or gift—was the zamindar. The drafters of the Permanent Settlement were convinced that a series of favorable consequences would flow from this single transformation. The principal change, they thought, would be the redirection of the interests and energies of the little kings from local warfare and intrigue to agrarian management and investment. In short, the zamindars would become the rural gentry, sources of both local stability and a steady flow of revenue.

The extension of the Permanent Settlement in Madras Presidency has never been examined with great care by historians, who have been, as a rule, far more impressed by that settlement's initial formulation in Bengal and by the far more original contribution of Madras in the *ryotwari* settlement, in which settlements were made not with local lords but with leading cultivators.[10] But virtually one-third of the area of Madras Presidency was settled with zamindars, and however much this settlement was a reflex of Governor General Charles Cornwallis's operation in Bengal, the significance of this southern reflex is deserving of some consideration. The terms and operations of the southern settlement were based on those devised in Bengal, and, by the turn of the century, the enthusiasm that had accompanied the initial drafting of the Permanent Settlement in 1793 was still little diminished and not yet under attack by the southern-based advocates of *ryotwari* tenure. But at the same time, the actual drafters of the Madras settlement had many reservations about their handiwork, and they were by no means apologists for the little kings whom they converted into zamindars on the Bengal model. While they shared some of the same hopes as those who had prophesied the creation of a new gentried class in Bengal, they also had rather low opinions of the men who were intended to be made into gentry.

Stephen R. Lushington, who was Collector of Poligar Peshkash during 1799–1803, the crucial years of the formulation of the Permanent Settlement, was one of the most severe critics of the *palaiyakkarars,* and yet he seems never to have given public expression to any doubts about the wisdom of the Permanent Settlement.[11] Lushington advanced the following conclusions about their origins.

> First, that the pretension which the Poligars advance to their present lands, on the ground of ancient immemorial possession, have little foundation. Secondly, that they were created about 300 years ago, by the policy of the hindoo Government, for the protection of the country and the support of the Sovereign; and that in the time of Tirumala Naicke, 160 years ago, they had not degenerated from the original purpose of the institution.

He thus saw their existence, and by extension their property rights, as totally contingent on an arrangement with a sovereign ruler, and he therefore accorded full authority to the British East India Company to develop an appropriate policy for them. Moreover, his characterization of the *palaiyakkarars* was hardly flattering.

> Their insolent tyranny in the absence of authority is as proverbial as their treacherous intrigue in the presence of it, and . . . your records teem with relations of their delight in times of tumult and disorder,

when all their favorite passions of tyrannising over the country and
of contempt for their rulers may with impunity be indulged.

The tyranny of the *palaiyakkarars* could be explained by two principal
factors. First, claimed Lushington, "the assumed power and state set
up by these people is most attended to and we believe will be found the
principal cause for their turbulence." Of primary concern to Lushington
were the forts, guns, and stores that they used to "overcome their weaker
neighbors," though he was also concerned about other signs of "false
pride." The second source for the *palaiyakkarars'* despotic activity rested,
according to Lushington, in their illegal appropriation of "desha cawel"
(*tecakkaval*)—the rights to provide protection to the countryside, which
rights justified the collecting of taxes ("in money or in grain, cattle,
etc.") of a sort. This he saw as one of their most invidious means of
oppression. Lushington recommended that the desha cawel right should
be abolished as soon as possible. He further recommended that the
palaiyakkarars' forts should be demolished, their firearms appropriated,
and the tribute exacted from them increased. Without firearms they would
not be able to collect the desha cawel fees, and with a higher tribute
they would have fewer resources to justify their arrogance and support
their establishment. The higher tribute was justified as a commutation
of desha cawel.

The East India Company followed these recommendations. A report
of 1803 explained the adoption of such a policy in terms that congrat-
ulated the Company's enlightened attitude and "progressive approach."[12]
The Company insisted on the "absolute suppression of the military
power" of the *palaiyakkarars,* and on the "substitution of a pecuniary
tribute more proportionate than the ordinary peishcush, to the resources
of the poligar countries, and more adequate to the public demand, for
defraying the expenses of general protection and government." In particular, the "demolition of the poligar forts" and the "discontinuance
of their military retinues" were cited as evidence of the "efficient exercise
of the authority of government" by the British. But, we might ask, why
stop here? If the *palaiyakkarars* were such a scourge, why not make
settlements with the principal *ryots,* as was done later in the nineteenth
century in many parts of Madras Presidency.

The reason why not was succinctly stated in a Minute of the Board
of Revenue, dated January 5, 1818.

The ancient zamindars and polygars were in fact the nobility of the country, and though the origin of their tenures would not bear too minute a scrutiny, they were connected with the people by ties which it was more politic, more liberal, and more just to strengthen, than to dissolve[;] . . . when the attachment of the people to their native chieftains and the local situation of many zamindaries are considered, it may be greatly doubted whether such a policy [of reducing them to pensioners] would not have been as unwise as it would have been ungenerous, and at the time perhaps impracticable.[13]

The question of whether their decision had more to do with wisdom than with generosity notwithstanding, it seems never to have occurred to officials such as Lushington, who worked in the areas of the *palaiyakkarars,* that the local chiefs were not the appropriate agents with whom settlements should be made. When opposition to the Permanent Settlement mounted in years subsequent to its enactment in Madras in 1803, the principal opponents were men who worked in areas, such as the Baramahal, where the traditional structure of political authority had already been significantly eroded by the revenue and political policies of the Muslim rulers of *Srirankapattinam.*[14] It can be further argued that a major impetus behind the *ryotwari* settlement came not from actual experience in India, but from the changing intellectual climate of Britain in the early nineteenth century.[15]

But in 1803 it was the firm intention of the president and members of the Board of Revenue that the zamindars should be constituted "proprietors of their respective estates" on the basis "of the principles on which the permanent settlement has been established in Bengal."[16] The board believed that the security afforded by the Permanent Settlement in Madras would have even more dramatic consequences than in Bengal, where a "more regular form of government . . . has been gradually established."[17] So while they wished to estimate the permanent peshkash according to the "probable improvement in the course of a short period under the system of property and security about to take place,"[18] their fundamental justification for the permanence of the settlement was, as in Bengal, its "productive principle,"

that the possession of property and the sure enjoyment of the benefits deriveable from it, will awaken and stimulate industry, promote agriculture, extend improvement, establish credit, and augment the general wealth, and prosperity.[19]

Even so, Lushington's constant complaint was that the turmoil of the eighteenth century, particularly when combined with the monopoly of revenue records held by corrupt village officers, made it difficult to establish any proper notion of what the revenue assessment should be. The British view of the second half of the eighteenth century allowed them to see decadence everywhere. Lushington's assurance that there had been a system of regular payments was based more on conviction than historical evidence.

Lushington further believed that the alienation of extensive tracts of land as *inam* benefits was nothing more than an established mode of tax evasion, rather than a vital component of the precolonial political process.[20] He was in fact wrong to suggest that the *inam* tracts were given away to reduce the tax roles, even as Eric Stokes, far more recently, was mistaken to see *inams* as having swelled "to an unnatural extent" because of the "long period of disturbed political conditions and unstable central authority" in the period prior to the nineteenth century.[21] Lushington, of course, wished to characterize the *inams* as forms of tax evasion because he was directly charged with the collection of the poligar peshkash as well as with the elimination, to the extent possible, of military tenures. In cases where *inams* were seen as straightforward remunerative grants for military service, the East India Company shared his belief that tribute on those lands could be assessed because of the commutation of military service, which was no longer seen as necessary.[22] In remaining cases, the *inams* were continued, but it was believed that a great amount of potentially taxable land was unnecessarily, though for the moment unavoidably, exempt. Perhaps in compensation, though more probably because it was thought that many other potential sources of income were being covered up, the British determined the figure for the average amount of peshkash to be collected on the basis of collections after 1792, when they had taken over the administration of the *palaiyakkarars* and had doubled both the amount and frequency of the average collections over what they had been only a decade before.

The more general theoretical question that emerged in the Permanent Settlement concerned the sense in which the rights of the zamindars would be "proprietary." This question was never adequately resolved, and gave birth to immense practical difficulties in the years to come.

The permanent proprietary right was to be extended to zamindars and other landholders and to "their heirs and successors" in order to end the practices of tax farming, revenue augmentation, and dispossession that had been "so fruitful a source of uncertainty and disquietude." However, this proprietary right was not to be absolute. First, as we have seen, it was dependent on the proper and punctual payment of peshkash. Default in revenue would give the British a free hand to assume the estate. Second, this right was not to infringe upon the established rights of the "undertenantry." Third, the government reserved to itself many rights over sources of revenue, including all *inam* lands. However, the assumption of control over *inam* lands was not to be construed to mean that the zamindars could no longer alienate land. According to article 7 of the deed,

> You shall be at free liberty to transfer without the previous consent of Government or of any other authority, to whomsoever you may think proper, either by sale, gift, or otherwise, your proprietary right in the whole or in any part of your zamindary.

The zamindar had only to register any such transfer in the collector's office and to be consistent with the principles of native law in the provisions of his alienation. The ultimate consideration, however, was that no alienation could reduce the amount of the permanent peshkash, for which the "whole Zamindary shall continue to be answerable . . . as if no such transact had occurred."

However abridged the nature of the zamindars' proprietary rights, it is clear that the single greatest innovation afforded by the Permanent Settlement was the establishment, to use Ranajit Guha's phrase, of a "rule of property."[23] Property was now to govern political relations. In the case of the Permanent Settlement, the *ksatra* (the encompassing lordship of all land) of the king was to be translated into a title, or *patta,* indicating legal ownership of land. (The term *patta* was previously used to mean a title, usually of some heroic and/or royal association, as well kingship itself; the coronation festival for kings was called the *pattapicekam.*) The land rights of the cultivators were deemed under this system to be tenancy rights rather than proprietary rights. Thomas Munro was correct to assert that

> we have, in our anxiety to make everything as English as possible in a country which resembles England in nothing, attempted to create

at once throughout extensive provinces, a kind of landed property which had never existed in them.[24]

As Munro predicted, the nineteenth century did not witness the actual creation of a landed gentry, as many had hoped, but rather, at least in British terms, a steady deterioration of the state of agrarian affairs.

Indeed, many of the estates went immediately into arrears. The zamindars spent their energies in diverse avenues of local intrigue and in running up debts, litigating in courts over succession and other issues of property and office, and alienating increasing amounts of land from the local tax base. In an excellent analysis, Pamela Price has shown that these new activities were neither mindlessly corrupt nor totally divorced from earlier Tamil ideas of kingship.[25] Price writes of the same Tamil zamindari examined here, noting that a combination of strategic action and the continued acceptance of precolonial rules and beliefs made for a complicated patchwork of zamindari politics. She adds that "the principles of authoritative rule in the political system of the zamindaries lent themselves more to the 'diffusion of power and scattering of resources' characteristic of traditional Indian politics than to behavior of the sort expected by the British.[26]

Not only were the expectations of the Permanent Settlement often unfulfilled, so, too, were its terms. Time and again the British bailed the zamindars out from desperate positions of improvidence and indebtedness. The estate of Uttumalai is a good case in point. In 1836 the collector of Tinnevelly District investigated the resources of this estate, which had been in arrears for some years. His initial suspicion was that the value of the estate might have been overestimated by Lushington at the time the permanent peshkash was instituted, but at the end of his investigation he concluded that the estate could not be "expected to rise to its intrinsic value at once."[27] However, he also noted that as long as the present zamindar was in any way connected with the estate, it was not likely that it would ever attain this value. The collector thus recommended that the government assume the estate, arguing that "the feudal feeling that exists in an Old Estate always operates powerfully to prevent inhabitants from complaining and seeking redress," but adding that he had no doubt the zamindar was "widely disliked." Nonetheless, the Board of Revenue finally decided to restore the estate to the zamindar, even against the outrage of the collector.[28] In similar cases, the government for the most part restrained the enthusiasm of collectors who believed the government could do a much better job of managing estates, arguing instead "the acknowledged expediency of preserving the ancient aristocracy of the country."[29] Most estates were preserved from extinction in spite of their failure to conform to the principles of management espoused by the British government.

The preservation of moribund estates was conducted in the face of mounting criticism of the Permanent Settlement by prominent members of government such as Thomas Munro. Munro, in particular, was concerned that the government had "relinquished the rights which the sovereign always possessed in the soil," though he went on to argue his theory that, in most cases, the real owners were the cultivators and not the zamindars.[30] A. D. Campbell, onetime secretary to the Board of Revenue, was insistent that the provisions of the Permanent Settlement be interpreted to include a statement of proprietary rights for the cultivator.[31] But in spite of these loudly voiced concerns, the zamindars continued, for a very long time and with no restraint at all, to engage in activities that were prejudicial to tenants. The very permanence of the settlement, combined with the continuing sense that the old "feudal feeling" could prove dangerous if not respected, prevailed over the concerns of the newly ascendant group of British administrators, at least for those areas where the Permanent Settlement had been made. But one of the greatest problems of the settlement was yet to be fully realized. Not only did the zamindars shirk their new roles as capitalist gentry and act contrary to the interests of their tenants, they also behaved in ways prejudicial to the future positions of their own successors and heirs. The alienation of land, of course, resulted in the erosion of the tax base of the zamindary estate, not only for the life of the relevant zamindar, but for all future generations. Calculated to meet the needs of a colonial revenue state rather than being set in relation to a dynamically defined set of goals, demands, and strategic contexts, the tax base was now a fixed, bureaucratically defined entity. I will now examine the delicate balance achieved by the newly constructed legal system, poised between the desire to maintain the proprietary perquisites of zamindars and the felt need to secure the cross-generational permanence of the settlement, all against the backdrop of a steady demand for revenue.

The Law and Authority

The Permanent Settlement had established a rule of property, or so it seemed. As the British set up the framework and institutions of colonial governance, it became increasingly clear that property itself was to be governed by law. Law, of course, was seen as a counterbalance to the capricious exercise of political power. Stated in ideal terms, law was to be autonomous from the workings of the colonial state.[32] The importation of law into India was intended to secure the loyalties and protect the rights of all its citizens.

While the law was vested with the "rule over property" and had such an esteemed position in the structure of British rule, at first it was not at all clear what law in India was to be. The British assumed that law in India had comprised two things, Hindu law and Muslim law, a somewhat preposterous claim given the variability of Indian legal traditions. Even so staunch an advocate of the law as James Mill was sharply critical of the efforts of Sir William Jones to codify Indian law. He characterized Jones's efforts as "a disorderly compilation of loose, vague, stupid or unintelligible quotations and maxims: selected arbitrarily from books of law, books of devotion, and books of poetry; attended with a commentary which only adds to the mass of absurdity and darkness; a farrago by which nothing is defined, nothing established."[33] Mill's venom was directed at Indian law and at the Orientalists' sanctification of it under the Cornwallis system, not at the law itself or the principles of legal codification. Other, less Eurocentric critics such as J. H. Nelson of Madras were critical of the reliance on Brahmanic codes (and pundits) to formulate codes for non-Brahmans,[34] who constituted 97 percent of the population in the south.

While all these criticisms rang true, the real problem was far more fundamental and lay in the very institutionalization and codification of the law. All of these critics shared a belief in the necessary autonomy of law. However, in pre-British Hindu India, the law, however much it was codified in various legal traditions, was in practice embedded in the structure of political authority and measured against *dharma,* a principle of order that was both natural and moral. As Robert Lingat notes, "The classical legal system of India substitutes the notion of *authority* for that of legality. The precepts of *smrti* are an authority because in them was seen the expression of a law in the sense in which that word is used in the natural sciences, a law which rules human activity."[35] Nonetheless, the king has the duty of imposing the law, for the law does not impose itself, at least not immediately. The imposition of law entails the interpretation of law according to each context of its application. The authority of the interpreter, and thus the interpretation, does not, however, yield a system of codes and precedents that can, at least independently, orient future legal decisions. Authority continues to be invested in the complex but integral relationship of the authoritative interpreter and *dharma*. As Lingat explains, although the judgments of the king are "really law-in-action, they remain singular and unrelated, staccato, without any future."[36] While the king is constrained by the principles of *dharma*, he is at the same time enjoined to maintain *dharma*, and as such he becomes the embodiment of the law. As Clifford Geertz has said, "In the Indic world Law was one but its expressions many."[37]

In British law, in contrast, not only were codification and precedent crucial, but law was also seen as most just and most effective when it was self-regulating and, to the extent possible, autonomous from the state. The law was not to pursue goals at variance with those of the state. In India, the British considered the development of legal codes to be part of a larger reform of native customs. However, as Eric Stokes has written, "The administration of the law was not ... to be understood as the actions of executive officers vested with discretionary powers, but solely as the operation of the judicial process in the courts."[38] Indeed, however much the drafting of the legal codes and regulations was ultimately controlled by interests of the colonial state, it is indisputable that the daily exercise of the law had a peculiar, if partial, autonomy from government, often frustrating members of council and the Board of Revenue to the point of utter distraction.

But was this seeming operational autonomy of any real historical significance? How much was the law controlled by the state, and did the law ever, in fact, operate in ways that ran counter to the state's interests? In a recent and penetrating article, David Washbrook examined this question and concluded that the law was far from autonomous in practice, its autonomy nothing more than a legal fiction, its practice "pure farce."[39] The effective operation of law as an autonomous domain was belied by its selective application and by the constant manufacture of acts and regulations to direct and constrain the free play of legal norms and procedures. Further, law never accomplished what it putatively set out to do, for example, never bringing into existence a genuinely free market in property.

While Washbrook's critique of the nineteenth-century operation of law in India seems indisputable, his general approach fails to explain the immense effort that went into the creation of legal institutions, nor does it prepare us for what is to come: the story of how the British attempted, with extremely limited success, to use law to gain control over the zamindaries and, in particular, to curb the steady alienation of land by the zamindars. Washbrook's argument dismantles the colonial myth of the autonomy of law, but it neglects the cultural impact of the introduction of British law in India,[40] where the rituals of legal practice created significant if ultimately unreal taxonomies of power and control, and where the rhetorical reification of the Permanent Settlement's necessary fictions found its effective institutional base. Law was as powerful an arm of the state as it was precisely because it appeared, even to the colonizers, to be as powerful, and as autonomous, as it did. I will now examine this paradox as it surrounds the history of the law in episodes concerning the newly constituted landlords of the southern Tamil countryside.

The Gift Colonized

Under the Permanent Settlement, the zamindars were invested neither with political nor with legal authority. Political authority, in the form of British rule, had made them proprietors of their estates, and their proprietary rights were to be protected and regulated by the legal authority of nascent institutions and hastily conceived and executed codes of jurisprudence. This complex background oriented a great number of issues in the nineteenth century, from disputes over succession and the division of property to the problem of alienation. In cases that concerned zamindaries, the problems of adjudication became particularly byzantine because, while the properties of joint families were seen by ordinary Hindu law to be partible estates, "the theory as to ancient Zemindaries has always been that they are in the nature of regalities or principalities, the property attached to which is inseparable from the regal or princely office."[41] Zamindaries were impartible because, in mock recognition of precolonial political succession, the estates were seen as impartible "principalities." Or rather, loosening the trope as much as possible, the estates were only "in the nature of regalities or principalities."

But for reasons that had less to do with the perceived ancient status of zamindaries than with British theories about the fundamental nature of property, the deed of Permanent Settlement put few restrictions on the power of the zamindar to alienate, "by sale, gift, or otherwise," any part of the zamindari estate. Little did the drafters of the Permanent Settlement suspect that the ambiguities of this clause would haunt their administrative successors for at least a century, for instead of accumulating more property, the zamindars disbursed it. Instead of always managing the new estates with an eye to bringing new lands into the tax rolls, the zamindars continued to act as if they were, indeed, in the nature of kings, remitting taxes and giving lands on tax-free leases.

One of the principal activities of the British in relation to the zamindars was to use every possible opportunity to initiate or support suits that had the objective of reversing this massive political entropy, of resuming the tax-free lands and assuring the long-term viability (that is, the permanence) of their zamindari settlement. In this British attempt to control alienation, two legal questions quickly developed as major issues: the first had to do with the status of certain alienations made before 1803, and the second with those made after 1803, when successors to zamindari titles began to complain about the encumbrances on the estates handed down by their predecessors. It is interesting that whenever zamindars tried to resume alienated lands that had been granted before 1803, the legal decision, and British legal opinion, generally ruled against the zamindar on the grounds that tradition must be preserved. However, 1803 was the cutoff point. The entire force of British action and opinion was in favor of restricting, once it became clear that the new political economy was not working, any new alienations. Tradition, in short, was to be freeze dried and decaffeinated.

The law, however, did not cooperate. In retrospect, it is astounding that such fundamental questions as the hereditary nature of alienations and the future reversionary rights of zamindars had not been addressed, nor the problems concerning them anticipated, in the Permanent Settlement. The drafters of the settlement simply assumed that the fixed nature of the peshkash would restrict excessive gifts of land, but they could not have been more mistaken. Alienations were made to attain religious merit, to establish political alliances, to reward services, and to pay off debts. Alienations were made because, in spite of the changing nature of the political system, the traffic of the political process continued to be in gifts of land. While many of the reasons behind these new gifts were shifted in the changed and demilitarized nineteenth century, the cultural logic of the gift continued to prevail.

The consequences of this continuity were startling to the British all over India, as they saw the maintenance of the dominant landed classes in their privileged position as crucial to the stability of the agrarian economy. Long before the British passed legislation in 1900 in the Punjab to restrict the transfer of land from "peasants" to "moneylenders," they fought battles in southern India for one zamindar after another in trying to resume land alienated by zamindari predecessors to groups such as the Cettiyars, whose merchant associations and usurious activities made them inappropriate and undesirable landholders in British eyes. No sooner, of course, did a zamindar win his battle than he set the stage for a subsequent confrontation by alienating more land to new people and sometimes new groups.

In 1871, J. D. Mayne, the acting advocate general, was asked to give his opinion about the status of two alienations in Ramnad, and his response thereafter became much cited as a general authoritative position on all such matters.[42] The first question he addressed had to do with identifying what restrictions existed as to the zamindar's rights of alienation, and this question rapidly turned him to a consideration of the possible restrictions constituted by Hindu law. Did the application of Hindu law, for example, mean that the zamindar could neither encumber nor alienate beyond the period of his own life? In this respect, the ordinary statutes of Hindu law dictated that, as one's heirs became at birth coparceners, a Hindu proprietor could not, without his heirs' consent, or "unless under circumstance of necessity," alienate more than his own interest in the estate. But, as Mayne observed, the zamindari is not an ordinary Hindu estate. In an ordinary estate, the father and sons are actual joint owners in possession, but a zamindary is "impartible." The implications of this were clear enough to Mayne. Hindu law provided no counterbalance to the deed of Permanent Settlement. Alienations could not be controlled unless they were successfully contested by the appointed heir before the end of the period specified by the statute of limitations.[43] The question then arose of whether the period should begin from the date of the grant (or, perhaps, its registration in the collector's office) or from the date of accession of an heir who might desire to resume his predecessor's alienations. Mayne reviewed a number of High Court decisions and interpreted them as stipulating expressly that the former option was to be taken as the intent of the law, in spite of his realization that this left the heir with few options unless he succeeded to the estate before the expiration of the period of limitation. Mayne therefore offered no hope for success to the collector in recovering certain alienations on behalf of a minor zamindar.

While the government had every right to resume lands granted on service tenures, permanent leases with no quid pro quo other than a quit rent were, for the most part, not resumable. Nonetheless, this did not worry Mayne, unencumbered as he was by the more overarching concerns of the government. As he wrote,

> Government has no ground for the alarm expressed.... No act of the Zemindar in alienating his assets, by lease or otherwise, can in any degree diminish the security for the public revenue.... The public demand...takes precedence of all other encumbrances, and in the event of either attachment or sale, the Collector in the former case and the purchases in the latter case, are in no way bound by any alienation or dimunition of the assets of the Zemindary.

But, Mayne's assurances notwithstanding, the concern of the British government was to keep such a turn of events from happening. The government was as concerned about public order as about the public demand (that is, revenue), both of which were seen as indissolubly linked and dependent on the preservation of local elites. This ideal union seemed constantly to come unhinged, as we shall see in two cases from Ramnad in which Mayne's principles were put to the test.

The first case concerns the alienation of two *taluks* in Ramnad Zamindari, the first in 1858 (the initial grant of which was confirmed in 1863) and the second in 1863. The first alienation was made by the then minor zamindar's adoptive mother, and the confirmation and the grant of 1863 were made by the zamindar when he came of age. The recipient of both alienations was Ponnucami Tevar, eldest son of the original grantor's sister, and brother of her adopted son, the minor zamindar. Ponnucami Tevar was also the manager of Ramnad Zamindari between 1858 and 1868, and a man of very considerable influence. He attained this influence for the same reasons given for granting the two *taluks* to him: his services as estate manager and his legal support and efforts in getting the adoption approved, which had entailed a long-fought succession case. By 1868, the year of Ponnucami's dismissal as manager, he had involved the estate in debts of at least fourteen and a half *lakhs,* and he left office in a cloud of accusations about this corruption. In 1873, shortly after the death of the zamindar, the Board of Revenue considered what legal steps could be taken to reappropriate, on behalf of the new minor zamindar, the considerable lands that had been alienated to Ponnucami.[44]

The legal questions involved turned out to be extremely delicate. The period specified by the statute of limitations had run out for the 1858 grant unless it could be shown that the 1863 confirmation was the legal date of the grant, and this was unlikely. Even if Hindu law respecting inheritance was invoked as relevant to the case, all of the alienations had been before the birth of the minor on whose behalf the suits were being instituted. The conclusion of the Government Pleader, J. W. Handley, was therefore that the government's argument must be that, from the principle of "impartibility," it should "follow that until the Raj is extinct the property must remain for the Raja to take, and hence that the holder of the Raj for the time being can neither encumber nor alienate beyond the period of his own life."[45] In taking this position, Handley was aware that, while there was some legal precedent, it would perhaps be "difficult to reconcile the extensive power of alienation allowed by later cases for family necessities with the dictum in its widest sense." But he was equally aware that if the government lost this case, there would be nothing at all to restrict alienation, even of an entire estate by a zamindar. This was a terrifying prospect, and Handley felt sure that the only evidence necessary to win the suit would be documentation of undue influence by Ponnucami Tevar in securing the grants.

Handley's opinion was used to justify the institution of a suit for recovery of the two *taluks* against the descendents of Ponnucami Tevar (who had died in 1869) in late 1873.[46] The government's suit, claiming that Ponnucami, who had received proper remuneration for having acted as manager, "fraudulently induced [the late zamindar and his mother] to grant the said villages to him without any proper consideration," was based on the facts that the grants were not properly registered and that "by Hindu law, and the custom of the zemindari, . . . the late Zemindar had only a life interest in the zemindari, and [n]either he nor his adoptive mother had power to alienate this or any portion of the said zemindari beyond the period of their lives." In the judgment, rendered on February 12, 1874, the government lost its case.

According to the judge, who echoed much of Mayne's original opinion, even if general Hindu law was followed, there would be no restriction on alienation for those who had no coparceners. As for the particular case of zamindaries, the judge noted that the only obvious difference was that succession was governed by primogeniture, and thus the estate was impartible. But he disputed Handley's claim that alienability depends on partibility, even though he admitted that "the result of course may be a Zemindar without a Zemindary." He went on to say that even if the zamindari was considered on absolutely separate grounds as, or as analogous to, a kingdom, he did not "understand why even a kingdom should be absolutely inalienable by an absolute monarch, much less a tributary principality, which was the utmost dignity to which Ramnad ever attained." Neither did he understand the claim that the zamindar had only a "life interest," citing as grounds that legal precedent had indubitably established the opposite in a variety of cases. The judge concluded his opinion by saying that nonregistration was, in this case, not an issue, and that he saw no evidence of exercise of undue influence by Ponnucami in securing the grants. Once again, alienation carried the day.

The second case to be considered here concerns zamindari lands rented at favorable rates, many on permanent leases. In Ramnad these leases were called *cowles,* and the leader of the battle against their legality was Lee-Warner, the special assistant collector. In 1873, he successfully urged the collector, with the sanction of the Court of Wards, to issue a notice to all *cowledars* in Ramnad that their leases were to be canceled and their villages to be resumed by the government on behalf of the minor zamindar. Some of the *cowledars* immediately gave up their lands, but others, particularly those of some means, decided to contest the legality of the proclamation. It was at this point that J. A. Boyle entered the scene, and in October, 1873, he wrote a report suggesting that the government's case was untenable.[47] Even the test case selected by Lee-Warner for legal advice met with the negative opinion of Handley, who wrote that the possible justifications for the permanent lease were more various than Lee-Warner had thought.[48] Boyle also noted that Lee-Warner had a special but unjustified distaste for the Chetties (Cettiyars) who acquired leases in return for unpaid loans, speaking as he did "with the vulgar dislike of usurers." In addition, and for much the same reason, Boyle saw nothing fraudulent in other grants to relatives and palace servants: the zamindar had no money to part with, only land. Boyles noted with evident pleasure that the *cowle* villages were generally far more prosperous than most of the other villages of the estate, and protested that, instead of lamenting all the lost revenue, the British should realize that the villages became prosperous only after their grant as *cowles,* another argument in their favor. Indeed, the very classes that were to be prevented from holding land proved to be better land managers than the traditional agricultural classes.

Lee-Warner, in his own cynical fashion, appreciated the political nature of the leases. He noted that, in 1866, Ponnucami Tevar had run into difficulties, and that he had attempted to put down opposing factions "partly by the distribution of heavy largess to all his dependents, partly by many settlements of accounts with the Chetties."[49] Leaving aside fascinating questions about Ponnucami's managership,[50] we can nonetheless recognize the conflict between "traditional" modes of political action (however different this largess was from the royal gifts that came before) and British expectations about the functioning of the new agrarian system. This conflict was both mediated and accentuated by the role of the legal system, which in this case seemed to prevent the British from "rationalizing" (in Max Weber's sense) their bureaucratic control, even as it maintained, however paradoxically, the status quo.

The government did not give up easily. Between 1873 and 1882, the British were able to recover 104 villages in Ramnad "forming part of the alienations made subsequent to the Permanent settlement...either on the expiry of the leases or by court decree."[51] This included the fourteen villages of Palaiyampatti and Pantalkuti that were recovered under the provisions of the Act of 1876, a direct administrative response to the failures in legal cases such as Ponnucami Tevar's. The act provided for the subdivision and separate assessment of Peshkash on alienated lands within permanently settled estates. This provision was to apply "except when the quit rent paid to the estates was greater than the proportionate peshkash which would be payable after separation," thus displaying the true magnanimous intent of the government.[52] As for service and religious grants, the government followed the basic provision that had been laid down in their settlement of *inams* in 1859.

In disposing of grants for religious and charitable purposes due consideration has been shewn for the feelings of the zemindars' families, and they have been resumed only in those cases in which the purposes were not daily fulfilled.[53]

Little by little, the Court of Wards appeared to be regaining "control" of the estate. But in spite of all the recoveries, in 1886, there remained another 323 unrecovered alienated villages out of a total number of 2,168 villages in the whole estate.[54]

The fundamental problem for the British was that the Court of Wards could exercise control only when there was a minor zamindar.

And, when these zamindars came of age, instead of taking advantage of the great benefits of British litigation on their behalf, they proceeded to alienate even more land. When the report on success in recovering alienations was written in 1886, three years were left before the minor, Baskara Cetupati, was to attain his majority. Lee-Warner, who had been instrumental not only in pressing forward the interests of Baskara's estate but in establishing a number of other agrarian reforms, anticipated what might happen and wrote, in 1874, his assessment of what would be best for the estate.

> Among other contingencies which might clear the path of reform (if it is not looking too far forward) it is just possible that the successor to the estate becoming as he grows up convinced of the hereditary inaptitude of his family for administration, may desire to leave his estate under management and become a pensioner of Government. Such an alienation would be valid if the recent judgement in the Madura Civil Court is to be relied upon, and with regard to all that I know of the life of the late Zemindar (who was considered to be a "gentle man among Maravars") and the antecedents of his family and ruin of this country, I cannot conceive a juster proposition for the Government to entertain; for I regard it as the remotest contingence of all, that the present boy when he succeeds to rule his estate will have the firmness or grasp of mind to reason out that his own happiness is intimately bound up with the welfare and prosperity of his tenants; and his first act after ascension to power, as Sethoopathy, would be to cancel this work and deluge the villages again with dependents and officials of all sorts. All the family traditions and Zennanah traning point this way.[55]

The acceptance of Lee-Warner's proposal would have been tantamount to dismantling the Permanent Settlement, leaving only a pensioned king to live a life devoid of both power and property. But Lee-Warner did give expression to the fundamental cleavage between the old political system and the new, and realized more perspicaciously than many that the attempted synthesis of the Permanent Settlement had been a failure. The reasons for its failure were, in part, also the reasons why Lee-Warner's advice fell on deaf ears: the old cultural system, however truncated and transformed, lived on because it helped satisfy another and different British aim, the protection of the native aristocracy and the status quo. The British were most reluctant, particularly after the great rebellion in 1857, to give the impression that they were undermining the authority and position of this local elite, however unattainable their goals of agrarian reform, and however much the old regime political system had been emptied of genuine power.

Law and the Colonial State

Although on one level the attempts of the British to deal with the contradictions of colonial rule were inept, on another level we must recognize their skill in managing to maintain order in spite of their many failures. For all their misunderstanding and ineptitude, the British were remarkably successful in stemming disorder. Indeed, under the terms of the Permanent Settlement, they presented themselves as the salvation of the old regime at the very same time they were busy dismantling it. As we have seen recurrently in the administrative and legal history of the Permanent Settlement, this capacity to pursue simultaneously the contradictory pursuits of revenue and order was matched by the successful management of the contradictory position of the law's supposed autonomy. While the "rule of property" was ushered in by the Permanent Settlement, the Raj not only preserved two levels of proprietary interest, but also controlled very carefully the introduction of a free-market economy. Zamindars were propped up and merchants were kept out.

The Permanent Settlement provides one of the clearest examples of the British institutional reification of their concept of the old regime within the framework of a new, "progressive" system governed by the overarching principles of order and revenue. The old regime continued in the sense that terms such as *kingdom,* far from containing any political content, were now used in the context of legal debate, in this particular instance to provide a classificatory distinction between properties that were partible and those that were impartible. But the old regime was dismantled and discontinued as a political process. Boundaries became fixed, relationships became bureaucratically codified, warfare was abolished, and gifts no longer constituted political relations. The fixity of the revenue demand was both a metaphor of this change and the fundamental cornerstone of the new regime. To maintain both the revenue demand and local social order, kings—and kingdoms—were subordinated to the discursive and institutional structures of the new colonial legal system.

Furthermore, the new structures were repeatedly hailed as examples of the British concern with pressing forward the interests of the zamindars. Even when the British tried to stem alienation, they did so by suing on behalf of minor zamindars when estates were under the control of the Court of Wards. Both the victories and the defeats of the legal process seemed to herald the continuing sovereignty of the new landlords, even while their very implication in most of these cases was caused by their systematic violation of the new colonial political economy. Nonetheless, the old moral economy underwent change, for under the terms of the Permanent Settlement, with military *inams* resumed and religious *inams* separated from their corporate and political contexts, gifts were not the same. Gifts of land might, indeed, pay off political debts, but no longer could they sustain the old relations of service, loyalty, and honor.

Law neither eradicated gifts nor did it create a fully capitalist market in land. It did, however, provide both an ideological form of legitimation and a diffuse institutional means for the control of colonial society. The British were able to freeze their reified conception of the old regime only because the existence of the law provided a structural replacement for politics. Law courts thus provided new battlefields for the Rajas of old, where titles to kingdoms and rights to kingly activities could once again be won and lost.[56] Gifts could be made, or rather allowed after the fact to have legal validity, but only if they were given for reasons deemed satisfactory in British courts of law, which proposed new taxonomies of gifts and new ideas of political expediency for the construction of what would, and what would not, be legitimate zamindari activity. Nevertheless, the law only partly succeeded in defining new logics, as it only partly succeeded in implementing the new political economy. But in this failure lay success, for the failure of the British to use the law as effectively as Lee-Warner so devoutly wished allowed the law to succeed in preserving, and at the same time subtly controlling and transforming, the Permanent Settlement.

While the partial failure of the law to create new forms and meanings gave rise to the possibility of successful realization of certain colonial aspirations, the partial autonomy of the law, far from demonstrating the loftiness of British ideals and the liberality of their institutions, worked to rationalize and legitimate the colonial system. Law had a political effect far more important than its economic one. The endless legal dramas were compelling fictions and served to marginalize the participants at the very moments they were included most vigorously in the colonial system. By losing some measure of control over the management of estates, the British gained all the more control over the old elites, who could be barely cognizant of the extent of their displacement.

For this very reason, law worked powerfully at the level of discourse. Situated as it was at the very highest level of cultural production and hegemonic influence, law provided a set of discursive structures that, because of their real implications for the lives of the descendants of old elites, put all other discourse—about the nature of both property and sovereignty—in relation to itself. The little kings, while they continued old forms of sovereignty by giving gifts, now had to justify these alienations in terms not of the language of old—where honor, protection, loyalty, kinship, service, property, and privilege had specific relational and operational meanings—but in new terms of legal argument and adjudication. Succession disputes privileged new forms of conquest and legitimation, where the ability to influence a judge became more important than the capacity to mobilize the support and loyalty of one's military nobles and retainers. Disputes over alienation were now couched in the language of the zamindar's life interest in his estate, in arbitrarily conceived and imposed statutes of limitation, and in taxonomies of alienation that defined "service" in quasi-bureaucratic language. These taxonomies not only separated "personal" from "public" service, but even set off "religious" from "nonreligious" grants, in total violation of earlier, precolonial meanings. For example, in preserving certain religious *inams,* the British, in fact, appropriated the right to define and decide whether Hindu religious functions, themselves previously important components of a total social and political formation, were being properly performed. The partial autonomy of law in the structure of British colonialism made the discourse of the law all the more significant. The law appeared to be all-powerful, even when it was not, and it was often the case that the zamindar saw himself as having locus standi only in the British courts of law, which appeared to mediate all relations between landlords and the state.

Law thus worked both ideologically and institutionally to permit the persistence of contradictions in colonial governance. Law courts provided an arena for political dispute that was as all-consuming for some of its litigants as it was nonthreatening to the state. Old concerns continued, of course, but they were now deflected and displaced by the state's appropriation of the political position of the zamindars and they had now to be argued in the language of the colonizers. Precisely because of the persistence of old concerns in this new arena, rapid change did not take place. The political economy that the British announced would accompany the introduction of property rights was actually invoked only for the purpose of extracting revenue, not for creating a fully capitalist market in land. At the same time, the law steadily chipped away at the conceptual and institutional linkages that gave the old regime its integrity and its dynamic. Nineteenth-century gifts took place within the vortex of a cultural lag, in which none of the systematic features of the gift as a mode of statecraft and locality integration could continue. Law was, thus, both one of the major reasons for the British failure to achieve a complete change of rural society, and the means by which the changes that were achieved were accomplished with so little disruption. The death of the old regime happened not with the swift slice of the guillotine, but with the slow and blunted chops of colonial contradictions, leaving a legacy that postindependent India must continue to deal with even today.

Law cannot, therefore, be dismissed as epiphenomenal to the study of colonialism, even if there were significant tensions between the formal rhetoric and the discursive reality of the law.[57] It was law that provided the institutional context for the partial—though of course changed—continuance of aspects of the old regime, rendering those aspects troublesome but never fundamentally threatening to British rule in India. The mechanisms that brought about the curious combination of continuity and change cannot be explained without examining the peculiar and often paradoxical position of the law in the history of colonialism.[58] A great many contradictions can be seen to render the picture of social change under colonialism more complex than has usually been accepted. In the case of the vestigial domains of South India—the little kingdoms that, in the eighteenth century, had constituted one of the most serious challenges to British hegemony in Madras—a study of law provides us with a particularly clear window through which to view these contradictions, and perhaps with one of the major keys for understanding why these contradictions never became explosively antagonistic. Law—with all its discourse and its drama, its autonomy and its inutility—was certainly one of the most important, convincing, and successful cultural forms of colonialism. That it was often successful in spite of itself was perhaps its greatest triumph.

NOTES

This article was first published with the title "From Little King to Landlord: Property, Law, and the Gift under the Madras Permanent Settlement," in the April, 1986, issue of *CSSH*.

1. For a collection of some of the best writing in this mode, see H. L. Gates, ed., *Race, Writing, and Difference* (Chicago: University of Chicago Press, 1986). For a more recent critical review of this literature, see Gates, "Critical Fanonism," *Critical Inquiry* 17, no. 8 (Spring, 1991): 457–70. Although I agree with Gates about the problems of global theorizing, Gates himself seems to miss the obvious fact that he has trouble with theorists whose postcolonial referent is South Asia. For a recent sympathetic review of the work of some of the most important contributors to colonial discourse theory, see Robert Young, *White Mythologies* (London: Routledge, 1990). My quarrel here is not with the effect of work in colonial discourse on literary and cultural studies, but with the adequacy of some of this work for coming to terms with the text of colonialism itself.

2. As Marx aptly wrote, "In Bengal [the British] created a caricature of large-scale English landed estates; in southeastern India a caricature of small parcelled property; in the northwest they did all they could to transform the Indian economic community with common ownership of land into a caricature of itself" (*Capital* [Moscow: Progress Publishers, 1974], 3:334n). For more recent views, see Tom G. Kessinger, *Vilyatpur 1848–1968: Social and Economic Change in a North Indian Village* (Berkeley: University of California Press, 1974); Walter C. Neale, "Land Is to Rule," in *Land Control and Social Structure in Indian History*, ed. R. E. Frykenberg (Madison: University of Wisconsin Press, 1969); Gananath Obeyesekere, *Land Tenure in Village Ceylon: A Sociological and Historical Study* (Cambridge: Cambridge University Press, 1967); Burton Stein, *Peasant State and Society in Medieval South India* (Delhi: Oxford University Press, 1980).

3. See the discussion of these two terms in David Ludden, *Peasant History in South India* (Princeton: Princeton University Press, 1985).

4. See W. H. Bayley and W. Huddleston, eds., *Paper in Mirasi Right: Selected from the Records of the Government and Published by Permission* (Madras, 1862); Brian Murton, "Key People in the Countryside: Decision Makers in Interior Tamil Nadu in the Late Eighteenth Century," *Indian Economic and Social History Review* 10, no. 2 (1973): 169–79.

5. Robert Lingat, *The Classical Law of India* (Berkeley: University of Cal-

ifornia Press, 1973), 212. My stress on the term *ksatra* derives from conversations with Burton Stein. My particular sense of the way in which the king's mastery or lordship of land was constituted in medieval India is also influenced by the work of Ronald Inden, e.g., his "Lordship and Caste in Hindu Discourse," mimeograph, 1980.

6. See Kessinger, *Vilyatpur*, Washbrook, "Law, State, and Agrarian Society," *Modern Asian Studies* 15, no. 3 (1981): 649–721.

7. See Nicholas B. Dirks, *The Hollow Crown: Ethnohistory of an Indian Kingdom* (Cambridge: Cambridge University Press, 1988).

8. K. Rajayyan, *South Indian Rebellion: The First War of Independence* (Mysore: Rao and Raghavan, 1971).

9. *Tinnevelly Collectorate Records*, Tamil Nadu Archives, Madras.

10. For an excellent recent study (published after this article was originally written) of the *ryotwari* settlement, and its relationship to arguments for and against the permanent settlement, see Burton Stein, *Thomas Munro* (Delhi: Oxford University Press, 1989).

11. *Collector's Report Regarding the Tinnevelly Poligars and Sequestered Pollams, 1799–1801*, Tamil Nadu Archives, Madras.

12. In P. K. Gnanasundara Mudaliyar, *Note on the Permanent Settlement* (Madras: Government Press, 1940).

13. Mudaliyar, *Permanent Settlement*, par. 369.

14. Tipu Sultan had commenced a systematic attempt to remove the local *palaiyakkarars* and replace them with revenue officials called *amildars*. Often, rather than risking local revolt by directly attacking the *palaiyakkarars*, he would invite them to Srirankapattinam, his capital, give them honorary posts in the army, settle their families there as well, and protect them with armed guards, which made them, in essence, captives. Tipu even resumed many of the local *inams* in the Baramahal and had *brahmadeyam* lands assessed in 1784. See Walter Kelly Firminger, ed., *The Fifth Report on East India Company Affairs—1812* (Calcutta: R. Cambray and Company, 1918), 3:350–82; *The Baramahal Records; or, The Ancient Records of Salem District, Madras* (Madras: Government Press, 1907), sec. 5.

15. Burton Stein, "Munro Sahib and Elements of the Political Structure of Early Nineteenth-Century South India," manuscript, 28–37.

16. Letter from Board of Revenue to Collector Lushington, September 4, 1799, in *Correspondence between Mr. S. R. Lushington, Collector of Ramnad and Poligar Peshcush and the Board of Revenue and the Special Commission on the Permanent Settlement of the Southern Pollams and of Ramnad and Shevagungah Zemindaries in the District of Madura* (Madura: Collectorate Press, n.d.), ASO (D)304, Tamil Nadu Archives, Madras. The only major difficulties that the Board of Revenue saw when enunciating this policy in 1799 involved

determining the proper amount of peshkash and ascertaining the "rights of the Talookdars, or under Tenantry throughout the different districts, that in confirming the proprietary rights of the Zemindars we may not violate the ascertained right of other individuals."

17. Deed of Permanent Settlement, art. 9 (reprinted in *Correspondence,* 68).

18. Deed of Permanent Settlement, art. 7.

19. Deed of Permanent Settlement, art. 10.

20. *Alienation* is a British term that means the transfer of property, titles, or goods from one person to another, by gift or sale, or even deceit. I use this term here because it was the term most generally used in British records for all the transfers involved in *inam* gifts or in gifts where some diminution of the tax burden was entailed.

21. Eric Stokes, *Peasant and Raj* (Cambridge: Cambridge University Press, 1978), 60.

22. In the end, the usual principle followed by Lushington, as for example in Ramnad, was to take two-thirds of the average collections of the six previous years (*Proceedings of the Board of Revenue,* Madras, no. 2234, March 25, 1850, Tamil Nadu Archives, Madras [hereafter cited *PBR*]). In zamindaries where actual rebellion took place, such as Civakankai, the determination of peshkash proved more difficult, because previous collections had been "irregular." In Civakankai, Lushington simply "Proposed for its Peishcush, and Government acceded to this proposal, two-thirds of the Ramnad zemindary peishcush on the grounds that originally the Zemindaries of Ramnad and Shivagungah formed one state, the revenues of which had been divided by the then Raja in the proportion of Ramnad three-fifths and Shivagungah two-fifths." Letter from Collector Lushington to the Board of Revenue, September 30, 1802, in *Correspondence.*

23. Ranajit Guha, *A Rule of Property for Bengal: An Essay on the Idea of the Permanent Settlement* (Mouton: Paris, 1963).

24. Minutes of December 31, 1824, in Mudaliyar, *Permanent Settlement,* 82.

25. See Pamela Price, "Raja-dharma in Ramnad, Land Litigation, and Largess," *Contributions to Indian Sociology* 13, no. 2 (July–December, 1979): 207–40. For the most thorough and insightful treatment of north Indian landlords, see Thomas Metcalf, *Land, Landlords, and the British Raj* (Berkeley: University of California Press, 1979). For an analysis that shares the kind of expection that accompanies the Permanent Settlement—that the opportunity of security should be greeted by local investment and the subsequent generation of a group of landed capitalists—see Christopher Baker, "Tamilnad Estates in the Twentieth Century," *Indian Economic and Social History Review* 13, no. 1 (1976): 1–44.

26. Price, "Raja-dharma," 208. Nonetheless, Price seems to assume that the only reason these nonmaterial strategic concerns continued to have such salience was that Ramnad was so poor and dry (237). In so arguing, she fails to persuade

us of the continuing force of precolonial political forms and the role of British colonial intervention in making the continuance of the old regime all the more powerful.

27. Letter from R. Eden to Board of Revenue, October 14, 1836, in *Selections from Old Records: Papers Relating to Zamindaries, Mittahs, etc., Tinnevelly District, Board Sent* (Madras: Government Press, 1934), 8.

28. Letter from E. P. Thompson to Board of Revenue, May 30, 1839, in *Selections from Old Records,* 38.

29. Extract from a letter from the Court of Directors, May 9, 1838, no. 5, in *Selections from Old Records: Papers Relating to Zamindaries, Mittahs, etc., Tinnevelly District, Board Received* (Madras: Government Press, 1934), 17.

30. Minutes of December 31, 1824, in Mudaliyar, *Permanent Settlement,* 82.

31. Reprinted in Mudaliyar, *Permanent Settlement,* 78.

32. See Eric Stokes, *The English Utilitarians and India* (London: Oxford University Press, 1959).

33. James Mill, *The History of British India* (London: J. Madden, 1820), 5:513.

34. J. Duncan M. Derrett, "J. H. Nelson: A Forgotten Administrator-Historian of India," in *Essays in Classical and Modern Hindu Law,* ed. J. D. M. Derrett (Leiden: Brill, 1977), 2:354–73.

35. Lingat, *Classical Law,* 257–58.

36. Lingat, *Classical Law,* 259.

37. Clifford Geertz, *Local Knowledge* (New York: Basic Books, 1983), 196.

38. Stokes, *English Utilitarians,* 235.

39. Washbrook, "Law, State, and Agrarian Society," 657–58, 665.

40. See Arjun Appadurai, *Worship and Conflict under Colonial Rule* (Cambridge: Cambridge University Press, 1981). Appadurai argues that the British were profoundly ambivalent about questions of change and preservation, wishing to regularize their administration of India while altering as little of "Indian tradition" (as they defined it) as possible (166–67). Appadurai demonstrates that, in spite of this ambivalence, the British brought about profound changes involving the shift of law from a royal and administrative context to a colonial and bureaucratic one, and often entailing major changes in the legal basis and social constitutions of religious communities.

41. *PBR,* no. 1863, September 17, 1873.

42. *PBR,* no. 2104, May 22, 1871.

43. As stipulated under Act XIV of 1859, sec. 1, clause 14, Madras Regulations.

44. *PBR,* no. 747, May 8, 1873.

45. *PBR,* no. 1863, September 17, 1873.

46. District Court of Madura, original suit no. 21 of 1873. I am grateful to Pamela Price for making the transcript of this case available to me.

47. *PBR,* no. 389, February 21, 1874.

48. *PBR,* no. 1116, May 12, 1874.

49. *PBR,* no. 3490, December 2, 1874.

50. See Price, "Raja-dharma."

51. *Proceedings of the Court of Wards,* Madras, no. 874, July 24, 1886.

52. *Court of Wards,* no. 1684, November 4, 1887.

53. *Court of Wards.*

54. *Court of Wards,* no. 874, July 24, 1886.

55. *Court of Wards,* no. 2060, August 3, 1874.

56. Ventures of this kind occurred only at the upper level of society. Even today, many disputes continue to be solved within the framework of traditional local procedures for dispute arbitration. In areas of Tamil Nadu where I worked, local assemblies called *kuttams* continue to play an important role in certain areas. In fact, it is often considered to be a sign of the demise of these institutions, and of local society in general, when the law courts are frequented. The characterization of Indians as unusually litigious is based on the extraordinarily rapid penetration of legal institutions into certain areas of Indian society. This effect was due to the transfer of all cases concerning landholding to the legal domain and to the uncertain classificatory command the newly created legal codes have over foreign systems of landholding. But most other areas of civil law continued to be dealt with effectively in local assemblies, where the purpose of arbitration was not to punish offenders but, rather, to reestablish communal harmony—and hierarchy. Landholding had been summarily removed from its previous contextualization within the same communal institutions.

57. This is the clear implication of Washbrook's paper. Once Washbrook judges the law to be a mere accomplice of the economic interests of the colonial state, he lets the law drop from his analysis. Because he is more concerned with criticizing the global history of capitalism than the specific history of colonialism in India, he does not identify the cultural, social, and political factors that made the transition to colonialism so disruptive. Accordingly, it is hardly surprising that Washbrook does not seriously consider the nature and significance of the introduction of the colonial law beyond its demonstrable economic effects, or lack of them. However, elsewhere Washbrook has concerned himself with the mechanisms through which the law eroded the corporate institutions of the old regime in South India even while it seemed to invoke these institutions. Washbrook cites, as an example, the fact that laws demanding written consensus on each property transaction within a village actually worked to reduce significantly the openness and dynamism of village society. See David Washbrook, "Colonialism, Underdevelopment, and the Making of a Backward Economy: The Case of South India, 1770–1870" (Paper presented to Humanities Seminar, California Institute of Technology, April 30, 1984).

58. For a detailed examination of the role of the law in the history of zam-

indaries in southern India, see Pamela G. Price, "Resources and Rule in Zamindari Southern India, 1802–1903: Sivagangai and Ramnad as Kingdoms under the Raj" (Ph.D. diss., University of Wisconsin, 1979). Of particular interest is her discussion of succession disputes (chap. 5, 132–75).

Colonizing Time: Work Rhythms and Labor Conflict in Colonial Mombasa

Frederick Cooper

Colonizing space was one question, colonizing time another. Britain, France, and the other colonizing powers sent their armies across the African continent at the end of the nineteenth century, concentrating forces sufficiently to subdue kingdoms and intimidate villages into acknowledging the sovereignty of a distant power. The content of that sovereignty, however, remained problematic. At the time of conquest, industrial capitalism in Europe had reached a stage of great complexity and considerable—if hardly unchallenged—self-confidence: Europeans thought they knew what kind of economic structures would lead to progress in the colonies as well as at home.

This article is about the effort of a colonial power to induce African workers to adapt to the work rhythms of industrial capitalism: to the idea that work should be steady and regular and carefully controlled. It focuses on two moments when a colonial state—Kenya—made a concerted attempt to impose such a model of time on a particular social milieu, one at the beginning of the colonial era, the other at the end. In the first round, the Kenya government successfully asserted its power over the wide spaces of a portion of Africa, but could not impose its vision within the workplace of its most valuable and vulnerable port. In the second, the colonial state—with considerable difficulty—imposed its work rhythms on a tiny proportion of the Kenyan work force, but, as it did so, it helped to shape a discourse on African society that separated—more starkly than ever before—the restructured milieu from the undisciplined work culture outside it.

Remaking time in the 1940s and 1950s also remade space, not in the

209

sense of a broad imperialist sweep across the continent, but in the sense of compartmentalizing Africa. Once dock work demanded a regular, full-time commitment from workers and once its rewards made a job too valuable to give up, dockworkers' life chances became sharply distinguished from the working population that did not have access to such jobs, and whose growing presence in the cities officials could not prevent. Meanwhile, the very process of thinking through a policy toward such workers led officials increasingly to dichotomize the "modern" world they thought they were creating from the "traditional" world they thought they were separating it from. Dualism became a defining characteristic of social analysis within the colonial bureaucracy, and in the social sciences concerned with Africa as well. The important changes in the terms of international discourse on Africa reflected not just the evolution of academic disciplines and world politics, but the effects of local transformations and global frustrations in the late colonial era.[1]

The significance of the question of time in the development of industrial capitalism was the focus of a now famous article by E. P. Thompson (1967). He argued that, at one time, European cultivators and peasants shared with people in parts of the world now described as undeveloped an attitude toward time and work discipline vastly different from that which came to dominate European society. It was not that people worked less or with less motivation, but that their notions of discipline were geared around the notion of "task time." When something had to be done, it was, and so effort varied seasonally and in other ways, while work rhythms were integrated into patterns of social life. The work rhythms of modern Europe—"clock time"— were not natural characteristics of a particular culture, but historical developments, consequences of the rise of wage labor and the imposition of discipline from above. The capitalist bought his laborer's time and insisted that he get his precise due. The notion of clock time was vigorously insinuated into daily life: from the highly visible clock to the factory bell to the commercialization of timepieces to the regular rhythms of school periods to the practice of clocking-in, as workers' arrivals and departures were coded onto a card. When workers started to demand extra payments for overtime it was a sign that they "had accepted the categories of their employers and learned to fight back within them. They had learned their lesson, that time is money, only too well" (Thompson 1967, 86).

More recently, some scholars, while acknowledging the overall trend, have argued that Thompson treated it in too linear a manner. The establishment of work routines in particular industries involved variety, pragmatism, and bargaining, and, in some industries, workers were more successful in maintaining task orientation and partial control over work organization than Thompson allows. The clock—and the dichotomy of work and leisure—has not so fully come to dominate the rhythms of family and community life; multiple rhythms continue to coexist (Whipp 1987).

Nevertheless, it is clear that the clash of different notions of time and work occurred in the context of colonization, particularly as certain colonial regimes tried to harness the labor power of the colonized. Keletso Atkins (1988) has argued that Zulu workers in mid-nineteenth-century South Africa had an identifiable work culture, only it was not the work culture of the white conquerors and employers. The confrontation of alternative conceptions of work time, however, was read by white commentators as the laziness of the African.

I argue that the contestation over time was, in fact, a long one, its outcome hardly determined by the formal imposition of colonial rule; that there were more than two alternative ways of organizing the working day and the working life and African workers explored, individually and collectively, a series of new forms; that the ultimate imposition of the colonial construction of time discipline in the docks of Mombasa was obtained only through the narrowing of the spatial arena to which it applied; and that officials' changing notions of time and space in Africa reflected their failures as much as their successes.

Time and Work Discipline in Coastal Kenyan Slave Society

Time and work were contested before the advent of colonial conquerors and managers. A particularly important site of confrontation was the coast of what is now Kenya, part of a belt of fertile territory often no more than ten miles deep, with (in places) a range of hills followed by an arid region on one side, and the Indian Ocean on the other. Coastal society gazed toward the interior of Africa and out to sea. The regional language, Swahili, shared its basic structure with the largest language group in Africa, but included a substantial component of loanwords, mainly Arabic, in its vocabulary.

The seaborne commercial linkages of the coast provided the starting point for the large-scale development of export agriculture using slave labor during the nineteenth century. Arab immigrants and indigenous—

Muslim, Swahili-speaking—inhabitants of coastal towns took advantage of new opportunities, buying slaves in a market that had expanded to serve export needs and selling cloves, grain, and dried coconut in an Indian Ocean–wide system of exchange. In coastal Kenya, large plantations, sometimes with hundreds of slaves, were founded by people from a variety of local and immigrant communal groups in the relatively open spaces around Malindi. In Mombasa, with a higher population, less room to expand, and a longer tradition of urban life, the expansion of agricultural production took place on a smaller and less intensive scale: aside from a small number of plantations, a few slaves supplemented the labor of their owners, or else a group of slaves was settled on a farm near the city, cultivating more or less on their own while their urban owner checked up on them occasionally and oversaw the harvest (Cooper 1977; Sheriff 1987).

Slave labor—especially in the large grain estates of Malindi—has left a deep impression in the memories of local people. Research conducted some sixty-five years after the colonial regime abolished slavery in 1907 revealed that descendants of slaves and slaveowners agreed that there were customary expectations and limitations placed on field labor, but the two categories of informants interpreted them in quite different ways. All agreed that slaves labored in gangs under close supervision by a hierarchy of overseers—themselves slaves—and the owner. They agreed that the customary unit of daily labor was the *ngwe,* named after a length of rope used to measure a plot of ground. But they disagreed over how long weeding an *ngwe* took: the descendants of free people claimed it required a morning, the descendants of slaves insisted it took all day. Who was correct is less interesting than the fact that, generations after the actual experience, the transmitted memories were still sharp enough for people to disagree.[2]

Slavery's work week was five days: all sources agree that this was generally accepted. Slaves were given small plots on which they could build their own huts and grow their own food. Near Mombasa, owners' intervention in the agricultural labor process was often intermittent. Meanwhile, urban slaves frequently hired themselves out as port carriers, artisans, or caravan porters, paying about half of their wages to their owners. Turn-of-the-century land registers reveal that many slaves owned their own small huts: the urban master-slave relationship was not a question of the daily intimacy of power but largely a matter of cash payments (Cooper 1977, 184–87, 229).

Informants of slave descent remembered that discipline on plantations was enforced with the *kiboko,* a whip made of hippopotamus hide; informants from formerly slaveholding communal groups generally claimed that planters were lenient and—in accordance with Islamic norms—benevolent, but do not deny that slaves were punished. Where coastal slaveholders differed from their Western Hemisphere counterparts was in the weakness of coercive capabilities beyond the plantation. Malindi—where work routines were the most demanding—had only a tiny garrison of mercenary soldiers under an official representing the Sultan of Zanzibar. The collective authority of slaveholders also had its limitations. While within a town like Mombasa or Malindi the slaveholders from differing communal groups respected each other's rights in human property, the same was not true of a number of maverick potentates who had moved away from the towns with their followers and slaves. Rival communal groups even armed their slaves for their periodic conflicts. The need to count on slaves as more than field hands limited the extent to which coercive sanctions could be the ultimate basis of plantation discipline (Cooper 1977, 176–80, 190–92).

As in all slave societies, the vulnerability of slaves followed from the fact that they had been alienated from the places and communities of birth (Patterson 1982). In coastal society, anyone without a place, however lowly, in a recognized communal group was in an anomalous and dangerous situation. The other side of this dependence was the efforts of slaves to counter it: escape took place frequently, but it had to have a collective element to it. Runaways created maroon villages in the hinterland behind the fertile coastal belt; others joined the entourages of potentates hostile to the Sultanate of Zanzibar; others, by the 1870s, fled to Christian missions, where they entered a new sort of community and a new sort of discipline. For slaves who did not escape, there is evidence that many resisted the cultural onslaught of their owners, keeping up the dances, the initiation rites, and other practices of their home societies, and maintaining—even sixty-five years after abolition—a form of self-identification that countered the idea that they could only be inferior members of coastal society: *Wanyasa.* This was a generic label, after the Lake Nyasa region from which the majority had been taken, and in its affirmation of a hinterland identification negated the dualities of slaveholder hegemony: Muslim-pagan, civilized-heathen, coast-interior (Cooper 1981).

Had Nyasa identity developed over time and across generations, the horizontal ties among slaves could have become closer than the vertical ties with their owners. This accounts for a strong tendency among slaveholders to manumit second-generation slaves or to find special roles for them within the entourage: as overseer, as a trader on the master's behalf, as autonomous worker or artisan paying occasional money or fealty to the owner. That meant that the labor force had to be reproduced by the continual importation of slaves.[3] Most of the men and women who were clearing an *ngwe* per day, five days a week, in Malindi's fields had been born in far-away parts of Africa and had themselves experienced the trauma of the slave trade.

Colonial Conquest, Emancipation, and Work Discipline

The form of reproduction of the slave labor force was the slaveholders' greatest vulnerability. The slave trade also provided the most vivid symbolism in European anti-slavery propaganda of the horrors associated with slavery. David Livingstone's voyages in the 1860s in the Lake Nyasa region portrayed a large area where villages lived in constant fear of slave raiders, where people retreated in defensive isolation, and, hence, where the slave trade presented "an unsurmountable barrier to all moral and commercial progress" (Livingstone 1865, 595). The image of Africa as a slave-ridden continent, however exaggerated, entered European discourse as a marker of the contrast between Africa's tyranny and backwardness and Europe's capacity for benign progress. At the great conclaves in Berlin in 1884 and Brussels in 1889–90 at which European powers agreed on the rules for competing for African territory, leaders declared themselves willing to make action against African slave trading a basic standard of morality in imperial endeavors (Cooper 1980, 1989).

As conquest proceeded, emancipating slaves was thus an imperative, even as officials, learning more and more about the complexities of the societies they were taking over, came quickly to doubt their own capacity to abolish slavery while maintaining order and productivity. They realized that work discipline was embedded in a social system, and that tampering with any part of it posed risks. Even missionaries were concerned that if slaves were freed but not subjected to close control they "would tend to produce a demoralized and dangerous class of people, such as would be sure in the future to embarrass the good government and to mar the prosperity of the country." An official worried that "if a large number of slaves are liberated at one time, they are apt to break loose, loot shops and shambas [farms] and commit all sorts of excesses."[4]

The Kenya government—having taken power in 1895 after a British chartered company had ineffectually administered the coastal zone since 1888—hesitated. A rebellion by one of the dissident coastal communal groups (with its entourage of clients, ex-slaves, and slaves) made officials even more uncertain that the colonial state was strong enough to superintend abolition. So it was not until 1907—ten years after slavery was abolished in the closely connected British colony on Zanzibar—that slavery was finally abolished.

The Zanzibar Precedent

The Zanzibari experience had a great deal to do with how emancipation proceeded in coastal Kenya. The largely Arab slaveholders of Zanzibar had achieved a near monopoly of the world's supply of cloves by the mid-nineteenth century. After the British takeover in 1890, officials did not question that slaveholders should retain the property rights in land and productive trees that they had under Islamic law. Nor did they question the need for a managerial class to superintend production: the option of allowing ex-slaves to cultivate on their own, as peasants, was not seriously considered. Under the Zanzibar emancipation decree of 1897, slaveholders were paid compensation money to ease their transition from slave to wage labor. The decree attempted, however, to make a compromise between the radical implications of the British view of slavery—that labor be "free"—and the conservative implications of officials' view of class—that order and production required a class of landowners and managers. Ex-slaves, under the decree that freed them, would lose the plots of land they had and be declared vagrant unless they agreed to a contract with a landowner, attested to in court. Officials used the intimidating atmosphere of the courts where freedom papers were granted to impose model contracts: ex-slaves would work three days per week (versus the customary five of slave days), all year, in exchange for a subsistence plot and a place to build a home. In fact, ex-slaves agreed to the contracts and did not, in general, do the three days labor. Taking advantage of the new possibilities for mobility among plantations, for finding vacant, nonclove land, or for casual labor in towns—while planters could no longer reproduce their labor force via slave imports—ex-slaves were able to reach an understanding with landlords that gave them access to land in exchange for vague responsibilities to do some work and be part of the landowners' "people" (Cooper 1980, chap. 3).

Landowners desperate for some kind of sway over ex-slaves, as much as ex-slaves themselves, subverted British notions of contractually specific obligations and regular work. They did not refuse ex-slaves who had reneged on previous contracts, and British officials lacked the coercive power to undertake massive evictions and vagrancy prosecutions. This inability reinforced landowners' tendency to act within more familiar norms: to cultivate long-term ties of dependency rather than contractual obligations. These ties made British views of regularity and their wish that the "sanction of the sack" would maintain labor discipline increasingly irrelevant. Within a few years of emancipation, an official was, typically, lamenting, "Steady, regular work is just what your slave or free slave dislikes very much."[5]

Zanzibar's clove output was saved by a very different allocation of time, quite different from the regularity of wage labor discipline that British officials had tried to instill. Short-term migrants from nonclove areas of the islands (who had been marginalized by the slave economy) began to pick cloves, working for only a few weeks each year. Long-term migrants from German Africa—where the end of the slave trade, ivory trade, and porterage had ruined forms in which young men could acquire cash—began to come for periods of two to three years, weeding the plantations throughout the year. Ex-slaves filled in the crevices. So clove production actually rose, even as officials lamented the *way* the work was done.

Land and Labor in Postabolition Kenya

This precedent established in Zanzibar reduced the Kenya government's willingness to try to superintend a direct transition from slave to wage labor. By 1907, however, the slaves had already gone a long way to free themselves. They took advantage of the British presence to undermine the subtle relations of dependency of a slave society. The end of the slave trade meant that the slave population could no longer be reproduced; the Pax Britannica meant that people could leave plantations without fear for their lives; railway construction and other colonial projects created alternative employment. The slow but steady exodus of slave labor meant a readjustment of labor conditions for those who stayed:

slaves devoted more time (and space) to their own cultivation and less to the landowners' fields.

When abolition came to Kenya in 1907—allowing slaveholders to claim compensation for slaves whose services they lost—it in effect ratified the freedom slaves had already effectively claimed, while legitimating the efforts of landowners to get the slaves of other landowners to squat on their land. The reality of the situation (on both sides of 1907) was that a tied labor system was giving way to competition between landowners for increasingly mobile workers, and squatters paid only a modest rent or provided vaguely specified labor services. People who lived in the hinterland behind the more fertile coastal belt—belonging to nine distinct political and communal groups later collectively known as Mijikenda (nine villages)—began to join ex-slaves as squatters on coastal estates. Near Mombasa, both ex-slaves and Mijikenda established a symbiosis between urban and rural activities, seeking casual labor, mainly on the docks, which would provide cash for a day's work but which would not compromise participation in agriculture (Cooper 1980, chap. 5).

The planters had lost their once effective control over labor. Land was another question. In 1905, as an official Land Committee sat, the coast promised to stand alongside the Highlands as one of the twin poles of a European-dominated economy. The committee—anxious to legitimate private ownership of land—did not wish to flout Islamic law as it did African systems of land tenure, yet it feared that confusion over titles would make productive investment too risky. As a result, the government set out to establish the *legal* structure for capitalist development: it called for the systematic survey and adjudication of all claims to land ownership in the coastal belt, and it insisted that all transactions be registered. Behind the legalistic approach lay another assumption: that the fair operations of the market would result in the transfer of a considerable proportion of the land to the most efficient producers, who were assumed to be white.

The survey, carried out between 1910 and 1922, discriminated in favor of those with written deeds or oral evidence of continued ownership from established leaders from the former slaveholding community. The people who lost most were those whose claims derived from membership in a communal group or from a relationship such as clientage or, indeed, slavery. While slaves had formerly been allowed to use small plots on their owners' estates and people who were converted to Islam and became personal followers of an established Muslim had been given rights to pieces of the patron's land, such bases of claims to land were consistently rejected. They were thus to be landless and their labor power, in theory, became available to old and new landowners who wished to purchase it.

Europeans did acquire substantial tracts of land by purchase from planters who could no longer plant or as concessions from the government, but members of the old landowning groups of Arab or local origin still retained title to the largest portion (Cooper 1980, chap. 5). The European plantation experiment, meanwhile, proved a fiasco. Land speculation was based on the potential of rubber, and a a number of estates were started, but even at their peak, well under a third of the plantations' land was planted. Then in 1912, the rubber boom collapsed (largely because of the success of Malaya's rubber plantations), and with it the British hopes that a coastal plantation zone would flourish.

Even in its productive phase, European plantations were unable to recruit local labor, despite numerous attempts and considerable pressure from colonial officials. Coastal people would seek to become squatters or they would work for indigenous landowners, who made no demands about length of service. European planters insisted on a contract of at least several months duration, and commitment to full-time, carefully monitored labor for that length of time would have jeopardized what was most important: acquiring long-term, secure access to land, as squatters on the coast plain or as members of a communal group in the hinterland. For labor, the plantations had to look upcountry, where denser European settlement and a higher level of intimidation was pushing labor out (Cooper 1980, 244–48).

What collapsed on the old plantations was not so much agriculture as the British fantasy of agricultural wage labor. Regional exchange—between different parts of the coast and between Mombasa and the rural areas around it—became more intense, more varied, more ramified. Exports were more modest, but coconut products and grain continued to be sent forth. But the people who worked had gained at the expense of the people who owned. In most cases, landowners could only extract a modest rent and a share of the harvest of coconut trees on their plantations; they could not control the production process. Squatters grew and directly sold modest surpluses of grain. The tension in the relationship of squatters and landowners came out in the issue of planting new trees, especially coconut trees. Landlords lacked the cash to pay laborers for an investment that would take years to pay off and did not want tenants to plant for fear that, under coastal customs, the tenant would acquire rights to the tree; squatters, for their part, feared that making permanent improvements in the land would only encourage landowners to evict them. So an uneasy standoff ensued.

Officials periodically expressed displeasure at the squatters and never recognized the contribution they were making to the regional and export agriculture. They feared their presence would compromise the system of individual land tenure and discourage new purchasers of land, particularly Europeans. Even squatters who were reviving grain production on former plantation lands were accused by the governor of leading a "useless and degenerate existence."[6] In the government blueprint, the coastal zone was for private ownership and wage labor agriculture; the Mijikenda migrants belonged in their hinterland homeland—now labeled a "reserve"—and should only come forth when they had a definite arrangement to work. A government attempt to evict squatters from a fertile region north of Malindi—as late as 1914—resulted in a major rebellion and a famine that officials were obliged to relieve. Shortly thereafter, squatters returned to the area where their huts had been burned and fields destroyed, and this time officials gave up: the renewed presence of squatters—welcomed by the hapless Arab landlords of the area—heralded a modest revival of grain exports (Cooper 1980; Brantley 1981).

Urban Labor: The Virtues and Dangers of Casual Labor

The urban labor market of Mombasa developed relatively smoothly in the era of emancipation and expansion, while the rural labor market did not. In the days of slavery, urban slaveholders frequently had their slaves seek day labor; employers gave the slave a piece of paper with their earnings on it to inform the owner what he or she should expect the slave to turn over: this practice gave the Swahili name to day labor that remains with it to the present: *kazi ya kibarua* (work of the little letter).

The labor market of Mombasa adjusted well because employers willingly accepted labor power in the units in which coastal Africans wanted to provide it: by the day. Even as the tonnage of steamers entering Mombasa doubled between 1903 and 1913—accelerated by the completion of the railway to Kisumu in 1901—casual workers were getting the job done. The work was hard and the hours long, but casual workers in the port could earn as much in ten days as unskilled contract workers—who had no control over when they worked—could earn in a month.

Ex-slaves and Mijikenda found that periods of urban casual labor in the city complemented squatting and cultivating in rural areas.

Employers, given the fluctuating nature of shipping, found day labor served their interests too: they could adjust their wage bill to actual needs. But officials felt the same unease that their brethren in London had in regard to casual labor there (Stedman Jones 1971), and their anxieties appear in the preamble to a 1898 vagrancy decree that

> aim[ed] at checking, not only the influx into the town of Mombasa of idle and criminal runaway slaves, but also of disreputable free people of all sorts, who come to get an "odd job" on the railway, then throw up their work when tired of it, or are discharged, and take to drink and rioting, thus augmenting to an undesirable extent the disorderly floating population of Mombasa.[7]

But it would only be in the late 1940s that a serious attempt would be made to change the system of casual labor.

Nonetheless, day labor represented a dangerous standoff for both sides. Too few workers and employers risked being unable to meet demands on busy days, too many workers and the laborers risked being unable to work enough days to get through each month. During World War I, the escalating demand for African workers led to shortages in the port. Officials saw the solution in "systematic labour (without days off whenever they feel inclined) while any man not working at the port would be available for work elsewhere."[8] They devised a registration scheme intended to draw the necessary dichotomy between a worker and a nonworker: wages would be fixed and men could lose their registration for failing to work.

But the scheme ran up against a reality rather different from the anarchic and anomic images suggested by the term *casual labor*. The work gangs and the gang leaders had no interest in a registration scheme; the companies were too anxious about their ties to gangs and to the intermediaries who presented them with preconstituted work groups— and who could withdraw entire gangs—to cooperate fully in a scheme that would necessarily antagonize the independent-minded dockers. They participated in a variety of evasions of the registration system. At bottom lay the fear that dockers—with access to nonwage resources and a wider casual labor market in Mombasa as well as some forms of collective organization—would withdraw their labor altogether. In the end, the scheme failed, and only increased daily wages kept the port going.[9]

In the 1920s, the casual labor market turned in the opposite direction: more upcountry migration, the stagnation of coastal agriculture, and the modest pace of expansion meant that dockers were less likely to find work when they sought it. Tensions surfaced between coastal and upcountry workers, although the importance of networks to constituting work gangs maintained coastal predominance in dock labor.

Complaints of labor shortages in Mombasa ceased even before the depression of the early 1930s. But that did not lessen the other dimension of the casual labor problem: the kind of work situation and society casual labor entailed. In 1930, the *Mombasa Times* editorialized about the threat of workers, who "in virtue of the very casual nature of their job, relapse into that crime that is so easily absorbed from surroundings which are as casual as the labour itself." The "loose living and evil associations of casual home life" contrasted with the "cleaner life, the discipline, the counter attraction of a well-ordered existence" that seemed the more appropriate virtues for an African labor force. Officials also wrote frequently about the lack of "discipline," and about the dangers of "an almost featureless mass of humanity" moving into and out of jobs.[10]

Only later would officials realize that their imagery was all wrong. Casual labor was, in fact, quite organized, but not by employers. Shipping companies did not hire directly but developed relationships with men known as *serangs,* usually from the Swahili-speaking community of the coast, who in turn developed relationships with a group of men. The *serangs* thus supplied employers with a ready-made work gang, and in many phases of dock work they supervised the gang on the job. The gangs were often paid as a collectivity in accordance with the weight of cargo they moved, dividing the money among themselves. They thus had every incentive to work rapidly. The gangs were relatively stable, and their solidarity was reinforced by participation in the Beni dance societies typical of colonial cities in eastern and central Africa. In Mombasa, these dance groups were organized, often by *serangs,* around the work gangs and they competed each Sunday. Although not exclusively worker organizations, the Beni societies—especially two called Scotchi and Settla—were closely associated with dockworkers. Settla's "admiral," in 1934, was chief *serang* for the shorehandling company in the port. These societies, as their names and officers' titles suggest, carried out a kind of mocking commentary on the power structure of colonial society, even as they provided recreational outlets and vehicles for cementing relationships among city dwellers (Ranger 1975; Cooper 1987, 34–40).

While the overall labor market of Mombasa was affected by up-country migration, the social cohesion of the dock labor gangs and the dock work culture kept port daily labor largely in the hands of coastal people. Ex-slaves, Mijikenda, the less well off elements of Mombasa's Swahili-speaking population, and Swahili-speaking migrants from other coastal towns contributed the majority of the dockers (Cooper 1987, 40). The work gangs were far from the anonymous and ever-changing units of labor power suggested by the term *casual labor.*

Time and the Limits of Conquest

The colonial regime did not face the task of transforming a pristine "precolonial concept of time." The temporality of the labor process had already been transformed by the development of plantation slavery. Work rhythms—and the limits of discipline—were a question of power, and as slaveholders' power faded in the decade before formal abolition, the limits were redefined again. As the colonial regime sought to remake time in one direction, ex-slaves sought to remake it in another, and squatting, crop production, short-term agricultural labor, and urban casual labor all became part of a complex testing of new limits and defining of new expectations among ex-slaves, ex-slaveholders, Miji-kenda, upcountry migrants, and colonial officials.

The absence of a work force fully dependent on wage employment and subject to time discipline and the sanction of the sack is not alto-gether a bad thing for capitalists. Such patterns have, indeed, been taken to be characteristic of colonial capitalism. Casual laborers, migrant work-ers whose families remained in their natal villages, and agricultural laborers who produced their own food did not have to be paid a wage sufficient to pay the costs of their own reproduction; their unpaid labor on subsistence plots or that of their family members subsidized the money wage and lowered the labor value embodied in export crops (Meillassoux 1975). Such an interpretation comes close to being a tautology: capitalism cannot fail to triumph, for its inability to alienate people from the means of production or to exercise control over workers' time is taken to be the triumph of colonial or peripheral capitalism. Yet the conditions under which different variants of wage labor production are most profitable are more specific, and—more important—the forms of social and economic organization that colonizers saw as progressive and profitable are not the same as the abstract, ex post facto reconstruction of what capital logic in a colonial situation should have been.

In coastal East Africa, the record of officials' intentions, before the fact, is clear enough: success for them would have been turning slaves into a landless proletariat, mediated perhaps by contracts and labor tenancy, but certainly extinguishing all *rights* of access to land and certainly implying landlord control over the labor process itself. Yet it is not clear—in this or many other cases—whether capitalists and officials in the early colonial era had much choice over the kind of labor force they could get: African labor power was hard to detach from the soil and it came forth in small units (see also Cooper 1983).

It was after the fact that British colonial officials—most notably Frederick Lugard—began to make a virtue of their failures. Lugard himself, as ruler of northern Nigeria, had seen a landowning indigenous elite as worthy intermediaries whose cultural practices—as he saw them—should be respected, and he had insisted that the key to a prosperous agrarian future was to reinforce their ownership of land and convert their slaves into proletarians, producing under their direct supervision. Instead, the capitalists-to-be preferred to extort tribute from peasants and slaves alike, leading to such disorder that Lugard left Nigeria to be replaced by a governor with less reformist ambition, and who promptly reversed land policy, in effect eliminating freehold tenancy and accepting the existence of smallholder production out of which the colonial state, local elites, and merchants would squeeze a surplus by various means (Lennihan 1982). Lugard later espoused the virtues of indirect rule and a conservationist approach to African society: he had the genius to define failure as success (Lugard 1922; Phillips 1989). In coastal Kenya, officials backed off from the universality of their transformative goals but not from their desirability. They pinned the blame for the shortcomings of their labor and land policies on the coast and for its apparent stagnation (which did not take into account whether ex-slaves were living better or worse) on the slaves themselves. "A human being accustomed to slavery, when freed, seems to have lost all incentive to work," commented the East Africa Commission in 1925 in its postmortem on the coastal region.[11]

In Mombasa, a certain measure of successful transition was not accepted as such. The urban labor market had adjusted with remarkable smoothness to the rapid growth of East Africa's major port, the com-

pletion of a railway to Uganda, the growth of settler and African production upcountry, and the refocusing of import-export trade from a
series of small ports to a single large one. Except during World War I,
there were no notable transport bottlenecks. The reason the adjustment
was smooth was that men from the coastal region—ex-slaves, Mijikenda,
and others—were quite willing to work as long as they had some control
over time. Just as they rejected the contractually defined labor interval
of coastal rubber or sisal plantations, they left long-term labor to upcountry migrants, who, having paid high migration costs and distanced themselves from their own land and their own communities, were willing to
work steadily for a period of months or years to earn something to take
home. Coastal people integrated labor into their lives, not the other way
around, and so concentrated in the casual labor force.

But officials' comments—from the preamble to the 1897 vagrancy statute to the attacks on "casualism" in 1930— suggest that this condition
remained problematic in British eyes, even when the job seemed to be getting done. The nature of the comments reveals how much colonial officials
saw labor as a coherent system, in which regularity and discipline were
intrinsic parts, regardless of the local context. The ideal labor system in
offical eyes was a cultural construct, not just a series of cost-minimizing
strategies, and the colonial elite of Mombasa felt anxious and insecure
with the structure of labor they had. In the 1920s and 1930s, their anxiety
did not propel them to act. But at the end of the 1930s, Africans began to
strike, and while none of the strikes brought forth a demand for more
steady work, the very fact that colonial control was now being contested
led officials to a concerted campaign to reassert control in the way they
understood it: over the laborers' time.

Recolonizing Time: The Struggle over Dock Labor

Such fears could be put out of mind for a time. But the fact that they had
been articulated gave officials a context in which the first serious labor
conflicts in the port could be interpreted. The casual labor problem was
never very far away from official explanations of the strikes, and the
demarcation of an urban working class—clearly separated from the dangerous classes of the city—became the critical element of a solution.

The Crisis of Control

The first strike occurred in 1934, just as commerce began to pick up following the Depression. Casual laborers—fighting a wage cut—were at the

heart of the four-day strike. Their gains were limited, but the discipline of the strikers—without a trade union—made an impression. Officials sought an explanation within the Swahili milieu of the Mombasa working population. In particular, they blamed the Beni dance societies that were particularly popular with dockers; these, they thought, provided a communications network capable of organizing collective action. The district officials, however imperfect their understanding of how the 1934 strike was organized, had latched onto a significant fact: the mobilization of casual labor was a social process, and the relationships and the cultural forms to which it gave rise were being developed by workers themselves in ways that companies and officials could not control. The gangs and the *serangs* would one day be a focus of the port companies' efforts to reassert control.[12]

The Beni dance societies do not appear to have been a factor in the general strike of 1939. The strike reflected the common experience of being a worker in Mombasa. It transcended individual workplaces, and drew much of its strength from the residential area where most workers lived, Majengo. It began on July 19 with a sit-down strike by workers in the Public Works Department, which was settled when officials quickly granted them a three shillings per month housing allowance. Both the strikes and the solution then rolled through the city, affecting one employer after another. On August 1, it reached the port, where the casual gangs were again instrumental, and the entire port shut down; "bands of strikers" circulated in Majengo. On August 3, workers began to drift back. The one large segment of the working population that did not strike was the railway workers. They were unique in having housing provided for them, a fact that not only made them less vulnerable to the rapidly escalating cost of a room, but implied that they risked a home as well as a job should they strike and that they were not part of the vibrant life of Majengo (Cooper 1987, 45–50).

Housing became the prime culprit of an administration that had been badly frightened. In their correspondence and in the report of the Commission of Enquiry that followed, officials began to think their way through the fragility and danger of the cheap labor system. If the immediate grievance could be palliated with a housing allowance, resolution demanded that scarce housing resources be devoted to a working population that actually worked. Only days after the strike, the Principal Labour Officer suggested that "the regular worker should be substituted for the irregular worker," and the District Officer insisted, "casual labour is the danger point."[13] In London, Frederick Pedler—a rising star in the Colonial Office—saw the solution in bringing European models of labor organization to Africa: "Before long East Africa will have to change over—probably very suddenly—from low grade labour and very low wages to something much nearer the standard of European manual labour and the European labourer's wage." The Secretary of State for the Colonies agreed, and made it clear that the other side of developing a more compact, efficient, and better paid labor force was expelling everyone else from the city.[14]

The Commission of Enquiry drew its conclusions: casual labor in the port should be abolished. Their argument never concerned the productivity of casual laborers; it was not an argument about work but about workers. The need to keep a pool of semi-idle men in town undermined any hope of solving the housing crisis. The "idlers and stiffs" on whom the Commission blamed the strike could not be distinguished from authentic workers. Regular employment, improved housing, and massive expulsions were all necessary to reassert control (Kenya 1939). In this way, the commisssion hoped that within a particular space—the city of Mombasa—labor time could be controlled.

The companies were not yet ready to move. The stevedoring firms sharply rejected decasualization, insisting that port labor was casual by necessity. But quietly, the shorehandling company signed 150 workers onto monthly terms.

More jolts were soon to come. As in much of British Africa, World War II was a period of unprecedented labor conflict, marked by a cycle of inflation, challenge, and anxious concessions to striking workers. A series of short strikes rolled rapidly through Mombasa in 1942, and officials barely averted a general strike in 1945. A parallel series of tribunals and commissions met threats with timely cost of living bonuses and increased allowances of different sorts, while trying to place their actions in the light of an ideology of basic needs and objective determination of living standards. But as the recalculations of the budget of the single African worker went on, the actual wage increases followed a pattern of agitation (Cooper 1987, 57–78).

The inquiry by a committee headed by Arthur Phillips, whose appointment helped to avert a general strike in 1945, did the usual calculations yet again, but went further. It attempted to come to grips with the new reality that capital and the state faced in Mombasa. Its investigations revealed that a substantial portion of workers, particularly in the railway, had worked for the same employer for years. Yet it also found that the wages of the overwhelming majority of workers clustered near the bottom of a limited job hierarchy. While policymakers kept thinking about the "raw migrant," 80 percent of the lower paid workers the committee examined were married and more and more unskilled workers were aspiring to a "civilized standard of living." The committee thought it was observing the "emergence of [an] urbanized working class," and it feared "the beginnings of class-consciousness, complicated by race-consciousness" (Kenya 1945, 49, 53, 65).

The "system of 'cheap' Migrant Labour," the committee argued, was dangerous and it was not cheap. The system pushed all workers into similar conditions in which collective action was likely to spread; it brought the effects of rural malnutrition into the urban workplace; and it immunized workers against the "sanction of the Sack." The only way of building an orderly and productive working class was to insure that its reproduction took place within the city, under the aegis of a capitalist economy and a colonial state. The committee took the word that had long expressed colonial officials' misgivings about taking Africans out of rural society and reversed its implications: "There seems to be no escaping the fact that the evils which are commonly attributed to 'detribalisation' can only be cured by more complete detribalisation" (Kenya 1945, 50).

The government did Phillips the honor of suppressing his report; the concrete result of its effort was a thirty-five shillings per month wage increase. But Mombasa's workers were willing to teach more lessons. In January, 1947, they shut down the entire city for twelve days in a general strike involving some 15,000 workers crossing the divisions between casual and long-term workers, coastal people, and upcountry migrants. Again, no trade union was involved, and collective action grew out of the social networks of Majengo, which the colonial government did not understand, and expressed itself during the course of the strike in daily meetings in a football field. Renamed *Kiwanja cha Maskini,* 'the field of the poor,' this location became the organizational and symbolic focus of the strike: thousands of people gathered each day. There, during the course of the strike, was born the African Workers Federation (AWF). This organization, in the months after the strike, attempted to give coherence and leadership to the mass unity that had developed: rejecting any concessions that favored only some workers, it sought to become a union of all African workers. Its leader, Chege Kibachia, addressed weekly meetings of up to 2,000 people at Kiwanja cha Maskini and attempted to extend the movement beyond Mombasa (Cooper 1987, 78–88).

That was what frightened officials more than anything: the masses, led, might prove even more effective than they had without formal organization. But the repression of the AWF did not begin until its base was undercut. The usual poststrike tribunal and wage increases began at last to pay the costs of fostering a differentiated working class. The first installment applied only to 5,000 monthly workers—a point with which the AWF took issue—and the second, while it was broader, sought to separate out a corps of long-term workers by paying bonuses to workers with six months experience and higher wages to those with five years continuous service to one employer. The AWF seemed taken aback by the complex award and—sticking to its vision of a unified working class—failed to develop a coherent politics around the fact that the award was a material and symbolic victory for strikers. Attendance at its weekly meetings fell, and in August the state was ready to attack: Kibachia was arrested and deported to a part of Kenya where there was no working class to organize.[15]

There were, thus, two sides to the government's reaction to the challenge of Mombasa's workers, the repression of the AWF being only one. The other was to seek to fracture the urban mass that had made the general strike general and the AWF a mass organization: that meant restructuring the meaning of a working life. A differentiated working class could only exist if African workers were identified with particular occupations over their entire working lives; they could not move into and out of jobs that provided them with no security and no future. The two arguments came together in the contention of Kenya's Trade Union Advisor that, under Chege Kibachia's aegis, "You could be a baker, a tailor or a candle-stick maker, it didn't matter what your occupation was, if you wanted to join, The African Workers' Federation would only be too pleased to accept you."[16] Anything but an occupationally structured trade union was thus condemned. But it was precisely the fluid world of work as it actually existed that the AWF was trying to address. Casual labor—in Mombasa's most vital activity—was incompatible with officials' underlying concept of work.

Migrancy, Culture, and the Case for Restructuring Labor

The critique of casual labor in Mombasa, in fact, became the entering wedge for a wider critique of migrant labor. This discussion has been analyzed elsewhere (Cooper 1987, chap. 4), and can only be summarized here. The crux of the case against casual labor was that it precluded the socialization and acculturation of African workers—issues that were even more central than those of training and skill development. The urban masses were dangerous as well as inefficient, and if enough bad workers could not be safely packed into cities, the question of how to make good workers became acute. Casual workers, however, could not be disciplined by the "sanction of the sack," and they never stayed around long enough to be acculturated. Instead, they undermined, by their daily choice between toil and idleness, the lessons being taught the more stable elements of the city's working class. The arguments of officials were both reformist and authoritarian: a compact body of workers should be given the benefits of improved wages and better housing; they should be closely supervised, expected to provide high levels of output; and everyone else should be expelled from the city.

The argument soon became one about African culture: the reproduction of urban workers within the precapitalist economies of rural Africa was reproducing the wrong kind of African working class. The argument began with nutrition—inadequate food in childhood, a consequence of ignorance as much as poverty, ruined African workers for life. African women, above all, had to be taught modern ideas about food. The influential "African Labour Efficiency Survey" of 1947 extended the concern into a condemnation of African society in an industrial age: "He [the African worker] is ineffective in many industrial techniques by the very nature of his birth, his upbringing, and his native culture." The study expressed faith that a transformation could be effected, but it required a total remaking of culture. It thus implied the redefinition of time on and off the job: efficiency became a question of "how to influence the conduct and effort of men in respect of their life-at-work." Within the workplace, the idea of time discipline had to be taught.

The East African has not been bent under the discipline of organized work. In his primitive economy, the steady, continuous labor is carried out by women. . . . Though the tasks he performed were prescribed by tribal law and custom, he could do them in his own way and at his own speed, for to him time had no economic value. . . . To work steadily and continuously at the will and direction of another was one of the hard lessons he had to learn when he began to work for Europeans. (Northcott 1949, 7, 12–13, 15)

These arguments were debated by officials and settlers in the Legislative Council from the late 1940s to the mid-1950s. White farmers did not have much faith in the possibilities of lifetime socialization, and they did not want to pay the cost. Top officials, particularly in the Labour Department, remained convinced that productivity and order both demanded restructuring, but they were willing to focus their arguments where the risks of disorder seemed highest and the milieu the most demanding—urban and industrial labor. There, what was needed was an entirely new work ethic, and that implied the total separation of the African industrial worker from the milieu of his upbringing. As the Committee on African Wages argued in 1954, work discipline required such measures "as will induce the African to sever his ties with tribal life and virtually start afresh in a new environment.... We cannot *hope* to produce an effective African labour force until we have first removed the African from the enervating and retarding influence of his economic and cultural background" (Kenya 1954, 11, 16).

Dualism had come to the fore in colonial sociology: the interplay of urban and rural milieus intrinsic to casual and migratory labor had to give way to their stark separation in space and in the way time was used in each.

Such a separation would have its costs. The Secretary of State for the Colonies, Oliver Lyttleton, accepted the idea that wages had to cover the costs of bringing up new generations of workers in the city, and he rejected the old system of paying "bachelor" wages that forced the costs of reproducing the working class onto rural African societies. He insisted that "even where the 'bachelor' wage still represents the supply price of labour, it may be below the level of wages necessary to secure efficient production."[17] For this Conservative minister, even the dictates of the labor market had to give way before the imperious necessity of shaping and reproducing the right sort of African working class. Making the working day productive and safe required reshaping the working life.

The Decasualization of the Docks

Implementing such a program was a complex, contradictory, and conflictual process, involving not only an effort to separate the lives of urban workers from rural Africa but an attempt to build a differentiated working class within the city. At the most general level of government policy, the new policy was implemented by instituting an urban minimum wage for "adults" 1.67 times what became called the "youth" minimum wage—which was supposed to apply to new, presumably unmarried workers. The higher minimum wage, in officials' eyes, would embody the commitment to the reproduction of the working class.[18]

This was obviously not going very far. The key was how particular occupational structures were to be redefined, and the main test—like the most dramatic African challenge—was already underway in Mombasa. The decasualization of dock labor represents a remarkable case of a program of social engineering that was actually implemented. It transformed the way dockers worked, turning the working day into the working month, and—ultimately—into the working life. In transforming the meaning of work time for dockers, it transformed their relationship to other Africans involved in the complex interplay of Mombasa and its hinterland, of wage labor and farming, of dock work and other urban activities. A docker became a docker. And in so doing, dockers' life situation was slowly separated from that of the rest of the people of Mombasa, with whom they had recently made common cause. At the same time, the port companies remade the structure of supervision in the dockyards, undermining the role—and hence the power—of the labor gangs and the gang leaders, creating a pattern of top-down authority.

The first step was aimed, above all, at enabling officials to expel the idle from Mombasa. In 1944, dockers were made to register, with the idea that this would allow authorities to identify people whom it would not expel. In the event, authorities lacked the coercive capacity of their South African counterparts to keep expelled people from drifting back. And the registration scheme, at that stage, was not used to enforce a new pattern of work discipline on the dockers. Some 4,000 men were registered to insure that an average of 1,500 dockers would be available each day, and when port usage increased, so too did the pool—to over 6,500. Officials feared that too rigorous standards of performance would cause independent-minded dockers to abandon their trade altogether, so that dockers were only called on to work ten days per month in order to retain their registrations. Dockers native to the coastal region—the majority—were considered particularly prone to leave and were treated with particular diffidence: they could retain their registration even if they only worked five days per month.[19]

Steady work had never been a demand of the dockworkers; better pay for daily labor, the end of arbitrary discipline, and more recognition for long service within the framework of work routines are the demands that emerge from such sources as the testimony to the post-1947 tribunal. And officials saw even their tentative registration schemes faced with "stubborn resistance" from port workers.[20]

Meanwhile, however, the shorehandling firm increased its monthly employees from 970 to 1,212 between January and September, 1947. The stevedoring firms, however, responded to labor shortages by swelling the casual labor pool.

Finally, in the midst of a crisis over port congestion in 1952, the government Labour Department decided to act. The registration requirement was raised to fifteen shifts per month, then to twenty the next year. Between 1952 and 1954, officials forced unsteady workers off the list, despite a "spate of protests."[21] In 1954, the hiring of casual workers was centralized and the pool divided between stevedores and shorehandlers, each of whom was called on via a single queuing system. In 1957, dockers began to collect a small attendance bonus whenever they reported for work but found that none was available (Cooper 1987, chap. 4).

And so at last, the working behavior of dockworkers began to change, as table 1 reveals. By 1954, then, the large majority of "casual" dockworkers were putting in the characteristic work month of advanced capitalism. Those who did not were subject to deregistration, and by 1958, 99 percent of those still on the rolls were doing their twenty shifts. By then, many were doing more: some 40 percent of the stevedores and 35 percent of the shorehandlers worked over thirty shifts in the month of July, 1958.[22]

As casual labor became less casual, the companies dispensed more and more with the bother of the daily hiring process. Table 2 shows the shift from daily to monthly terms in the 1950s. Such workers were eligible for retirement gratuities based on seniority, and by the late 1950s the question of pension plans for regular workers was on the agenda of the Kenya government. The choice facing dockworkers, wherever they came

TABLE 1. Working Patterns of Casual Workers

Date	Days Worked per Month (in percentage)			
	Under 5	5–14	15–19	Over 20
September, 1946	24	34	17	25
September, 1947	40	27	13	20
September, 1954	27		3	70

Sources: Progress Report No. 2 on Phillips Report, ca. January, 1947, and Progress Report No. 3 on Phillips Report, incl. LO to LC 23 August, 1948, LAB 9/1838; Labour Department, Memorandum on Casual Labor Scheme, Mombasa, October, 1954, LAB 9/217.

TABLE 2. Casual and Monthly Dockworkers, as of December 31

	1953	1955	1957	1958	1959
Monthly	1,683	2,614	3,079	3,077	4,432
Casual	4,800	4,254	2,268	1,783	1,030

Source: Labour Department, Annual Report (1959), 11.

TABLE 3. Comparison of Lowest Wage Rates (in shillings)

	1938	1947	1958
Government and municipality (monthly)	16.00	40.00	87.00[a]
Railway (monthly)	20.00	35.50	87.00[a]
Shorehandlers (monthly)	40.00	54.50	152.25
Shorehandlers (daily)	1.50	2.75	7.20
Stevedores (daily)	2.00	3.25	7.60
Casual shorehandlers (monthly)[b]	18.00	38.50	156.20
Casual stevedores (monthly)[b]	24.00	45.50	167.20

Source: Mombasa Social Survey 1958, 274; the wages for casuals in 1947 have been revised because the survey used pre-Tribunal figures.

[a] Plus free housing (Sh 21); Sh 108 should be used for comparison with casual workers, who were not housed.

[b] Earnings for casual workers are based on 12 shifts per month in 1938, 14 shifts in 1947, and 22 shifts in 1958.

from and whatever they wanted, was between working regularly or not working at all.[23]

The port companies and the Labour Department had created a distinct corps of dockers; in theory, they were to be separated from other workers not only by strict work rules but by a distinct wage structure. For dockers, that objective was to a large extent met. In the city as a whole, however, the idea of a family wage sufficient to wean workers from the "enervating" influence of rural life was less clear. What stands out above all is the transition in dockers' position from the middle of a narrow wage hierarchy to the top of an expanded one. As table 3 suggests, they were pulling well ahead of other government and transport workers.

The new work rules in effect forced casual workers to earn more; their ability to trade money for time was taken away. Workers who chose to exceed the requirement could earn well above the standard for other manual workers: the 40 percent of stevedores who worked at least thirty shifts in 1958 would have earned over Sh 228. When Kenya became independent in 1963, the floor wage for dockworkers was Sh 254.13 per month and the average was Sh 350, three times the official minimum adult wage for Mombasa. At that time, 79 percent of agricultural workers were earning less than Sh 100.[24]

The point to be stressed is the growing differentiation of the African work force, not that dockers were privileged by any other standard, such as comparison with whites. In 1960, in fact, 99 percent of wage-earning whites in Kenya earned more than the average docker; about half the whites earned at least ten times as much.[25]

Improved wages went along with increased managerial control over workers' time. And they went along with tightening authority in the workplace itself. Centralized hiring of casual workers eliminated the basis for the work gangs' solidarity. After 1954, the gangs were constituted by management each day from workers taken on in the order in which they had queued up. The *serang* became a kind of low-grade foreman. With that, the internalized discipline of the gangs—who in several important operations had been paid collectively depending on their performance—gave way to top-down authority. Output thus depended on the capacity of supervisors to observe performance and use the "sanction of the sack." It was, on the face of it, a fundamental change in the nature of work discipline. Workers were not being paid for collective output, but for individual time, and the only sanctions supervisors had within the time block sold to management by the workers were negative ones, mainly the threat of firing.

But this was rarely carried out, probably because labor relations were strained enough owing to the changed structure of authority on the docks. A series of wildcat strikes between 1957 and 1959 broke out over such issues as abusive behavior by supervisors and revisions—without consultation—of the role of certain specialists. There was one last episode in the struggle over time. In 1959, two wildcat strikes took place just as management was about to install a system of clocking in: workers would have to have their cards punched by a machine to mark their times of arrival and exit. It was an issue of great symbolic importance—as it often was in Western societies. "If you as much as mention clocking in," commented one official, "everyone practically faints."[26] It was an issue, however, of far more concern to the rank and file than to leaders of the fledgling Dockworkers Union, who were apparently caught unaware by the strike and the sentiment behind it. The strike delayed the implementation of clocking in, but the union leaders did not take it up effectively, and management eventually got its way. By decade's end, management had obtained the control over time and over the labor process that it had sought. It was less sure that it was getting the performance out of workers that it had expected to be a consequence: measures of productivity were uncertain and officials were not sure that it had, in fact, increased (Kenya 1959; Cooper 1987, chap. 5).

But the state had succeeded in still another way—in demarcating a narrower terrain of contestation. The wildcat strikes, to be sure, were unexpected and undesired, and the Dockworkers Union, founded in 1954, slowly proved to be rather more effective than expected in setting forth wage claims, although it had a mixed record in coming to grips with the conflicts over the labor process that so upset the rank and file. But all these uncertainties were confined to the docks.

In 1955, before the union was effective, wage grievances in the docks had led to a strike that almost spilled into other industries, mainly in the port area of Mombasa. But the young trade unionist Tom Mboya had come to town from Nairobi. He chastened the workers—at a mass meeting that seemed to echo the style of the 1947 general strike—for striking without authorization from a union or following proper collective bargaining procedures. The crowd nearly roughed him up for his pains. But he was able to convey the sense of mass threat—which made a deep and personal impact on him—to the previously recalcitrant management side, and the dispute slowly entered the arena of bureaucratic structures and carefully prepared memoranda in which Mboya knew how to operate. Along the way, negotiations focused exclusively on dockworkers, leaving the other workers of Mombasa to fend for themselves.[27] The 30 percent raise Mboya eventually won convinced the dockworkers that his style of trade unionism had something to add to their own militant tradition, and, in its aftermath, Mboya helped to organize the Dockworkers Union on a more stable and effective basis. But the 1955 strike represented a critical transition: it came in the midst of a parting of the ways between dockers and the rest of the Mombasa working class, and the weight of the new definition of jobs, of the new wage structure, and of the new way of conducting collective bargaining proved too great for the older tradition of unity to triumph. The 1947 strike proved to be the last general strike in Mombasa's history.

The decasualization policy had been intended to decrease the circulation of workers into and out of jobs, and the rigid structures that kept dockers at work also made it increasingly difficult for new men to enter the docks. Kenya's labor force, in the late 1950s, was increasingly divided between those who had stable jobs and those who stood little chance of getting them. In one of the first official recognitions of the unemployment problem in Kenya, A. G. Dalgleish felt obliged to note that even if relatively high urban wages contributed to rising unemployment, they were aimed "very properly, to encourage the development of the family unit as an integral feature of stabilized African labor in urban areas."[28] The separation of a stable working class from the rest of Kenyan society was not an undesirable side effect of economic change, but its very purpose.

Anthropologist David Parkin, working among Giriama from coastal Kenya in the 1970s, found that men associate security and control over one's destiny with *kazi ya mwezi,* a permanent job, and look at *kazi ya barua* ('daily work') as uncertain. Parkin claims that "this folk distinction between preferences completely reverses the notion of many social scientists who see permanent monthly wage employment as leading to irreversible dependency and less control by the wage earner over his labour...." Parkin fails to note how recent this preference is: Giriama and other coastal peoples had, even as late as 1958, constituted 76 percent of the stevedores and 59 percent of the shorehandlers, and it was precisely these workers who had had to be pressured into working steadily (Parkin 1979, 234; Mombasa Social Survey 1958, 351).

If the evidence that the reformed authority structure of the Mombasa docks actually increased productivity was uncertain, at least the process gave officials—unsure of whether they really held the levers of power—the confidence that they had followed the best lessons of Western experience in developing the institutions required for modern industrial capitalism. In labeling daily workers "casual," employers and officials had given—without analyzing the labor process itself—a reason for anxiety and concern. By labeling another form of labor "stable," they gave themselves a reason for hope, without necessarily realizing at what social level the stability was manifest. Officials looked to the day when a working class would be self-reproducing, when new generations of workers would not experience the "backward" culture of rural Kenya.

There never was much hope or possibility that such policies would affect all Kenyans: even in theory, the entire agricultural sector was segregated from the stabilization policy of 1954. The application of time discipline and occupational discipline to the dockworkers and the limited array of workers like them meant that their life course would be separated from that of other Kenyans. Agricultural workers, especially those who had no access to land, often came to see the chance—however small—

of a regular, or even an irregular, urban job as more attractive than what their segment of the labor market had to offer them. If various social ties and economic activities crossed this divide, the segmentation of the labor market was nonetheless an important aspect of postindependence Kenya (House and Rempel 1976).

Dockers lived alongside other urbanites who had little chance of achieving their degree of job security, and, predictably, leaders of the Dockworkers Union began to be accused, in the early 1960s, of ethnic favoritism in deciding who was to have access to the now-valued jobs.[29] Access to housing similarly became a tense issue, and so did another consequence of unequal access to resources: urban criminality. All these tensions had their roots in the colonial state's efforts to resolve the tensions of an earlier era, when dockers moved into and out of their jobs and shared their residences and the experience of generalized poverty with the mass of city dwellers. The segmentation of labor was not a policy that independent Kenya, any more than the colonial regime, wanted to give up. The alternative of a mass labor force sharing its common misery had been tried before.

Dualism in Late Colonial Discourse

The triumph of time discipline took place through the narrowing of the arena that was being transformed. The very process of reasoning by which officials convinced themselves that an array of urban, industrial, and transportation occupations could be restructured also convinced officials that they could do so only by starkly separating the reformed milieu from the rest of Africa. The dualism of colonial industrial sociology in the mid-1950s was echoed in such fields as economics. In 1954, as Mombasa's casual labor pool was being reconstructed and as a government committee pondered how to separate African workers from their "enervating" cultural background, W. Arthur Lewis published his labor surplus theory of economic development. Lewis divided undeveloped countries into two sectors, a backward one where the marginal product of labor was zero and a modern one where labor was productive. He saw development in the movement of labor from the one to the other (Lewis 1954). Lewis's two-sector model was part of the increasingly salient and harsh division in social science and colonial policy between "traditional" and "modern." The traditional African no longer seemed a quaint, "natural" figure, whose conservatism could remain harmlessly compatible with colonial order but stood accused of being an obstacle to a progress along Western lines that now seemed attainable.

As the social engineers set forth their vision of a modern, acultural social order for Africa, a bitter conflict raged in upcountry Kenya, embracing rural areas and the seedy, desperate neighborhoods of Nairobi where "casualism" still reigned. In 1952, the Mau Mau Emergency was declared in central Kenya. Kenya's rulers—convinced they were bringing modern industrial relations, economic growth, and agricultural improvement to their colony—had no clear way of analyzing the grievances of people burdened by soil conservation programs or displaced from settler farms in the midst of rationalizing production. Nor did they understand the anger of squatters, expelled from white farms, who found in their areas of origin a class of accumulating Africans eager to shed their social obligations. The roots of the Mau Mau Emergency were complex, but the official interpretation was simpler: the Kikuyu people of central Kenya, unable to take the streams of social change, had fallen into an atavistic rebellion against progress. They had gone collectively mad, egging each other on with a "primitive" oath to tribal unity and terrorizing Europeans and Christian, progressive Kenyans.

The supposed savagery of Mau Mau rationalized the countersavagery of its repression. All the while, the firm program of rationalizing time and discipline in urban labor and bringing Africans into a modern system of industrial relations served as a vivid counterfoil for the British construction of Mau Mau as an atavistic revolt and for its brutal suppression.[30]

By the time the rebellion was over, the weight of direct British intervention and the burden of protecting white settlers had grown intolerable. The dualism of 1950s thinking on social—as well as political—questions in Africa was crucial in helping British officials convince themselves that they could, indeed, find modern African parliamentarians, modern Africans trade unionists, and modern African workers who could continue to promote progress, with its attendant linkages to Western society and the world economy, and who could take over the task of containing those Africans who had not yet made the transition.[31]

The docks of Mombasa became the harbingers of a world of work that was, in the late colonial and postcolonial years, increasingly regulated and rationalized, where unions bargained with managers, where hours and working conditions were kept within standards familiar to any European industrial sociologist. Outside of that world, the unreformed domain—where the labor regulations, organization charts, and time discipline of advanced capitalism did not rule—came eventually to be known as the "informal sector." There was nothing particularly new about what went on there: in the Victorian age it would have been called the "residuum" and in early twentieth-century Mombasa it was referred to as "casualism." Like indirect rule a half-century previously, the informal sector concept of the postcolonial era attached a neutral label to an unsubdued domain. Leaders of the fragile polities of African states saw the informal sector as both dangerous and useful; international agencies eventually came to see it as a locus of cheap, labor-intensive production that could animate African economies (International Labour Organization 1972).

What the promoters of informal economies did not understand, but which local officials could not ignore, was that production did not take place in a black box—with inputs going in and outputs emerging, at market prices—but as a social process. The informal sector was not particularly informal: social networks tied together owners, workers, and commercial partners. The social basis of production was more varied, more complex, more ramified than the direct relationship of buyers and sellers of labor power; the labor process generated relationships as well as commodities; and these relationships constituted both a reminder that the postcolonial city did not live up to the modernist fantasy and that the owners of capital and the rulers of the state did not control—or even understand—the web of connections among the urban population (Cooper 1983, 40–43).

The lessons of the late colonial era are important here: colonial officials, faced with the strike wave of 1939–47, did not move—for the second time in their short period of rule—to remake the organization of labor because that system had failed to get vital tasks done. They did not calculate, with any precision, the costs of casual versus monthly labor, and did not follow up the program of decasualization with attempts to measure changes in how efficiently cargo was handled. Time discipline was, in official eyes, a cultural and political concept: this was what modern capitalist organization was supposed to look like; this was the way in which managers could exercise control; this was the way in which a labor force could be made predictable, the way in which its behavior could be kept within familiar bounds. Casual labor—and the informal sector in another era—presented social, political, and ideological dangers as well as economic possibilities.

What is curious about the discourses of the late colonial and early independence era are their silences. The actual lives of African workers in Mombasa in the 1950s remained unexamined, just as the labeling of a dimension of the urban economy of Nairobi in the 1970s as "informal" obviated the need to probe what the relations of production actually were. The rationale behind stabilization implied that performance in the workplace was shaped by the way a working class was reproduced, by the milieu in which children and young men were socialized and accul-turated. Yet officials did not choose to examine that milieu, to study the social processes of work and reproduction. In the heat of the 1947 strike, a social survey of Mombasa had been proposed. It was not, in fact, performed until 1958, did not probe workers' family and community life in any depth, and was never published.[32] Perhaps colonial bureaucrats—challenged by workers, nationalists, and international opinion—needed their new vision of labor so much that they could not examine it too deeply. The imposed formal structure of work time itself stood for a reassertion of control over dock labor, and success could be claimed in those terms. The intimacies of the labor process—and its wider social and political nexus—were gingerly left unexamined.[33]

In the port of Mombasa, the colonization of time succeeded in a narrow social space, and, as it did, contributed to the development of a sociological and political language in which the African worker stood as a universal, cultureless being, separated from a dangerous, culturally specific milieu that surrounded the workplace. Such a vision, ultimately, proved incompatible with the concrete problems of exercising power over a colonized society, but its effect on the terms in which social policy and social change could be discussed in newly independent nations and in global organizations proved more lasting and more powerful.

NOTES

1. I have written elsewhere on each of the critical episodes in the Kenyan state's attempts to transform the nature of work, and this article brings them into a single framework (Cooper 1977, 1980, 1987). The following abbreviations are used in these notes: CP (Coast Province) and LAB (Labour), both from the Kenya National Archives, Nairobi, and CO (Colonial Office), from the Public Record Office, London.

2. Field work on this topic was conducted in Mombasa and Malindi in 1972–73. There is also written evidence from European visitors in the 1870s and 1890s

to confirm the existence of the gang system and the pattern of cultivating fixed areas each day. See Cooper 1977, 170–71.

3. This was typical of Africa's large-scale slave establishments, where rulers were rarely confident of their ability to cope with a rigidly defined slave class. See Meillassoux 1986.

4. W. E. Taylor to Henry Binns, July 26, 1895, Parliamentary Papers 1896, 59:395, p. 18; Piggott to Hardinge, August 1, 1895, Foreign Office Confidential Prints 6761, 262.

5. District and Consular Report on Pemba (1900), 12.

6. Belfield to Harcourt, May 4, 1914, CO 533/136.

7. Hardinge to Salisbury, January 16, 1898, Foreign Office Confidential Prints 7024, 122.

8. Captain O. F. Watkins, Carrier Section, to General Staff Officer, December 21, 1915, CP 38/603.

9. See the extensive correspondence from 1916 to 1919 in CP 38/603 and CP 38/611.

10. *Mombasa Times,* January 29, 1930; Mombasa District, *Annual Report* (1927, 1929).

11. East Africa Commission 1925, 37.

12. See especially Inspector of Police to Asst. Supt. of Police, July 10, 1934; District Commissioner, Mombasa, Memorandum on Port Strike, July 5–7, 1934, LAB 5/25. On Beni, see Ranger 1975.

13. Principal Labour Officer to Chief Secretary, August 9, 1939, LAB 9/1835; District Officer to Commission of Enquiry, September 19, 1939, in Kenya 1939, 74.

14. Frederick Pedler, Minute, August 18, 1939, CO 533/513/38397/2; Malcolm MacDonald to Governor of Kenya, November 18, 1939, CO 533/513/38397/2.

15. A particularly valuable document on the history of the AWF is the transcript of the deportation hearing, found in CO 537/2109.

16. James Patrick, "Memorandum on Trade Unions—Development and Policy—Kenya," n.d. [1949], Fabian Colonial Bureau Papers, 118/1, 5, Rhodes House, Oxford University.

17. Oliver Lyttleton, Circular Letter, June 2, 1954, EST 26/26/1, copy in Railway Archives, Nairobi.

18. Legislative Council Debates 63 (December 16–17, 1954), cc. 1207–1355.

19. "Casual Labour, Mombasa," incl. LO to LC, February 27, 1946, LAB 9/1053.

20. Progress Report No. 3 on Phillips Report, August 23, 1948, LAB 9/1838; Senior Labour Officer, Coast, to Labour Commissioner, October 26, 1950, LAB 9/221. See also the testimony of various workers to the poststrike tribunal in LAB 5/28 and LAB 5/29.

21. Minutes of Meeting of Management Committee of Port Casual Labour Scheme, January 25, 1954, LAB 9/220.

22. Mombasa Social Survey 1958.

23. Coastal people in 1958 made up 76 percent of the casual stevedore pool and 59 percent of the casual shorehandlers (Mombasa Social Survey 1958, 351).

24. Labour Department, *Annual Report* (1963); Kenya 1971, 33.

25. Kenya 1961, 17.

26. *East African Standard,* September 16, 1959. See also *East African Standard,* January 20 and 21, 1959, and Deputy Labour Commissioner, Note on stoppage of work, January 20, 1959, LAB 10/345.

27. A blow-by-blow account is found in the 1955 strike file, Railway Archives, Nairobi. Mboya's own reactions are described in his report to his Federation (reprinted in Singh 1980, 140, 154–59) and his autobiography (Mboya 1963, 33).

28. Dalgleish 1960, 6–8, 20–22.

29. Dennis Akumu, leader of the Dockworkers Union from 1958 to 1965, was accused of getting jobs for people from his own ethnic group (the Luo, of western Kenya) and discriminating against coastal people. Akumu had, in fact, gone to some trouble to diversify the leadership of the union. But the accusation was virtually inevitable, given the all-or-nothing quality that the few thousand jobs in the docks had acquired (Sandbrook 1975, 116–17, 135–36; Stren 1978, 79–87).

30. The modernizing fantasy for Kenya was spelled out at considerable length and in regard to many dimensions of social policy—from urban housing to agrarian class structure—in the Report of the East Africa Royal Commission (London, 1955), written even as the rebels were being processed through concentration camps and "cured" of their madness. The official version of Mau Mau as "anti-modern," it must be said, was self-serving but not entirely wrong: Mau Mau ideology opposed a radical particularism—with its mythic appeals to the Kikuyu past—against the claim that the squatters' disenfranchisement was a necessary part of the universal drive to human progress. The clash of discourses and some recent interpretations of Mau Mau are analyzed in Cooper 1988.

31. This issue will be taken up in my forthcoming study, tentatively entitled "Decolonization and African Society: The Labor Question in French and British Africa, 1935-1960."

32. Mombasa Social Survey 1958. Even in the important laboratory where African urban anthropology was developed, the Central African Copperbelt, serious research in mining communities only began around 1950, by which time the decisions regarding stabilization had already been made and officials had become comfortable with their postwar vision of labor reform. The early

efforts of Copperbelt anthropologists to study mine towns were blocked by the mining companies (Brown 1979).

33. There were investigations into the quality of supervision and such questions (Kenya 1959), but little curiosity from the management point of view about what is now called the politics of production (Burawoy 1985).

BIBLIOGRAPHY

Atkins, Keletso. 1988. "'Kafir Time': Preindustrial Temporal Concepts and Labour Discipline in Nineteenth Century Colonial Natal." *Journal of African History* 29:229–44.

Brantley, Cynthia. 1981. *The Giriama and Colonial Resistance in Kenya.* Berkeley: University of California Press.

Burawoy, Michael. 1985. *The Politics of Production.* London: Verso.

Brown, Richard. 1979. "Passages in the Life of a White Anthropologist: Max Gluckman in Northern Rhodesia." *Journal of African History* 20:525–41.

Cooper, Frederick. 1977. *Plantation Slavery on the East Coast of Africa.* New Haven: Yale University Press.

———. 1980. *From Slaves to Squatters: Plantation Labor and Agriculture in Zanzibar and Coastal Kenya, 1890–1925.* New Haven: Yale University Press.

———. 1981. "Islam and Cultural Hegemony: The Ideology of Slaveowners on the East African Coast." In *The Ideology of Slavery in Africa,* ed. Paul E. Lovejoy, 271–308. Beverly Hills: Sage.

———. 1983. "Urban Space, Industrial Time, and Wage Labor in Africa." In *Struggle for the City: Migrant Labor, Capital, and the State in Urban Africa,* ed. Frederick Cooper, 7–50. Beverly Hills: Sage.

———. 1987. *On the African Waterfront: Urban Disorder and the Transformation of Work in Colonial Mombasa.* New Haven: Yale University Press.

———. 1988. "Mau Mau and the Discourses of Decolonization." *Journal of African History* 29:313–20.

———. 1989. "From Free Labor to Family Allowances: Labor and African Society in Colonial Discourse." *American Ethnologist* 16:745–65.

Dalgleish, A.G. 1960. *Survey of Unemployment.* Nairobi: Government Printer.

East Africa Commission. 1925. *Report.* London: Government Printer.

House, William, and Henry Rempel. 1976. "Labour Market Segmentation in Kenya." *East African Economic Review* 8:35–54.

International Labour Organization. 1972. *Employment, Incomes, and Equality.* Geneva: International Labour Organization.

Kenya. 1939. "Report of the Commission of Inquiry Appointed to Examine the Labour Conditions in Mombasa." Nairobi: Government Printer.

———. 1945. "Report of the Committee of Inquiry into Labour Unrest at Mombasa." Nairobi: Government Printer.

————. 1954. "Report of the Committee on African Wages." Nairobi: Government Printer.

————. 1959. "Report of a Board of Inquiry Appointed to Inquire into Employment in the Port of Mombasa." Nairobi: Government Printer.

————. 1961. *Reported Employment and Wages in Kenya, 1946–1960.* Nairobi: Government Printer.

————. 1971. Employment and Earnings, 1963, 1967. Nairobi: Government Printer.

Lennihan, Louise, 1982. "Rights in Men and Rights in Land: Slavery, Labor, and Smallholder Agriculture in Northern Nigeria." *Slavery and Abolition* 3:111–39.

Lewis, W. Arthur. 1954. "Economic Development with Unlimited Supplies of Labour." *The Manchester School* 22:139–91.

Livingstone, David. 1865. *Narrative of an Expedition to the Zambesi and Its Tributaries.* London: Murray.

Lugard, Frederick. 1922. *The Dual Mandate in British Tropical Africa.* London: Blackwood.

Meillassoux, Claude. 1975. *Femmes, greniers et capitaux.* Paris: Maspero.

————. 1986. *L'Anthropologie de l'esclavage: le ventre de fer et d'argent.* Paris: PUF.

Mboya, Tom. 1963. *Freedom and After.* Boston: Little, Brown.

Mombasa Social Survey. 1958. Mimeograph.

Northcott, C. H. 1949. *African Labour Efficiency Survey.* Colonial Research Publications, no. 3. London: HMS0.

Parkin, David. 1979. "The Categorization of Work: Cases from Coastal Kenya." *Social Anthropology of Work,* ed. Sandra Wallman, 317–36. London: Academic Press.

Patterson, Orlando. 1982. *Slavery and Social Death.* Cambridge, Mass.: Harvard University Press.

Phillips, Anne. 1989. *The Enigma of Colonialism: British Policy in West Africa.* Bloomington: Indiana University Press.

Ranger, Terence. 1975. *Dance and Society in Eastern Africa, 1890–1970: The Beni Ngoma.* Berkeley: University of California Press.

Sandbrook, Richard. 1975. *Proletarians and African Capitalism: The Kenyan Case, 1960–1972.* Cambridge: Cambridge University Press.

Sheriff, Abdul. 1987. *Slaves, Spices and Ivory in Zanzibar: Integration of an East African Commercial Empire into the World Economy, 1770–1873.* London: Jane Currey.

Singh, Makhan. 1980. *1952–56: Crucial Years of Kenya Trade Unions.* Nairobi: Uzima.

Stedman Jones, Gareth. 1971. *Outcast London.* Oxford: Oxford University Press.

Stren, Richard. 1978. *Housing the Urban Poor in Africa: Policy, Politics, and Bureaucracy in Mombasa.* Berkeley: Center for International Studies.

Thompson, E. P. 1967. "Time, Work Discipline, and Industrial Capitalism." *Past and Present* 38:56–97.

Whipp, Richard. 1987. "'A Time to Every Purpose': An Essay on Time and Work." In *The Historical Meanings of Work,* ed. Patrick Joyce, 210–36. Cambridge: Cambridge University Press.

India's Development Regime

David Ludden

Economic development appears to be a process of quantitative growth and structural change that, like growth and differentiation among cells, occurs in the object world, independent of the numbers that measure it and the conditions that affect it. Economic measurements enable analysts to test the impact of variables on economies; thus, the impact of state policies can be assigned causal influence on economic development. The success of policies in promoting development can be gauged and steps prescribed to promote economic growth, as a biologist or doctor might prescribe a regimen to enhance the health and maturation of cells or people.

Development discourse sustains analogies like these because it relies on organic imagery and science. Like science, it is implicated in histories of power that make the modern world (Adas 1989; Foucault 1973 and 1979; Headrick 1988; Noble 1991). "Underdeveloped" and "developing" imply immaturity and unrealized potential; development discourse is replete with the assumption that the realization of potential lies in mature capitalism. For example, in *The International Encyclopedia of the Social Sciences,* scholars make this assumption a definition and construct history accordingly.

> As a distinctive epoch in economic organization, modern economic growth, or development, dates from the eighteenth century, when its beginnings in Western Europe can be clearly discerned. It may be defined as a rapid and sustained rise in real output per head and attendant shifts in the technological, economic, and demographic characteristics of a society. (Easterlin 1968, 395)

Imperial politicians project power from the heights of capitalist maturity and routinely speak as adults talking about children, in the rhetoric of national superiority, responsibility, philanthropy, and self-defense, none better than Harry Truman in his 1949 inaugural address, which put world development on America's agenda.

> . . . we must embark on a bold new program for making the benefits of our scientific advances and industrial progress available for the improvement and growth of underdeveloped areas.
>
> More than half of the people in the world are living in conditions approaching misery. Their food is inadequate. They are victims of disease. Their economic life is primitive and stagnant. Their poverty is a handicap and a threat both to them and to more prosperous areas. . . .
>
> I believe we should make available to peace-loving peoples the benefits of our store of technical knowledge in order to help them realize their aspirations for a better life. And, in cooperation with other nations, we should foster capital investment in areas needing development. (Quoted in Nieuwenhuijze 1969, 15)

In this way, the language of history and politics defines the world by development, its absence, and its spread from the West. Europe is its birthplace; capitalist expansion, its vehicle; a scenario embedded in theories and narratives of world history from Hegel, Marx, and Weber to Toynbee, McNeill, and Wallerstein.

On this intellectual terrain, a venerable opposition accepts that Europe spawned capitalism and development but inverts the assessment of Europe's impact on the Third World. Against the imagery of global progress fathered by capitalist modernity arise counterimages of dependency, exploitation, immiseration, and backwardness forced on the Third World by capitalist imperialism. Even early efforts to measure Europe's impact on world development (such as Mulhall 1880) confronted work that demonstrated Europe's toxic powers, such as that by Dadabhai Naoroji (Chandra 1966, 1–55), work that now forms an oppositional genre endowed with classics like Walter Rodney's *How Europe Underdeveloped Africa*. Theorized into world history (Amin 1974; Castro 1984; Gunder-Frank 1969; Nkrumah 1965; Sau 1978; Stavrianos 1981), this genre informs debate on the new international economic order and on Third World history (Ludden 1990; Washbrook 1990).

Such opposition divides a world of images and counterimages; it marks a cultural boundary within a world development regime with many borders and many actors—from banks, multinationals, governments, and international bodies, to parties, scientists, publicists, think tanks, disciplines, lobbies, and rebels—that constitutes development discourse today. This world regime is a legacy of colonialism and, with the decline of the Second World of socialist powers, appears clearly as a reincarnation of the nineteenth-century regime composed of capitalist empires and colonial domains. That such a continuity unifies an epoch so ruptured by war, revolution, and nationalist victories suggests that historians should look long and hard for solid substrata on which ephemeral landscapes are built and for logics that create order across epochs fractured by upheaval.

Scholars tend to follow history across fractures marked by the end of colonial rule either in forms of material power or of cultural representations, as do Joe Stork and Edward Said in their respective treatments of oil and orientalism in the Middle East (Said 1978; Stork 1976). Though the history of India is being divided on such lines (Narayanan 1988; O'Hanlon and Washbrook 1991; Prakash 1990b), there have been efforts to combine these approaches theoretically (Perlin 1988) and in studies of institutions sustained by material and cultural forces that persist across the colonial divide (Pandey 1990; Prakash 1990a; Washbrook 1989). In this latter vein, I consider here an institutional complex—a development regime—created by colonial capitalism and by bourgeois nationalism as a vital force in the cultural and material life of India. This article is the first step in a long research enterprise. It seeks to delineate the broad outlines of trends and transitions that have produced the institutional environment within which people in India make their living, particularly people who work the land. Its analytical framework is suggested by a proclamation made by Max Weber at one of his more polemical moments, in his inaugural lecture at Freiburg, in May, 1895.

Processes of economic development are in the final analysis also *power struggles,* and the ultimate and decisive interests at whose service economic policy must place itself are the interests of national *power,* where these interests are in question. (Weber 1980, 438; italics in original)

Development Regimes

India's national planning apparatus did not exist in colonial times. The Planning Commission and its constellation of scholars, politicans, and administrators face conditions unique to the years after 1947, before which India was a different territory with different endowments, part of an empire managed for Britain's national interest. Independence brought new possibilities and partition's disruption, added to a universal franchise and popular expectations attending independence, put pressures on the government that were unknown before 1947. In 1950, the Planning Commission assumed intellectual responsibility for a mixed economy conceived by Indian nationalists for India's national interest. Independence drastically changed the conduct and meaning of Indian development, altered India's place in the world economy, put elections and planning into the tangle of representative politics, and tied the state to the domestic economy more tightly than ever before. Within twenty years, India had undergone its own industrial revolution and had become a manufacturing giant (Thorner 1970).

Even so, material conditions that planners face even today describe massive continuities across this century: the calculus of poverty was not changed substantially by independence, the economy remains dominated by agriculture and small-scale enterprise, land scarcity and rapid population growth amid slow increases in nonagricultural employment and income define a geological stratum underlying change since 1947. In material terms, change wrought by planned development has occurred inside substantial long-term continuity (Das 1987; Ranade 1982, Preface; Rudolph and Rudolph 1987, 10; Tomlinson 1988, 126).

Discourse on India's economic development shows a continuity that reaches far back into colonial times. It is dominated by debate over the impact of state policy (as measured statistically by experts who control data) and theories admissable in such debates. Experts and expertise judge governments and policies; they express their political commitments through arguments about the best route toward progressive futures. Since 1970, debates have emerged in India much like those that raged in 1820, 1850, and 1870, and pitted nationalists against imperialism and its intellectual allies from the 1870s to the 1960s. "Establishment" experts highlight progress, explain it by policy success, and explain shortfalls by reference to problems outside state control. A "loyal opposition" blames policy and implementation for economic shortfalls yet stresses the viability of the system within which development is pursued. A "radical opposition" attributes economic failure, measured by data showing negligible or negative progress, to the nature of the system itself (Charlesworth 1982; Jha 1980; Lal 1988; Tomlinson 1988).

Unities in development discourse arise from stability in policy debates amid slow change in material conditions. But, as Weber argued, development discourse is also constituted by national power, whose stabilizing influence becomes more striking the closer we look, when we see that development science and politics dissolve into one another. On the surface, disinterested sciences seem to create development data, debate, research, and policy. But sciences do not talk about the impact of variables on development from a position outside power struggles. They talk inside an empirical and analytic environment created by states. Development data derive from the state. Better data means more state power. Whether it be reliable revenue data in the early nineteenth century, modern statistics after 1870, or the more detailed data that allowed sectoral input-output formulas to multiply from ten to forty between India's first and seventh five-year plans, enhanced state power over data, arising from more comprehensive state surveillance and cognitive manipulation of human activity, generates the substance of development discourse. Reliable data depends on labor discipline and supervision; ideal data would require power to observe and measure "down to the finest grain of the social body" (Foucault 1973, 57). Development discourse depends, in addition, on the premise that states exert directive power in human affairs; how to exert that power is what debates are about. Expertise thus stands outside its subject matter—the economy, society, or nation—by virtue of its ability to observe objects of analysis within the ambience of the state's measuring, managing, and manipulating apparatus, a cultural offspring of its power.

Many modern states and governments have grounded their legitimacy, in significant measure, on their ability to effect development. In India, from the start of colonialism, a development discourse has informed policy debate and provided a language of legitimacy for the state. The British Empire, as much as Indian nationalists and postcolonial states, pursued a development mission that imperialism posed as philanthropy and "moral and material progress," much like Harry Truman (Adas 1989; Halstead 1983). Since the early nineteenth century, the terms that have defined progress, participants in policy debate, and the audiences that have shaped debate have changed dramatically. But they share cognitive terrain that has remained remarkably stable. Its major landmarks include (1) ruling powers that claim progress as a goal, (2) a "people" whose condition must be improved, (3) an ideology of science that controls principles and techniques to effect and measure progress, and (4) self-declared, enlightened leaders who would use state power for development and compete for power with claims of their ability to effect progress. These are components of political rhetoric and development sciences that collapse into one another within a modern cultural formation that pervades colonialism and nationalism alike.

From this perspective, technical talk about economic growth, development, and planning is not so much about science and progress as about power, specifically state power in a development regime. A development regime is an institutionalized configuration of power within a state system ideologically committed to progress that draws its material sustenance from the conduct of development. In such regimes, the language of science represents development as a process occurring in the object world, outside the state and its constellation of experts and expertise. Science informs policy, but instrumental functions of science for any one regime are less essential than its constitutive force in all regimes of this kind. For all such regimes rest on the assertion that something "out there" is being developed by powers detached, standing above, outside, looking down through the eyes of science. The ideology of science serves this type of regime by cognitive concealment, hiding its institutional character and interests, its stake in development, and its power to invent development in its own terms. The character of a regime disappears in language that constructs the regime as an embodiment and instrument of progress. The "economy" and "living conditions" disappear as abstractions substantiated by regimes themselves, to reappear as real objects to be rationally manipulated for their own good, for growth and improvement. Development disappears as a system of power and appears, instead, to be a concatenation of variables in the object world.

The development regime is a child of capitalist empire. Early capitalism compelled productivity-enhancing investment as no mode of production had before (Brenner 1986). It provided an ideology of progress and scientific measurement in which the state became an enlightened representative of progressive forces and morally responsible for their propagation. Empire provided an "other" of development, its object world. When capitalist states acquired new territory, they exerted power in the name of progress. Underproductive resources had to be developed. Past systems of resource control had to be denigrated, dismantled, and replaced by rational policy and social order designed by enlightened rulers to benefit people victimized by their past. In the age of revolution—the half-century after 1770—one such regime evolved in India, a contemporary of those in Europe and the United States.

Subordination and Rationality

Colonialism construed India as an "other" on the frontier of European expansion. But classes that emerged in India over centuries of commercialization and state formation before 1800 formed the basis of India's development regime. A compulsive record keeping that is characteristic of such regimes produced a paper trail wherein we see that many preconditions for the regime were in place when the East India Company's military expansion began. Pervasive commercialism allowed an infinite number of objects to be assigned market values. States were sustained by the appropriation and increase of exchange values. Competing rulers stiffened and deepened powers to appropriate revenue amid early-modern military competition. Popular prosperity was measurable and seen as the responsibility of rulers whose power did not arise from natural affinites to "the people," rulers who could be judged accordingly, and to whom loyalty could be assigned costs and benefits. In the commercialized polities of eighteenth-century India, a huge number of specialists measured, computed, commuted, and recorded the rules and values that made states and markets work. These specialists provided the information base of the colonial state (Bayly 1983; Frykenberg 1965; Ludden 1988; Perlin 1977; Raychaudhuri and Habib 1982; Stein 1989; Subrahmanyam 1990).

The English East India Company competed in India's eighteenth-century state system, acquired state power in Bengal in 1757, and, after 1784, accelerated its military expansion and administrative centralization. War and rationalization went hand in hand. Military victory depended on data about enemy assets and capabilities, terrain, supply lines, and the potential profits of conquest. The fruits of victory had to be assessed, collected, and commuted for the company's far-flung transactions. Accurate observation, measures, assessment, communication, and computation were means and ends of victory; their reliability required a disciplining of labor within power relations more military than commercial. Putting this system of power in place was the work of men who subordinated Indians to Europeans and trade to governance, men who disciplined colonial knowledge.

In this transformation of power over knowledge, India's development regime was born. Government imagined itself rationality and progress. Disorder "out there" in the world of Indian politics and tradition became an "other" to be vanquished by conquest and by analyzing India empirically to bring it into the history of the new regime, to transform it for the good of people victimized by their past. The company's opposition, the old regime, was India "from time immemorial." The progressive order of company Raj was to be India's future. Progress meant standardization and centralization; efficiency required a chain of command to subordinate knowledge about India to scientific intellect. After 1790, under Cornwallis, new attention was especially paid to native intermediaries in the information system who stood between the Court of Directors and its Indian subjects (Stein 1989). To subordinate these native intermediaries required Europeans to appropriate knowledge locked in the minds of Indian commercial, judicial, military, and revenue specialists. By doing so, Europeans converted Indian knowledge into English language forms that were systematic, scientific, and accessible to the kind of truth testing that was becoming the pride of Europe (Adas 1989). Centralization also required data to be created by government that had never been produced by Indian rulers; such data constituted new kinds of facts for a new kind of regime. India was thus reorganized politically and empirically, and the two reorganizations sustained one another.

Company men on the colonial frontier made it happen. James Rennell was surveying harbors for the Royal Navy when the company hired him to survey routes from Calcutta to the Bay of Bengal in 1763. He became Surveyor General of Bengal the very next year. When he left India, in 1777, he put India on the map in his *Map of Hindoostan,* whose accompanying *Memoir* was not superseded as a compendium of geographical data for decades, though Rennell stopped revising it in 1793, because, as he says in the preface, data was accumulating too fast with the expansion of company power. In the preface he also relates that the market for his *Memoir* came from English curiosity about company wars. That progress in geography rested on British arms is also illustrated by the lithograph adorning his *Map,* which shows surveying and mapmaking tools on the ground and European civilians in the shadow of Britannia, as she receives texts, one labeled "Shastas" (Shastras), Hindu law books. The lithograph is homage to Britannia's power to gather knowledge for European science and commerce, yet also shows that Indians (particularly Brahmans) possessed knowledge that Europeans needed. With each company victory, however, more Britons surveyed the interior. Scientific measurement displaced native accounts. In 1808, Rennell looked back to the 1770s and told a gathering of surveyors, "At that day we were compelled to receive information from others respecting the interior of the country, but in your time you *explored* for *yourselves*" (Phillimore 1954–56, frontispiece; italics in original).

Colin Mackenzie, Francis Buchanan, and Benjamin Heyne explored for themselves. Mackenzie's orders of 1799 demand "a statistical account of the whole country" of Mysore. Land revenue was central, but data were now needed for a wide range of purposes. Wellesley needed empirical ammunition to fight his critics and Buchanan provided plenty in reports of oppressions by Tipu Sultan. Buchanan's orders in 1800 direct his attention to living conditions and the impact of state policy; by measuring the negative impact of Tipu's reign, Buchanan helped justify company expansion (Vicziany 1986). Heyne—a botanist like Buchanan—was ordered to collect useful plants for study and propagation in a proposed botanical garden. He was also to attend to vegetables, their soils, means of cultivation, and potential use as food for the poor. Horses and cattle merit special attention, with means to improve and propagate breeds. He was also to judge if land tenures, farming techniques, and machineries for cultivation and irrigation he observed might be used elsewhere (Buchanan 1870, 1956).

These surveyors explored "for themselves," but worked under military orders and depended on locals. Their reports inhabit the space between science and lore: contrary to orders, they digress constantly into local curiosities that were thrust into their work by local specialists who captured their imagination and regulated access to information. Mackenzie compiled a vast collection of native lore (Mahalingam 1972) that was largely unauthorized (Dirks, personal communication). The others were not committed to local knowledge as such, they simply relied on locals and reported accordingly. Their motley reports jumble varieties of data together that would soon be segregated by the system of colonial knowledge, a jumble that reflects the character of local expertise (Ludden forthcoming a). Heyne's 1802 report takes a step toward systematizing by being organized in response to queries on thirty-one topics that include thermometer and barometer readings, thunder, prevailing winds, earthquakes, rainfall, soils, topography, minerals, implements, coins, weights and measures, trade, production, shares of produce allowed to farmers, modes of farming, prices, dress, and languages (Heyne 1814). Movement toward systematic classification is visible in all the early survey documents. But early surveyors cooked their reports with one part scientific discipline, one part military discipline, and eight parts local wisdom, to produce an Anglo-Indian creole form of colonial knowledge that would survive for about twenty years. They explored India under company arms and orders, and they subordinated locals to the status of informants; yet their texts indicate that the knowledge the company Raj most needed still lay substantially outside its command.

Thomas Munro and William Jones brought power over knowledge more firmly into European hands. Cornwallis appointed Munro to assist another soldier, Alexander Read, in administering territory ceded by Tipu Sultan in 1792. Appointing military men to such civilian posts was part of his strategy to discipline company administration (Stokes 1980) and subordinate native intermediaries, a job he felt Madras civilians could not do, because they had "allow[ed] . . . management . . . to fall into the hands of *dubashes* [native agents] . . . calculated for being the most cruel instruments of rapine and extortion" (Stein 1989, 38). Munro proceeded to advance his career—until he died while serving as Governor of Madras in 1826—by applying the "political principle of destroying any and all intermediary authority between the company and the cultivator as the best assurance of the securing of control by the company over its new dominions." He sought "nothing less than the completion, by administrative means, of . . . military conquest . . . " (Stein 1989, 59–60). Thus, the *Ryotwari* System was born. In Bengal, Indian civil law had similar origins. In 1784, soon after his arrival as a judge in Calcutta, William Jones wrote to Warren Hastings, "I can no longer bear to be at the mercy of our Pundits, who deal out Hindu law as they please . . . " (Mukherjee 1968, 118). As a remedy, he proposed to Cornwallis (who once wrote, "Every native of Hindustan, I verily believe, is corrupt" [Spear 1979, 88]) that he be commissioned to compile a "Digest of Hindu and Mohammadan laws." He argued that "if we give judgment only from the opinions of native lawyers . . . we can never be sure, that we have not been deceived by them." But "if we had a complete digest of Hindu and Mohammadan laws . . . we . . . should never perhaps, be led astray by the Pandits or Maulavi's [*sic*] . . . " (Cannon 1970, 2:795). His proposal was accepted and Jones pursued "his greatest desire," to be "the legislator of the Indians" (Mukherjee 1968, 112).

By 1820, Jones, Munro, and their colleagues had reversed the power-knowledge relationship etched in Rennell's lithograph. They founded a regimen that put the power to measure justice and material resources increasingly in the hands of the state. Regimentation began with war and proceeded, as Europeans learned Indian languages and Indians learned English, to appropriate local expertise and standardize knowledge in the statistical ledgers of revenue settlements and codifications of law. Munro and Jones were among the men who fathered disciplines that have increased cognitive control of India ever since—systems of administration, law, statistics, ethnography, history, archaeology, moral debate, and description (as in gazetteers)—based on principles of standardized definition, measurement, and order, guided by rules of state. At one level, this disciplining of knowledge was colonial, in that it put British officers in control. But colonial knowledge also formed a regimen of cognition, collection, and transmission of facts that universalized as it concealed state power. Control of the state would be contested and change hands, but its regimentation of knowledge became permanent (Ludden forthcoming b).

State and Economy

India's development regime evolved in stages measured by the growing state power to standardize, unify, classify, count, list, compare, and compute systematically. Colonial empiricism entailed a discipline of numbers that rationalized India with statistics. For this, monetary trends are basic. In 1800, hundreds of coins of many metals and provenance, as well as perishable media such as cowry shells, circulated in India (Perlin 1987). Local combinations of coins and the local influence of natural events such as drought and human events such as war complicated evaluations and commutations in a context where calculations of value were linked inextricably to local measures of weight, volume, distance, and area. This kept thousands of specialists at work whose expertise had to be local. Localized conjunctures conditioned all transactions and all forms of knowledge. Money transactions were pervasive and widespread but embedded in local legal practice, social custom, and tax routines. Highly context-sensitive transactions were difficult to manipulate from afar, impossible to render systematic. The standardization of measures in the nineteenth century integrated localities into a transactional system that constituted India as a cognitive terrain for development.

Subordinating India to the silver rupee lowered transaction costs. It eliminated money changers and their expertise and created a more simplified, centralized monetary system as the state accumulated wealth and knowledge, becoming the most powerful actor in the transactional system. The standard measure of value in a single currency proceeded with standard measures of area, weight, volume, and distance applied in the marketplace, tax records, surveys, and land records in contracts—indeed, in all types of transactions. As a whole, the process describes a transformation of knowledge and power throughout social life—in private calculations of dowry and in public court disputes, in secret bazaar deals and great debates on the morality of government. By 1900, all transactions involving measurement were linked together by a language of standards spoken everywhere in the Indian transactional system. In the short run, as the rupee conquered the monetary system, its power, combined with silver exports to pay company debts, drove down prices and added discomfort to the disruptions of company military conquest. By the 1850s, these effects were reversed. But the integration by standard measure of India's transactional system—which implicated trade, religion, language, and law, as much as politics—was not reversible. It became an institutional regimen of numbers born under colonialism but not of it. The erasure of localism as the definitive feature of India's transactional environment was irreversible; it produced the cultural possibility of talking about India in the language of systems, and the cultural reality of India as a systemic unity.

The colonial regime thus reconfigured India within an empirical regimentation of measurement that was not itself essentially colonial. Extractive by intent and effect, colonialism discriminated left and right and made shifting alliances to sustain its control. Yet, as a whole, the transformation of transactions propelled by the colonial state steadily, massively, and permanently increased the importance of the state, commercial exchange, money, and people who accumulated exchange values. The expansion of money-measured transactions and the scope of commercial exchange pushed only in one direction; it steadily increased the capacity of bureaucrats, policymakers, politicians, reformers, and experts to capture and manipulate that central cognitive invention of capitalism, "the economy." An Indian national economy thus emerged in the nineteenth century as a bounded and coherent entity within a global capitalist system dominated by the British Empire.

Inside the Empire, India's national economy acquired a life of its own, whose improvement became a preoccupation of policymakers by 1820, when James Mill and Ram Mohan Roy equally indicate the emergence of

India as a unified object of reformist thought (Majeed 1990; Sarkar 1965). The measurements of progress were those of capitalism, articulations of the state and the market. This articulation sustained a discourse of economic policy formation that became so conventionalized as to itself constitute an institutional component of India's development regime. From Edmund Burke to Dadabhai Naoroji, Romesh Chandra Dutt and beyond, policy critics enshrined the state and the market in their discourse by focusing on taxation, tax expenditures, and state policies affecting capital accumulation. From Cornwallis through a hundred years of Indian National Congress policy declarations (Cotton 1968; Mill 1818; Ranade 1982; Stein 1989; Zaidi 1985), critics attacked tax policies and proposed more progressive ways for the state to tax and spend taxes. Those in power defended themselves by showing how their powers to tax and spend taxes were used for the good of the people. Debates turned on two types of measure—of state expenditure and economic prosperity—linked rhetorically and theoretically to general well-being. The classic maneuver of critical attack came to be the attribution of a measurably negative economic phenomenon to the effects of state policy. Company minds attacked Indian rulers, who were said to have caused poverty because their brutish self-indulgence sucked resources from the economy for useless royal display (Dirks 1987; Price 1979). Critics of the company attacked its excessive and regressive land taxation as well as its failure to invest in India's infrastructure of transportation and irrigation (Ludden 1985, 116–19; Stokes 1971). Indian economic nationalism emerged in this critical tradition when Naoroji and Dutt attributed famine and poverty to excessive imperial taxation and to the drain of capital from India (Chandra 1966; Ganguli 1977; Mishra 1988). Throughout, the power of criticism relied on the power to measure progress in official statistics representing India's national economic life.

This continuity in the logic of critical maneuver hides dramatic change in the nature of the powers and terms that measure progress. Company Raj shifted these measures from calculations of mercantile profit toward those of commercial growth generally, a shift begun by Burke that continued to the 1850s. Debates propelling this shift focused on revenue and related systems of property law that would promote commerce and, thus, the general welfare. Such debates were about development as constituted by early colonial capitalism (Ambirajan 1968; Stokes 1959). For the company to calculate revenue accurately, collect it at lower cost, and use it to activate commerce were development goals. Ideas about government responsibility for progress spawned a critique of corruption, waste, and bureaucratic inefficiency that became a permanent cultural feature of India's development regime. The goal of progress, measured by numbers drawn from the market, spawned a critique of the government's impact on the growth and distribution of wealth that has increased in scope and sophistication ever since.

The company's failure to generate progress became obvious in the 1840s. The midcentury restructuring of the colonial state occurred during debates covering four decades that stimulated the creation of new institutions of measurement and control, which became foundations for India's modern development regime and relegated company Raj to the past. By 1880, the state had become a huge investor in India, manned by an ever larger and more disciplined bureaucracy, which conceived itself the custodian of public welfare. Measures of progress disciplined by departmental regimentation came to include statistics of state expenditure on roads, railways, ports, irrigation, famine relief, education, public health, prisons, and other categories of "moral and material progress." Volumes printed by the state publicized the statistical product of bureaucratic labor deployed to enumerate population, prices, occupations, output, irrigation, railway traffic, imports and exports—raw material for economic analysis—aggregated for India as a whole and available for every district in British India, thereby rendering India an economic whole by the sum of its identically empirical parts. During the rise of this new apparatus of cognition, relying on its data and demanding more, imperial commissions on torture, famine, riots, debt, trade, finance, and other subjects multiplied along with private and specialized department studies on every policy topic and public debates on all topics pertaining to public welfare promulgated by lecturers, newspapers, books, and pamphlets. State institutions conditioned all this inquiry and debate, by state-disciplined labor that produced data, by the state's design and dissemination of data, and by state certification of factual authority, all of which made India into an empirical terrain as it made the state appear progressive and responsible.

When Congress first met, in 1885, the development Raj was in place. Subsequently it became an ever bigger if not better Raj. More state responsibility for the economy meant more state power, surveillance, and data; more accountable, specialized, supervised, bureaucrats; more paperwork; and more taxation, direct and indirect, which, by 1900, touched every sector of the economy and involved government at every level (Tinker 1954). By 1900, institutional foundations of the state information apparatus and the surrounding constellation of public debate and expertise that sustain India's development regime today were in place. They produced statistics about almost anything: population, production, wages, prices, rainfall, soil types, village boundaries, property values, tax liability, mortality, morbidity, livestock, railway traffic, prisoners, ethnic groups, bank assets, and industrial output. In place were private and public experts to process data and make policy, and a massive bureaucracy for implementation. By 1900, the government had the power to value, demarcate, judge, and survey assets, transactions, and conflicts in every corner of British India; it had rendered India systematic. The Raj was a "rule by record" (Smith 1985) in the hands of English-educated urbanites, Indian nationalists among them.

As the development Raj matured, so did its criticism by nationalist political economists. With high imperialism and the scramble for Africa, Indian economic nationalism emerged in the world of competition among industrial capitalist nations after 1870. One self-declared economic nationalist, Max Weber, expressed (at Freiburg) the contemporary character of political economy, his self-professed discipline, and also that of his Indian nationalist peers, Naoroji, Dutt, and Mahadev Govind Ranade.

As a science of explanation and analysis political economy is *international,* but as soon as it makes *value judgments* it is bound up with the distinct imprint of humanity we find in our own nature. . . . The economic policy of a German state, and the standard of value adopted by a German economic theorist, can therefore be nothing other than a German policy and a German standard. . . . We do not have peace and human happiness to bequeath to posterity, but rather the *eternal struggle* for the maintenance and improvement by careful cultivation of our national character. . . . The science of political economy is a *political* science. It is a servant of politics, not the day-to-day politics of the individuals and classes who happen to be ruling at a particular time, but the lasting power-political interests of the nation. . . . (1980, 437–38, 442)

Calling himself "a bourgeois scholar," Weber implied that economic nationalism was the ideology of a struggling bourgeoisie, which he, "a member of the bourgeois classes . . . brought up to share their views," endeavored to render more potent so that the German bourgeoisie could make a credible "claim to political leadership" (442–48). In this context, Naoroji, Dutt, and Ranade unmasked British India as a machinery of British self-interest that was impoverishing India, denying it the means of progress, and denying its masses, plagued by famine, even the bare means of survival. In addition to high taxation and the drain of wealth from India, they criticized the destruction by laissez-faire trade policies of Indian manufacturing, a standard theme of protectionism. They forth-rightly agreed with arguments by what Ranade called "Anglo-Indian Thinkers," Britons who engaged India in imperial policy debates. Ranade emphasized that he deployed the same political economy that guided governments and divided policymakers in Europe and the United States. In all respects but one—its colonial status—India constituted a national economy like any in the West, a fact made clear in Ranade's 1892 lecture, "Indian Political Economy," to which he appended "extracts [to] show that the views embodied in the foregoing paper are not confined to the Native Community only" (1982, 24).

Expressed in political economy by bourgeois interests, economic nationalism turned against Empire in the heyday of imperialism and counterposed to empire the national interest not only of India, but also of Britain (Hobson 1901). India originated a specifically *colonial* eco-nomic nationalism whose genius was relentless concentration on the state as a decisive and responsible engine of progress. Whereas laissez-faire was, for imperial minds, a mechanism for taking the state cognitively out of the economy; and whereas generations of classical and neoclassical economists have treated the economy and state as separate spheres har-monized by subordinating states analytically and politically to market discipline; Indian nationalism constitutes the state as the prime mover in development. Until 1920, nationalists represented India's national interest by struggling to improve imperial policy. The fixity of nationalist thought on the state as the engine of progress remained after 1920, despite Mohandas Gandhi's influence, and in 1947, Jawaharlal Nehru's govern-ment made the original nationalist critique of imperial policy the cen-terpiece of India's development program. Though Girish Mishra may overstate continuities between early nationalists and Nehru, reading Ranade sustains this impression, as it was surely intended to do by the Government of India, which reprinted Ranade's lectures in 1982. Mishra reports Naoroji "was convinced that without an active intervention of the state, Indian economy could not develop," and that he wanted to allow private enterprise, both Indian and foreign, "but within a well-formulated policy discipline." Mishra attributes the idea of a mixed economy to Naoroji, who argued that "Indian entrepreneurs needed encouragement and guidance...by the State" (Mishra 1988, 12-19). Ranade also argued, in "Indian Political Economy," that India possessed unique national characteristics that made the state a primary economic agent, especially for industry; and he advocated "state factories" in the iron industry (1982, 63-90). The need to protect India from foreign capital was stressed by nationalists, who, like Bipan Chandra Pal, warned that "the introduction of foreign, and mostly British, capital for working out the natural resources of the country, instead of being a help, is, in fact, the greatest hindrance to all real improvement in the economic condition of the people" (Chandra 1966, 97ff.; Mishra 1988, 19).

Indian nationalism began as a critique of policy. It became a critique of British power by its being denied a voice in government. Queen Victoria's late years saw something new in India—a clash of nationalisms—in a context of similar clashes that were driving European imperialism toward world war. Viewed as a political economy of nationhood devised within a real Indian national economy, Indian nationalism appears not as a derivative discourse (Chatterjee 1986) but, rather (despite—or as suggested by—condescension from the likes of Lord Curzon), a cultural product of nineteenth-century capitalism, on the same plane with bourgeois nationalisms in the West, with which it has much in common, but from which it is distinguished, as Congress leaders were painfully aware, by extreme political weakness and a lack of means for real political expression. British imperial nationalism denied that expression absolutely; even the idea offended British orderliness. The need for more British control of Indians—who were still identified with inefficiency and corruption—was a dominant theme of Victorian empire (Cohen 1971; Cohn 1983, 1985; Yang 1985). Control by British capital of the Indian economy became more domineering as the Raj matured (Bagchi 1972; Harnetty 1972; Kling 1976; Thorner 1950; Washbrook 1981). In 1892, the ever-tight imperial budget induced the government to order that high civil service posts be kept to the minimum that was "absolutely necessary to fill the supervising and controlling offices for which Europeans are required" (Stokes 1980, 155). Indian nationalism faced its political struggle with theory grounded in a bourgeois experience of discrimination and subordination and in bourgeois identification of itself with a nation suffering under a foreign yoke; both were bolstered by official orientalism and the racism highlighted by outbursts like the Ilbert Bill and Rowlatt Acts.

In this light, it seems logical that Indian nationalism never seriously proposed reversing the trend of expanding state power that was well established in 1885. Quite the contrary. When its economic program began to emerge, Congress promised that its state would do everything the British were doing, but do it better, and do more. Its intentions in this line emerged in the 1930s and are explicit in its 1945 election manifesto.

> The most vital and urgent of India's problems is how to remove the curse of poverty and raise the standard of the masses.... For this purpose, it will be necessary to plan and coordinate social advance in all its many fields, to prevent the concentration of wealth and power in the hands of individuals and groups, to prevent vested interests inimical to society from growing, and to have social control of mineral resources, means of transportation and the principal methods of production and distribution in land, industry and in other departments of national activity, so that free India may develop into a cooperative commonwealth. The State must own or control key and basic industries and services, mineral resources, railways, waterways, shipping, and other means of public transport. Currency and exchange, banking and insurance, must be regulated in the national interest. (Zaidi 1985, 71–72)

At independence, national objectives thus included not only increasing India's national income and employment, price stability, and balance of payments stability, but reducing economic inequality among classes and regions, and attaining national self-reliance (Chaudhuri 1979; Frankel 1978, 71–113; Zaidi 1985, 79–91).

Culture and State Power

India's development regime evolved on coherent, consistent lines after 1870, the trend being toward more ramified and centralized state power. This trend was not inevitable. Removing its opposition meant military conquest for most of the nineteenth century; after 1945, it meant partition and reconquest of Telengana and Kashmir. All along, the regime has sustained a growing, coercive apparatus that it deploys in proportion to the militance of opposition, as well as growing costs to "discipline and punish" resistance (Guha 1983). It was not, however, high protection costs (Bowles and Gintis 1986) that inspired Gandhians to cajole Congress toward making India "a federation of village republics." It was a philosophy of government harmonized with what Gandhi believed to be India's spiritual essence. A blueprint for the new state on these lines was published in 1946, S. N. Agarwal's *Gandhian Constitution for Free India*. But in 1947, when B. N. Rau, constitutional adviser to the government, "circulated an elaborate questionnaire to all members of the Central and Provincial Legislatures, . . . he received exactly one reply," so strong apparently was political consensus that a blueprint for the new constitution existed in the 1935 Government of India Act. Yet the Planning Commission was not indicated in the 1935 act or the Constitution: this centralizing fiat of the Nehru government, with the prime minister as chairman, was a bold boost to the long-term trend. The commission's power to plan resource allocations to states made it controversial in the early years, but it became part of the Nehru government's centralized unification of India that was both logical and "long foreshadowed" (Thorner 1970, 138) by Congress's declarations (Frankel 1978; Tinker 1962, 155, 158, 163–65). The long-term growth trend of state power and centralization has been sustained since 1947. One commentator has argued recently that " . . . the system inherited from colonial times was in many ways more decentralized than centralized. With the arrival of democratically elected governments . . . the balance was heavily tilted toward centralization" (Mukarji 1989, 468).

Independence altered the meaning of state power. Yet movement across the colonial divide along a trajectory of state centralization suggests that there are logics of agency and structural change at work *inside India* that sustain the trend (Callinicos 1988; Giddens 1979). We can call these logics cultural in that they seem to underlie patterns of action and ideology without being expressed in them directly. They concern the interaction of state and society.

Lloyd Rudolph and Susanne Hoeber Rudolph suggest that the cultural drive behind India's high "stateness" comes from precolonial imperial tradition (1987, 72–73). Indeed, patterns of discourse alive for many centuries support a sense of there being a popular presumption in India that rulers are responsible for the people, that state rituals effect control over evil and embody well-being, and that the state is a privileged site for honor and rank in society. All this would support the idea that more state power is good. The personal distribution of largess at sites of state power and the popular personification of the state in charismatic politicians remain prominent parts of Indian political culture. Yet there is no ancient cultural injunction that the state "remove the curse of poverty," "prevent vested interests inimical to society from growing," or "plan and coordinate social advance." Precolonial states had little control of production and distribution and what they did have came through social intermediation unregulated by the state. Precolonial political culture produced multiple, overlapping levels and arenas of authority more than centralized states. Even the Mughal state was more patrimonial than bureaucratic, and its centralization was more ideological than operative. From medieval to late precolonial times, centralization was episodic. Precolonial traditions hardly sustain India's "stateness" and may better explain its opposition (Blake 1979; Dirks 1987; Dumont 1981; Fox 1971; Heesterman 1985; Kulke 1982; Stein 1980; Wink 1986).

The cultural logic of the Indian state's centralizing trend did begin to emerge before the Company Raj, in regimes such as those of Haider Ali and Tipu Sultan, which strove to subdue intermediaries between rulers and producers with powers not firmly established until colonial times. After 1800, a new cultural logic emerged within interactions among officials and social actors who controlled the means of production. A cultural formation arose in the conduct of conquest, negotiation, accommodation, dispute, expectation, precedent, resistance, evaluation, and moral injunction—in short, from discourses of power—articulating forms of class power and state power that came into being in relation to one another. By pervading social transactions, a colonial capitalism endowed with a compelling state-building imperative *inside India* articulated cultural expressions of class power, above all, perhaps, in the property rights that the state defined more widely and minutely each year. A cultural drive toward a centralizing state thus arose with India's development regime, in the articulations of capitalist class and colonial state formation.

Interactions of state and social power in the production process define promising terrain for studies of culture in this development regime. Interactions between the state and the classes that expanded their productive powers under colonialism hold particular promise, and especially continuity in these interactions after independence. For example, without passing judgement on the overall impact of imperial power on India's economy (Habib 1985), we can focus on the twin facts that the colonial state was a domineering presence for Indian capital and that substantial capitalist interests arose in colonial India, some industrial, others concentrated in trade and finance, and others situated in between, as in the handloom industry (Baker 1984; Ray 1972; Rudner 1989; Timberg 1978). The empire nurtured Indian capital's expansion into Burma and South Africa (where Gandhi began his career) and became more nurturing of Indian industrial capital as Indian nationalism put industrialization high on its agenda. Big capital became a major player in the late colonial economy and the nationalist movement (Markovits 1985; Tomlinson 1978). It is thus intriguing that the nationalist critique of imperialism was transformed into a national industrial program that made the state itself India's great capitalist. From critique and defeat of empire arose a national version of the colonial state's relation to capital. State planning assumed the dominant position after 1950 for national, rather than colonial, purposes and to protect Indian capitalists from the foreign threats from abroad to which empire had subjected them. The national interest made the state's relation to capital once again nurturing and constricting; it merely juggled the old terms of this relationship (Chaudhuri 1979).

That this relationship was thus reconfigured by national leaders who stressed industrial growth to counteract the legacy of empire (Mishra 1988) indicates a continuous logic in the state's relation with capital. One way to unravel it would be to look through the state's eyes. Congress's affirmation of the state's primacy as an instrument and embodiment of the national interest may itself explain the increase in state power represented by India's "organized sector." To reach its development goals, the new state had to enhance its power to pull the levers controlling the economy, so the increase of its power became a goal and measure of development. That the state would not only refuse to give up levers it held in 1947, but take more in its grip, seems logical. Big capital may also be seen as a potential competitor of the state, potentially "inimical to society." This logic, of course, depends on a prior identification of the state rather than capital with the Indian national interest, a principle that was certainly propagated by Congress. So, like the colonial state, the national state defines and measures development in terms of itself and measures progress by its own accomplishments.

But looking "at economic development from above," concentrating on the logics of state, we may, as Weber warned, "involuntarily become their apologist" (or, we might add, merely critics). This approach also renders capital passive and misses interactive dynamics between the state and capital wherein we might find more compelling cultural possibilities. Looking "more from below . . . at the great spectacle of the emancipatory struggles of rising classes emerging from the chaos of economic interest, we may observe the way the balance of economic power shifts in their favour" (Weber 1980, 441). It does indeed seem that nationalism did work in favor of Indian capital along the trend line of state centralization, enough so that many capitalists had reasons to support the trend. Capital being "competition among capitals" (Callinicos 1988, 192ff.), and there being reasons for state centralization other than to court capital, no conspiracy theory is worth pursuing. But a route worth pursuing is suggested by the argument that India's bourgeoisie emerged as a distinctive interest with no regional identity, so that, unlike other interests expressed by nationalism, it *only* identified politically with the nation. Its class subculture yearned for protection from foreign capital and to expand into a huge domestic economy that the Congress Raj promised to enlarge further, while the most powerful capitalists would have hoped to shape the national rules of competition in their favor. Thus, capital had reasons to seek state nurturing and protection, to support national economic integration and centralization. At the same time, as one author has noted, the Hindi-speaking, North Indian electoral "heartland" had no bourgeoisie of its own, so that protectively nurturing capital was a means to subordinate capital to "the Prussia of India [where] it [is] easy . . . to slip into the feeling that to talk of any other than a pan-Indian identity is antinational" (D. N. 1989). The conjunction of state and capitalist interests does seem to have shifted economic power in favor of India's big industrial firms after 1950 (Thorner 1970).

Agriculture and State Power

As capitalism invented the economy, it also envisioned agriculture as a domain of political economy, and the cultural assumption of state responsibility for development was established first for the agricultural economy. To create a domain for progress, the colonial regime separated "economy" and "society" in the manner of liberalism (Bowles and Gintis 1986). It viewed society as a complex of traditions whose reformation had to be balanced with conservation to maintain its social hierarchy and stability (Bayly 1988; Washbrook 1981), but defined the agricultural economy as autonomous and open for progressive intervention, to which the colonial regime was compelled. Indian agricultural products were critical for British industry, agrarian profits fed the imperial treasury, and abundant crops in markets subsidized imperial wages. Food crises threatened law and order and the revenue. In addition, in India as Britain, agrarian prosperity was identified with popular well-being; the Indian peasantry became identified with the vast masses over whom the colonial state had responsibility to rule justly. Such considerations indicate why colonial social policy wavered between reform and conservation as the principle of agrarian economic policy remained constant: the state strove to increase commodity production.

In Munro's time, policy focused on institutionalizing the state's relations with landowners on progressive lines. The initial tendency was to construct zaminder landlord rights over tenant farmers, whose production would increase given incentives to invest provided by a permanently fixed state revenue demand on landlords. This permanent limitation of state taxation came originally from a desire to secure the landed gentry and from the state's inability to bear the full cost of tax collection; but it was later revalorized by nationalists who sought to limit state demand from farmers hard pressed by taxes that were drained away from India (Dutt 1901). The nationalists challenged any upward revision of tax demands on agriculture but worked inside the legal principle, established in Munro's day, that the state itself was the landlord in India, under which farmers worked as tenants, so that taxation was rent that rose with land values. Thus, where taxes could be revised, the state (in theory) had an interest in investments to raise productivity. For Munro, low rent in cash and the elimination of intermediaries was nurture enough for farmers who would follow the yeoman path to enrichment. But by 1850 it was obvious that progress required direct state investment, especially in irrigation, which was understood then as being complementary to military pacification in the strengthening of empire (Bawa 1986, 210) and which soon became a weapon of imperial self-defense against nationalist critics (Bhutani 1976; Dutt 1874, 1900, 1901; Raghavaiyangar 1892). This midcentury move to direct state expenditure in productivity and security institutionalized state responsibility for agrarian prosperity. Reassessments of land revenue became moments for measuring agricultural progress as a function of state policy. In such moments of public scrutiny— above all, famine commission proceedings—agricultural development debates began.

These debates rested on a textual construction of agriculture with statistics. Unlike East Asia and Europe, India's literati did not generate a textual corpus on agricultural improvement before 1800. In Europe and China, the literati wrote agricultural calendars, manuals, and technical compendiums that indicate they controlled farm output and key inputs—above all, labor—more closely than their Indian counterparts. In China, officials, many themselves landlords, wrote texts printed and distributed by the state, and, as in Europe, texts disproportionately treat the most profitable crops (Needham 1986, 47–85). Such textualization was a managerial act that established an instrumental attitude toward farming, and in early modern Europe, as landowners gained new powers over production, they deployed a more domineering instrumentalism. Capitalism wrote a new kind of agricultural text. In the old text, authors gleaned knowledge from peasants; farm practice was expertise. But capitalist Europe disseminated progressive techniques authorized by science, which invented a new agricultural semantics. Peasant wisdom became folklore. Experts spoke the language of laboratory, model farm, efficiency, and statistics. The discourse of scientific agriculture overspread India, Europe, and the United States simultaneously in the nineteenth century (Ludden forthcoming a).

We have seen that the company began to know agrarian India during surveys at the end of the eighteenth century. By 1805, survey and revenue officers produced Anglo-Indian agricultural knowledge designed by government orders and by scientific training. Heyne's report of 1802 moves toward a system of representation that soon became standard with Buchanan's statistical tables on Bengal. Systematically, codified agriculture made input-output statistics a distinct domain of data, separating agricultural data from the morass of local knowledge. The revenue bureaucracy was a primary venue for codifying agriculture. Records replete with localism were kept in villages and towns, but reports moving up the chain of command were abstracted and purged of localism. Data for decision making at the higher echelons needed to cover a widening range of variation in standardized terms. So records sent from Madras to Calcutta and from India to London lost more and more localism, until metropolitan minds imbibed data compiled in terms applicable over the widest range of variation, the whole world. By 1840, the world was open to English enterprise and London sought data on crops, labor, and production from around the globe in uniform, economical English and statistical terms. As Egyptian, American, and Indian cotton simultaneously preoccupied London; as railway, telegraph, and steamship lowered transport costs; as print technologies lowered information costs; the imperial data-gathering machine rendered the world in statistical tables.

By 1880, agricultural statistics were as modern in India as in England and the United States, and the state's discursive power over agriculture was likewise set in its modern mold. The U.S. Department of Agriculture, founded in 1862, was "the first government agency created specifically to serve the interests of a special clientele" (Mann 1990, 136). The same can be said for India, but the colonial state represented its service to farmers with paternal condescension. State power over technologies of progress nested happily in the language of domination. Lord Mayo founded the Madras Agriculture Department and set its tone in 1869.

> For generations to come the progress of India . . . must be directly dependent on her progress in agriculture. . . . There is perhaps no country in the world in which the State has so immediate and direct an interest in such questions. . . . Throughout the greater part of India, every measure for the improvement of the land enhances the value of the property of the State. The duties which in England are performed by a good landlord fall in India, in a great measure, upon the government. Speaking generally, the only Indian landlord who can command the requisite knowledge is the state. (Manak 1979, 27)

In 1880, the Madras Government produced an *Agricultural Classbook* (Robertson 1880) and, in 1883, it held an Agricultural Exhibition. The state no longer simply told Europeans how to manage farms in India (Greenaway 1864; Robertson 1880; Royle 1851). It became *the* expert on agriculture in India and defined the style and substance of agricultural expertise (Moreland 1904, 1913; Pogson 1883; Randhawa 1980; Schrottky 1876; Shah 1888). The *Moral and Material Progress Report* for 1907–8 declared that "thirty years of experience and record gathering since the institution of the Departments of Agriculture lead to the recognition that Government's primary task was to apply European scientific methods to Indian agriculture" (Manak 1979, 73).

Agriculture thus became an object for development by being abstracted from society and culture, broken into input-output data, translated out of vernaculars into the English of scientific semantics, and projected back onto farmers by institutions that imagined localities only as identically empirical units, passive under their gaze, objects of observation and responsibility. Thus it became necessary to talk about the "average village" or "typical peasant" in statistical terms. Developing agriculture in the farm world of capitalism transformed agricultural knowledge in India by changing its mode of production, shifting its creative locus to the metropolis, and obliterating local experience as an active agent in the formation of expertise. The state became the embodiment of agricultural progress.

Indian nationalists entered this discourse and looked out onto a national economy where farmers needed help. The rural masses faced difficult conditions, not only natural scarcities of water, but scarcities of grazing land and fuel caused by agricultural expansion and deforestation, which could be rectified by progressive government management of the landscape. Farmers also suffered a scarcity of knowledge and means to increase productivity. In 1901, Congress made its first major commitment to the state's scientific machinery for agricultural improvement, resolving, "that the Government should be pleased to bestow its first and undivided attention upon the department of agriculture and adopt all those measures for its improvement and development which have been made in America, Russia, Holland, Belgium, and several other countries so successfully in that direction" (Zaidi 1985, 34). Government was moving in that direction already (in response to an outcry over famines); its accomplishments are duly recorded in the *Report of the Royal Commission on Agriculture in India* in 1928.

The Government of India has produced more monumental and detailed studies, plans, projects, projections, and assessments of progress ever since. The Congress manifesto of 1945 declared: "Agriculture has to be improved on scientific lines" (Zaidi 1985, 72). And toward that end, in 1947, Congress composed its first program for agriculture, which laid the groundwork for subsequent efforts and indicates some contours of the postcolonial transition. It expresses the rationale for state centralization as a vehicle for agricultural development and also continuing state paternalism toward farmers, a sentiment that today connects India's development elite with their peers in the world development regime.

The individual peasant is generally so ill equipped that he cannot be expected to assume complete responsibility for better farming. Implements, manure, seeds, bullocks, and such other essential equipment should therefore be made available to him by a Central Agency.... With a view immediately to raise the standard of efficiency and culture of the agricultural population, the Provincial Governments should organise and maintain schools and demonstration farms to provide refresher courses and to ensure that Kisan youths and skilled Kisans are educated and trained in the most efficient and practical modern methods of agriculture.... (Zaidi 1985, 81–83)

Here we see lines of continuity between imperial developmentalism and the accumulation of state power in independent India. India's development regime has increasingly bolstered the state as an engine of agricultural progress with state control over technologies that only it can provide to farmers, such as irrigation works, electrical hookups, and productivity-enhancing inputs such as those of the Green Revolution. The cultural assumption of state responsibility for agricultural progress established under the colonial regime gave nationalists leverage against the colonial state and a means to mobilize farmers who understood the state as a component of their livelihood. When in power, such farmers and the national government alike saw the fulfilment of the promise of independence as an increase in the state's power to provide productivity-enhancing inputs to farmers who would increase India's agricultural prosperity.

In the Congress program of 1947, we also see the state as a teacher with privileged access to the knowledge that farmers need. The reversal of the power-knowledge relation depicted in Rennell's lithograph, which began in Munro's day and matured into the edifying spectacle of agricultural exhibitions, became state responsibility to teach India's farmers how to farm. Schools, extension programs, and "development communications" via satellite broadcasts to village televisions became, at once, vehicles for disseminating useful knowledge and a means to elevate the state as rationality, as the originator of the power to effect progress. Rarely has the connection between progress, state-controlled technology, and the personal hand of imperious politicians been as blatant as in the 1989 election campaign, when Rajiv Gandhi's government used state television to portray his dynastic heritage as a national icon (Farmer n.d.). The centralized state as a teacher is more effective and culturally acceptable in the guise of a disinterested authority speaking the language of science, in which decisions about the allocation of resources are rendered in terms of efficiency, rationality, and national interest. Education for development thus constructs the state as a teacher who knows best and makes hard central planning decisions on scientific grounds.

Since before 1850, scientific consensus has taken the "peasant farmer" or "the actual cultivator" (Bagchi 1989, 828) as the elemental unit of agricultural progress in India. For a century thereafter, under colonialism, evidence piled up showing that peasant production suffered not only from scarcities (of irrigation, capital, land, tools, skills, market access, and the like) but also from exploitative social relations in which nonproducers controlled what peasants needed and charged extortionate rates for peasant access to the necessary means of production. Scarcities were thus made worse by limitations placed on farm productivity by exploitative social relations. The central tendency in scientific thought became that the state should remove obstacles to increased productivity by lowering the cost of productive resources for peasants with state provisioning and legislation. This was the justification for tenancy reform, which gave tenants more security of tenure and limited rental increases by landlords, while maintaining the colonial sanctity of zamindari rights (Ludden 1984). Along with cooperative credit experiments (Catanach 1970), the colonial state enacted restrictions on power of foreclosure to prevent moneylenders from taking peasant land (Barrier 1979). The same development logic that worked for government reform efforts also gave nationalists leverage against the empire: as India's great landlord, the imperial state extracted excessive and regressive rents and then took them out of the Indian national economy, exacerbating the capital shortage that plagued farmers. Nationalists depicted British rule as the exploitation of farmers and a brake on productivity and progress (Chandra 1966; Charlesworth 1982; McLane 1963–64). Nationalism itself became a vehicle of agricultural development.

Participation by farmers in the nationalist movement focused primarily on issues already institutionalized in their interactions with the state: taxes, rents, and property rights. Struggles from below on these issues were constant features of the colonial regime, dramatized and raised to higher significance by nationalism. The farmers most central to the nationalist movement agitated to enhance their productive powers by forcing the state to remove more obstacles to more profitable agriculture (Epstein 1988; Hardiman 1981). Their nationalism geared itself to the creation of a regime more attuned to their interests, and, in the process, they challenged the Congress on the legal basis of landlordism and moneylending. They also pushed Congress to its most radical measure, announced in 1945:

The reform of the land system, which is so urgently needed in India, involves the removal of intermediaries between the peasant and the

State. The rights of such intermediaries should therefore be acquired on payment of equitable compensation. (Zaidi 1985, 72)

Thus, the national regime sought not only to provide knowledge and technology that would increase farm productivity but also to reform property rights and social relations to benefit farmers. "The removal of intermediaries" resonates with the language of Munro and Jones, who understood it to mean an increase in centralized state power and rationality; these, in 1947, were so pervasive and accepted as to be unquestioned. Putting peasant and state face to face, with no mediating institutions between them, did, however, imply that the state would become part of every farm's operation. State action would be critical in determining the cost of the farmer's access to the means of production. The sustenance of the state would, in turn, depend on its ability to work on the farmer's behalf. Amiya Kumar Bagchi describes the intricacy of this interdependence.

The failure to carry out thoroughgoing land reforms which would vest the ownership and management of the land in the hands of the actual cultivators [means] that traders and moneylenders [can] continue to prosper by exacting extortionate margins on goods sold or bought and charging usurious interest rates on loans to the poor in the countryside. These conditions also facilitate political coalitions between landlords, traders, and moneylenders blocking the process of reforms to endow peasants with the incentive and wherewithal to produce more and meet the needs of industrialisation. . . . When the farm sector is dominated by landlords, the rate of growth of agricultural output interacts with such factors as luxury consumption of the rich, the tendency to speculation whenever the harvest is poor, the extremely skewed distribution of credit, and public support for farm prices to produce a constricting limit on industrial growth. (1989, 828)

Within this interdependence, cultural sustenance for state power from below comes from farmers. The state defines property rights and did abolish zamindari, though it has yet to effect the radical land reform that Bagchi prescribes (Herring 1986). The state controls input and output prices, has effectively eliminated agricultural taxation since 1950, and subsidizes productivity-enhancing investment. The state is deeply entrenched in the culture of farming, and farmers rest their livelihood on the work of the state as much as on the rain. Many small farmers do resemble peasants in their reliance on family labor, but this typifies agrarian capitalism (Mann 1990). The ability of farmers to operate profitably within India's history of capitalist development is well attested (Baker 1984; Harriss 1982; Islam 1985; Ludden 1984), while there is little doubt that colonial and national regimes alike delivered fruits of science to agricultural profit-makers more than to subsistence-oriented peasants (Mann 1989; Pray 1978; Thorner 1968). It is reasonable, therefore, to argue that the culture of farming that sustains the trend of state power in India is not a peasant culture, though some people articulate the state-farmer relationship by using the term *peasant* (to translate *Kisan,* for example). The farming culture of India's development regime is that of a diverse and differentiated agrarian petty bourgeoisie, which has been rising in economic and cultural power since late precolonial times, in constant interaction with the state, whose powers are integral to its own (Stein 1991). Its political powers were local in the nineteenth century and expanded through channels of colonial politics into provincial capitals (Ludden 1985; Washbrook 1976). Since the 1920s, the size and political strength of this class have been sufficient that it has never lacked strong national spokesmen (Byres 1988; Shankardass 1986). This class formation and its articulations with state power in India are secrets well kept by the discourse of development (Jha 1980) and allied historical sociology (Guha 1983).

Conclusion

This discussion does not seek to diminish the importance of Indian independence, but, rather, to put its representation as progress in comparative perspective. There is no measurement of change versus continuity attempted here; nor any measurement of change after 1947 by comparison with what came before. My goal is rather to put the means to measure and evaluate in such areas into a context in which colonialism and nationalism are embedded. For, as Weber indicates, the study of economic development suffers a generic subordination to the nation-state as its vehicle and measure of progress. Compulsions to measure change and find causes for forward and backward movements, for the acceleration and stagnation of progress, are attributes of development regimes, engendered by capitalism.

Or I could say gendered by capitalism, for the attribution of male and female traits to imperial and colonial nations is a cultural legacy of orientalism that Edward Said has made famous, and this obscures the extent to which India has participated in capitalism, not, as Immanuel Wallerstein would have it, suspended between core and periphery (Washbrook 1990), but on the same plane as Europe and the United States. Measuring the ups and downs, the richer and poorer, the less and more powerful, is all part of world capitalist culture and is expressed in many idioms, including those of gender and "semiperiphery." An imperial subjugation of India sustained British power there. But India's development regime reveals another history, of transformations that start before colonialism and run to the present, which indicate parallel trajectories of class and state formation in India and the West, as well as a distinctive Indian "stateness." The significance of the state for capitalism in India best explains why historians are so divided over the economic assessment of colonialism: for in the horrors engendered by the colonial state lie the glories of the national state (Habib 1985). Its state culture of bourgeois socialism may be the most distinctive feature of India's development regime.

I have not considered all the reasons for this distinctiveness, nor have I measured it comparatively. The rise of India's urban middle class and its intelligentsia have not been discussed. But their cultural fixation on the state and political role in sustaining its power are discussed elsewhere (Haynes 1990; Rudra 1989). I have not talked about so-called subaltern subcultures, modes of resistance to state power, or struggles that often seem capable of tearing India apart. These fit into the category of suppressed oppositions and countermovements to the trends and transitions I have discussed. Subalterns are subordinated, resistance has not reduced state power, and when threatened, the state within India's development regime has galvanized support to increase its power to suppress opposition. These matters could be considered as cultural toleration for high protection costs or by reference to the fact that this regime has succeeded in defending and extending bourgeois privileges and private property rights for a very long time.

As Bagchi indicates, the endless extension of private property and powers of market access to material resources is a hallmark of planning that nestles neatly inside India's state socialism. For, as Congress proclamations and quotes from Nehru would indicate, Indian socialism is the "extension of democracy" from the political into the social and economic realms, which means the representation through elections of society by a state that manages national economic development. That politically decisive segments of society consist of an urban bourgeoisie with its employees, an urban petite bourgeoisie, and an agrarian petite bourgeoisie with its employees and dependents, suggests the extent of cultural support for private property rights and their protection. The Indian state has thus managed a virtually endless multiplication of property rights, an endless expansion of commodity production and consumerism. As the state becomes more critical in the livelihood of every class segment in India, however, it will necessarily become the site of increasing competition, which may require increased protection costs and even more coercive state power.

In India, colonialism remains a constituent of a regime geared toward increasing state control over the terms of capitalist development, because colonialism makes the nation-state inherently progressive. In this cultural construction, India's regime continues to occupy the same space as regimes in Europe and the United States, which are similarly served by historians who authorize progress. The language of science constructs and measures the progress demarcated by the history of these regimes, so that each increment of national power is a step forward, each diminution of national wealth, a step back. Today, the government in India is as determined as in the United States or in Victoria's Britain to portray itself as the engine of progress and to conceal its power to define progress in terms of itself. Development regimes verify themselves by expansion, movement, and growth, measured in economic statistics that are a surrogate, among nations, for expanding imperial frontiers. The big numbers measuring growth and economic power are the machismo of development regimes. Best to make yours look bigger by comparison to your temporal and spatial neighbor. Colonialism and nationalism alike verify themselves by their invention of a new regime as a dawn following dark days past when a retrograde old regime stymied progress. Development regimes hire historians to make themselves look good.

Past "others" to be dispelled from the new-age present entail present "others," obstacles to the progress embodied by a new regime but inherited from the old. In British India, the present "other" was traditional India as described by orientalism, which constructed the opposition to modernity. "India from time immemorial" appears in colonial literature as the dark-age past against which progress was measured, and as the home of colonial modernity's regrettable "others," retrograde realities that, despite its best efforts, the Raj could not dispel: caste, famine, poverty, religious conflict, and primitive technology. Similarly, in India today, history is officially the study of old regimes and ends in 1947. In India as elsewhere, history concentrates on the genealogy of the nation-state (Ludden 1986) and especially on struggles against a colonialism that left behind present "others" that oppose national progress. These retrograde "others" are an amalgam of precolonial elements preserved by colonialism and colonial creations dumped on India: semi-feudalism, caste prejudice, deindustrialization, cultural alienation, bureaucratic rigidity, and communalism, to cite prominent examples.

In this respect, history does not concern the past so much as a present regime defined by its opposition to old regimes and to its past and present "others." The inscription of discontinuity and fracture across history, in which colonial past and national present appear in stark contrast to one another, seems to be the sound and fury of development regimes, which reproduce themselves with proclamations that time is linear and humankind moving forward, to celebrate new beginnings and the passing of old regimes. Though in the dominant ideology of the Indian state, colonialism stands for the past to be vanquished by national progress, the national state has like its colonial predecessor turned its guns against those who oppose the trajectory of its development regime.

NOTE

This article was written with the assistance of financial support from the National Endowment for the Humanities. Inspired by conversations with Joel Kaye, Victoria Farmer, Madhavi Kale, Robb Gregg, Burton Stein, and Tosun Aricanli, I have benefited from readings and comments by S. Ambirajan, Nicholas Dirks, David Gilmartin, David Washbrook, and the Research Triangle South Asia Colloquium.

REFERENCES

Adas, Michael. 1989. *Machines as the Measure of Men: Science, Technology, and Ideologies of Western Dominance.* Ithaca.

Ambirajan, S. 1968. *Classical Political Economy and British Policy in India.* Cambridge.

Amin, Samir. 1974. *Accumulation on a World Scale.* New York.

Bagchi, Amiya Kumar. 1972. *Private Investment in India, 1900–1939.* Cambridge.

Bagchi, Amiya Kumar. 1989. "Development Planning." In *The New Palgrave:*

A Dictionary of Economics, ed. Murray Milgate, Peter Newman, and John Eatwell, 826–29. London.

Baker, Christopher John. 1984. *An Indian Rural Economy: The Tamilnad Countryside, 1880–1955.* Oxford.

Barrier, N. G. 1979. "The Formulation and Enactment of the Punjab Alienation of Land Bill." *Punjab Past and Present* 13 (1): 193–215.

Bawa, Satinder Singh, ed. 1986. *The Letters of the First Viscount Hardinge of Lahore to Lady Hardinge and Sir Walter and Lady James: 1844–1847.* London.

Bayly, C. A. 1983. *Rulers, Townsmen, and Bazaars: North Indian Society in the Age of British Expansion.* Cambridge.

Bayly, C. A. 1988. *Indian Society and the Making of the British Empire.* Cambridge.

Bhutani, V. C. 1976. *The Apotheosis of Imperialism: Indian Land Economy under Curzon.* New Delhi.

Blake, Stephen P. 1979. "The Patrimonial-Bureaucratic Empire of the Mughals." *Journal of Asian Studies* 39 (1): 77–94.

Bowles, Samuel, and Herbert Gintis. 1986. *Democracy and Capitalism: Property, Community, and the Contradictions of Modern Social Thought.* New York.

Brenner, Robert. 1986. "The Social Basis of Economic Development." In *Analytical Marxism,* ed. John Roemer, 23–53. Cambridge.

Buchanan, Francis Hamilton. 1870. *A Journey from Madras through the Countries of Mysore, Canara, and Malabar.* Madras.

Buchanan, Francis Hamilton. 1956. *Journey through the Northern Parts of Kanara.* Delhi.

Byres, Terence J. 1988. "Charan Singh (1902–87): An Assessment." *Journal of Peasant Studies* 15 (2): 139–89.

Callinicos, Alex. 1988. *Making History: Agency, Structure, and Change in Social Theory.* Ithaca.

Cannon, Garland, ed. 1970. *The Letters of Sir William Jones.* 2 vols. Oxford.

Castro, Fidel. 1984. *The World Crisis: Its Economic and Social Impact on the Underdeveloped Countries.* London.

Catanach, Ian. 1970. *Rural Credit in Western India, 1875–1930: Rural Credit and the Cooperative Movement in the Bombay Presidency.* Berkeley.

Chandra, Bipan. 1966. *The Rise and Growth of Economic Nationalism in India: 1880–1905.* New Delhi.

Charlesworth, Neil. 1982. *British Rule and the Indian Economy, 1800–1914.* London.

Chatterjee, Partha. 1986. *Nationalist Thought and the Colonial World: A Derivative Discourse?* London.

Chaudhuri, Pramit. 1979. *India's Economy: Poverty and Development.* New York.

Cohen, Stephen P. 1971. *The Indian Army and Its Contribution to the Development of a Nation.* Berkeley.

Cohn, Bernard S. 1983. "Representing Authority in Victorian India." In *The Invention of Tradition,* ed. E. J. Hobsbawm and T. O. Ranger, 165–209. Cambridge.

Cohn, Bernard S. 1985. "The Command of Language and the Language of Command." In *Subaltern Studies,* ed. Ranajit Guha, 4:276–329.

Cotton, Arthur T. 1968. *Lectures on Irrigation Works in India.* Vijayawada.

Cotton, Lady Hope. 1900. *General Sir Arthur Cotton: His Life and Work.* London.

Darling, Sir Malcolm. 1925. *The Punjab Peasant in Prosperity and Debt.* Delhi.

Das, Arvind N. 1987. "Changel: Three Centuries of an Indian Village." *Journal of Peasant Studies* 15 (1): 3–60.

Dirks, Nicholas B. 1987. *The Hollow Crown: Ethnohistory of an Indian Kingdom.* Cambridge.

D. N. 1989. "Indian Big Bourgeoisie and the National Question: The Formative Phase." *Economic and Political Weekly,* March 4, 1989, 454–56.

Dumont, Louis. 1981. *Homo Hierarchicus: The Caste System and Its Implications.* Chicago.

Dutt, Romesh Chandra. 1874. *Peasantry of Bengal.* Calcutta.

Dutt, Romesh Chandra. 1900. *Open Letters to Lord Curzon on Famines and Land Assessments in India.* London.

Dutt, Romesh Chandra. 1901. *The Economic History of India.* Calcutta.

Easterlin, Richard. 1968. "Economic Growth." In *International Encyclopedia of the Social Sciences,* ed. David Sills, 395–408. New York.

Epstein, S. J. M. 1988. *The Earthy Soil: Bombay Peasants and the Indian Nationalist Movement, 1919–1947.* Delhi.

Farmer, Victoria L. N.d. "The Limits of Image Making: Doordarshan and the 1989 Lok Sabha Elections." In *Democracy and Development in South Asia,* ed. Ayesha Jalal and Sugata Bose. Delhi (forthcoming).

Foucault, Michel. 1973. *The Birth of the Clinic.* New York.

Foucault, Michel. 1979. *Discipline and Punish: The Birth of the Prison.* New York.

Fox, Richard. 1971. *Kin, Clan, Raja, and Rule.* Berkeley.

Frankel, Francine. 1978. *India's Political Economy, 1947–1977: The Gradual Revolution.* Princeton.

Frykenburg, Robert Eric. 1965. *Guntur District, 1788–1848: A History of Local Influence and Central Authority in South India.* Oxford.

Ganguli, B. N. 1977. *Indian Economic Thought—Nineteenth-Century Perspectives.* New Delhi.

Giddens, Anthony. 1979. *Central Problems in Social Theory: Action, Structure, and Contradiction in Social Analysis.* Berkeley.

Greenaway, T. 1864. *Farming in India, Considered as a Pursuit for European Settlers of a Superior Class, with Plans for the Construction of Dams, Weirs, Tanks, and Sluices.* London.

Guha, Ranajit. 1983. *Elementary Aspects of Peasant Insurgency in Colonial India*. Delhi.

Guha, Ranajit, ed. 1982–89. *Subaltern Studies: Writings on South Asian History and Society*. 6 vols. Delhi.

Gunder-Frank, Andre. 1969. *Capitalism and Underdevelopment in Latin America*. New York.

Habib, Irfan. 1985. "Studying a Colonial Economy—Without Perceiving Colonialism." *Modern Asian Studies* 19 (3): 355–82.

Halstead, John P. 1983. *The Second British Empire: Trade, Philanthropy, and Good Government, 1820–1890*. Westport.

Hardiman, David. 1981. *Peasant Nationalists of Gujarat: Kheda District, 1917–1934*. Delhi.

Harnetty, Peter. 1972. *The Imperialism of Free Trade: India and Lancashire in the Mid-Nineteenth Century*. Manchester.

Harriss, John. 1982. *Capitalism and Peasant Farming: Agrarian Structure and Ideology in Northern Tamil Nadu*. Bombay.

Haynes, Douglas. 1990. *Rhetoric and Ritual in Colonial India: The Shaping of a Public Culture in Surat City, 1852–1928*. Berkeley.

Headrick, Daniel R. 1988. *The Tentacles of Progress: Technological Transfer in the Age of Imperialism, 1850–1940*. New York.

Heesterman, J. C. 1985. *The Inner Conflict of Tradition: Essays in Indian Ritual, Kingship, and Society*. Chicago.

Herring, Ronald. 1986. *Land to the Tiller: Agrarian Reform in South Asia*. New Haven.

Heyne, Benjamin. 1814. *Tracts Historical and Statistical on India*. London.

Hobson, J. A. 1901. *Imperialism*. London.

Indian National Congress. 1969. *Resolutions on Economic Policy, Programme and Allied Matters (1924–1969)*. New Delhi.

Islam, M. M. 1985. "M. L. Darling and the Punjab Peasant in Prosperity and Debt: A Fresh Look." *Journal of Peasant Studies* 13 (1): 83–98.

Jha, Prem Shankar. 1980. *India: A Political Economy of Stagnation*. Bombay.

Kling, Blair. 1976. *Partner in Empire: Dwarkanath Tagore and the Age of Enterprise in Eastern India*. Berkeley.

Kulke, Hermann. 1982. "Fragmentation and Segmentation versus Integration? Reflections on the Concepts of Indian Feudalism and the Segmentary State in Indian History." *Studies in History* 4 (2): 237–64.

Lal, Deepak. 1988. *The Hindu Equilibrium, I: Cultural Stability and Economic Stagnation, India, ca. 1500 B.C.-A.D. 1980*. Oxford.

Ludden, David. 1984. "Productive Power in Agriculture: A Survey of Work on the Local History of British India." In *Agrarian Power and Agricultural Productivity in South Asia*, ed. Meghnad Desai, 51–100. Berkeley.

Ludden, David. 1985. *Peasant History in South India*. Princeton.

Ludden, David. 1986. "Historians and Nation States." *Perspectives, The American Historical Association Newsletter,* 24 (4): 12–14.

Ludden, David. 1988. "Agrarian Commercialism in Eighteenth-Century South India: Evidence from the 1823 Tirunelveli Census." *Indian Economic and Social History Review* 25 (4): 493–519.

Ludden, David. 1990. "World Economy and Village India, 1600–1900: Exploring the Agrarian History of Capitalism." In *South Asia and World Capitalism,* ed. Sugata Bose. Delhi.

Ludden, David. Forthcoming a. "Archaic Formations of Agricultural Knowledge in South India." In *Agricultural Discourse in South Asia,* ed. Arjun Appadurai.

Ludden, David. Forthcoming b. "Orientalist Empiricism: Transformations of Colonial Knowledge." In *Orientalism and Beyond: Perspectives from South Asia,* ed. Carol Breckenridge and Peter Van der Veer.

Mahalingam, T. V. 1972. *Mackenzie Manuscripts: Summaries of the Historical Manuscripts in the Mackenzie Collection.* Madras.

Majeed, J. 1990. "James Mill's 'The History of British India' and Utilitarianism as a Rhetoric of Reform." *Modern Asian Studies* 24 (2): 209–24.

Manak, Elizabeth. 1979. "Formulation of Agricultural Policy in Imperial India, 1872–1929: A Case Study of Madras Presidency." Ph.D. diss., University of Hawaii.

Mann, Prem S. 1989. "Green Revolution Revisited: The Adoption of High Yielding Variety Wheat Seeds in India." *Journal of Development Studies* 26 (1): 131–44.

Mann, Susan Archer. 1990. *Agrarian Capitalism in Theory and Practice.* Chapel Hill.

Markovits, Claude. 1985. *Indian Business and Nationalist Politics, 1931–1939: The Indigenous Capitalist Class and the Rise of the Congress Party.* Cambridge.

McLane, John R. 1963–64. "Peasants, Moneylenders, and Nationalists at the End of the Nineteenth Century." *Indian Economic and Social History Review* 1 (1): 67–73.

Mill, James. 1818. *The History of British India.* 6 vols. London.

Mishra, Girish. 1988. *Nehru and the Congress Economic Policies.* New Delhi.

Moreland, William H. 1904. *The Agriculture of the United Provinces: An Introduction for the Use of Landholders and Officials.* Allahabad.

Moreland, William H. 1913. *Notes on the Agricultural Conditions and Problems of the United Provinces, Revised up to 1911.* Allahabad.

Mukarji, Nirmal. 1989. "Decentralization below the State Level: Need for a New System of Governance." *Economic and Political Weekly,* March 4, 467–72.

Mukherjee, S. N. 1968. *Sir William Jones: A Study in Eighteenth-Century British Attitudes to India.* London.

Mulhall, Michael G. 1880. *The Progress of the World in Arts, Agriculture, Commerce, Manufacture, Instruction, Railways, and Public Wealth.* London.

Naoroji, Dadabhai. 1901. *Poverty and Un-British Rule in India.* London.

Narayanan, M. G. S. 1988. "The Role of Peasants in the Early History of Tamilakam in South India." *Social Scientist* 16 (9): 17–45.

Needham, Joseph, ed. 1986. *Science and Civilisation in China.* vol. 6., pt. 2. Cambridge.

Nieuwenhuijze, C. A. O. van. 1969. *Development: A Challenge to Whom?* The Hague.

Nkrumah, Kwame. 1965. *Neocolonialism: The Last Stage of Imperialism.* New York.

Noble, David F. 1991. *A World without Women: The Clerical Culture of Western Science.* New York.

O'Hanlon, Rosalind, and David Washbrook. 1991. "After Orientalism: Cultural Criticism and Politics in the Third World." *Comparative Studies in Society and History* 33 (4).

Pandey, Gyanendra. 1990. *The Construction of Communalism in Colonial North India.* Delhi.

Perlin, Frank. 1977. "Of White Whale and Countrymen in the Eighteenth Century Maratha Deccan: Extended Class Relations, Rights, and the Problem of Rural Autonomy under the Old Regime." *Journal of Peasant Studies* 5 (2): 172–237.

Perlin, Frank. 1987. "Money Use in Late Precolonial India and the International Trade in Currency Media." In *The Imperial Monetary System of Mughal India,* ed. John Richards, 232–73. Delhi.

Perlin, Frank. 1988. "The Material and the Cultural: An Attempt to Transcend the Present Impasse." *Modern Asian Studies* 22: 383–416.

Phillimore, R. H. 1954–56. *Historical Records of the Survey of India.* 4 vols. Dehra Dun.

Pogson, Frederick. 1883. *A Manual for Agriculture in India.* Calcutta.

Prakash, Gyan. 1990a. *Bonded Histories: Genealogies of Labor Servitude in Colonial India.* Cambridge.

Prakash, Gyan. 1990b. "Writing Post-Orientalist Histories of the Third World: Perspectives from Indian Historiography." *Comparative Studies in Society and History* 32 (2): 383–408.

Pray, Carl. 1978. "The Economics of Agricultural Research in British Punjab." Ph.D. diss., University of Pennsylvania.

Price, Pamela G. 1979. "Rajadharma in Ramnad: Land Litigation and Largess." *Contributions to Indian Sociology* 13 (2): 207–39.

Raghavaiyangar, S. Srinivasa. 1892. *Memorandum on the Progress of the Madras Presidency during the Last Fifty Years of British Administration.* Madras.

Ranade, Mahadev Govind. 1898. "Indian Political Economy." In Ranade 1982, 1–28.

Ranade, M. G. 1982. *Essays on Indian Economics: A Collection of Essays and Speeches.* Rev. ed. New Delhi.

Randhawa, M. S. 1980. *A History of Agriculture in India.* New Delhi.

Ray, Rajat. 1972. *Industrialization in India: Growth and Conflict in the Private Corporate Sector, 1914–1947.* Delhi.

Raychaudhuri, Tapan, and Irfan Habib, eds. 1982. *The Cambridge Economic History of India.* Cambridge.

Rennell, James. 1793. *Memoir of a Map of Hindoostan.* London.

Robertson, William R. 1880. *An Agricultural Classbook for the Use of Schools in South India.* Madras.

Rodney, Walter. 1982. *How Europe Underdeveloped Africa.* Washington.

Royle, J. Forbes. 1851. *On the Culture and Commerce of Cotton in India.* London.

Rudner, David. 1989. "Banker's Trust and the Culture of Banking among the Nattukottai Chettiars of Colonial South India." *Modern Asian Studies* 23:417–58.

Rudolph, Lloyd I., and Susanne Hoeber Rudolph. 1987. *In Pursuit of Lakshmi: A Political Economy of the Indian State.* Chicago.

Rudra, Ashok. 1989. "Emergence of the Intelligentsia as a Ruling Class in India." *Economic and Political Weekly,* January 21, 151–55.

Said, Edward S. 1978. *Orientalism.* New York.

Sarkar, Susobhan Chandra. 1965. *Rammohun Roy on Indian Economy.* Calcutta.

Sau, Rajit. 1978. *Unequal Exchange, Imperialism, and Underdevelopment: An Essay on the Political Economy of World Capitalism.* Calcutta.

Schrottky, Eugene C. 1876. *The Principles of Rational Agriculture Applied to India and Its Staple Products.* Bombay.

Shah, D. A. 1920. *A Historical Summary and Critical Examination of the Indian Point of View in Economics.* Bombay.

Shah, Motilal Kashal Chand. 1888. *Principles of Agriculture for India.* Ahmedabad.

Shankardass, Rani Dhavan. 1986. "Spokesman for the Peasantry: The Case of Vallabhbhai Patel and Bardoli." *Studies in History* 2 (1): 47–70.

Smith, Richard S. 1985. "Rule-by-Records and Rule-by-Reports: Complementary Aspects of the British Imperial Rule of Law." *Contributions to Indian Sociology* 19 (1): 153–76.

Spear, Percival. 1979. *The Oxford History of Modern India, 1740–1975.* New York.

Stavrianos, L. S. 1981. *Global Rift: The Third World Comes of Age.* New York.

Stein, Burton. 1980. *Peasant State and Society in Medieval South India.* Delhi.

Stein, Burton. 1989. *Thomas Munro: The Origins of the Colonial State and His Vision of Empire.* Delhi.

Stein, Burton. 1991. "Toward an Indian Petty Bourgeoisie: Outline of an Approach." *Economic and Political Weekly,* January 26, 9–20.

Stokes, Eric. 1959. *The English Utilitarians and India.* Oxford.

Stokes, Eric. 1971. "The First Century of British Colonial Rule in India: Social Revolution or Social Stagnation." *Past and Present* 58:136–59.

Stokes, Eric. 1978. *The Peasant and the Raj: Studies in Agrarian Society and Peasant Rebellion in Colonial India.* Cambridge.

Stokes, Eric. 1980. "Bureaucracy and Ideology in Britain and India in the Nineteenth Century." *Transactions of the Royal Historical Society* 5 (30): 131–56.

Stork, Joe. 1976. *Middle East Oil and the Energy Crisis.* New York.

Subrahmanyam, Sanjay, ed. 1990. *Merchants, Markets, and the State in Early Modern India.* Delhi.

Thorner, Daniel. 1950. *Investment in Empire: British Railway and Steam Shipping Enterprise in India, 1825–1849.* Philadelphia.

Thorner, Daniel. 1968. "The Emergence of Capitalist Agriculture in India." In Thorner 1980, 328–56.

Thorner, Daniel. 1970. "Consequences of Independence for the Economy of India." In Thorner 1980, 136–50.

Thorner, Daniel. 1980. *The Making of Modern India.* New Delhi.

Timberg, Thomas. 1978. *The Marwaris: From Traders to Industrialists.* New Delhi.

Tinker, Hugh. 1954. *The Foundations of Local Self-Government in India, Pakistan, and Burma.* London.

Tinker, Hugh. 1962. "Tradition and Experiment in Forms of Government." In *Politics and Society in India,* ed. C. H. Phillips, 155–86. New York.

Tomlinson, B. R. 1978. "Private Foreign Investment in India, 1920–1950." *Modern Asian Studies* 12 (4): 655–77.

Tomlinson, B. R. 1979. *The Political Economy of the Raj, 1914–1947: The Economics of Decolonization.* London.

Tomlinson, B. R. 1988. "The Historical Roots of Indian Poverty: Issues in the Economic and Social History of Modern South Asia, 1880–1960." *Modern Asian Studies* 22:123–40.

Vicziany, Marika. 1986. "Imperialism, Botany, and Statistics in Early Nineteenth-Century India: The Surveys of Francis Buchanan (1762–1829)." *Modern Asian Studies* 20:625–60.

Wallerstein, Immanuel. 1983. *Historical Capitalism.* London.

Washbrook, David A. 1976. *The Emergence of Provincial Politics: The Madras Presidency, 1870–1920.* Cambridge.

Washbrook, David A. 1981. "Law, State, and Agrarian Society in Colonial India." *Modern Asian Studies* 15 (3): 649–721.

Washbrook, David A. 1988. "Progress and Problems: South Asian Economic and Social History, ca. 1720–1860." *Modern Asian Studies* 22 (1): 57–96.

Washbrook, David A. 1989. "Caste, Class, and Dominance in Modern Tamil Nadu." In *Dominance and State Power in Modern India: Decline of a Social Order,* ed. Francine R. Frankel and M. S. A. Rao, 1:204–64. Delhi.

Washbrook, David A. 1990. "South Asia, the World System, and World Capitalism." *Journal of Asian Studies* 49 (3): 479–508.

Weber, Max. 1980. "The Nation-State and Economic Policy (Freiburg Address)." *Economy and Society* 9 (4): 428–49.

Wink, Andre. 1986. *Land and Sovereignty in India: Agrarian Society and Politics under the Eighteenth-Century Maratha Swarajya.* Cambridge.

Yang, Anand A., ed. 1985. *Crime and Criminality in British India.* Tucson.

Zaidi, A. Moin, ed. 1985. *A Tryst with Destiny: A Study of Economic Policy Resolutions of the INC Passed during the Last One Hundred Years.* New Delhi.

Orientalism and the
Exhibitionary Order

Timothy Mitchell

It is no longer unusual to suggest that the construction of the colonial order is related to the elaboration of modern forms of representation and knowledge. The relationship has been most closely examined in the critique of Orientalism. The Western artistic and scholarly portrayal of the non-West, in Edward Said's analysis, is not merely an ideological distortion convenient to an emergent global political order but a densely imbricated arrangement of imagery and expertise that organizes and produces the Orient as a political reality.[1] Three features define this Orientalist reality: it is understood as the product of unchanging racial or cultural essences; these essential characteristics are in each case the polar opposite of the West (passive rather than active, static rather than mobile, emotional rather than rational, chaotic rather than ordered); and the Oriental opposite or Other is, therefore, marked by a series of fundamental absences (of movement, reason, order, meaning, and so on). In terms of these three features—essentialism, otherness, and absence— the colonial world can be mastered, and colonial mastery will, in turn, reinscribe and reinforce these defining features.

Orientalism, however, has always been part of something larger. The nineteenth-century image of the Orient was constructed not just in Oriental studies, romantic novels, and colonial administrations, but in all the new procedures with which Europeans began to organize the representation of the world, from museums and world exhibitions to architecture, schooling, tourism, the fashion industry, and the commodification of everyday life. In 1889, to give an indication of the scale of these processes, 32 million people visited the Exposition Universelle, built that year in Paris to commemorate the centenary of the Revolution and to demonstrate French commercial and imperial power.[2] The consolidation of the global hegemony of the West, economically and politically, can be connected not just to the imagery of Orientalism but to all the new machinery for rendering up and laying out the meaning of the world, so characteristic of the imperial age.

The new apparatus of representation, particularly the world exhibitions, gave a central place to the representation of the non-Western world, and several studies have pointed out the importance of this construction of otherness to the manufacture of national identity and imperial purpose.[3] But is there, perhaps, some more integral relationship between representation, as a modern technique of meaning and order, and the construction of otherness so important to the colonial project? One perspective from which to explore this question is provided by the accounts of non-Western visitors to nineteenth-century Europe. An Egyptian delegation to the Eighth International Congress of Orientalists, for example, held in Stockholm in the summer of 1889, traveled to Sweden via Paris and paused there to visit the Exposition Universelle, leaving us a detailed description of their encounter with the representation of their own otherness. Beginning with this and other accounts written by visitors from the Middle East, I examine the distinctiveness of the modern representational order exemplified by the world exhibition. What Arab writers found in the West, I will argue, were not just exhibitions and representations of the world, but the world itself being ordered up as an endless exhibition. This world-as-exhibition was a place where the artificial, the model, and the plan were employed to generate an unprecedented effect of order and certainty. It is not the artificiality of the exhibitionary order that matters, however, so much as the contrasting effect of an external reality that the artificial and the model create—a reality characterized, like Orientalism's Orient, by essentialism, otherness, and absence. In the second half of the article, I examine this connection between the world-as-exhibition and Orientalism, through a rereading of European travel accounts of the nineteenth-century Middle East. The features of the kind of Orient these writings construct—above all its characteristic absences—are not merely motifs convenient to colonial mastery, I argue, but necessary elements of the order of representation itself.

La rue du Caire

The four members of the Egyptian delegation to the Stockholm Orientalist conference spent several days in Paris, climbing twice the height (as they were told) of the Great Pyramid in Alexandre Eiffel's new tower, and exploring the city and exhibition laid out beneath. Only one thing disturbed them. The Egyptian exhibit had been built by the French to represent a street in medieval Cairo, made of houses with overhanging upper stories and a mosque like that of Qaitbay. "It was intended," one of the Egyptians wrote, "to resemble the old aspect of Cairo." So carefully was this done, he noted, that "even the paint on the buildings was made dirty."[4] The exhibit had also been made carefully chaotic. In contrast to the geometric layout of the rest of the exhibition, the imitation street was arranged in the haphazard manner of the bazaar. The way was crowded with shops and stalls, where Frenchmen, dressed as Orientals, sold perfumes, pastries, and tarbushes. To complete the effect of the Orient, the French organizers had imported from Cairo fifty Egyptian donkeys, together with their drivers and the requisite number of grooms, farriers, and saddlers. The donkeys gave rides (for the price of one franc) up and down the street, resulting in a clamor and confusion so lifelike, the director of the exhibition was obliged to issue an order restricting the donkeys to a certain number at each hour of the day. The Egyptian visitors were disgusted by all this and stayed away. Their final embarrassment had been to enter the door of the mosque and discover that, like the rest of the street, it had been erected as what the Europeans called a facade. "Its external form was all that there was of the mosque. As for the interior, it had been set up as a coffee house, where Egyptian girls performed dances with young males, and dervishes whirled."[5]

After eighteen days in Paris, the Egyptian delegation traveled on to Stockholm to attend the Congress of Orientalists. Together with other non-European delegates, the Egyptians were received with hospitality—and a great curiosity. As though they were still in Paris, they found themselves something of an exhibit. "*Bona fide* Orientals," wrote a European participant in the Congress, "were stared at as in a Barnum's all-world show: the good Scandinavian people seemed to think that it was a collection of *Orientals,* not of *Orientalists.*"[6] Some of the Orientalists themselves seemed to delight in the role of showmen. At an earlier congress, in Berlin, we are told that "the grotesque idea was started of producing natives of Oriental countries as illustrations of a paper: thus the Boden Professor of Sanskrit at Oxford produced a real live Indian Pandit, and made him go through the ritual of Brahmanical prayer and worship before a hilarious assembly.... Professor Max Müller of Oxford produced two rival Japanese priests, who exhibited their gifts; it had the appearance of two showmen exhibiting their monkeys."[7] At the Stockholm Congress, the Egyptians were invited to participate as scholars, but when they used their own language to do so they again found themselves treated as exhibits. "I have heard nothing so unworthy of a sensible man," complained an Oxford scholar, "as . . . the whistling howls emitted by an Arabic student of El-Azhar of Cairo. Such exhibitions at Congresses are mischievous and degrading."[8]

The exhibition and the congress were not the only examples of this European mischief. As Europe consolidated its colonial power, non-European visitors found themselves continually being placed on exhibit or made the careful object of European curiosity. The degradation they were made to suffer seemed as necessary to these spectacles as the scaffolded facades or the curious crowds of onlookers. The facades, the onlookers, and the degradation seemed all to belong to the organizing of an exhibit, to a particularly European concern with rendering the world up to be viewed. Of what, exactly, did this exhibitionary process consist?

An Object-World

To begin with, Middle Eastern visitors found Europeans a curious people, with an uncontainable eagerness to stand and stare. "One of the characteristics of the French is to stare and get excited at everything new," wrote an Egyptian scholar who spent five years in Paris in the 1820s, in the first description of nineteenth-century Europe to be published in Arabic.[9] The "curiosity" of the European is encountered in almost every subsequent Middle Eastern account. Toward the end of the nineteenth century, when one or two Egyptian writers adopted the realistic style of the novel and made the journey to Europe their first topic, their stories would often evoke the peculiar experience of the West by describing an individual surrounded and stared at, like an object on exhibit. "Whenever he paused outside a shop or showroom," the protagonist in one such story found on his first day in Paris, "a large number of people would surround him, both men and women, staring at his dress and appearance."[10]

In the second place, this curious attitude that is described in Arabic accounts was connected with what one might call a corresponding *object-ness*. The curiosity of the observing subject was something demanded by a diversity of mechanisms for rendering things up as its object—beginning with the Middle Eastern visitor himself. The members of an Egyptian student mission sent to Paris in the 1820s were confined to the college where they lived and allowed out only to visit museums and the theater—where they found themselves parodied in vaudeville as objects of entertainment for the French public.[11] "They construct the stage as the play demands," explained one of the students. "For example, if they want to imitate a sultan and the things that happen to him, they set up the stage in the form of a palace and portray him in person. If for instance they want to play the Shah of Persia, they dress someone in the clothes of the Persian monarch and then put him there and sit him on a throne."[12] Even Middle Eastern monarchs who came in person to Europe were liable to be incorporated into its theatrical machinery. When the Khedive of Egypt visited Paris to attend the Exposition Universelle of 1867, he found that the Egyptian exhibit had been built to simulate medieval Cairo in the form of a royal palace. The Khedive stayed in the imitation palace during his visit and became a part of the exhibition, receiving visitors with medieval hospitality.[13]

Visitors to Europe found not only themselves rendered up as objects to be viewed. The Arabic account of the student mission to Paris devoted several pages to the Parisian phenomenon of *"le spectacle,"* a word for which its author knew of no Arabic equivalent. Besides the Opéra and the Opéra-Comique, among the different kinds of spectacle he described were "places in which they represent for the person the view of a town or a country or the like," such as "the Panorama, the Cosmorama, the Diorama, the Europorama and the Uranorama." In a panorama of Cairo, he explained in illustration, "it is as though you were looking from on top of the minaret of Sultan Hasan, for example, with al-Rumaila and the rest of the city beneath you."[14]

The effect of such spectacles was to set the world up as a picture. They ordered it up as an object on display to be investigated and experienced by the dominating European gaze. An Orientalist of the same period, the great French scholar Sylvestre de Sacy, wanted the scholarly picturing of the Orient to make available to European inspection a similar kind of object-world. He had planned to establish a museum, which was to be

a vast depot of objects of all kinds, of drawings, of original books, maps, accounts of voyages, all offered to those who wish to give themselves to the study of [the Orient]; in such a way that each of these students would be able to feel himself transported as if by enchantment into the midst of, say, a Mongolian tribe or of the Chinese race, whichever he might have made the object of his studies.[15]

As part of a more ambitious plan in England for "the education of the people," a proposal was made to set up "an ethnological institution, with very extensive grounds" where "within the same enclosure" were to be kept "specimens in pairs of the various races." The natives on exhibit, it was said,

> should construct their own dwellings according to the architectural ideas of their several countries; their . . . mode of life should be their own. The forms of industry prevalent in their nation or tribe they should be required to practise; and their ideas, opinions, habits, and superstitions should be permitted to perpetuate themselves. . . . To go from one division of this establishment to another would be like travelling into a new country.[16]

The world exhibitions of the second half of the century offered the visitor exactly this educational encounter, with natives and their artifacts arranged to provide the direct experience of a colonized object-world. In planning the layout of the 1889 Paris Exhibition, it was decided that the visitor "before entering the temple of modern life" should pass through an exhibit of all human history, "as a gateway to the exposition and a noble preface." Entitled "Histoire du Travail," or, more fully, "Exposition retrospective du travail et des sciences anthropologiques," the display would demonstrate the history of human labor by means of "objects and things themselves." It would have "nothing vague about it," it was said, "because it will consist of an *object lesson*."[17]

Arabic accounts of the modern West became accounts of these curious object-worlds. By the last decade of the nineteenth century, more than half the descriptions of journeys to Europe published in Cairo were written to describe visits to a world exhibition or an international congress of Orientalists.[18] Such accounts devote hundreds of pages to describing the peculiar order and technique of these events—the curious crowds of spectators, the organization of panoramas and perspectives, the arrangement of natives in mock colonial villages, the display of new inventions and commodities, the architecture of iron and glass, the systems of classification, the calculations of statistics, the lectures, the plans, and the guide books—in short, the entire method of organization that we think of as representation.

The World-as-Exhibition

In the third place, then, the effect of objectness was a matter not just of visual arrangement around a curious spectator, but of representation. What reduced the world to a system of objects was the way their careful organization enabled them to evoke some larger meaning, such as History or Empire or Progress. This machinery of representation was not confined to the exhibition and the congress. Almost everywhere that Middle Eastern visitors went they seemed to encounter the arrangement of things to stand for something larger. They visited the new museums, and saw the cultures of the world portrayed in the form of objects arranged under glass, in the order of their evolution. They were taken to the theater, a place where Europeans represented to themselves their history, as several Egyptian writers explained. They spent afternoons in the public gardens, carefully organized "to bring together the trees and plants of every part of the world," as another Arab writer put it. And, inevitably, they took trips to the zoo, a product of nineteenth-century colonial penetration of the Orient, as Theodor Adorno wrote, that "paid symbolic tribute in the form of animals."[19]

The Europe one reads about in Arabic accounts was a place of spectacle and visual arrangement, of the organization of everything and everything organized to represent, to recall, like the exhibition, a larger meaning. Characteristic of the way Europeans seemed to live was their preoccupation with what an Egyptian author described as *"intizam al-manzar,"* the organization of the view.[20] Beyond the exhibition and the congress, beyond the museum and the zoo, everywhere that non-European visitors went—the streets of the modern city with their meaningful facades, the countryside encountered typically in the form of a model farm exhibiting new machinery and cultivation methods, even the Alps once the funicular was built—they found the technique and sensation to be the same.[21] Everything seemed to be set up before one as though it were the model or the picture of something. Everything was arranged before an observing subject into a system of signification, declaring itself to be a mere object, a mere "signifier of" something further.

The exhibition, therefore, could be read in such accounts as epitomizing the strange character of the West, a place where one was continually pressed into service as a spectator by a world ordered so as to represent. In exhibitions, the traveler from the Middle East could describe the curious way of addressing the world increasingly encountered in modern Europe, a particular relationship between the individual and a world of "objects" that Europeans seemed to take as the experience of the real. This reality effect was a world increasingly rendered up to the individual according to the way in which, and to the extent to which, it could be made to stand before him or her as an exhibit. Non-Europeans encountered in Europe what one might call, echoing a phrase from Heidegger, the age of the world exhibition, or rather, the age of the world-as-exhibition.[22] The world-as-exhibition means not an exhibition of the world but the world organized and grasped as though it were an exhibition.

The Certainty of Representation

"England is at present the greatest Oriental Empire which the world has ever known," proclaimed the president of the 1892 Orientalist Congress at its opening session. His words reflected the political certainty of the imperial age. "She knows not only how to conquer, but how to rule."[23] The endless spectacles of the world-as-exhibition were not just reflections of this certainty but the means of its production, by their technique of rendering imperial truth and cultural difference in "objective" form.

Three aspects of this kind of certainty can be illustrated from the accounts of the world exhibition. First there was the apparent realism of the representation. The model or display always seemed to stand in perfect correspondence to the external world, a correspondence that was frequently noted in Middle Eastern accounts. As the Egyptian visitor had remarked, "Even the paint on the buildings was made dirty." One of the most impressive exhibits at the 1889 exhibition in Paris was a panorama of the city. As described by an Arab visitor, this consisted of a viewing platform on which one stood, encircled by images of the city. The images were mounted and illuminated in such a way that the observer felt himself standing at the center of the city itself, which seemed to materialize around him as a single, solid object "not differing from reality in any way."[24]

In the second place, the model, however realistic, always remained distinguishable from the reality it claimed to represent. Even though the paint was made dirty and the donkeys were brought from Cairo, the medieval Egyptian street at the Paris exhibition remained only a Parisian copy of the Oriental original. The certainty of representation depended on this deliberate difference in time and displacement in space that separated the representation from the real thing. It also depended on the position of the visitor—the tourist in the imitation street or the figure on the viewing platform. The representation of reality was always an exhibit set up for an observer in its midst, an observing European gaze surrounded by and yet excluded from the exhibition's careful order. The more the exhibit drew in and encircled the visitor, the more the gaze was set apart from it, as the mind (in our Cartesian imagery) is said to be set apart from the material world it observes. The separation is suggested in a description of the Egyptian exhibit at the Paris Exhibition of 1867.

A museum inside a pharaonic temple represented Antiquity, a palace richly decorated in the Arab style represented the Middle Ages, a caravanserai of merchants and performers portrayed in real life the customs of today. Weapons from the Sudan, the skins of wild monsters, perfumes, poisons and medicinal plants transport us directly to the tropics. Pottery from Assiut and Aswan, filigree and cloth of silk and gold invite us to touch with our fingers a strange civilization. All the races subject to the Vice-Roy were personified by individuals selected with care. We rubbed shoulders with the fellah, we made way before the Bedouin of the Libyan desert on their beautiful white dromedaries. This sumptuous display spoke to the mind as to the eyes; it expressed a political idea.[25]

The remarkable realism of such displays made the Orient into an object the visitor could almost touch. Yet to the observing eye, surrounded by the display but excluded from it by the status of visitor, it remained a mere representation, the picture of some further reality. Thus, two parallel pairs of distinctions were maintained, between the visitor and the exhibit and between the exhibit and what it expressed. The representation seemed set apart from the political reality it claimed to portray as the observing mind seems set apart from what it observes.

Third, the distinction between the system of exhibits or representations and the exterior meaning they portrayed was imitated, within the exhibition, by distinguishing between the exhibits themselves and the plan of the exhibition. The visitor would encounter, set apart from the objects

on display, an abundance of catalogs, plans, sign posts, programs, guide-
books, instructions, educational talks, and compilations of statistics.
The Egyptian exhibit at the 1867 exhibition, for example, was accompanied by a guidebook containing an outline of the country's history—
divided, like the exhibit to which it referred, into the ancient, medieval,
and modern—together with a "notice statistique sur le territoire, la
population, les forces productives, le commerce, l'effective militaire et
naval, l'organisation financière, l'instruction publique, etc. de l'Egypte"
compiled by the Commission Impériale in Paris.[26] To provide such outlines, guides, tables, and plans, which were essential to the educational
aspect of the exhibition, involved processes of representation that are
no different from those at work in the construction of the exhibits themselves. But the practical distinction that was maintained between the
exhibit and the plan, between the objects and their catalog, reinforced
the effect of two distinct orders of being—the order of things and the
order of their meaning, of representation and reality.

Despite the careful ways in which it was constructed, however, there
was something paradoxical about this distinction between the simulated
and the real, and about the certainty that depends on it. In Paris, it
was not always easy to tell where the exhibition ended and the world
itself began. The boundaries of the exhibition were clearly marked, of
course, with high perimeter walls and monumental gates. But, as Middle
Eastern visitors had continually discovered, there was much about the
organization of the "real world" outside, with its museums and department stores, its street facades and Alpine scenes, that resembled the
world exhibition. Despite the determined efforts to isolate the exhibition
as merely an artificial representation of a reality outside, the real world
beyond the gates turned out to be more and more like an extension of
the exhibition. Yet this extended exhibition continued to present itself
as a series of mere representations, representing a reality beyond. We
should think of it, therefore, not so much as an exhibition but as a kind
of labyrinth, the labyrinth that, as Derrida says, includes in itself its
own exits.[27] But then, maybe the exhibitions whose exits led only to
further exhibitions were becoming at once so realistic and so extensive
that no one ever realized that the real world they promised was not there.

The Labyrinth without Exits

To see the uncertainty of what seemed, at first, the clear distinction
between the simulated and the real, one can begin again inside the world

exhibition, back at the Egyptian bazaar. Part of the shock of the Egyptians came from just how real the street claimed to be: not simply that the paint was made dirty, that the donkeys were from Cairo, and that the Egyptian pastries on sale were said to taste like the real thing, but that one paid for them with what we call *"real* money." The commercialism of the donkey rides, the bazaar stalls, and the dancing girls seemed no different from the commercialism of the world outside. With so disorienting an experience as entering the facade of a mosque to find oneself inside an Oriental cafe that served real customers what seemed to be real coffee, where, exactly, lay the line between the artificial and the real, the representation and the reality?

Exhibitions were coming to resemble the commercial machinery of the rest of the city. This machinery, in turn, was rapidly changing in places such as London and Paris, to imitate the architecture and technique of the exhibition. Small, individually owned shops, often based on local crafts, were giving way to the larger apparatus of shopping arcades and department stores. According to the *Illustrated Guide to Paris* (a book supplying, like an exhibition program, the plan and meaning of the place), each of these new establishments formed "a city, indeed a world in miniature."[28] The Egyptian accounts of Europe contain several descriptions of these commercial worlds-in-miniature, where the real world, as at the exhibition, was something organized by the representation of its commodities. The department stores were described as "large and well organized," with their merchandise "arranged in perfect order, set in rows on shelves with everything symmetrical and precisely positioned." Non-European visitors would remark especially on the panes of glass, inside the stores and along the gas-lit arcades. "The merchandise is all arranged behind sheets of clear glass, in the most remarkable order.... Its dazzling appearance draws thousands of onlookers."[29] The glass panels inserted themselves between the visitors and the goods on display, setting up the former as mere onlookers and endowing the goods with the distance that is the source, one might say, of their objectness. Just as exhibitions had become commercialized, the machinery of commerce was becoming a further means of engineering the real, indistinguishable from that of the exhibition.

Something of the experience of the strangely ordered world of modern commerce and consumers is indicated in the first fictional account of Europe to be published in Arabic. Appearing in 1882, it tells the story of two Egyptians who travel to France and England in the company of an English Orientalist. On their first day in Paris, the two Egyptians wander accidentally into the vast, gas-lit premises of a wholesale supplier. Inside the building they find long corridors, each leading into another. They walk from one corridor to the next, and after a while begin to search for the way out. Turning a corner they see what looks like an exit, with people approaching from the other side. But it turns out to be a mirror, which covers the entire width and height of the wall, and the people approaching are merely their own reflections. They turn down another passage and then another, but each one ends only in a mirror. As they make their way through the corridors of the building, they pass groups of people at work. "The people were busy setting out merchandise, sorting it and putting it into boxes and cases. They stared at the two of them in silence as they passed, standing quite still, not leaving their places or interrupting their work." After wandering silently for some time through the building, the two Egyptians realize they have lost their way completely and begin going from room to room looking for an exit. "But no one interfered with them," we are told, "or came up to them to ask if they were lost." Eventually they are rescued by the manager of the store, who proceeds to explain to them how it is organized, pointing out that, in the objects being sorted and packed, the produce of every country in the world is represented.[30] The West, it appears, is a place organized as a system of commodities, values, meanings, and representations, forming signs that reflect one another in a labyrinth without exits.

The Effect of the Real

The conventional critique of this world of representation and commodification stresses its artificiality. We imagine ourselves caught up in a hall of mirrors from which we cannot find a way out. We cannot find the door that leads back to the real world outside; we have lost touch with reality. This kind of critique remains complicitous with the world-as-exhibition, which is built to persuade us that such a simple door exists. The exhibition does not cut us off from reality. It persuades us that the world is divided neatly into two realms, the exhibition and the real world, thereby creating the effect of a reality from which we now feel cut off. It is not the artificiality of the world-as-exhibition that should concern us, but the contrasting effect of a lost reality to which such supposed artificiality gives rise. This reality, which we take to be something obvious and natural, is in fact something novel and unusual. It appears as a place completely external to the exhibition: that is, a pristine realm existing prior to all representation, which means prior to all intervention by the self, to all construction, mixing, or intermediation, to all the forms of imitation, displacement, and difference that give rise to meaning.

This external reality, it can be noted, bears a peculiar relationship to the Orientalist portrayal of the Orient. Like the Orient, it appears that it simply "is." It is a place of mere being, where essences are untouched by history, by intervention, by difference. Such an essentialized world lacks, by definition, what the exhibition supplies—the dimension of meaning. It lacks the plan or program that supplies reality with its historical and cultural order. The techniques of the world exhibition build into an exterior world this supposed lack, this original meaninglessness and disorder, just as colonialism introduces it to the Orient. The Orient, it could be said, is the pure form of the novel kind of external reality to which the world-as-exhibition gives rise.

Before further examining this connection between the features of Orientalism and the kind of external reality produced by the world-as-exhibition, it is worth recalling that world exhibitions and the new large-scale commercial life of European cities were aspects of a political and economic transformation that was not limited to Europe itself. The new department stores were the first establishments to keep large quantities of merchandise in stock, in the form of standardized textiles and clothing. The stockpiling, together with the introduction of advertising (the word was coined at the time of the great exhibitions, Walter Benjamin reminds us) and the new European industry of "fashion" (on which several Middle Eastern writers commented) were all connected with the boom in textile production.[31] The textile boom was an aspect of other changes, such as new ways of harvesting and treating cotton, new machinery for the manufacture of textiles, the resulting increase in profits, and the reinvestment of profit abroad in further cotton production. At the other end from the exhibition and the department store, these wider changes extended to include places such as the southern United States, India, and the Nile valley.

Since the latter part of the eighteenth century, the Nile valley had been undergoing a transformation associated principally with the European textile industry.[32] From a country that formed one of the hubs in the commerce of the Ottoman world and beyond and that produced and exported its own food and its own textiles, Egypt was turning into a country whose economy was dominated by the production of a single commodity, raw cotton, for the global textile industry of Europe.[33] The changes associated with this growth and concentration in exports included an enormous growth in imports, principally of textile products and food, the extension throughout the country of a network of roads, telegraphs, police stations, railways, ports, and permanent irrigation canals, a new relationship to the land (which became a privately owned commodity concentrated in the hands of a small, powerful, and increasingly wealthy social class), the influx of Europeans (seeking to make fortunes, transform agricultural production or make the country a model of colonial order), the building and rebuilding of towns and cities as centers of the new European-dominated commercial life, and the migration to these urban centers of tens of thousands of the increasingly impoverished rural poor. In the nineteenth century, no other place in the world was transformed on a greater scale to serve the production of a single commodity.

Elsewhere I have examined in detail how the modern means of colonizing a country that this transformation required—new military methods, the reordering of agricultural production, systems of organized schooling, the rebuilding of cities, new forms of communication, the transformation of writing, and so on—all represented the techniques of ordering up an object-world to create the novel effect of a world divided in two: on the one hand a material dimension of things themselves, and on the other a seemingly separate dimension of their order or meaning.[34] Thus it can be shown, I think, that the strange, binary order of the world-as-exhibition was already being extended through a variety of techniques to places like the Middle East. If, as I have been suggesting, this binary division was, in fact, uncertain and it was hard to tell on close inspection where the exhibition ended and reality began, then this uncertainty extended well beyond the supposed limits of the West. Yet at the same time as these paradoxical but enormously powerful methods of the exhibition were spreading across the southern and eastern shores of the Mediterranean, the world exhibitions began to portray, outside the world-as-exhibition and lacking by definition the meaning and order that exhibitions supply, an essentialized and exotic Orient.

There are three features of this binary world that I have tried to outline in the preceding pages. First, there is its remarkable claim to certainty or truth: the apparent certainty with which everything seems ordered and represented, calculated and rendered unambiguous—ultimately, what seems its political decidedness. Second, there is the paradoxical nature of this decidedness: the certainty exists as the seemingly determined correspondence between mere representations and reality; yet the real world, like the world outside the exhibition, despite everything the exhibition promises, turns out to consist only of further representations of this "reality." Third, there is its colonial nature: the age of the exhibition was necessarily the colonial age, the age of world economy and global power in which we live, since what was to be made available as exhibit was reality, the world itself.

To draw out the colonial nature of these methods of order and truth and thus their relationship to Orientalism, I am now going to move on to the Middle East. The Orient, as I have suggested, was the great "external reality" of modern Europe—the most common object of its exhibitions, the great signified. By the 1860s, Thomas Cook, who had launched the modern tourist industry by organizing excursion trains (with the Midland Railway Company) to visit the first of the great exhibitions, at the Crystal Palace in 1851, was offering excursions to visit not exhibits of the East, but the "East itself." If Europe was becoming the world-as-exhibition, what happened to Europeans who went abroad—to visit places whose images invariably they had already encountered in books, spectacles, and exhibitions? How did they experience the so-called real world such images had depicted, when the reality was a place whose life was not lived, or at least not yet, as if the world were an exhibition?

The East Itself

"So here we are in Egypt," wrote Gustave Flaubert, in a letter from Cairo in January, 1850.

> What can I say about it all? What can I write you? As yet I am scarcely over the initial bedazzlement . . . each detail reaches out to grip you; it pinches you; and the more you concentrate on it the less you grasp the whole. Then gradually all this becomes harmonious and the pieces fall into place of themselves, in accordance with the laws of perspective. But the first days, by God, it is such a bewildering chaos of colours. . . . "[35]

Flaubert experiences Cairo as a visual turmoil. What can he write about the place? That it is a chaos of color and detail that refuses to compose itself as a picture. The disorienting experience of a Cairo street, in other words, with its arguments in unknown languages, strangers who brush past in strange clothes, unusual colors, and unfamiliar sounds and smells, is expressed as an absence of pictorial order. There is no distance, this means, between oneself and the view, and the eyes are reduced to organs of touch: "Each detail reaches out to grip you." Without a separation of the self from a picture, moreover, what becomes impossible is to grasp "the whole." The experience of the world as a picture set up before a subject is linked to the unusual conception of the world as an enframed totality, something that forms a structure or system. Subsequently, coming to terms with this disorientation and recovering one's self-possession is expressed again in pictorial terms. The world arranges itself into a picture and achieves a visual order, "in accordance with the laws of perspective."

Flaubert's experience suggests a paradoxical answer to my question concerning what happened to Europeans who "left" the exhibition. Although they thought of themselves as moving from the pictures or exhibits to the real thing, they went on trying—like Flaubert—to grasp the real thing as a picture. How could they do otherwise, since they took reality itself to be picturelike? The real is that which is grasped in terms of a distinction between a picture and what it represents, so nothing else would have been, quite literally, thinkable.

Among European writers who traveled to the Middle East in the middle and latter part of the nineteenth century, one very frequently finds the experience of its strangeness expressed in terms of the problem of forming a picture. It was as though to make sense of it meant to stand back and make a drawing or take a photograph of it; which for many of them actually it did. "Every year that passes," an Egyptian wrote, "you see thousands of Europeans traveling all over the world, and everything they come across they make a picture of."[36] Flaubert traveled in Egypt on a photographic mission with Maxime du Camp, the results of which were expected to be "quite special in character" it was remarked at the Institut de France, "thanks to the aid of this modern traveling companion, efficient, rapid, and always scrupulously exact."[37] The chemically etched correspondence between photographic image and reality would provide a new, almost mechanical kind of certainty.

Like the photographer, the writer wanted to reproduce a picture of things "exactly as they are," of "the East itself in its vital actual reality."[38] Flaubert was preceded in Egypt by Edward Lane, whose innovative *Account of the Manners and Customs of the Modern Egyptians,* published in 1835, was a product of the same search for a pictorial certainty of representation. The book's "singular power of description and minute accuracy" made it, in the words of his nephew, Orientalist Stanley Poole, "the most perfect picture of a people's life that has ever been written."[39] "Very few men," added his grandnephew, the Orientalist Stanley Lane-Poole, "have possessed in equal degree the power of minutely describing a scene or a monument, so that the pencil might almost restore it without a fault after the lapse of years. . . . The objects stand before you as you read, and this not by the use of imaginative language, but by the plain simple description."[40]

Lane, in fact, did not begin as a writer but as a professional artist and engraver, and had first traveled to Egypt in 1825 with a new apparatus called the camera lucida, a drawing device with a prism that projected an exact image of the object on to paper. He had planned to publish the drawings he made and the accompanying descriptions in an eight-volume work entitled "An Exhaustive Description of Egypt," but had been unable to find a publisher whose printing techniques could reproduce the minute and mechanical accuracy of the illustrations. Subsequently he published the part dealing with contemporary Egypt, rewritten as the famous ethnographic description of the modern Egyptians.[41]

The problem for the photographer or writer visiting the Middle East, however, was not just to make an accurate picture of the East but to set up the East as a picture. One can copy or represent only what appears already to exist representationally—as a picture. The problem, in other words, was to create a distance between oneself and the world and thus constitute it as something picturelike—as an object on exhibit. This required what was now called a "point of view," a position set apart and outside. While in Cairo, Edward Lane lived near one of the city's gates, outside which there was a large hill with a tower and military telegraph on top. This elevated position commanded "a most magnificent view of the city and suburbs and the citadel," Lane wrote. "Soon after my arrival I made a very elaborate drawing of the scene, with the camera lucida. From no other spot can so good a view of the metropolis . . . be obtained."[42]

These spots were difficult to find in a world where, unlike the West, such "objectivity" was not yet built in. Besides the military observation tower used by Lane, visitors to the Middle East would appropriate whatever buildings and monuments were available in order to obtain the necessary viewpoint. The Great Pyramid at Giza had now become a viewing platform. Teams of Bedouin were organized to heave and push the writer or tourist—guidebook in hand—to the top, where two more Bedouin would carry the European on their shoulders to all four corners, to observe the view. At the end of the century, an Egyptian novel satirized the westernizing pretensions among members of the Egyptian upper middle class, by having one such character spend a day climbing the pyramids at Giza to see the view.[43] The minaret presented itself similarly to even the most respectable European as a viewing tower, from which to sneak a panoptic gaze over a Muslim town. "The mobbing I got at *Shoomlo*," complained Jeremy Bentham on his visit to the Middle East, "only for taking a peep at the town from a thing they call a *minaret* . . . has canceled any claims they might have had upon me for the dinner they gave me at the *divan,* had it been better than it was."[44]

Bentham can remind us of one more similarity between writer and camera, and of what it meant, therefore, to grasp the world as though it were a picture or exhibition. The point of view was not just a place set apart, outside the world or above it. Ideally, it was a position from where, like the authorities in Bentham's panopticon, one could see and yet not be seen. The photographer, invisible beneath his black cloth as he eyed the world through his camera's gaze, in this respect typified the kind of presence desired by the European in the Middle East, whether as tourist, writer, or, indeed, colonial power.[45] The ordinary European tourist, dressed (according to the advice in *Murray's Handbook for Travellers in Lower and Upper Egypt,* already in its seventh edition by 1888) in either "a common felt helmet or wide-awake, with a turban of white muslin wound around it" or alternatively a pith helmet, together with a blue or green veil and "coloured-glass spectacles with gauze sides," possessed the same invisible gaze.[46] The ability to see without being seen confirmed one's separation from the world, and constituted at the same time a position of power.

The writer, too, wished to see without being seen. The representation of the Orient, in its attempt to be detached and objective, would seek to eliminate from the picture the presence of the European observer. Indeed, to represent something as Oriental, as Edward Said has argued, one sought to excise the European presence altogether.[47] "Many thanks for the local details you sent me," wrote Théophile Gautier to Gérard de Nerval in Cairo, who was supplying him with firsthand material for his Oriental scenarios at the Paris Opéra. "But how the devil was I to have included among the walk-on's of the Opéra these Englishmen dressed in raincoats, with their quilted cotton hats and their green veils to protect themselves against ophthalmia?" Representation was not to represent the voyeur, the seeing eye that made representation possible.[48] To establish the objectness of the Orient, as a picture-reality containing no sign of the increasingly pervasive European presence, required that the presence itself, ideally, become invisible.

Participant Observation

Yet this was where the paradox began. At the same time as the European wished to elide himself in order to constitute the world as something not-himself, something other and objectlike, he also wanted to experience it as though it were the real thing. Like visitors to an exhibition or scholars in Sacy's Orientalist museum, travelers wanted to feel themselves "transported . . . into the very midst" of their Oriental object-world, and to "touch with their fingers a strange civilization." In his journal, Edward Lane wrote of wanting "to throw myself entirely among strangers, . . . to adopt their language, their customs, and their dress."[49] This kind of immersion was to make possible the profusion of ethnographic detail in writers such as Lane, and produce in their work the effect of a direct and immediate experience of the Orient. In Lane, and even more so in writers such as Flaubert and Nerval, the desire for this immediacy of the real became a desire for direct and physical contact with the exotic, the bizarre, and the erotic.

There was a contradiction, therefore, between the need to separate oneself from the world and render it up as an object of representation, and the desire to lose oneself within this object-world and experience it directly; a contradiction that world exhibitions, with their profusion of exotic detail and yet their clear distinction between visitor and exhibit, were built to accommodate and overcome. In fact, "experience," in this sense, depends upon the structure of the exhibition. The problem in a place such as Cairo, which had not been built to provide the experience of an exhibition, was to fulfill such a double desire. On his first day in Cairo, Gérard de Nerval met a French "painter" equipped with a daguerreotype, who "suggested that I come with him to choose a point of view." Agreeing to accompany him, Nerval decided "to have myself taken to the most labyrinthine point of the city, abandon the painter to his tasks, and then wander off haphazardly, without interpreter or companion." But within the labyrinth of the city, where Nerval hoped to immerse himself in the exotic and finally experience "without interpreter" the real Orient, they were unable to find any point from which to take the picture. They followed one crowded, twisting street after another, looking without success for a suitable viewpoint, until eventually the profusion of noises and people subsided and the streets became "more silent, more dusty, more deserted, the mosques fallen in decay and here and there a building in collapse." In the end they found themselves outside the city, "somewhere in the suburbs, on the other side of the canal from the main sections of the town." Here at last, amid the silence and the ruins, the photographer was able to set up his device and portray the Oriental city.[50]

Said reminds us that it was Edward Lane who claimed to have found the ideal device for meeting this double demand, to immerse oneself and yet stand apart. The device was that of hiding beneath a deliberate disguise, rather like the tourist in colored spectacles or the photographer beneath his cloth. In order "to escape exciting, in strangers, any suspicion of . . . being a person who had no right to intrude among them," Lane explained, he adopted the dress and feigned the religious belief of the local Muslim inhabitants of Cairo. The dissimulation allowed him to gain the confidence of his Egyptian informants, making it possible to observe them in their own presence without himself being observed. His ethnographic writing seems to acquire the authority of this presence, this direct experience of the real. But at the same time, as Said points out, in a preface to the ethnography, Lane carefully explains his deception to the European reader, thus assuring the reader of his absolute distance from the Egyptians. The distance assured by the deception is what gives his experience its "objectivity."[51]

The curious double position of the European, as participant-observer, makes it possible to experience the Orient as though one were the visitor to an exhibition. Unaware that the Orient has not been arranged as an exhibition, the visitor nevertheless attempts to carry out the characteristic cognitive maneuver of the modern subject, who separates himself from an object-world and observes it from a position that is invisible and set apart. From there, like the modern anthropologist or social scientist, one transfers into the object the principles of one's relation to it and, as Pierre Bourdieu says, "conceives of it as a totality intended for cognition alone." The world is grasped, inevitably, in terms of a distinction between the object—the "thing itself" as the European says—and its meaning, with no sense of the historical peculiarity of this effect we call the "thing itself" or of this realm that we call "meaning." In terms of this distinction, the scholar can grasp the world as an exhibition, as a representation—"in the sense of idealist philosophy, but also as used in painting or the theatre," and people's lives appear as no more than "stage parts . . . or the implementing of plans."[52] We must add to what Bourdieu says that the anthropologist, like the tourist and the Orientalist writer, had come to the Middle East from Europe, a world (as we have seen) that was being set up as a system of theaters and exhibitions that demand this kind of cognitive maneuver. They came from a place, in other words, in which ordinary people were beginning to live as tourists or anthropologists, addressing an object-world as the endless representation of some further meaning or reality, and experiencing personhood as the playing of a cultural stage part or the implementation of a plan.

The Orient That Escapes

This, then, was the contradiction of Orientalism. Europeans brought to the Middle East the cognitive habits of the world-as-exhibition, and tried to grasp the Orient as something picturelike. On the other hand, they came to experience a "reality" that invariably they had already seen represented in an exhibition. They thought of themselves, therefore, as actually moving from the exhibit or picture to the experience of the real thing. This was literally the case with Théophile Gautier, who lived in Paris writing his Orientalist scenarios for the Opéra-Comique and championing the cause of Orientalist painting. He finally set off for Egypt in 1869 after being inspired to see the real thing by a visit to the Egyptian exhibit at the 1867 Exposition Universelle. But in this respect Gautier was no exception. Europeans in general arrived in the Orient after seeing plans and models—in pictures, exhibitions, museums, and books—of which they were seeking the original; and their purpose was always explained in these terms.

Orientalism's contradiction exemplifies the paradoxical nature of the world-as-exhibition. The exhibition persuades people that the world is divided into two realms—the representation and the original, the exhibit and the external reality, the text and the world. Everything seems organized as if this were the case. But "reality," it turns out, means that which can be represented, that which presents itself as an exhibit before an observer. The so-called real world "outside" is something experienced and grasped only as a series of further representations, an extended exhibition. Visitors to the Orient conceived of themselves as traveling to "the East itself in its vital actual reality."[53] But the reality they sought there was simply that which could be pictured or accurately represented— that which stands apart as something distinct from an observing subject and is grasped in terms of a corresponding distinction between representation and reality. In the end, the European tried to grasp the Orient as though it were an exhibition of itself.

This paradox produced the symptomatic features of the Orientalist portrayal of the Orient. First of all, as we have already seen with Flaubert and Nerval, since the Middle East had not yet been organized representationally, to Europeans it appeared to suffer from an essential lack. It lacked those effects they knew as order and meaning—making the task of representing it almost impossible and the results disappointing. "Think of it no more!" wrote Nerval to Gautier, of the Cairo they had dreamed of describing. "That Cairo lies beneath the ashes and dirt . . . dust-laden and dumb." Nothing encountered in those Oriental streets quite matched up to the reality they had seen represented in Paris. Not even the cafes looked genuine. "I really wanted to set the scene for you here," Nerval explained, in an attempt to describe a typical Cairene street for one of Gautier's Parisian stage sets, "but . . . it is only in Paris that one finds cafés so Oriental."[54] "To create imaginary Egyptians as they are usually seen in the theater is not difficult," wrote Egyptologist Mariette Pasha, another supplier of Oriental detail for the Paris stage, in this case the opera *Aida*. But "to make a scholarly as well as a picturesque mise-en-scene," accurately representing the Orient, was almost impossible. "I did not suspect the immensity of the details. . . . I am literally losing my mind."[55]

Herman Melville, who visited the Middle East in the winter of 1856– 57, felt the usual need to find a point of view from which to observe an Oriental city and experienced the usual difficulties. Rather than an exhibition of something, Cairo seemed like some temporary market or carnival—"one booth and Bartholomew Fair," he called it. Like Nerval, Melville wrote of wanting to withdraw from the "maze" of streets, in order to see the place as a picture or plan. Visiting Istanbul, he complained in his journal that there was "no plan to streets. Perfect labyrinth. Narrow. Close, shut in. If one could but get *up* aloft. . . . But no. No names to the streets. . . . No numbers. No anything."[56] Like Nerval, Melville could find no point of view within the city and, therefore, no picture. What this meant, in turn, was that there seemed to be no plan. As at the world exhibitions, the separation of an observer from an object-world was something a European needed to experience in terms of a plan. He expected there to be something that was somehow set apart from "things themselves" as a guidebook, a sign, or a map that supplied the meaning and order of what was laid out before him. In the Middle Eastern city, nothing seemed to have been arranged to stand apart and address itself in this way to the outsider, to the observing subject. There were no names to the streets and no street signs, no open spaces with imposing facades, and no maps.[57] The city refused to offer itself in this way as a representation of something, because it had not been built as one. It had not been arranged, like an exhibition, to effect our strange distinction between the city on the one hand and on the other its meaning or plan.

The apparent absence of order and meaning led the European visitor to despair completely of finding "real Egypt," the Orient that could be represented. "I will find at the Opéra the real Cairo," wrote Nerval, ". . . the Orient that escapes me." In the end, only the Orient one finds in Paris, the simulation of what is itself a series of representations to begin with, can offer a satisfying spectacle. As he moved on toward the towns of Palestine, Nerval remembered Cairo as something no more solid or real than facades of an exhibition or the painted scenery of a theater set. "Just as well that the six months I spent there are over; it is already nothing, I have seen so many places collapse behind my steps, like stage sets; what do I have left from them? An image as confused as that of a dream: the best of what one finds there, I already knew by heart."[58]

The second feature of the Orient was that it became a place the European felt he "already knew by heart" on arrival. "Familiar to me from days of early childhood are the forms of the Egyptian pyramids," wrote Alexander Kinglake in *Eōthen.* "Now, as I approached them from the banks of the Nile, I had no print, no picture before me, and yet the old shapes were there; there was no change: they were as I had always known them." Gautier, for his part, wrote that if the visitor to Egypt "has long inhabited in his dreams" a certain town, he will carry in his head "an imaginary map, difficult indeed to erase even when he finds himself facing the reality." His own map of Cairo, he explained, "built with the materials of *A Thousand and One Nights,* arranges itself around Marilhat's *Place de l'Ezbekieh,* a remarkable and violent painting. . . ." The attentive European, wrote Flaubert in Cairo, "*rediscovers* here much more than he discovers."[59]

The Orient was something one only ever rediscovered. Lacking the visual order of an exhibition and the accompanying system of signs, the meaning and order of the Orient had to be brought in from outside, or so the colonial European assumed. The only way to grasp it representationally, as the picture of something, was to grasp it as the reoccurrence of a picture one had seen before, or according to the lines of a map one already carried in one's head, or as the reiteration of an earlier description. How far this repetition could go was illustrated by Gautier, the champion of Orientalist art, when he was finally inspired, by the 1867 Paris exhibition, to leave Paris and visit Cairo to see the real thing. On his return from the Middle East he published an account of Egypt whose first chapter, entitled "Vue génerale," was, in fact, a description, in great detail, of the Egyptian exhibit at the Parisian world exhibition.[60]

The representation of the Orient obeyed, inevitably, this problematic and unrecognized logic, a logic determined not by any intellectual failure of the European mind but by its search for the certainty of representation—for an effect called "reality." What is problematic is not the logic itself but the failure to recognize its paradoxical nature. Europeans like Edward Lane had begun the drawing up of their "exhaustive description of Egypt," already determined to correct the earlier work of the French scientific mission's *Description de l'Egypte.* Later writers would then take themselves to the library of the French Institut in Cairo, and draw from and add to this body of description. Gérard de Nerval, collecting the material in Egypt he later published as *Voyage en Orient,* his life's major prose work, saw more of the library than of the rest of the country. After two months in Cairo, more than halfway through his stay, he wrote to his father that he had not even visited the pyramids. "Moreover I have no desire to see any place until after I have adequately informed myself from the books and memoires," he explained. Six weeks later he wrote again, saying that he was leaving the country even though he had not yet ventured outside Cairo and its environs.[61]

As a result, the bulk of *Voyage en Orient,* like so much of the literature of Orientalism, turns out to be a reworking or direct repetition of the "information" available in libraries, in Nerval's case mostly from Lane's *Manners and Customs of the Modern Egyptians.* Such repetition and reworking is what Edward Said has referred to as the citationary nature of Orientalism, its writings added to one another "as a restorer of old sketches might put a series of them together for the cumulative picture they implicitly represent." The Orient is put together as this "representation," and what is represented is not a real place but "a set of references, a congeries of characteristics, that seems to have its origin in a quotation, or a fragment of a text, or a citation from someone's work on the Orient, or some bit of previous imagining, or an amalgam of all these."[62] The "East itself" is not a place, despite the exhibition's promise, but a further series of representations, each one reannouncing the reality of the Orient but doing no more than referring backwards and forwards to all the others. It is the chain of references that produces the effect of the place. Robert Graves remarks wryly on this effect in *Goodbye to All That,* when he disembarks at Port Said in the 1920s to take up a job at the Egyptian University and is met by an English friend: "I still felt seasick," he writes, "but knew that I was in the East because he began talking about Kipling."[63]

In claiming that the "East itself" is not a place, I am not saying simply that Western representations created a distorted image of the real Orient; nor am I saying that the "real Orient" does not exist, and that there are no realities but only images and representations. Either statement would take for granted the strange way the West had come to live, as though the world were divided in this way into two: into a realm of "mere" representations opposed to an essentialized realm of "the real"; into exhibitions opposed to an external reality; into an order of models, descriptions, texts, and meanings opposed to an order of originals, of things in themselves.[64] What we already suspected in the streets of Paris, concerning this division, is confirmed by the journey to the Orient: what seems excluded from the exhibition as the real or the outside turns out to be only that which can be represented, that which occurs in exhibitionlike form—in other words, a further extension of that labyrinth that we call an exhibition. What matters about this labyrinth is not that we never reach the real, never find the promised exit, but that such a notion of the real, such a system of truth, continues to convince us.

The case of Orientalism shows us, moreover, how this supposed distinction between a realm of representation and an external reality corresponds to another apparent division of the world, into the West and the non-West. In the binary terms of the world-as-exhibition, reality is the effect of an external realm of pure existence, untouched by the self and by the processes that construct meaning and order. The Orient is a similar effect. It appears as an essentialized realm originally outside and untouched by the West, lacking the meaning and order that only colonialism can bring. Orientalism, it follows, is not just a nineteenth-century instance of some general historical problem of how one culture portrays another, nor just an aspect of colonial domination, but part of a method of order and truth essential to the peculiar nature of the modern world.

NOTES

This is a revised and extended version of "The World as Exhibition," *Comparative Studies in Society and History* 31, no. 2 (April, 1989): 217–36, much of which was drawn from the first chapter of *Colonising Egypt* (Cambridge: Cambridge University Press, 1988). I am indebted to Lila Abu-Lughod, Stefania Pandolfo, and the participants in the Conference on Colonialism and Culture held at the University of Michigan in May, 1989, for their comments on earlier versions.

1. Edward Said, *Orientalism* (New York: Pantheon, 1978).

2. Tony Bennett, "The Exhibitionary Complex," *New Formations* 4 (Spring, 1988): 96. Unfortunately, this insightful article came to my attention only as I was completing the revisions to this article.

3. See especially Robert W. Rydell, *All the World's a Fair: Visions of Empire at American International Expositions, 1876–1916* (Chicago: University of Chicago Press, 1984); see also Bennett, "Exhibitionary Complex."

4. Muhammad Amin Fikri, *Irshad al-alibba' ila mahasin Urubba* (Cairo, 1892), 128.

5. Fikri, *Irshad,* 128–29, 136.

6. R. N. Crust, "The International Congresses of Orientalists," *Hellas* 6 (1897): 359.

7. Crust, "International Congresses," 351.

8. Crust, "International Congresses," 359.

9. Rifa'a al-Tahtawi, *al-A'mal al-kamila* (Beirut: al-Mu'assasa al-Arabiyya li-l-Dirasat wa-l-Nashr, 1973), 2:76.

10. Ali Mubarak, *Alam al-din* (Alexandria, 1882), 816. The "curiosity" of the European is something of a theme for Orientalist writers, who contrast it with the "general lack of curiosity" of non-Europeans. Such curiosity is assumed to be the natural, unfettered relation of a person to the world, emerging in Europe once the loosening of "theological bonds" had brought about "the freeing of human minds" (Bernard Lewis, *The Muslim Discovery of Europe* [London: Weidenfeld and Nicholson, 1982], 299). See Mitchell, *Colonising Egypt,* 4–5, for a critique of this sort of argument and its own "theological" assumptions.

11. Alain Silvera, "The First Egyptian Student Mission to France under Muhammad Ali," in *Modern Egypt: Studies in Politics and Society,* ed. Elie Kedourie and Sylvia G. Haim (London: Frank Cass, 1980), 13.

12. Tahtawi, *al-A'mal,* 2:177, 119–20.

13. Georges Douin, *Histoire du règne du Khédive Ismaïl* (Rome: Royal Egyptian Geographical Society, 1934), 2:4–5.

14. Tahtawi, *al-A'mal,* 2:121.

15. Quoted in Said, *Orientalism,* 165.

16. James Augustus St. John, *The Education of the People* (London: Chapman and Hall, 1858), 82–83.

17. "Les origines et le plan de l'exposition," in *L'Exposition de Paris de 1889,* no. 3 (December 15, 1889): 18.

18. On Egyptian writing about Europe in the nineteenth century, see Ibrahim Abu-Lughod, *Arab Rediscovery of Europe* (Princeton: Princeton University Press, 1963); Anouar Louca, *Voyageurs et écrivains égyptiens en France au XIXe siècle* (Paris: Didier, 1970); Mitchell, *Colonising Egypt,* 7–13, 180 n. 14.

19. Theodor Adorno, *Minima Moralia: Reflections from a Damaged Life* (London: Verso, 1978), 116; on the theater, see, for example, Muhammad al-Muwaylihi, *Hadith Isa ibn Hisham, aw fatra min al-zaman,* 2d ed. (Cairo: al-Maktaba al-Azhariyya, 1911), 434, and Tahtawi, *al-A'mal,* 2:119–20; on the public garden and the zoo, Muhammad al-Sanusi al-Tunisi, *al-Istitla'at al-barisiya fi ma'rad sanat 1889* (Tunis: n.p., 1891), 37.

20. Mubarak, *Alam al-din,* 817.

21. The model farm outside Paris is described in Mubarak, *Alam al-din,* 1008–42; the visual effect of the street in Mubarak, *Alam al-din,* 964, and Idwar Ilyas, *Mashahid Uruba wa-Amirka* (Cairo: al-Muqtataf, 1900), 268; the new funicular at Lucerne and the European passion for panoramas in Fikri, *Irshad,* 98.

22. Martin Heidegger, "The Age of the World Picture," in *The Question Concerning Technology and Other Essays* (New York: Harper and Row, 1977).

23. International Congress of Orientalists, *Transactions of the Ninth Congress, 1892* (London: International Congress of Orientalists, 1893), 1:35.

24. Al-Sanusi, *al-Istitla'at,* 242.

25. Edmond About, *Le fellah: souvenirs d'Egypte* (Paris: Hachette, 1869), 47–48.

26. Charles Edmond, *L'Egypte à l'exposition universelle de 1867* (Paris: Dentu, 1867).

27. Jacques Derrida, *Speech and Phenomena and Other Essays on Husserl's Theory of Signs* (Evanston, Ill.: Northwestern University Press, 1973), 104. All of his subsequent writings, Derrida once remarked, "are only a commentary on the sentence about a labyrinth" ("Implications: Interview with Henri Ronse," in *Positions* [Chicago: University of Chicago Press, 1981], 5). My article, too, should be read as a commentary on that sentence.

28. Quoted in Walter Benjamin, "Paris, Capital of the Nineteenth Century," in *Reflections: Essays, Aphorisms, Autobiographical Writings* (New York: Harcourt Brace Jovanovich, 1978), 146–47.

29. Mubarak, *Alam al-din,* 818; Ilyas, *Mashahid Uruba,* 268.

30. Mubarak, *Alam al-din,* 829–30.

31. Benjamin, "Paris," 146, 152; Tahtawi, *al-A'mal,* 2:76.

32. See André Raymond, *Artisans et commerçants au Caire au XVIIIe siècle* (Damascus: Institut français de Damas, 1973), 1:173–202; Roger Owen, *The Middle East in the World Economy 1800–1914* (London: Methuen, 1981).

33. By the eve of World War I, cotton accounted for more than 92 percent of the total value of Egypt's exports (Roger Owen, *Cotton and the Egyptian Economy* [Oxford: Oxford University Press, 1969], 307).

34. See Mitchell, *Colonising Egypt.*

35. Gustave Flaubert, *Flaubert in Egypt: A Sensibility on Tour,* trans. Francis Steegmuller (London: Michael Haag, 1983), 79.

36. Mubarak, *Alam al-din,* 308.

37. Flaubert, *Flaubert in Egypt,* 23.

38. Eliot Warburton, author of *The Crescent and the Cross: or Romance and Realities of Eastern Travel* (1845), describing Alexander Kinglake's *Eōthen, or Traces of Travel Brought Home from the East* (London, 1844; reprint ed., J. M. Dent, 1908); cited in *The Oxford Companion to English Literature,* 5th ed. (Oxford: Oxford University Press, 1985), s.v. "Kinglake."

39. Edward Lane, *An Account of the Manners and Customs of the Modern Egyptians,* reprint ed. (London: J. M. Dent, 1908), vii, xvii.

40. Stanley Lane-Poole, "Memoir," in Edward Lane, *An Arabic-English Lexicon,* reprint ed. (Beirut: Librairie du Liban, 1980), 5:xii.

41. Leila Ahmed, *Edward W. Lane: A Study of His Life and Work* (London: Longmans, 1978); John D. Wortham, *The Genesis of British Egyptology, 1549–1906* (Norman, Okla.: University of Oklahoma Press, 1971), 65.

42. Quoted in Ahmed, *Edward Lane,* 26.

43. Muwaylihi, *Isa ibn Hisham,* 405–17.

44. Jeremy Bentham, *The Complete Works,* ed. John Bowring (Edinburgh: Tait, 1838–43), 4:65–66.

45. Cf. Malek Alloula, *The Colonial Harem* (Minneapolis: University of Minnesota Press, 1986).

46. *Murray's Handbook for Travellers in Lower and Upper Egypt* (London: John Murray, 1888).

47. Said, *Orientalism,* 160–61, 168, 239. My subsequent analysis is much indebted to Said's work.

48. J. M. Carré, *Voyageurs et écrivains français en Egypte,* 2d ed. (Cairo: Institut Français d'Archéologie Orientale, 1956), 2:191.

49. Quoted in Lane, *Arabic-English Lexicon,* 5:vii.

50. Gérard de Nerval, *Oeuvres,* ed. Albert Béguin and Jean Richer, vol. 1, *Voyage en Orient* [1851], ed. Michel Jeanneret (Paris: Gallimard 1952), 172–74.

51. Said, *Orientalism,* 160–64.

52. Pierre Bourdieu, *Outline of a Theory of Practice* (Cambridge: Cambridge University Press, 1977), 2, 96. On "visualism" in anthropology, see Johannes Fabian, *Time and the Other: How Anthropology Makes Its Object* (New York: Columbia University Press, 1983), 105–41; James Clifford, "Partial Truths," in *Writing Culture: The Poetics and Politics of Ethnography,* ed. James Clifford and George E. Marcus (Berkeley: University of California Press, 1986), 11–12.

53. Warburton, *Oxford Companion to English Literature,* s.v. "Kinglake."

54. Gérard de Nerval, *Oeuvres,* 1:878–79.

55. Hans Busch, ed. and trans., *Verdi's Aida: The History of an Opera in Letters and Documents* (Minneapolis: University of Minnesota Press, 1978), 33–36.

56. Herman Melville, *Journal of a Visit to the Levant, October 11, 1856–May 6, 1857,* ed. Howard C. Horsford (Princeton: Princeton University Press, 1955), 79, 114.

57. See Mitchell, *Colonising Egypt,* 161–79; Stefania Pandolfo, "The Voyeur in the Old City: Two Postcards from French Morocco," paper presented at the Department of Anthropology, Princeton University, October, 1983.

58. Gérard de Nerval, *Oeuvres,* 1:878–79, 882, 883.

59. Kinglake, *Eōthen,* 280; Théophile Gautier, *Oeuvres complètes* (Paris: Charpentier, 1880–1903), vol. 20, *L'Orient,* 2:187; Flaubert, *Flaubert in Egypt,* 81.

60. Gautier, *L'Orient,* 2:91–122.

61. Gérard de Nerval, *Oeuvres,* 1:862, 867.

62. Said, *Orientalism,* 176–77.

63. Robert Graves, *Goodbye to All That* (Harmondsworth: Penguin Books, 1960), 265.

64. Cf. Jacques Derrida, "The Double Session," in *Dissemination* (Chicago: University of Chicago Press, 1981), 191–92, *Speech and Phenomena,* and "Implications."

Rethinking Colonial Categories: European Communities and the Boundaries of Rule

Ann Laura Stoler

In 1945, Bronislaw Malinowski urged anthropology to abandon what he called its "one-column entries" on African societies and to study instead the "no-man's land of change," to attend to the "aggressive and con-quering" European communities as well as native ones, and to be aware that "European interests and intentions" were rarely unified but more often "at war" (1966, 14–15). Four decades later, few of us have heeded his prompting or really examined his claim.[1]

The anthropology of colonialism has been a prolific yet selective proj-ect, challenging some of the boundaries of the discipline but remaining surprisingly respectful of others. As part of the more general political enterprise in the early 1970s, we reexamined how colonial politics affected both the theory and method of ethnography and the histories of our subjects.[2] Influenced by the work of Andre Frank and Immanuel Wallerstein, we investigated how the structural constraints of colonial capitalism not only shaped indigenous changes in community and class, but by turns destroyed, preserved, and froze traditional relations of power and production, and as frequently reinvented and conjured them up (Asad 1975b; Scott 1976; Foster-Carter 1978; Hobsbawm and Ranger 1983).

Initially this work looked to the impact of colonialism on various domains of indigenous agrarian structure, household economy, kinship organization, and community life (Steward 1956; Wolf 1959; Geertz 1968; Mintz 1974; Etienne and Leacock 1980). A second wave, turning away from the determinism that some of that approach applied, sought to identify the active agency of colonized populations as they engaged and resisted colonial impositions, thereby transforming the terms of that encounter. The contours of these communities and the cultural practices of their inhabitants (exemplified in the preservation of "little traditions," "reconstituted peasantries," and "moral economies") have appeared double-edged—explainable neither solely by their functional utility to colonialism nor by their defiance of it, but as the product of a historically layered colonial encounter (Rosaldo 1980; Taussig 1980; Wasserstrom 1980; Comaroff 1985; Stoler 1985a; Roseberry 1986).

In attending to both global processes and local practices, the units of analysis have also shifted to the extra village, regional, national, and global ties that bind seemingly discrete peasant populations to the world economy (Nash 1981; Vincent 1982; Roseberry 1983), and to a rejection of the notion that categories such as nation, tribe, and culture are, as Eric Wolf puts it, "internally homogenous and externally distinctive and bounded objects" (1982, 6). Curiously, in spite of this innovation, the objects of our study, if not the units of our analysis, have remained much the same. Where we have attended to world market forces and examined European images of the Other, we have done so better to explain the impact of perceptions and policy on people, on a particular subject community, on our ethnographic subject—the colonized (Asad 1975b; Clammer 1975; Alatas 1977; Sahlins 1981; Sider 1987). And even where we have probed the nature of colonial discourse and the politics of its language, the texts are often assumed to express a shared European mentality, the sentiments of a unified, conquering elite (Alatas 1977; Todorov 1985).

With few exceptions, even when we have attended to concrete capitalist relations of production and exchange, we have taken colonialism and its European agents as an abstract force, as a *structure* imposed on local *practice.* The terms *colonial state, colonial policy, foreign capital,* and *the white enclave* are often used interchangeably, as if they captured one and the same thing. While such a treatment encourages certain lines of novel enquiry, it closes off others. The makers of metropole policy become conflated with its local practitioners. Company executives and their clerks appear as a seamless community of class and colonial interests whose internal discrepancies are seen as relatively inconsequential, whose divisions are blurred.[3] In South Africa, and in white settler communities more generally, where conflicts between imperial design and local European interests are overt, such glosses are less frequent, but these communities are rarely the objects of our ethnographies.[4]

More sensitized to the class, ethnic, and gender distinctions among the colonized, anthropologists have taken the politically constructed dichotomy of colonizer and colonized as a given, rather than as a historically shifting pair of social categories that needs to be explained. Certainly this is not to suggest that anthropologists have not attended to the ambiguity and manipulation of racial classification (Harris and Kotak 1963; Harris 1964, 1970; Mintz 1971; Dominguez 1986). But this interest has rarely been coupled with a focus on European communities, or the powerful cultural idioms of domination in which they invest (see, for example, Tanner 1964).[5] As a result, colonizers and their communities are frequently treated as diverse but unproblematic, viewed as unified in a fashion that would disturb our ethnographic sensibilities if applied to ruling elites of the colonized. Finally, the assumption that colonial political agendas are self-evident precludes our examination of the cultural politics of the communities in which colonizers lived.

Colonial cultures were never direct translations of European society planted in the colonies, but unique cultural configurations, homespun creations in which European food, dress, housing, and morality were given new political meanings in the particular social order of colonial rule.[6] Formal dress codes, sumptuary laws, and military display did more than reiterate middle-class European visions and values. They were reactive to class tensions in the metropole, and created what Benedict Anderson calls a "tropical gothic," a "middle-class aristocracy" that cultivated the colonials' differences from the colonized, while maintaining social distinctions among themselves (1983, 137). The point is that colonial projects and the European populations to which they gave rise were based on new constructions of Europeanness; they were artificial groupings—demographically, occupationally, and politically distinct. Not only white settlers but the more transient European residents in the colonies were occupied with social and political concerns that often pitted them against policymakers in the metropole as much as against the colonized (Emmanuel 1972, 89; Hughes 1987).[7] Colonizers themselves, however, were neither by nature unified nor did they inevitably share common interests and fears; their boundaries—always marked by whom those in power considered legitimate progeny and whom they did not—were never clear. On the contrary, colonial Europeans constructed "imagined communities" as deftly as the nationalist colonized populations to whom they were opposed (Anderson 1983)—European communities that were consciously fashioned to overcome the economic and social disparities that would, in other contexts, separate and often set their members in conflict.

Racism is the classic foil invoked to mitigate such divisions and is thus a critical feature in the casting of colonial cultures, so much so that it is often seen as a virtually built-in and natural product of that encounter, essential to the social construction of an otherwise illegitimate and privileged access to property and power (Memmi 1973; Sartre 1976; Takaki 1983). But this view accords poorly with the fact that the *quality* and *intensity* of racism vary enormously in different colonial contexts and at different historical moments in any particular colonial encounter. In colonial situations as diverse as India, New Guinea, the Netherlands Indies, Cuba, Mexico, and South Africa, increasing knowledge, contact, and familiarity lead not to a diminution of racial discrimination but to an intensification of it over time, and to a rigidifying of boundaries. Understanding those sharpened racial pressures has entailed, among other things, identifying heightened forms of anticolonial resistance and increased demands by those given limited access to certain privileges but categorically denied others.

But colonial racism is more than an aspect of how people classify each other, how they fix and naturalize the differences between We and They. It is also, less clearly perhaps, part of how people identify the affinities that they share and how they define themselves in contexts where discrepant interests, ethnic differences, and class might otherwise weaken consensus (Lévi-Strauss 1983). In other words, it provides a way of creating the sense of (colonial) community and context that allows for colonial authority and for a particular set of relations of production and power. What I suggest here is that racist ideology, fear of the Other, preoccupation with white prestige, and obsession with protecting European women from sexual assault by Asian and black males were not simply justifications for continued European rule and white supremacy. They were part of a critical, class-based logic, statements not only about indigenous subversives, but directives aimed at dissenting European underlings in the colonies—and part of the apparatus that kept potentially subversive white colonials in line.

This is not to say that in the absence of white ruling-class manipulations, subordinate white colonials would necessarily have joined social forces and become politically allied with the colonized; nor is it to suggest that these subordinates were unwitting practitioners of racist policy.[8] Rather, I argue that these internal divisions augmented the intensity of racist practice, affected the terrains of contest, and intervened significantly in shaping social policies toward those rules. It is significant that racist rationales permeated the political strategies of *both* the corporate elite and their less-privileged European class opposition. In this article I draw on the case of a European community in North Sumatra in the late nineteenth and early twentieth centuries and use it to set out some of the issues that I think the anthropology of colonialism has not sufficiently addressed—how competing colonial agendas, based on distinct class and gender interests, shaped the politics of race and tensions of rule. In what follows I outline some of the social differences and antagonisms that divided the Deli community of East Sumatra and describe the material provisions and cultural conventions that were invoked to secure its unity. Within this context, the sexual and domestic arrangements of European staff were central issues, not private matters, but political and economic affairs that acted to sharpen or mute the categories of ruler and ruled. In the Sumatran case, the rights to marry and form families were a focal point of indigenous and European labor protest and of the strategies of corporate control.

Within the ranks of the European communities, I examine two disparate social groups closely linked to the European self-image of privilege and rule. First was the category of poor or impoverished whites. The efforts displayed to prevent their emergence in the colony, forbid their entry, and expedite their repatriation reveal a wider set of colonial concerns and policies. The second category, white women, represented a threat of a different order. The overwhelming uniformity with which white women were barred from early colonial enterprises and the heightened racism that usually accompanied their entry is cited for a wide range of colonial situations. As we shall see, attitudes toward poor whites and white women were intimately tied: both were categories that defined and threatened the boundaries of European (white male) prestige and control. The reasons these categories had such political saliency will be clearer if we look first at some of the more general divisions and commonalities that characterized the community of colonizers on Sumatra's East Coast.

The Making of Colonial Community in Deli

The case of Sumatra's plantation belt—or Deli, as it was known during the first half of the twentieth century—is particularly interesting on several counts. Deli was, first of all, pioneered on a scale unparalleled elsewhere in the Indies. Opened by the Dutch in the late nineteenth century, it rapidly emerged as one of the most lucrative investment sites in Southeast Asia. Covering a fertile lowland plain of some thirty thousand square kilometers, the plantation belt (*cultuurgebeid*) included nearly one million hectares of jungle and swiddens converted within several decades into tobacco, rubber, tea, and oil-palm estates leased to foreign companies. Unlike the case in Java, where sugar and tobacco were interposed between rice fields, in North Sumatra, estate holdings were laid out with contiguous borders, the complexes ranging anywhere from one thousand to several thousand hectares.

Distant and largely autonomous from the Dutch colonial heartland in Java, the foreign community of the plantation belt developed a specific character during its late nineteenth-century expansion: a multinational European membership (rather than a predominantly Dutch one as on Java), an extensive system of concubinage well into the twentieth century, a high level of labor violence, and what has been described as the most marked degree of social discrimination in the Netherlands Indies (Bagley 1973, 44). This emphasis on rigid social markings and strict class lines has been attributed in part to Deli's proximity to the more socially rigid British Straits colonies and to the large number of British planters in East Sumatra (Marinus 1929; Bagley 1973). Deli was frequently contrasted with the more lax, and less discriminatory, largely Dutch-colonial culture in Java, whose members were said to have mixed more willingly and adapted more easily to local custom.

But British influence aside, there were other features of plantation expansion in Sumatra that rendered Deli and the Deliaan (the Deli planter) unique. Unlike Java, where Dutch hegemony was established in the seventeenth century, most of the Sumatran plantation belt came under the political and economic control of the Dutch only in the 1870s. It did so at a time when the colonial state administration had neither sufficient funds nor personnel to carry out the task. Thus, pacification of East Sumatra was made an international affair with investors from France, Belgium, Germany, Britain, and the United States at the forefront of the plantation effort. These early Deli planters were able to initiate and maintain a level of autonomy from state control over labor conditions and labor relations well into the twentieth century (Stoler 1985a). Given license to procure land and labor under an open-door policy, they were also granted the right to protect those assets as they saw fit through, among other things, an indentured labor system endorsed and formalized by the Dutch colonial state. Dependent more on Europe and the Straits settlements than on the Indies administration in Java for personnel and financial support, the early Deli planters were in sustained conflict with the colonial administration, demanding its protection while protesting its interference in labor affairs (Marinus 1929). But because the planters could claim prior and privileged knowledge of Deli's conditions, they easily circumvented or simply ignored the directives of the younger and less experienced government agents who were on relatively short-term assignments in this Indies outpost.[9]

What stands out in memoirs, the contemporary press, period novels, and government archives is the disjuncture between a dominant rhetoric of unity and a subjacent concern with the reality of sharp social and political division among the Europeans themselves. The proffered image of a rough and rugged cohort of men transforming the primeval forest into a civilized and profitable plantation belt captured the imagination not only of Deli's European population, but of colonials elsewhere in the Indies and in Southeast Asia. The notions that Deli was an "entirely different idea" (Nieuwenhuys 1978, 346–47) and that the Deliaan was a unique type appealed to a pioneering Protestant ethic in which success resulted from perseverance and hard work. Descriptions of this planter prototype emphasize and concur on several distinct features: diverse social background, uncompromising courage, and a disregard for class origin (Brandt 1948, 186; Székely 1979, 37).[10]

While descriptions of such pioneering personalities are commonplace in many colonial situations, our interest here is how this image played on the Deliaans themselves, contributing to a sense that privilege and profit were based on issues of *character,* not race or class.[11] But character itself was not derived directly from abstract and universal values. It was based on a concept of Europeanness that emphasized a bearing, standard of living, and set of cultural competencies to which all European community members had to subscribe and from which Asians were barred.[12]

Most accounts of Deli describe an early estate administration staffed with a motley assortment of inexperienced personnel drawn from the scions of failed business families, runaways from ill-fated love affairs, defunct aristocrats, and adventurers seeking to make their fortunes. This portrait was deeply romanticized, focusing more on the relatively few social marginals and fugitives than on the majority of lower middle-class and middle-class men for whom the Indies offered the hope of financial improvement (Clerkx 1961, 10–12; Nieuwenhuys 1982, 154). While the early boom years of tobacco growing may have allowed some to strike it rich, a much larger number of planters-cum-speculators went bankrupt when the international market failed. Some with good reputations became administrators for the larger companies that bought them out (Breman 1987, 63–67). For the most part, however, the dream of *haute-bourgeois* retirement was something realized by few Europeans employed on the estates. In the initial years when staff were trained on the spot, new recruits had some opportunity to work themselves up to high administrative positions. This became increasingly rare, however, as multinational companies took over the plantation belt after the turn of the century, and as greater technical and administrative skills were needed to fill higher echelon posts. In reality, the Deli planters were, for the most part, not gentlemen planters at all but bureaucrats, office workers, specialists, and field foremen in a rapidly expanding corporate hierarchy.

The distinctions among Europeans were most commonly couched in terms of the differences between *singkeh* ('greenhorns') and old hands, between the *assistenten* ('European field staff') and senior management, giving the latter legitimate claim to an authority and income based on earned seniority.[13] Implicit within this emphasis on age-related status was the principle that one could and would move naturally up the corporate ranks. But the evidence suggests that economic mobility was limited, and for dissenting personnel virtually impossible (*De Planter,* April 1, 1909, 19; Said 1976, 51–52; cf. Breman 1987, 65–66). The social and economic distance that divided estate directors, administrators, and higher personnel from those at the bottom was further accentuated in Deli by the virtual absence of Indo-Europeans, who on Java, in contrast, constituted much of the low-level office and field staff. Deli's planter elite prided itself on the maintenance of strict racial distinction, many companies even refusing to employ Indo-Europeans as clerks (Marinus 1929, 47).

Despite a public facade to the contrary, discontent within the lower ranks of the estate hierarchy was evident early in Deli's history. By 1909 it had become formalized in a union of European plantation employees (*Vakvereeniging voor Assistenten in Deli,* or VvAiD), the formation of which government officials in Batavia, plantation owners in Sumatra, and directors in Europe commonly viewed as *chantage* (*Kroniek* 1917, 39). Starting off with only two hundred members in 1909, the union grew to several thousand within ten years, reaching out from its primarily Dutch-speaking membership. Setting itself up in direct opposition to the powerful rubber- and tobacco-planters' associations and the press that represented those interests, the union founded an independent but widely read newspaper wherein members aired grievances, criticized government policies, and offered their own interpretations of labor legislation and the causes of labor violence in the plantation belt. While government reports and the planters' press attributed increased coolie assaults to the poor quality of European recruits, the employees' union was concerned with the strains that an indentured labor system placed on labor relations in general. Where the planters' press blamed labor violence on inappropriate mishandling of coolies by assistants, the latter pointed to excessive production quotas and the pressure placed on assistants to meet them. Where company executives advocated a change in recruitment practices and requirements used to select low-level staff, subordinate whites demanded improved living conditions, job security, and pensions for those already employed (*De Planter,* April 1, 1909, September 1, 1909).

The union publication, ironically entitled *De Planter* although union members were by definition not planters at all, not only fought against policies that affected employees' private lives, but lent support to various indigenous protests, railway strikes, and nationalist organizations (Said 1976, 51). Formed at a time when the nationalist movement was making its presence felt throughout the Indies and locally among Deli's Javanese estate workers, the Assistants' Union was able to force concessions during this period that would later have been impossible. For example, the 1917 Assistants' Ruling established by the government bureau accorded European field supervisors some protection from "coolie assaults," more job security, and directly addressed the assistants' concern with their dependence on the personal whims of their employers (Algemene Rijksarchief, Afdeeling II, Verbaal, January 19, 1921, no. 71). Plantation executives vehemently protested, arguing that it gave Deli a bad name and tainted its image as a united front.

The Marriage Restriction in Deli

We can get a sense of the sorts of issues that arose and the sorts of solutions that were sought by looking at one policy that was contested for nearly fifteen years, namely, the marriage prohibition on all incoming European plantation employees. In the late nineteenth century, the major tobacco companies neither accepted married applicants nor allowed them to take wives while in service.[14] Corporate authorities argued repeatedly that new European employees with families in tow would be unable to support them in a proper manner, risking the emergence of a "European proletariat in Deli" (*Sumatra Post* 1913; *Kroneik* 1917, 50). Eventually the antimarriage sanction was relaxed to a stipulation that an assistant could marry only after his first five years of service and then only if he had attained some demonstrable solvency. Concubinary arrangements with Javanese women, in contrast, were considered preferable because they posed little financial burden to low-salaried staff, and had the advantage of allowing newcomers to acquire the native language quickly and learn native customs. European marriages, on the other hand, threatened to take up too much time and too much salary. By refusing to employ married men, the estate industry virtually legislated a broad system of interracial concubinage into existence.

That system was not without its problems, however. Given the ratio of fewer than one Javanese woman for every ten Javanese and Chinese men, intense competition for sexual and domestic partners among the indigenous workers, and between them and their European supervisors, resulted in *vrouwen perkara* ('disputes over women'), barracks brawls, and assaults on white staff. In British Malaya during the same period, the comparative advantage of setting up households with native women as opposed to importing European women was actively weighed. While the use of prostitutes and the proliferation of Indo-European children were viewed as a blight on the community, these alternatives were considered less distressing than the impoverishment of white men, which could result from attempts to maintain a middle-class life-style with European wives (Butcher 1979, 93). In both instances, colonial morality was relative: interracial sexual activity was more easily tolerated than destitution. As Butcher notes, for Malaysia there was a "particular anathema with which the British regarded 'poor whites'" (1979, 26).

Nonetheless, the presence of white women was seen as exerting a civilizing, cultured, and restraining check on the rowdy, crude, and hard-drinking life-style for which Deli's European staff were infamous. Jacob Nienhuis, one of the pioneer planters, argued that marriages to European women would create more sociability (*gezelligheid*), provide better returns on labor, and encourage more applicants—this last because *het moederhart* ('a mothers' heart') in Europe would suffer less *angst* at permitting her child to depart for a place where "refined" society reigned (*De Planter,* May 1, 1909).[15]

Throughout the first ten years of *De Planter*'s publication, the assistants openly and vigorously protested the marriage restriction and the infringement on their civil rights that it represented. In fact, the marriage issue was a strategic focus for a wider set of demands. If estate directors feared that European marriages would impoverish their assistants, the assistants could then argue that improved wages, bonuses, job security, and pensions would ward off such an eventuality. Employing a language that appealed to the fears of the colonial elite, the assistants argued for a better standard of living, security from assault, protection of white prestige, and the right to choose their domestic arrangements on their own.

In 1920, after nearly a decade of steady protest, the marriage restriction was rescinded by the major companies, and large numbers of white women arrived in the East Coast Residency. Although the companies held that the change was now possible because Deli was sufficiently prosperous and the industry sufficiently secure to support European families in a proper manner, it is clear that this concession came at a crucial moment—when labor relations among Europeans had reached a new stage of tension, threatening European unity on the Deli estates. *De Planter*'s editor-in-chief, C. E. W. Krediet, having expressed open sympathy for indigenous strike actions and labor demands, was ousted from his post in 1920 and repatriated to Holland. Krediet was replaced by J. van den Brand, who had written a scathing critique of Deli's indentured-labor system in 1903 (leading to the establishment of a labor inspectorate to monitor working conditions on the Deli estates). But he, too, was relieved of his post by the governor general in less than a year and died a few months later (Said 1976, 51–52).

Corporate response to staff dissent, both indigenous and European, was strikingly similar. The recruitment of single male coolies from Java and a bachelor staff from Europe was replaced by a policy that encouraged married couples and promoted conditions that would allow for "family formation" by both European management and the Javanese rank and file. These parallel policies sharpened the divisions and accentuated racial distinctions more than ever. Thus, European recruits during the 1920s were upgraded with higher bonuses, better housing, more fringe benefits—an added share in the profits—and thus a stronger stake in the companies' cause.[16] For Javanese estate workers, single-family dwellings replaced barracks, and labor colonies included small subsistence plots that would allow for the semblance of village life and the reproduction of a local labor reserve.[17] In turn, the explanations of violence shifted their focus from the poor quality of low-level staff to the spread of dangerous communist and nationalist elements among the Javanese and Chinese recruits.

As indigenous resistance to Dutch rule heightened, the divisions within the European enclave were muted by additional reforms. European staff were thus advised to avoid confrontation by maintaining increased physical and social distance from their workers. For example, predawn roll calls, often the site of assaults on Europeans, had already been abolished (*Kroniek* 1917, 36). Throughout the 1920s, increasing emphasis was placed on a mediated chain of command: managers and their white staff were instructed to relay their orders through Javanese and Chinese foremen and through specific *tussenpersonen* ('go-betweens') delegated to the task, such that no European would have to risk the consequences of reprimanding a worker face to face. Low-level Europeans increasingly sought security in protection by the companies rather than in resistance to them.

Accompanying these changes in the material conditions of the lower management, the supposed commonalties of the European colonial experience in Deli were actively reinforced and affirmed. Although differences in income, housing, and social standing still set the lower echelon of the estate hierarchy off from those at the top, the myth of a Deliaan prototype highlighted their common interests. The evocation and reenactment of Deli's opening was celebrated in commemorative volumes issued by the various planters' associations and large companies every five, ten, and twenty-five years. These capsule corporate and personal histories produced a continual affirmation of economic success and heroic achievement. The East Coast of Sumatra Institute annually chronicled the expansion of the cultural infrastructure (tennis courts, theater troupes, social clubs, hill stations, and charities), assuring itself as well as its metropole investors that the European enclave was stable and strong.

The official discourse of colonial rule was laden with military metaphor, bolstered by uniforms, roll calls, and forms of deference and address that seemed designed as much to deter any break in the ranks as to impress the native population. A particularly strong iconographic expression of this created common history was the 1925 plan to build "a tomb of the unknown planter" in remembrance of those Europeans who had died by coolie assault or otherwise in the service of the industry (*Kroniek* 1925, 72). The idea that any European murdered (regardless of cause) was a hero emphasized the common enemy and shared threat. And homogenizing the past effectively blurred the vivid distinctions in the working conditions and experiences of the European community. As significant, it reiterated and enforced the differences that divided Asian workers from Europeans; it was, after all, in opposition to the archetypal plantation coolie that this unknown planter/soldier had pitted himself and died.

Custodians of Morality: Female Honor and White Prestige

From the outset, Deli's colonial community was defined in terms of cultural criteria that set it off from the colonized. Housing, dress codes, transport, food, clubs, conversation, recreation, and leaves marked a distinct social space in which Europeans were internally stratified but from which Asians were circumstantially and/or formally barred. However, when the colonial industry saw its position threatened, new measures were usually sought to identify its members, their affinities and common interests, along racial lines.

It is frequently argued that social and political differentiation of the colonized and colonizer intensified following the entry of European women. Some accounts claim that the increasing number of women in colonial settlements resulted in increased racism not only because of the native desire they excited and the chivalrous protection they therefore required, but because women were more avid racists in their own right. Thus, Percival Spear, writing on the social life of the English in eighteenth-century India, asserts that women "widened the racial gulf" by holding to "their insular whims and prejudices" (1963, 140). Similarly, Indian intellectual Ashis Nandy argues that "white women in India were generally more racist [than their men] because they unconsciously saw themselves as the sexual competitors of Indian men" (1983, 9–10).[18] Thomas Beidelman for colonial Tanganyika writes that "European wives and children created a new and less flexible domestic colonialism exhibiting overconcern with the sexual accessibility or vulnerability of wives, and with corresponding notions about the need for spatial and social segregation" (1982, 13). L. H. Gann and Peter Duignan baldly state that "it was the cheap steamship ticket for women that put an end to racial integration" in British Africa (1978, 242; also see O'Brien 1972, 59). In short, sources in which colonial women receive little or no mention accord to these otherwise marginal actors the primary responsibility for racial segregation.[19]

What stands out in many accounts is the fact that the arrival of women usually occurred in conjunction with some immediately prior or planned stabilization of colonial rule. The term *stabilization* is ambiguous; it may express either a securing of empire or a response to imperial vulnerability. In India, after the Sepoy Mutiny in 1857, the colonial community was stabilized and further segregated from indigenous contacts (Arnold 1983, 154). In New Guinea, large numbers of white women arrived in the 1920s when the colonial order was considered stable although nonetheless under attack by an increasing number of "acculturated" Papuans making their discontent with colonial policy more rigorously felt (Inglis 1975, 11). The white women's protection ordinance of 1926 rigidified racial divisions, but, more important, it represented a culmination of political tensions and was advocated not by women but by men (Inglis 1975, vii).

Thus the presence of European women did not inadvertently produce stronger racial divisions: rather, it was, in some cases, intended precisely to enforce the separation between Asians and whites. Colonial elite concern for the entry of white women was related, as James Boutilier argues, to "the real or imagined threat to superiority and status that miscegenation implied" (1984, 196). The arrival (and protection) of women was part of a wider response to problems of colonial control that often antedated the objections raised by European women to miscegenation. It was not sexual relations between European men and Asian women per se that were condemned, but this form of domestic arrangement and the social tensions to which it gave rise. The concubines and their Eurasian progeny came to be seen as a danger to the European community at large.[20]

White women arrived in large numbers in Deli in the 1920s, during the most profitable years of plantation economy, but also at a time of mounting resistance to estate labor conditions in particular and to colonial rule generally.[21] Their presence excused sharper racial divisions, but, more important, it also justified policies already in motion to tighten the European community, and to control those European men who blurred the naturalized categories of ruler and ruled. Entering this context, European women as the caretakers of male physical well-being and guardians of morality found their activities and the social space in which they could operate rigidly controlled (*De Planter,* April 9, 1910, 52; Groupe d'etudes coloniales 1910, 7).

Novels from Deli in the 1920s—the most famous a set written by the Dutch wife of a Hungarian estate manager—describe bored, inactive, and desperately lonely women, trapped on the estates and in the confines of their homes (Székely-Lulofs 1932, 1946). The books by women, however, also provide important insight into the highly stratified pecking order of European males—and their seige mentality vis-à-vis native labor. Unlike the male novelists of this period, who emphasize white comradery (despite the difficult, but temporary adjustments to becoming colonial managers), female authors highlight sustained social tensions deriving from relations of work, pressures for promotion, conflicts over sexual affairs, and hierarchies of class and race in the home.[22]

Whether or not white women exacerbated racial tensions, they certainly did not create them, as is sometimes implied.[23] On the other hand, we should not dismiss the fact that colonial women were committed to racial segregation for their own reasons and in their own right. In a context in which middle-class women's choices to live outside marriage and motherhood were more limited than in Europe, it is perhaps not surprising that these women championed a moral order that both restricted their husband's sexual activities and reconstituted the domestic domain as a site demanding their vigilance and control.

The coming of white women was part of a more general realignment of labor relations in the cultural politics of labor control. Such methods of stabilization invariably produced new arenas of vulnerability, creating more points of possible infringement, more places that could not be invaded, new demands for deference, thus legitimizing the coercive measures needed for control. On the other hand, as white women were made custodians of a distinct cultural and moral community, the protection of their honor became an issue with which all European men could agree and affirm their unity rather than their differences. In such a context, sexuality was politicized and charged. As in the post-Reconstruction U.S. South, where white men lynched blacks in the name of chivalry (Dowd Hall 1984), any attempted or perceived infringement of white female honor came to be seen as an assault on white supremacy and European rule (Barr 1976, 170; Ballhatchet 1980, 7). For example, in 1929, at a time when murders of European staff by indigenous workers occurred nearly every year, the killing of the wife of a European assistant by a

Javanese coolie was politicized in unprecedented fashion. The event was tied to "communist agitation," and explicitly interpreted as a threat to Dutch authority in the Indies at large (*Kroniek* 1929, 43–48).[24] As a direct consequence, army troops were reinforced in Deli, intelligence operations on the estates were expanded, and the fascist-linked Vaderlandsche Club increased its constituency, receiving added support for its repressive, conservative political agenda in the following years.

The Structuring of European Communities and the Problem of Poor Whites

What strikes us at first blush as artificial in the European colonial settlements is the inappropriate dress, food, and other markers of European culture that Anthony Burgess and George Orwell caricatured in their novels: the jungle planter sweating through a five-course dinner in formal attire. These cultural artifices were less important than the fact that these communities were constructed to sustain a particular structure and form. They were demographically and, therefore, socially skewed in several respects, the most obvious resulting from the absence of European women and children from the early colonial settlements and the enclosed social space that was delimited for them once they came.

Children were thought to be particularly susceptible to the dangers of tropical lethargy and disease, deemed a threat to all Europeans in the tropics (Price 1939, 6–8; Spencer and Thomas 1948, 637). By extension, they were also considered vulnerable to social contamination as they played with the children of native servants, easily acquiring the local language and deftly mimicking non-European gestures and social customs. While native nursemaids often reared the small children of European families, older children were invariably sent back to boarding schools in Europe, packed off to schools and vacation colonies in temperate hill-stations or, as in nineteenth-century Hawaii, confined with their mothers to walled courtyards in the latter's charge (*Kroniek* 1923, 78; Arnold 1983, 141; Grimshaw 1983, 508). Deli, like other colonial communities, often lacked a representation of young people in their impressionable years, namely, older children and adolescents (Mercier 1965, 287).

Among the men, there were also profound omissions. When possible, the European colonial elite restricted the presence of nonproductive men and of those individuals generally who might undermine the image of a healthy, empowered, and "vigorous" race (Groupe d'etudes coloniales 1910, 10). In Deli, the infirm, the aged, and the insane were quickly sent home. Insurgents were repatriated and the impoverished were zealously sheltered and supported until they, too, could be shipped out of the colony. In nineteenth-century India, the colonial state made every effort to institutionalize "unseemly" whites (in orphanages, workhouses, mental asylums, and old-age homes) for much of their lives, discreetly keeping them invisible from both Indians and Europeans alike (Arnold 1979, 113). Similarly, while various plans were devised in India and in the Netherlands Indies to establish agricultural settlements for poor Scottish and young Dutch farmers, successful opposition stressed the "loss of racial prestige and authority which . . . an 'influx' of poor whites would bring" (Arnold 1983, 139). In Sumatra, efforts to settle young Dutch farmers in the Batak highlands during the Great Depression were actively opposed by the local colonial elite as a "chimera" that would lead to "wretched [European] pauperism" (*Kroniek* 1933, 181).

The potential and actual presence of impoverished and "unfit" whites informed social policies in many colonial contexts. British, Dutch, and French colonial capitalists and state policymakers in the late nineteenth and early twentieth centuries designed pay scales, housing, medical facilities, marriage restrictions, and labor contracts such that the colonial venture remained a middle-class phenomenon. Some semblance of the middle-class ethic was made possible by the fact that wages were extremely low for native house servants and others who might provide services to European employers. Still, the amenities of a bourgeois existence were not within the reach of many Europeans who occupied the lowest level supervisory posts. While in some colonies, and in many parts of the Netherlands Indies, these positions were reserved for Indo-Europeans, on the Deli estates, as noted earlier, Indos were barred from low-level jobs in administrative service.

The presence of poor whites in the colonies was far more widespread than most colonial histories lead us to imagine. In nineteenth-century India, "nearly half the European population could be called poor whites"; nearly 6,000 of them were placed in workhouses by 1900 (Arnold 1979, 104, 122). In the Netherlands Indies, European pauperism was already a concern of the Dutch East Indies Company in the mid-eighteenth century. By the early 1900s, a profusion of government reports had identified tens of thousands of Eurasians ("Indos") and "full-blooded" Europeans as dangerously impoverished (*Encyclopaedie van Nederlandsch-Indie* 1919, 366–68). On Barbados, in the mid-nineteenth century, poor whites (called "red legs") made up more than three-quarters of the European population (Sheppard 1977, 43; Beckles 1986, 7). In French colonial communities in northern Africa, a vast population of "petits blancs" (a perjorative term for lower-class Europeans) included many poor whites of non-French European origin, whose political interests diverged from both the French colonial elite and from the skilled black Africans with whom they were in competition for jobs (Mercier 1965, 292–3; O'Brien 1972, 66–91; Leconte 1980, 71–83).

South Africa's poor-white population, conservatively estimated at 300,000 in the 1920s, was admittedly of a different order, but may serve as an instructive comparison (Albertyn 1932, vii). In a comprehensive investigation carried out during 1929–30, the Carnegie Commission attended specifically to the effects of increasing numbers of European paupers on the internal labor market, and on white prestige and rule. The commission concluded that wider class distinctions among Europeans were giving rise to more mixing between poor whites and "colored" groups: blacks were no longer calling poor white farmers "boss" but by their familiar, Christian names, and poor whites and "colored" were eating and drinking together, in short, displaying "no consciousness of the need for a segregation policy" (Albertyn 1932, 33–38). While South Africa represented the extreme of enforced separation, it was not an exception. British India and the Netherlands Indies were able to maintain less formalized apartheids because, in these colonies, the profusion of "unfit whites," the creation of settler communities, and, most important, the composition of the resident colonial population could all be controlled. The dangerous or destitute, unlike in South Africa, could simply be sent home. India and Sumatra experienced a poor-white problem of a different magnitude but the desire to contain it was motivated by similar priorities.

As early as 1891 a relief fund for "needy Europeans" was established in Deli to support bankrupt planters and their staff who were casualties of the crisis triggered by the halving of tobacco prices on the world market (*Kroniek* 1917, 51). At the end of World War I, the concern over white pauperism again loomed large. With the supply of goods from Europe severely diminished and the prices precipitously increased, many companies were forced to grant a temporary cost-of-living allowance to their lower salaried European personnel. Despite such efforts, "scores of Europeans without work and without means of support were at large and roaming around the administrative center of Medan" (*Kroniek* 1917, 49). Living on credit from Japanese hotels or on the hospitality of the native population, their inappropriate bearing and diminished standard of living were vigorously criticized as a direct threat to colonial prestige. Programs were devised to provide funds for the European poor, but the amounts were insufficient to support the number who fell below the *acceptable* European standard of living. During the malaise of 1921, relief funds were again collected to support the increasing number of European paupers (*armlastingen*) and vagrants (*landloopers*) until they could be sent home (*Kroniek* 1922, 50). Some, nonetheless, ended up in native villages when they had exhausted the largess of their European friends (Clerkx 1961, 13).

The white pauperism of the 1930s, however, like the Depression itself, was of crisis proportions (Kantoor van Arbeid 1935, 1–94). For the first time, repatriation was not an option as the metropole economies staggered in straits as serious as those in the colonies. The projected cost of reengaging personnel from Europe when the crisis passed was considered exorbitant, and many of these Europeans, in fact, had nowhere to go. In 1931, of the 240,000 Europeans in the Indies, 2,400 were unemployed (*Kroniek* 1930, 22). Other accounts estimated more than 5,500 unemployed Europeans in 1932, of which 3,238 were listed as "in straitened circumstances" (Furnivall 1944, 444). In Deli, the situation was worse. Of nearly 1,700 Europeans employed on the estates, half were dismissed within the first few years of the Depression; more than 400 of them were low-level staff (*Kroniek* 1931, 79).

The threat posed by large numbers of European paupers gave rise to a profusion of relief agencies and community efforts to feed, board, and maintain the unemployed at some semblance of a European standard. European hotel owners housed the unemployed for nominal rent, and hill-stations were converted into centers where courses were made available in modern languages and bookkeeping (*Kroniek* 1932, 82). Children of the unemployed received free schooling and free lunches. The Salvation Army boarded scores of families in abandoned hill-station villas and the Support Committee for European "Crisis-Victims," as they were called, provided funds to more than a thousand European adults and children. Remedies that were used in the United States and Europe to deal with the crisis—the "make-a-job" and "odd-job" campaigns to keep the working classes occupied at typically menial tasks, scavenging work, and public-utilites maintenance—were considered unsuitable for a middle-class colonial elite (Piven and Cloward 1971, 49–60). Nevertheless, some of the unemployed tried to help themselves, setting up spontaneous colonies on forestry reserves for small-scale agriculture and husbandry, but this was confined to a very small number (*Kroniek* 1932, 82). Impoverished Indo-Europeans fell between the cracks of both the indigenous support system and those of the Europeans. It is ironic that those who attempted to sustain themselves on subsistence farming were barred from doing so "owing to the traditional policy of excluding from agriculture all who ranked as Europeans" (Furnivall 1944, 444).

The handling of the worldwide crisis as it affected Deli served to accentuate certain local social distinctions and political alliances while downplaying others. First, and most important, it wiped out the dissident voice of subordinate whites in the estate hierarchy. In 1931, the assistants' union (VvAiD) was merged with the *Sumatra Cultuur Bond* that represented the companies' interests (*Kroniek* 1931, 80). Two years later, the 1917 Assistants' Ruling was abolished and absorbed into a Planters' Ruling that encompassed lower and higher level staff alike. Both moves severely undermined whatever was left of an independent politics for low-level staff. Affirming what planters called the "community of interest" in which all Europeans shared, company directors argued that an "economic class struggle" was not in the interests of the unemployed assistants, the owners of industry, or the colonial state (*Kroniek* 1933, 85). Second, the Depression produced a wave of reaction against the increasing number of non-Dutch Europeans employed as staff on the estates, and their recruitment was curtailed. Third, it created a more solid alliance between the plantation elite and the colonial administration. As the economy recovered in the mid-1930s, a more rationalized estate industry, devoid of indigenous "dangerous elements" and having an air of "military discipline," resumed full-scale operation (de Waard 1934, 272). Unemployment, however, did not disappear with the crisis. In 1935, nearly 20,000 Europeans who could no longer be classed as crisis victims remained out of work in the Netherlands Indies (*Kroniek* 1935, 94–96).

Exclusion and Enclosure of Colonial Categories

The preceding discussion points to a major problem with accounts that speak of *the* British in Malaya or *the* Dutch in the East Indies. It forces our attention to internal differences peculiar to each of these European

colonial communities and to their idiosyncratic membership requirements. Something as apparently basic as who could legally be deemed
a European differed across the colonial context, revealing discrepant and
changing criteria by which racial superiority and attendant European
privilege were assigned. For example, in the Netherlands Indies during
the early twentieth century, the legal category of "European" paralleled
only loosely the idea of ethnic European origin. Included within it were
Japanese, Jews, Arabs, Armenians, Filipinos, naturalized Javanese, the
Sudanese wives of Dutch-born bureaucrats, the recognized children of
mixed marriages, and Christian Africans, among others (van Marle 1952,
108). To acquire European legal equivalence (*gelijkgestelde*) in 1884, one
had to (1) be Christian, (2) speak and write Dutch, (3) have a European
upbringing and education, and (4) demonstrate a suitability for European
society—criteria that forty years earlier were far less specific (van Marle
1952, 98, 109). Or one could acquire European status simply by virtue
of marriage to or adoption by a European.

The distinctions that set the colonized apart from colonizer are further
complicated when we look at the movement of "Europeans" from one
colonial context to another. In British-ruled Malaya in the 1930s, for
instance, those designating themselves European outnumbered those who
were considered part of the colonizing community proper. The sons and
daughters of mixed marriages in Indochina and the Netherlands Indies—
persons often regarded as part of the native population in their home
countries—listed themselves as French, Dutch, or Portuguese when resident outside the colonies from which they came (Butcher 1979, 25). Such
shifting and arbitrary definitions should make us wary of taking "Europeans" and "colonizers" as synonymous categories.[25]

What is striking when we look to identify the contours and composition of any particular colonial community is the extent to which control
over sexuality and reproduction were at the core of defining colonial
privilege and its boundaries. Whether incoming European colonials married, lived, or bedded with native women, early colonial communities
commonly produced a quotidian world in which the dominant cultural
influence in the household was native (Taylor 1983, 16). The fact that
prohibitions against interracial marriage were commonly late rather than
early colonial inventions (in such diverse contexts as Mexico, Cuba,
India, Indonesia, and the U.S. South) suggests that it was not interracial
sexual contact that was seen as dangerous, but its public legitimation in
marriage. Similarly, it was not the progeny of such unions who were

problematic but the possibility that they might be recognized as heirs to a European inheritance. The point is obvious: colonial control and profits were secured by constantly readjusting the parameters of the European membership thereby limiting those who had access to property and privilege and those who did not.

Given such disparate origins and circumstances, it is clear that not all who were classed as European were colonial practitioners or colonialism's local agents; thousands were drawn from the middle ranks of the colonized and were neither "cultural brokers" nor natural "intermediaries." The populations that fell within these contradictory colonial locations were subject to a frequently shifting set of criteria that allowed them privilege at certain historical moments and pointedly excluded them at others. The point here is not to deny that sharp distinctions divided those who were ruled and those who did the ruling, but to highlight the fact that these divisions were not as easily (or permanently) drawn as the official discourse might lead one to imagine.

While Beidelman's contention that "anthropological curiosity [has] stopped at the color bar" (1982, 2) may be an exaggeration, much evidence supports his claim. For the most part, it has not been radical social scientists who have probed colonial mentalities nor political apologists who have cast the colonizer as victim, but colonized intellectuals who have attempted to broach the psychology and political economy of rulers and ruled. Franz Fanon (1963), Albert Memmi (1973), Aimé Césaire (1972), and Ashis Nandy (1983) have sought to identify a colonial consciousness that entraps the defenders of empire as well as the more passive middling participants. The colonial everyman they paint is often a politically conservative composite of middle-class moralism, what V. S. Naipaul calls B-rate mediocrity (1978, 65), hypermasculinity, guilt, alienation, and a passive acceptance of a system supporting violence. White women appear as racist accomplices, defined by proxy to their men.

Such caricatures effectively capture certain features of colonials but are analytically limiting. Some colonial administrations selected for mediocrity; others produced it. Middle-class moralism, as we have seen, is made up of a wide range of substitutable prohibitions and standards, and is meaningful only if we examine the changing political agenda to which it was applied. But what their combined sensibilities offer is a political project for which an understanding of racism, class tensions, sexual subordination, and the everyday cultural idioms of domination is essential to a goal of liberation. For anthropology, it suggests that we take seriously Memmi's insistence that colonialism creates both the colonizer and the colonized. We need to reexamine the internal structures of colonial authority, and to explore the salient features of European class and gender ideologies that were selectively refashioned to create and maintain the social distinctions of empire and the cultural boundaries of rule.

NOTES

This study was originally prepared for the American Ethnological Society Annual Meetings, Symposium on the Categories of Colonialism, May 1, 1987, San Antonio, Texas. Research funds were provided by the Graduate School of the University of Wisconsin. I thank Talal Asad, Frederick Cooper, Murray Edelman, Linda Gordon, Lawrence Hirschfeld, Gerda Lerner, Nancy Lutkehaus, and Aram Yengoyan for their thoughtful readings and useful criticisms of an earlier text. Steve Stern and Steve Feierman helped me ground comparative issues. I also wish to thank members of my graduate seminar on colonial cultures for allowing me to think out and clarify in that context many of the issues presented here.

1. Malinowski was certainly not alone in noting the conflicts of interest and distinctions among Europeans. On the contrary, Margaret Mead, for example, commented on the social tensions among officials, missionaries, and various planters and was acutely sensitive to the appropriate dress codes when encountering different sorts of whites in the colonies (1977, 62–63); also see Powdermaker 1966, 102–7. For the most part, however, such observations were anecdotal or personal asides and not considered relevant to the subject of ethnography. Malinowski's student, Hortense Powdermaker, is one of the few U.S. anthropologists who, in her work in both northern Rhodesia and Mississippi, attended specifically (if somewhat briefly, as she notes) to Europeans and white society, respectively (Powdermaker 1966, 183–98, 272–79).

2. See, for example, Gough 1968 and the important contributions in Dell Hymes 1969; Talal Asad 1975; Anthropological Research 1977; and Gerald Berreman 1981.

3. French students of colonial history, confronted with colonial territories in which *pieds noirs* (French born in the colonies) and *petits blancs* (lower-class whites) were a sizable political force, have tended to examine these divisions more thoroughly (Delavignette 1946; Nora 1961; Mercier 1965). Few French anthropologists have taken the lead suggested by George Balandier in 1951: to explore the internal structure of European communities and the construction of racial categories (1965, 47–49, 53). Other anthropological efforts to examine specific agents of colonialism (and sometimes the tensions among them) are

found, for example, in Beidelman 1982; Cohn 1983; Comaroff and Comaroff 1985, 1986; Gordon and Meggitt 1985; Mintz 1985; Breman 1987.

4. Vincent Crapanzano's study of whites in South Africa is a notable exception (1985).

5. Historians have been far more attentive to these issues, although nuanced studies of colonial Europeans are generally a genre distinct from those that deal with the social classifications of race and class. For example, a profusion of "community studies" of the British in India attend to the social rankings of colonial life, but not to the internal political tensions among the British themselves (see, e.g., Dodwell 1926; Spear 1963; Edwards 1969; Kincaid 1971). The numerous accounts of British and French interaction with the colonized and their philosophies of rule analyze the political priorities informing colonial policy, but rarely treat the everyday practice of colonial domination (for French imperialism, see Murphy 1968; Cohen 1980; on the British in Africa, see Gann and Duignan 1978). Efforts to go beyond the official debates and examine the distinct class interests within the colonial state include studies by Frederick Cooper (1980) and by John Lonsdale and Bruce Berman (1979). Since this article was written, several new works have appeared that provide rich case studies of European communities in colonial Africa, elaborating many of the themes addressed here (Callaway 1987; Kennedy 1987; Prochaska 1990).

Literature on the social construction of race in Latin America provides some insights into differentiation among European colonials (Degler 1971; Martinez-Alier 1974; Chance and Taylor 1977; Seed 1982), but focuses primarily on intermediary racial categories. Historical work on South African apartheid and Afrikaner nationalism raises the most salient and unresolved questions concerning class interests, racist discourse, and political affiliations among Europeans (O'Meara 1983; Thompson 1985; Marks and Trapido 1986).

6. I owe the term *homespun* to Scott Christensen, a participant in my seminar on colonial cultures. See also Malinowski's observation that the white settler "community is by no means a direct replica of its mother community at home" (1966, 14).

7. See, for example, B. J. Moore-Gilbert's (1986) excellent study, based on literary sources, of the conflicts and distinct social visions that divided British resident in India (Anglo-Indians) from British in the metropole.

8. There is, however, strong evidence that such forms of cooperation between European employees and indigenous workers did exist and were actively opposed by some colonial states and foreign companies. For example, during the rise of the Javanese labor movement in the 1920s, multiracial trade unions were promoted that, in the case of railway workers, included lower level Europeans and Indonesian workers (Ingelson 1981, 55). In South Africa, where working-class whites and blacks socialized at home and at work, urban planning in Johannesburg was

designed precisely to eradicate "interracial 'slum-yards'" and "increase the growing social distance between white and black miners" (van Onselen 1982, 39).

9. See Stoler 1985b for a discussion of how conflicts between local planters and Dutch government officials affected labor policy. For an analysis of the inconsistent interpretations of Sumatra's plantation violence made by Dutch administrative agents themselves in the late nineteenth century, see Stoler 1992.

10. Witness the number of novels, sketches, and memoirs describing the attributes of the "Deli planter" (e.g., Manders 1933; Kleian 1936; Gorter 1941; Brandt 1948; Petersen 1948; Székely 1979).

11. The relative importance of "character" vs. "class" in determining colonial status is something that apparently varied in different colonial contexts. References to character pervade the colonial literature but with often contradictory formulations. In New Guinea, "class distinctions disappeared and recognition of character took over" (Boutilier 1984, 179), whereas in the administrative service of the Ivory Coast in the 1920s, character was a class privilege defined by an Oxbridge arrogance if not education (Kuklick 1979, 26). Whereas character and not class origin allegedly marked the making of a Deli planter in the early twentieth century, in India at the same time "class distinctions within the British community became more sharply defined" (Woodcock 1969, 163). These differences may reflect historical variation or merely distinct rhetorical uses of the notion of "character." In any case, it is clear both that character served as a replacement for class as a social marker, and that it was defined by privileges that were, by and large, race and class specific. Cf. Robert Hughes (1987, 323), who states that, in the colonization of Australia, "the question of class was all pervasive and pathological."

On the significance of an accepted standard of living in shaping the contour of a European colonial community (in this case the British in Malaya), see Butcher 1979.

12. Thus, Henrika Kuklick notes that an Oxbridge education was required "not so much to receive occupational training as to acquire the social polish considered intrinsic to a commanding personality" (1979, 26). On the legal discourse about what role "character" played in distinguishing poor Indiesborn Europeans of mixed descent from those who were "really Dutch" see Stoler, n.d.a.

13. The transformation of a greenhorn into a seasoned planter is a central theme in a number of the memoirs and novels cited in n. 10.

14. This policy was by no means specific to Deli; it was simply enforced at a much later date there than elsewhere in the Indies. The migration of European women to the Dutch East Indies was actively discouraged from the seventeenth to mid-nineteenth centuries, and, until the late 1800s, European marriages in the army were basically restricted to the officer corps (Ming 1983; Taylor 1983, 26).

15. See also Nieuwenhuys 1982, 144 on the importance of maintaining a moral colonial society to assuage the fears of mothers in the Netherlands.

16. J. H. Marinus, for example, in describing the fact that distinctions between assistants and administrators were more striking thirty years earlier, writes: "The historical facts that the assistant might not ride in a four-wheeled carriage, nor wear a gray helmet, as did the administrator are long forgotten and something about which most of the young assistants today know nothing" (1929, 12, 112).

17. For a detailed discussion of the shift in corporate strategy to "family formation," or *gezinvorming,* see Stoler 1985a, 31–46.

18. Also see George Woodcock (1969, 163), who argues that, with the arrival of Englishwomen, "racial distinctions . . . became more sharply defined" and Hank Nelson (1982, 47), who asserts that new racial barriers were created when *kiaps* ('patrol officers') were accompanied by European wives.

19. More convincing accounts suggest rather that expatriate women were not only symbols of white male power but that they "served to define men in relationship to one another" (Elaine Silverman, quoted in Boutilier 1984, 196; Inglis 1975; Barr 1976). Boutilier argues further that the racist inclinations these women imported from Europe were not of their making, but derived from prejudices previously brought to the metropole by colonial men (Boutilier 1984).

20. Company and government authorities were concerned with interracial sexual contact but primarily as it related to prostitution. In the Netherlands Indies, for example, venereal disease had become endemic among subordinate white men. In 1930, it was estimated that more than 47,000 European men, mostly soldiers, were hospitalized with syphilis (de Braconier 1933, 923). New restrictions imposed on army barrack-concubinage apparently led to increased use of prostitutes and increased incidence of venereal disease. Concubinage and prostitution thus created different sorts of problems: While the latter was seen as a major source of European pauperism (by creating a large class of underprivileged barrack children), prostitution was condemned as a medical problem and social evil (Ming 1983, 74).

21. The number of European women in the Dutch East Indies rose from 18.7 to 40.6 percent of the total European population between 1905 and 1915 (Nieuwenhuys 1982, 166).

22. Compare, for example, the fiction of Madelon Székely-Lulofs (1932) with that of her husband Ladislao Székely (1979). Also see Jo Manders (1933), whose account of planter excesses won her much disfavor from those who deemed her portrait damaging to "colonial prestige at home and abroad" (Nieuwenhuys 1982, 173). On the hierarchy within African colonial communities and the constraints it imposed on European women's lives, see Knibiehler and Goutalier 1985, 133–36.

23. Also see Kuklick 1979; Lucas 1986.

24. For a more detailed account of this event and the political issues that surrounded it, see Stoler 1985a, 82–86; Stoler 1985b contrasts this 1929 reaction to the murder of an estate manager's wife sixty years earlier.

25. The alternating fluidity and rigidity with which these divisions were drawn is illustrated in June Nash's work on interracial marriage in sixteenth-century Mexico. Mixed marriages between Spanish men and Christianized Indian women were condoned by the colonial state until "the rising numbers of . . . mestizo progeny threatened the prerogatives of a narrowing elite sector" (Nash 1980, 141). By redefining the colonial categories to exclude mestizos from tribute rights and thus restrict their control over Indian labor (140–41), this segment of the population was forcibly marked off from the privileges that their parentage in other colonial contexts might have allowed. Also see Dominguez 1986 for an excellent historical analysis of social classification and its changing legal specification in creole Louisiana. For a comparative, and more extensive treatment, of the relationship of European sexual prohibitions to racial boundaries and the politics of colonial control, see Stoler 1991.

REFERENCES

Alatas, Syed Hussein. 1977. *The Myth of the Lazy Native.* London: Frank Cass.

Albertyn, J. R. 1932. *Die Armblanke ein Die Maatskappy: Verslag van die Carnegie-Kommissie.* Stellenbosch: Pro-ecclesia-drukkery.

Anderson, Benedict. 1983. *Imagined Communities: Reflections on the Origin and Spread of Nationalism.* London: Verso.

Anthropological Research. 1977. "Anthropological Research in British Colonies." *Anthropological Forum* 4(2): 1–112.

Arnold, David. 1979. "European Orphans and Vagrants in India in the Nineteenth Century." *Journal of Imperial and Commonwealth History* 7(2): 104–27.

———. 1983. "White Colonization and Labour in Nineteenth-Century India." *Journal of Imperial and Commonwealth History* 10(2): 133–58.

Asad, Talal. 1975a. "Two European Images of Non-European Rule." In *Anthropology and the Colonial Encounter,* ed. T. Asad, 103–20. London: Ithaca Press.

———. 1975b. *Anthropology and the Colonial Encounter.* London: Ithaca Press.

Bagley, Christopher. 1973. *The Dutch Plural Society: A Comparative Study in Race Relations.* London: Oxford University Press.

Balandier, George. 1965. "The Colonial Situation: A Theoretical Approach." In *Africa: Social Problems of Change and Conflict,* ed. Pierre L. van den Berghe, 34–61. San Francisco: Chandler.

Ballhatchet, Kenneth. 1980. *Race, Sex, and Class under the Raj: Imperial Attitudes and Policies and Their Critics, 1793-1905.* New York: St. Martin's Press.

Barr, Pat. 1976. *The Memsahibs: The Women of Victorian India.* London: Secker and Warburg.

Beckles, Hilary. 1986. "'Black Men in White Skins': The Formation of a White Proletariat in West Indian Slave Society." *Journal of Imperial and Commonwealth History* 15(1): 5-21.

Beidelman, T. O. 1982. *Colonial Evangelism.* Bloomington: Indiana University Press.

Berreman, Gerald. 1981. *The Politics of Truth: Essays in Critical Anthropology.* New Delhi: South Asian Publishers.

Boutilier, James. 1984. "European Women in the Solomon Islands, 1900-1942: Accommodation and Change on the Pacific Frontier." In *Rethinking Women's Roles: Perspectives from the Pacific,* ed. Denise O'Brien and Sharon Tiffany, 173-99. Berkeley: University of California Press.

Braconier, A. de. 1933. "Het Prostitutie-Vraagstuk in Nederlandsch-Indie." *Indische Gids* 55(2): 906-28.

Brandt, Willem. 1948. *De Aarde van Deli.* The Hague: van Hoeve.

Breman, Jan. 1987. *Koelies, Planters en Koloniale Politiek.* Dordrecht: Foris Publications.

Butcher, John G. 1979. *The British in Malaya, 1880-1941: The Social History of a European Community in Colonial Southeast Asia.* Kuala Lumpur: Oxford University Press.

Callaway, Helen. 1987. *Gender, Culture, and Empire: European Women in Colonial Nigeria.* Oxford: Macmillan Press.

Césaire, Aimé. 1972. *Discourse on Colonialism.* New York: Monthly Review Press.

Chance, John, and Taylor, William. 1977. "Estate and Class in a Colonial City: Oaxaca in 1792." *Comparative Studies in Society and History* 19(4): 454-87.

Clammer, John. 1975. "Colonialism and the Perception of Tradition." In *Anthropology and the Colonial Encounter,* ed. T. Asad, 199-222. London: Ithaca Press.

Clerkx, Lily. 1961. *Mensen in Deli.* Publicatie nr. 2. Amsterdam: Sociologisch-Historisch Seminarium voor Zuidoost-Azie.

Cohen, William B. 1980. *The French Encounter with Africans: White Response to Blacks, 1530-1880.* Bloomington: Indiana University Press.

Cohn, Bernard. 1983. "Representing Authority in Victorian India." In *The Invention of Tradition,* ed. E. Hobsbawm and T. Ranger, 165-210. Cambridge: Cambridge University Press.

Comaroff, Jean. 1985. *Body of Power, Spirit of Resistance.* Chicago: University of Chicago Press.

Comaroff, Jean, and Comaroff, John. 1986. "Christianity and Colonialism in South Africa." *American Ethnologist* 13(1): 1-22.

Cooper, Frederick. 1980. *From Slaves to Squatters: Plantation Labor and Agriculture in Zanzibar and Coastal Kenya, 1890–1925.* New Haven: Yale University Press.

Crapanzano, Vincent. 1985. *Waiting: The Whites of South Africa.* New York: Vintage.

Degler, Carl. 1971. *Neither Black nor White: Slavery and Race Relations in Brazil and the United States.* New York: Macmillan.

Delavignette, Robert. 1946. *Service africain.* Paris: Gallimard.

Deli Courant. Medan.

De Planter. 1909–22. Organ of the *Vakvereeniging voor Assistenten in Deli.* Medan.

Dixon, C. J. 1913. *De Assistent in Deli.* Amsterdam: J. H. de Bussy.

Dodwell, Henry. 1926. *The Nabobs of Madras.* London: Williams and Norgate.

Dominguez, Virginia. 1986. *White by Definition: Social Classification in Creole Louisiana.* New Brunswick: Rutgers University Press.

Dowd Hall, Jacquelyn. 1984. "'The Mind That Burns in Each Body': Women, Rape, and Racial Violence." *Southern Exposure* 12(6): 61–71.

Edwards, Michael. 1969. *Bound to Exile: The Victorians in India.* London: Sidgwick and Jackson.

Emmanuel, Arghiri. 1972. "White-Settler Colonialism and the Myth of Investment Imperialism." *New Left Review* 73 (May-June): 35–57.

Encyclopaedie van Nederlandsch-Indie. 1919. The Hague: M. Nijhoff and E. J. Brill.

Etienne, Mona, and Leacock, Eleanor. 1980. *Women and Colonization.* New York: Praeger.

Fanon, Franz. 1963. *The Wretched of the Earth.* New York: Grove.

Foster-Carter, Aidan. 1978. "The Modes of Production Controversy." *New Left Review* 107 (January-February): 47–78.

Foucault, Michel. 1980. *The History of Sexuality.* New York: Vintage.

Furnivall, J. S. 1944. *Netherlands India: A Study of Plural Economy.* New York: Macmillan.

Gann, L. H., and Duignan, Peter. 1978. *The Rulers of British Africa, 1870–1914.* Stanford: Stanford University Press.

Geertz, Clifford. 1968. *Agricultural Involution: The Processes of Ecological Change in Indonesia.* Berkeley: University of California Press.

Gordon, Robert, and Meggitt, Mervyn. 1985. "The Decline of the Kipas." In *Law and Order in the New Guinea Highlands: Encounters with Enga,* ed. R. Gordon and M. Meggitt, 39–70. Hanover: University Press of New England.

Gorter, H. 1941. *Delianen: Schetsen uit het plantersleven op Sumatra's Oostkust.* Amsterdam: L. J. Veen.

Gough, Kathleen. 1968. "Anthropology and Imperialism." *Current Anthropology* 9(5): 403–7.

Grimshaw, Patricia. 1983. "'Christian Woman, Pious Wife, Faithful Mother,

Devoted Missionary': Conflicts in Roles of American Missionary Women in Nineteenth-Century Hawaii." *Feminist Studies* 9(3): 489–521.

Groupe d'études coloniales. 1910. "La femme blanche au Congo." *Bulletin de la société belge d'études coloniales* 5 (May): 1–12.

Gutierrez, Ramon. 1985. "Honor Ideology, Marriage Negotiation, and Class-Gender Domination in New Mexico, 1690–1846." *Latin American Perspectives* 12(1): 81–104.

Harris, Marvin. 1964. *Patterns of Race in the Americas.* New York: Norton.

———. 1970. "Referential Ambiguity in the Calculus of Brazilian Racial Identity." *Southwestern Journal of Anthropology* 26(1): 1–14.

Harris, Marvin, and Kotak, Conrad. 1963. "The Structural Significance of Brazilian Racial Categories." *Sociologia* 25:203–9.

Hobsbawm, Eric, and Ranger, Terence, eds. 1983. *The Invention of Tradition.* Cambridge: Cambridge University Press.

Hughes, Robert. 1987. *The Fatal Shore.* New York: Knopf.

Hymes, Dell, ed. 1969. *Reinventing Anthropology.* New York: Vintage.

Ingelson, John. 1981. "'Bound Hand and Foot': Railway Workers and the 1923 Strike in Java." *Indonesia* 31 (April): 53–88.

Inglis, Amirah. 1975. *The White Women's Protection Ordinance: Sexual Anxiety and Politics in Papua.* London: Sussex University Press.

Kantoor van Arbeid. 1935. *Werkloosheid in Nederlandsch-Indie.* Batavia: Landsdrukkerij.

Kennedy, Dane. 1987. *Islands of White: Settler Society and Culture in Kenya and Southern Rhodesia, 1890–1939.* Durham: Duke University Press.

Kincaid, Dennis. 1971. *British Social Life in India, 1608–1937.* New York: Kennikat Press.

Kleian, J. 1936. *Deli-Planter.* The Hague: van Hoeve.

Knibiehler, Yvonne, and Goutalier, Regine. 1985. *La femme au temps des colonies.* Paris: Stock.

Kroniek [Chronicle]. 1916–39. Oostkust van Sumatra-Instituut. Amsterdam: J. H. de Bussy.

Kuklick, Henrika. 1979. *The Imperial Bureaucrat: The Colonial Administrative Service in the Gold Coast, 1920–1939.* Stanford: Hoover Institution Press.

Leconte, Daniel. 1980. *Les pieds noirs.* Paris: Seuil.

Lévi-Strauss, Claude. 1983. *Le regard éloigné.* Paris: Plon.

Lonsdale, John, and Berman, Bruce. 1979. "Coping with the Contradictions: The Development of the Colonial State in Kenya, 1895–1914." *Journal of African History* 20:487–505.

Lucas, Nicole. 1986. "Trouwverbod, inlandse huishoudsters en Europese vrouwen: Het concubinaat in de planterswereld aan Sumatra's Oostkust." In *Vrouwen in de Nederlandse kolonien,* ed. Jeske, Reijs, et. al., 78–97. Nijmegen: SUN.

Malinowski, B. 1966. "Dynamics of Culture Change." In *Social Change: The Colonial Situation,* ed. I. Wallerstein, 11–24. New York: Wiley.

Manders, Jo. 1933. *De Boedjang-Club.* The Hague: H. P. Leopold.

Marks, Shula, and Trapido, Stanley, eds. 1986. *The Politics of Race, Class, and Nationalism in Twentieth Century South Africa.* London: Longman.

Marle, A. van. 1952. "De groep der Europeanen in Nederlands-Indie." *Indonesie* 5(2): 77–121; 5(3): 314–41; 5(5): 481–507.

Martinez-Alier, Verena. 1974. *Marriage, Class, and Colour in Nineteenth-Century Cuba.* Cambridge: Cambridge University Press.

Marinus, J. H. 1929. *Veertig Jaren Ervaring in de Deli-Cultures.* Amsterdam: de Bussy.

Mead, Margaret. 1977. *Letters from the Field, 1925–1975.* New York: Harper and Row.

Memmi, Albert. 1973. *Portrait du colonisé.* Paris: Payot.

Mercier, Paul. 1965. "The European Community of Dakar." In *Africa: Social Problems of Change and Conflict,* ed. Pierre van den Berghe, 283–304. San Francisco: Chandler.

Ming, Hanneke. 1983. "Barracks-Concubinage in the Indies, 1887–1920." *Indonesia* 35 (April): 65–93.

Mintz, Sidney. 1971. "Groups, Group Boundaries, and the Perception of 'Race.'" *Comparative Studies in Society and History* 13 (Fall): 437–50.

———. 1974. *Caribbean Transformations.* Chicago: Aldine.

———. 1985. *Sweetness and Power: The Place of Sugar in Modern History.* New York: Penguin.

Moore-Gilbert, B. J. 1986. *Kipling and "Orientalism."* New York: St. Martin's Press.

Murphy, Agnes. 1968. *The Ideology of French Imperialism, 1871–1881.* New York: Howard Fertig.

Murray, Martin. 1980. *The Development of Capitalism in Colonial Indochina.* Berkeley: University of California Press.

Naipaul, V. S. 1978. *The Middle Passage.* London: Penguin.

Nandy, Ashis. 1983. *The Intimate Enemy: Loss and Recovery of Self under Colonialism.* Delhi: Oxford University Press.

Nash, June. 1980. "Aztec Women: The Transition from Status to Class in Empire and Colony." In *Women and Colonization: Anthropological Perspectives,* ed. Mona Etienne and Eleanor Leacock, 134–48. New York: Praeger.

———. 1981. "Ethnographic Aspects of the World Capitalist System." *Annual Review of Anthropology* 10:393–423.

Nelson, Hank. 1982. *Taim Bilong Masta: The Australian Involvement with Papua New Guinea.* Sydney: Australian Broadcasting Commission.

Nieuwenhuys, Roger. 1978. *Oost-Indische Spiegel.* Amsterdam: Querido.

———. 1982. *Mirror of the Indies: A History of Dutch Colonial Literature.*

Amherst: University of Massachusetts Press.

Nora, Pierre. 1961. *Les Francais d'Algerie.* Paris: Julliard.

O'Brien, Rita Cruise. 1972. *White Society in Black Africa: The French in Senegal.* London: Faber and Faber.

O'Meara, Dan. 1983. *Volkskapitalisme: Class, Capital, and Ideology in the Development of Afrikaner Nationalism, 1934–1948.* New York: Cambridge University Press.

Onselen, Charles van. 1982. *Studies in the Social and Economic History of the Witwatersrand 1886–1914.* Vol. 1. New York: Longman.

Petersen, Tscherning H. 1948. *Tropical Adventure.* London: J. Rolls.

Piven, Frances, and Cloward, Richard. 1971. *Regulating the Poor: The Functions of Public Welfare.* New York: Vintage.

Post, Ken. 1978. *Arise Ye Starvelings: The Jamaican Labour Rebellion of 1938 and Its Aftermath.* The Hague: Martinus Nijhoff.

Powdermaker, Hortense. 1966. *Stranger and Friend.* New York: Norton.

Price, A. Grenfell. 1939. *White Settlers in the Tropics.* New York: American Geographical Society.

Prochaska, David. 1990. *Making Algeria French: Colonialism in Bone, 1870–1920.* New York: Cambridge University Press.

Rosaldo, Renato. 1980. *Ilongot Headhunting, 1883–1974.* Stanford: Stanford University Press.

Roseberry, William. 1983. *Coffee and Capitalism in the Venezuelan Andes.* Austin: University of Texas Press.

———. 1986. "Images of the Peasant in the Consciousness of the Venezuelan Proletariat." In *Proletarians and Protest,* ed. Michael Hanagan and Charles Stephenson, 149–69. Westport, Conn.: Greenwood Press.

Sahlins, Marshall. 1981. *Historical Metaphors and Mythical Realities: Structure in the Early History of the Sandwich Islands Kingdom.* Ann Arbor: University of Michigan Press.

Said, H. Mohammad. 1976. *Sejarah Pers di Sumatera Utara.* Medan: Waspada.

Sartre, Jean-Paul. 1976. *Critique of Dialectical Reason.* London: New Left Books.

Scott, James C. 1976. *The Moral Economy of the Peasant.* New Haven: Yale University Press.

Seed, Patricia. 1982. "Social Dimensions of Race: Mexico City, 1753." *Hispanic American Historical Review* 62(4): 590–606.

Sheppard, Jill. 1977. *The "Redlegs" of Barbados.* New York: KTO Press.

Sider, Gerald. 1987. "When Parrots Learn to Talk, and Why They Can't: Domination, Deception and Self-Deception in Indian-White Relations." *Comparative Studies in Society and History* 29(1): 3–23.

Spear, Percival. 1963. *The Nabobs: A Study of Social Life of the English in the Eighteenth Century.* London: Oxford University Press.

Spencer, J. E., and Thomas, W. L. 1948. "The Hill Stations and Summer Resorts of the Orient." *Geographical Review* 38(4): 637–51.

Steward, Julian. 1956. *The People of Puerto Rico.* Urbana: University of Illinois Press.

Stoler, Ann. 1985a. *Capitalism and Confrontation in Sumatra's Plantation Belt, 1870–1979.* New Haven: Yale University Press.

———. 1985b. "Perceptions of Protest: Defining the Dangerous in Colonial Sumatra." *American Ethnologist* 12(4): 642–58.

———. 1986. "Plantation Politics and Protest on Sumatra's East Coast." *Journal of Peasant Studies* 13(2): 642–58.

———. 1991. "Carnal Knowledge and Imperial Power: Matrimony, Race, and Morality in Colonial Asia." In *Gender at the Crossroads: Feminist Anthropology in the Postmodern Era,* 51–101. ed. Micaela di Leonardo Berkeley: University of California Press.

———. 1992. "'In Cold Blood': Hierarchies of Credibility and the Politics of Colonial Narratives." *Representations* 37.

———. N.d. "Sexual Affronts and Racial Frontiers: European Identities and the Politics of Exclusion in Colonial Southeast Asia." *Comparative Studies in Society and History* (forthcoming).

Sumatra Post. Medan.

Sutherland, H. 1982. "Ethnicity and Access in Colonial Macassar." In *Papers of the Dutch-Indonesian Historical Conference,* 250–77. Dutch and Indonesian Steering Committees of the Indonesian Studies Programme. Leiden: Bureau of Indonesian Studies.

Székely, Ladislao. 1979. *Tropic Fever: The Adventures of a Planter in Sumatra.* Kuala Lumpur: Oxford in Asia.

Székely-Lulofs, Madelon. 1932. *Rubber.* Amsterdam: Elsevier.

———. 1946. *De Andere Wereld.* Amsterdam: Elsevier.

Takaki, Ronald. 1983. *Pau Hana: Plantation Life and Labor in Hawaii.* Honolulu: University of Hawaii Press.

Tanner, R. E. S. 1964. "Conflict within Small European Communities in Tanganyika." *Human Organization* 23(4): 319–27.

Taussig, Michael. 1980. *The Devil and Commodity Fetishism in South America.* Chapel Hill: University of North Carolina Press.

Taylor, Jean Gelman. 1983. *The Social World of Batavia: European and Eurasian in Dutch Asia.* Madison: University of Wisconsin Press.

Thompson, Leonard. 1985. *The Political Mythology of Apartheid.* New Haven: Yale University Press.

Todorov, Tzvetan. 1985. *The Conquest of America.* New York: Harper.

Vincent, Joan. 1982. *Teso in Transformation: The Political Economy of Peasant and Class in Eastern Africa.* Berkeley: University of California Press.

Waard, J. de. 1934. "De Oostkust van Sumatra." *Tijdschrift voor Economische*

Geographie 25:213–21, 255–75, 282–301.

Wasserstrom, Robert. 1980. "Ethnic Violence and Indigenous Protest: The Tzeltal (Maya) Rebellion of 1712." *Journal of Latin American Studies* 12(1): 1–19.

Wilkie, Mary. 1977. "Colonials, Marginals, and Immigrants: Contributions to a Theory of Ethnic Stratification." *Comparative Studies in Society and History* 19(1): 67–95.

Wolf, Eric. 1959. *Sons of the Shaking Earth*. Chicago: University of Chicago Press.

———. 1982. *Europe and the People without History*. Berkeley: University of California Press.

Woodcock, George. 1969. *The British in the Far East*. New York: Atheneum.

Writing Post-Orientalist Histories of the Third World: Indian Historiography Is Good to Think

Gyan Prakash

If the Third World has been configured by power, history as a category of knowledge has constituted the texture of this configuration. A profound sense of historical awareness guided the European colonial conquest of "peoples without history"; anticolonial nationalism responded to European rule by asserting its claim to history; and the identity of the postcolonial Third World rests on the experience of subjection to the master of history—Europe.[1] In view of history's prominence as a discursive mode of power, it does not appear surprising that the Third World figures prominently in the recent rethinking of the politics of history. But how should we understand this contemporary conjuncture of rethinking? What are the implications of the rethought history of the Third World? In current discussions of history and its politics, particularly since the publication of Edward Said's *Orientalism,*[2] the Third World is frequently resituated outside such binary oppositions as the Orient and the Occident, the East and the West, masculine and feminine. But because the present prominence of the Third World owes something to the current interest in decentered subjects, it is all too easy to slip into thinking that the Third World is the nonfoundational subject par excellence—useful primarily for exemplifying and contemplating decentered selves in the First World. I refer to this recuperative potential while also noting attempts to dissolve the binary oppositions that have "worlded" the Third World because I want to highlight the differentiated nature of the current conjuncture. This point is worth stressing because current discussions of poststructuralist theories and postmodern conditions—frequently lumped together uncritically—often either celebrate them with a heady sense of an

353

"epistemological internationalism" or disparage them as symptoms of a pernicious disease ("French flu" for some). Both cases attribute a singular political meaning to the current moment.

In this article, I examine the case for a more differentiated reading of histories influenced by the poststructuralist questioning of the idea of founding subjects. My examples are drawn from Indian history and I proceed by first reflecting on previous episodes in the discursive constitution of India. I suggest that, although historical writings record numerous attempts to fix India in such irreducible essences as religiosity, non-Westernness, nationhood, poverty, and underdevelopment, the very occurrence of such successive efforts speak eloquently of their failure to establish founding subjects. To speak of such failures, however, is not intended to make the obvious point that the essentialist constructions of India, as of any other category, rested on an epistemological quicksand. Rather, in highlighting the shifting constructions of India, my intention is to suggest that instability, contestation, and change were inherent in historiography's performance as a political discourse even as it narrativized India's history in terms of such unitary themes as the achievement of nationhood, the rise of capitalism, and the transition from "tradition" to "modernity." Such a reading of Indian historiography's functioning is consistent with the poststructuralist insistence that the singular and essentialist constructions cannot escape the effects of complex differences and differentiation that they obscure and straitjacket. But surely the discursive proliferation from the refiguration of history—or, as Peter De Bolla puts it, the "disfiguration" of what is given us as history[3]—that this perspective demands cannot but have discrepant politics. For just as historiography's shifting constructions (in spite of essentialisms) of India reveal historical writings as a differentiated political discourse, the disavowal of foundational histories also cannot but function as variant political practices. It is by recognizing the discrepant political implications formulated in the current conjuncture that we can understand it and postulate the refigurations that resist history's use in "worlding" the Third World. Simply put, if the positing of founding themes and subjects—religiosity, "tradition," "modernity," nation, class—have so far provided the discursive mode of constituting *and* resisting the subordination of the Third World, we must interrogate and understand the different political implications of the present rejection of these in order to deploy history as an enabling discourse. It is with this aim that I now turn to the analysis of Indian historiography as a political discourse, beginning with Orientalism.

Orientalism's India

Orientalism was a European enterprise from the very beginning. The scholars were Europeans; the audience was European; and the Indians figured as inert objects of knowledge. The Orientalist spoke for the Indian and represented the object in texts. Because the Indian was separated from the Orientalist knower, the Indian as object—as well as its representation—was construed to be outside and opposite of Self; thus, both the self and the Other, the rational and materialist British and the emotional and spiritual Indian, appeared as autonomous, ontological, and essential entities. Of course, the two essential entities, the spiritual India and the materialist West, made sense only in the context of each other and the traces of each in the other, which suggested that heterogeneity and difference lay beneath the binary opposition, although the process of rendering India into an object external both to its representation and to the knower concealed this difference. It also made the colonial relationship—the enabling condition of British Orientalism—appear as if it was irrelevant to the production of knowledge. As a result, although colonial dominance produced the East-West construct, it looked as if this binary opposition not only predated the colonial relationship but also accounted for it. In other words, Orientalist textual and institutional practices created the spiritual and sensuous Indian as an opposite of the materialist and rational British, and offered them as justifications for British conquest.

To be sure, these representations underwent considerable change over time, but Orientalism's basic procedures of knowledge remained remarkably stable. They were developed soon after the East India Company conquered Bengal in 1757. Since the company required that its officers have a knowledge about the conquered people, administrators learned Persian and Sanskrit and soon began to publish texts. Alexander Dow, an army officer, translated one of the standard Persian histories into English (*The History of Hindustan*) in 1768–71, and N. B. Halhead compiled and translated the Sanskrit *Dharmashastras* as *A Code of Gentoo Laws, or Ordinations of the Pundits* in 1776.[4] With the involvement of more officials—notably, William Jones, H. T. Colebrooke, John Shore, and Francis Gladwin—this process of learning

Sanskrit and Persian, as well as that of publishing texts and commentaries, gathered speed and led to the foundation of the Asiatic Society of Bengal in 1784. From then on, a number of research journals emerged—*Asiatik Researches* (1788), *Quarterly Journal* (1821), *Journal of the Asiatic Society* (1832). Orientalist knowledge spread to European universities, and scholars with no direct contact with India, Max Müller in London and the Romantics on the continent, saw Europe's origins or childhood in India.[5] In this developing discourse, the discovery of affinities between Sanskrit and European languages provided the premise for formulating the belief in an "Aryan race" from which the Europeans and Brahmans were seen to originate.[6] This search and discovery of European origins in the India of Sanskrit, the Brahmans, and texts essentialized and distanced India in two ways. First, because it embodied Europe's childhood, India was temporally separated from Europe's present and made incapable of achieving "progress." As an eternal child detached from time altogether, India was construed as an external object available to the Orientalist's gaze. Second, composed of language and texts, India appeared to be unchanging and passive. These distancing procedures overlooked the European world dominance that provided the conditions for the production of this knowledge and that had constituted the discursive dominance. The India of the Orientalist's knowledge emerged as Europe's Other, an essential and distanced entity knowable by the detached and distanced observation of the European Orientalist.

While essentialism, distancing, and the centrality of the opposition of Europe and India deployed in the formative phase of Orientalism outlived the early Orientalists, the specific configurations of knowledge did not. As the genuine respect and love for the Orient of William Jones gave way to the cold utilitarian scrutiny of James Mill, and then to missionary contempt, the picture changed.[7] Sanskrit, texts, and Brahmans were no longer attractive in the harsh light thrown by liberal reformers and critics. Instead, they became accountable for India's lack of civilization, moral obligations, good government, and historical change. Such revisions and refigurations of representations were occasioned by debates over such major policy questions as land revenue settlements, educational and administrative policies, and the renewal of the East India Company's charter.[8] These were occasions when the ideas current in Europe were most conspicuously applied to India. In the course of time, the application of Eurocentric ideas added to the stock of images available for representing India, but the on-the-spot official reports, Parliamentary inquiries and papers, and detailed surveys during the first half of the nineteenth century exponentially crowded the representational field. These became regularized and professionalized in the late nineteenth century, as linguistic, ethnological, archaeological, and Census surveys and District Gazetteers emerged. With these, the older India of Sanskrit, texts, and Brahmans was pushed off center by details on peasants, revenue, rent, caste, customs, tribes, popular religious practices, linguistic diversity, agro-economic regimes, male and female population, and other such topics. In this enlarged but crowded picture, the India of William Jones was less relevant.

The enormous growth, change, and increasing complexity of Orientalist knowledge was of crucial importance; for, committed as the British rule was to a government based on accurate knowledge of facts, changes in knowledge had direct implications for the technologies of rule. For example, when the ethnographic surveys and census operations commenced in the late nineteenth and the early twentieth centuries, they broke society into groups, households, and individuals, making them available for piecing together through statistics. Because the society aggregated from the new units was constituted by an apparently objective and culturally neutral classificatory system of individuals, households, and occupations, it became available to more extensive administrative penetration. This brought the older debates on the nature of Indian village communities, culminating in Baden-Powell's 1892 publication of *The Land Systems of British India,* to an end. The government no longer considered the indirect systems of rule—consisting of contractual agreements with village leaders—as necessary and it reached down to the individuals configured by their caste and tribal status.[9]

The discursive space for such changes in knowledge was provided by the Orientalist construction of India as an external object knowable through representations.[10] Because the government viewed knowledge contained in official documents as a representation of reality, or, in one official's words in 1860, as a "photograph of the actual state of the community,"[11] it was always possible to argue that the photograph did not represent the external reality adequately, thus requiring more adequate representations. This representational model of knowledge, coupled with the exigencies of colonial government, enabled the scholarly field of Orientalism, or Indology, to repeatedly refigure itself. The consequent refiguration, however, did not unsettle the authority of the Orientalist, the essentialization of India, and its representation as an object in binary opposition to Europe. The lines were drawn clearly, with separate authentic and autonomous essences—India and Europe (or England)—were clearly reflected in knowledge. The old Orientalist, buried in texts and devoted to learning Sanskrit and Persian, was replaced by the official, the scholar, and the modernizer. The new Orientalist administered the fruits of modern knowledge and government while being careful not to upset the Indian's presumed outmoded and traditionalist beliefs. Such actions and projections reaffirmed India's representation as a religiously driven social organism and found that the Indian's disinterest in modern politics and historical change was reflected in Sanskritic Hinduism and popular "animism." This representation allowed the British to see themselves as engaged in managing and changing such arenas as politics and economy in which the Indian social organism and thought was incapable of operating.[12]

Nationalist Historiography

The first significant challenge to this Orientalized India came from nationalism and nationalist historiography, albeit accompanied by a certain contradiction. While affirming the concept of an India essentialized in relation to Europe, the nationalist transformed it from passive to active, from dependent to sovereign, capable of relating to history and reason.[13] Nationalist historiographers accepted the patterns set for them by British scholarship. They accepted the periodization of Indian history into Hindu, Muslim, and British periods, later addressed as the ancient, medieval, and modern eras; relegated caste to sections on "Society," that is, to the history of society with politics left out; and reiterated the long and unchanging existence of a Sanskritic Indic civilization.

In the 1920s and the 1930s, when nationalism became a mass phenomenon, a professional Indian historiography emerged to contest British interpretations. It is significant that these historians chose ancient India as the ground for this contest. If some of the early Orientalists had seen Europe's origin in the India of the texts, the nationalists saw the origin of the modern nation in that same ancient India; for such historians, the old Orientalist scholarship's sympathetic remarks on the India of texts, such as Max Müller's studies, became objective and authoritative statements that affirmed India's great past.[14] Nationalist historians, such as H. C. Raychaudhuri, K. P. Jayaswal, Beni Prasad, R. C. Majumdar, and R. K. Mookerjee, studied ancient emperors and saw the rise of a nation-state in the creation of these ancient empires. Furthermore, as Romila Thapar points out, it was important for this historiography to claim that everything good in India—spirituality, Aryan origins, political ideas, art—had completely indigenous origins. In fact, Southeast Asian cultures were seen as outgrowths of the glorious Indian civilization, and the period of the Gupta empire (A.D. 320–540) came to symbolize the Golden Age when Hinduism prospered, national unity soared, and economic wealth, social harmony, and cultural achievements reached a state of plenitude. Later, the Muslims came (in the eleventh and twelfth centuries), and it was all downhill after that. These glorifications of classical India as Hindu India and of Hindu India as the originator of modern India arose in response to the dilemma that the nationalists faced. On the one hand, they thought of India as a nation-state in European terms—as a cradle for reason, progress, and modernity. On the other hand, the assertion of nationhood demanded the projection of a distance from Europe. For some, the answer lay in militant Hinduism. Thus, the Hindu nationalists claimed that the Vedic texts and ancient history had not only expressed India as a nation but had also displayed attributes that colonialism defined as exclusively European.

This abbreviated account of nationalist historiography does not do full justice to its achievements and complexity. These historians forced debates on sources and brought out much that was unknown, and regional histories came into focus. The assumption that all that was valuable in world civilizations originated in Greece was challenged. The Orientalist authority to speak for India was contested, and Hindu chauvinist interpretations did not go unquestioned. Jawaharlal Nehru's *The Discovery of India,* for example, was marked by an awareness of cultural and historical diversity, and argued that it was "undesirable to use Hindu or Hinduism for Indian culture."[15] Although for him, too, spirituality defined India's past essence and the Gupta age represented the blossoming of nationalism, the Hindu revivalist historiography was too parochial for his secular and cosmopolitan outlook. In place of a Hindu nation, the India that he discovered and presented was a secular entity, not a Hindu nation, that had cradled a variety of religions and sects through the centuries and had acquired a unity while surviving conquests and conflicts. His *Discovery of India* was a documentation of this unity through history; and, for him, the nationalist movement was designed to free this unity so that India could join the world-historical march toward modernity. In addition to the secular nationalist Nehru, there was Gandhi, for whom India's nationness lay in its nonmodern essence—a universal heritage that he felt the West had all but disowned in its drive toward materialist civilization.

Clearly, the differences between Nehru and the nationalist interpretations of Hindu chauvinist historians were important. There can be no doubt that the concept of India as essentially Sanskritic and Hindu—glorious in ancient times, then subjected to Muslim tyranny and degeneration in the Middle Ages that made it an easy target for British conquest—had and continues to have deadly implications in a multiethnic country such as India. While recognizing the importance of these differences, I also want to highlight that which was common to nationalism as a whole: the assumption that India was an undivided subject, that is, that it possessed a unitary self and a singular will that arose from its essence and was capable of autonomy and sovereignty. From this point of view, the task of history was to unleash this subjectivity from colonial control; and historiography was obliged to represent this unleashing. The nationalists acted on this assumption by questioning the authority of Orientalists. They accused the older Indological knowledge of biases and judged it as being inadequate for representing reality. In its place, nationalist historiography offered more adequate portraits. A good example of this was the interpretation of the 1857 revolt in North India. For British historians, mutiny was the right term because the revolt was nothing but an uprising of disaffected soldiers; calling it anything other than a mutiny meant conceding it some legitimacy. In 1909, a Hindu nationalist, Vinayak Damodar Savarkar, wrote a book entitled *The Indian War of Independence, 1857* and argued that it was a national revolt.[16] Nationalist historiography's commitment to the idea of India as an essential and undivided entity, and to knowledge as a more or less adequate representation of the real, underlay such revisions. In spite of such complicities in Orientalist procedures, nationalism broke the exclusivity of Indology as a European discipline. In the discourse of the nationalists, the objects of description did not owe their meanings only to their opposition to European essences; rather, it was the ontological being of India as a nation—no doubt barely visible and, for the most part in its history, enslaved—that was the most evident element in providing meaning to historical events and actors. So, when politicians spoke of a nation in the making, they were referring to the task of making the masses conscious of a nation already in existence as an objective reality.

The nationalist historiography's narrativization of Indian nationalism, brought to a successful conclusion in the achievement of independence in 1947, represents one trajectory in post-Orientalist history despite its complicity in many of the categories of thought and procedures of Orientalism. Burdened with the task of articulating an anticolonial national view, it could not but be different than Orientalism. Thus, the nationalists produced impressive scholarship on the "drain" of wealth from India to Britain, on the deindustrialization of the country by British manufacturing interests, the neglect of Indian industrialization, and other such questions.[17] For this historiography of economic nationalism, as for cultural and political nationalists, the subject was always India, and the interests of the nation were always at stake. Powerful pronouncements of these kinds established India as an active subject. Therefore, we need to recognize it as one of the ways in which the "Third World writes its own history." It is important to bear this contestatory aspect in mind (lest we overemphasize epistemological complicity at the expense of the contest between colonialism and nationalism) while also recognizing that the nationalist writing of history—both before and after independence—did not break free from two elements of the Orientalist canon. First, the nationalists, like the Orientalists, also assumed that India was an undivided entity but attributed it a sovereign and unitary will that was expressed in history. India now emerged as an active and undivided subject that had found its expression in the nation-state and transcended class and ethnic divisions rather than being the inert object of Orientalist representations. Second, India was given an ontological presence prior to and independent of its representations that followed the procedures of Orientalism. That such nationalism was contestatory while also being confined within the Orientalist "thematic" should not be surprising. As Partha Chatterjee argues, the nationalists opposed colonialism in the name of reason; by claiming that India's ancient history had followed, if not pioneered, a universal spirit leading to the nation-state, republicanism, economic development, and nationalism reaffirmed the cunning of reason; in asserting that, if liberated from colonial slavery, a "backward" country such as India could modernize itself, it reaffirmed the projects of modernity, making it ideologically incapable of transcending the Orientalist categories of thought.[18] Nationalism appropriated even Gandhi's antimodern ideology in its drive to create a nation-state devoted to modernization and turned him into a figure revered for his ability to appeal to the "irrational" peasants and for the mystical bond that he was seen to have with the masses. That historiography became a part of this project should cause no wonder. History, as a discipline, was, after all, an instrument of the post-Enlightenment regime of reason, and the Indian nationalist historians, being Western-educated elites engaged in the struggle for a modern nation-state, were its eager proponents.

The nation-state that came into being in 1947, therefore, was committed to a program of modernization. The belief that the British had deliberately deindustrialized India was common among the nationalists, and, for Nehru, the big hydroelectric projects and steel mills were to displace religious shrines as pilgrimage sites, and a modern sensibility founded on scientific thinking was to replace outmoded religious beliefs and superstitions. In line with this thinking, five-year economic plans got going; the diesel-driven pumps for irrigation began humming, new seed varieties were introduced, and the "green revolution" was launched; transitor radios invaded the countryside, and India was seen to be making rapid strides toward modernity in the 1960s and the early 1970s.

The Refigurations of Essentialized India

Nationalist historiography so discredited some of the specific representations of Orientalism that the image of a sensuous, inscrutable, and wholly spiritual India no longer enjoys academic prestige. More importantly, it made histories centered on India the norm. Postwar decolonization, anticolonial sentiments, and upsurges against neocolonialism also created a congenial political and intellectual climate for an orientation based on India. This orientation was institutionalized in the United States by the establishment of South Asia area studies programs in the 1950s. Scholarship founded on this basis did much to bring new evidence on history and culture to light by historians who moved rapidly from the study of imperial policies to "realities on the ground," and as social and cultural anthropologists broke new ground in the analysis of caste and village society. Implicit in these moves, however, was the search for an authentic India. With colonial rule over and cultural relativity ascendant, research centered on India assumed that an authentic history and culture unaffected by the knower's involvement in the object of knowledge could be recovered. This research naively assumed that its valorization of India freed the scholar from colonial discourses, released to write, as it were, on a clean slate. Acting on this assumption, the knower could once again be construed as separate from knowledge, thereby overlooking that this position itself had a long history; but because this scholarship did not recognize this history, it obviously could not reflect upon the consequences of its belief that the scholar was external to the object of inquiry. As a result, the operation of a whole battery of interests (academic disciplines, ideologies, institutional investments) was concealed, and old ideas reappeared in new guises. This was true, for instance, of the concept of a caste-driven and otherworldly India, which was reformulated as "traditional India" by the modernization theory in the 1960s. In the postcolonial context, the reappearance of such essentializations had two implications. First, insofar as a focus on India and cultural relativity enabled the represented object to appear as a vibrant and independent entity, the nationalist project was endorsed. Second, the attribution of this identity-in-itself also made an Orientalist refiguration possible. Anthropological studies in the 1950s and 1960s illustrate these two tendencies and are worth considering because they came to command a prominent place in South Asia area study programs quite early, preceding the recent liaison between history and anthropology by at least a decade.

Unlike the traditional Orientalists, anthropologists studied people instead of texts and observed culture in action rather than studying its textual remnants. Moreover, as a discipline that specialized in scrutinizing the Other, it was particularly suited to pursue studies centered on India. Studies of caste by anthropologists and, to a lesser extent, by historians influenced by them became the most prominent aspect of this scholarship.[19] Louis Dumont argued that caste, after all, was a vital part in envisioning the essence of India, and this was also the assumption in the vigorous debates and theorizing about its place.[20] After the publication of Dumont's *Homo Hierarchicus* in English, very few could resist the argument that caste was the centerpiece of Indian society. Even Marxists, who had always had some trouble dealing with the place of caste in their analysis of Indian society and history, were forced to take note and could no longer dismiss it as superstructural or as "false consciousness." For others, Dumont's all-encompassing theory provided a very elegant framework for explaining the forces of continuity, if not "unchangeability," in Indian history. All this is not to imply that studies on caste did not yield important insights. On the contrary, they did explode the older myths about the unchangeability of the caste system, show its links to economy and polity, and trace patterns of social mobility.[21] Imbued as these works were with a great deal of empathy for India, their depictions of vibrant realities fell in line with the nationalist celebration of India's autonomous and unitary subjectivity.

The attribution of cultural and social essences was, however, also open to Orientalist recuperation. The obsessive focus on caste, for instance, served to fix it as the one essence of India. In doing so, it shared the Orientalist project of constituting India as the Other—an Other whose difference from Self recuperated the latter as selfsame, autonomous, and sovereign. This was a far cry from the avant-garde ethnographic surrealism of Paris in the 1920s, when the Other had corroded the reality of Self.[22] The Paris of Louis Dumont in the 1960s, on the other hand, represented Homo hierarchicus (India) in affirming the reality of Homo aequalis (West). What was taken to be Dumont's distinct and crucial insight—namely that caste was a religious hierarchy that encompassed the economic and the political—turns out to be not all that different from the colonial view that India's essence lay in social organisms separated from the sphere of power.[23] In this respect, Dumont's work, the most celebrated and authoritative postwar anthropological scholarship on India, illustrates the vulnerability of essentialism to Orientalist refiguration.

These post-decolonization refigurations and recuperations in the scholarly field, particularly in anthropology, ought to be seen as materializations of a context marked by what may be called developmentalism. As new nations emerged from the shadow of colonial rule, the older project of colonial modernity was renovated and then deployed as economic development. As such, a new nation-state, India, looked at science and technology as universal forces and deployed them in transforming its society. The boom in postwar anthropological fieldwork and studies began and then pushed forward this reformulation of modernizing projects by providing a socioscientific knowledge of "traditional" social structures and beliefs targeted for modernization. The subdiscipline of economic development within the field of economics also emerged during these decades to formulate and further the modernization project by furnishing knowledge on the ways that existing economic institutions worked and by outlining strategies that could transform them. The area studies programs united these socio-scientific fields with Indological pursuits in creating knowledge that was no longer bounded by the old East-West definitions. Drawing regional rather than the old Orient-Occident boundaries, these area studies provided a distinct yet subtler understanding of cultural relativity, although they could not provide postcolonial scholarship with the means to escape nationalist and Orientalist essentialisms. Indeed, it was precisely the lens of cultural relativity that, as Johannes Fabian points out, made the world appear as culture gardens separated by boundary-maintaining values—as posited essences.[24] Furthermore, the erection of these boundaries visualized the separateness of the subject from the object and defended anthropology's claim to represent an external Other. In this regard, professional training and expertise allowed the researcher to claim that participant-observation protected the observer's externality that had been compromised in fieldwork. Conditioned by these methods of denying involvement in the construction of its object of knowledge, neither anthropology nor the area study programs could escape the nationalist and Orientalist recuperations of their essentialisms. These entities became represented as "traditional" beliefs and structures, which were posed in opposition to modernization and were useful both in formulating culturally sensitive development projects and in evolving "appropriate" technology. To be sure, the methodological conventions devised and the questions posed by anthropology, development studies, and area study programs cannot be reduced to some crude political determination: we can trace the particular configurations of these fields to the discussions and debates within them; these scholarly conventions and questions helped in configuring the postwar context of developmentalism—insofar as they highlighted essences (for example, Dumont's essentialization of ritual hierarchy) that could be evaluated for their adaptability to modernization.

Postnationalist Foundational Histories

It is a tribute to the resilience of the modernizing project inaugurated by Orientalism that the legitimacy of its proponents was challenged before its hegemony was threatened. Thus, nationalism accused colonialism of deliberately failing to live up to its own promise; Marxists, in turn, viewed both colonialism and nationalism as structurally incapable of fulfilling the tasks of modernization in the colonies. In Marxist analysis, the notion of India as an undivided subject, separated and observable in relation to an equally undivided Europe, was suspect because it denied the class relations underlying these entities. These class relations led to an unequal and uneven development that neither colonial rulers nor their nationalist successors could overcome; thus, the Marxists regarded the nationalist representation of India as an undivided and autonomous subject as ideological. A somewhat similar critique has been developed by social historians oriented toward world history. In their accounts, India is released from the restricting lens of national history and is placed in the larger focus of world history. Although the emergence of a professional Marxist historiography of India preceded the rise of world-history analysis in the late 1970s and early 1980s by roughly two decades, the two can be treated together because both interpret India in terms of a world-historical transition, despite the many differences between them. With their shared emphasis on political economy, they hold questions of production systems and political control to be of paramount importance in specifying the "third worldness" of India.

In the Marxist case, the issues relating to political economy were, above all, expressed by social classes. The consequent advocacy of class histories—often contesting Marx's writings on India—cracked the image of an undivided India. While other scholars approached India from the institutional context of an academic discipline, Marxists adopted the perspective of engaged critics that enabled them to adopt a combative stance vis-à-vis the disciplines of Indology and South Asia area studies. Convinced that nonclass histories suppress the history of the oppressed and stress consensus over conflict, Marxists wrote contestatory histories of domination, rebellions, and movements in which they accused others of biases and claimed that their own biases were true to the "real" world of class and mode of production.[25] In place of the notion of a homogeneous Indic civilization, the Marxists highlighted heterogeneity, change, and resistance.[26] Postcolonial Marxist historiography, in particular, replaced the undivided India of the nationalists with one divided by classes and class conflict; but because its inquiries were framed by a narrative about the transition of the mode of production, this scholarship viewed the activities of classes within the context of India's passage to capitalism (or, more accurately, to an aborted capitalist modernization). Take, for example, the Marxist readings of the so-called Bengal renaissance during the first half of the nineteenth century, when brilliant Bengali reformers defied conventions and produced new visions of Hinduism. Long heralded as the beginning of a new India (with one of the earliest reformers, Ram Mohun Roy, called "the father of modern India"), Marxist reinterpretations stressed the failure of this project.[27] Arguing against the widespread belief that this "renaissance" was entirely a Western influence, the existence of an indigenously born rationalism was discovered and shown to turn conservative through contact with the West. As for modernity inspired by the West and promoted by the Bengal renaissance, these scholars contended that, in the absence of an organic class to serve as its basis, the reformers could not but fail in their project. In short, the "renaissance" represents the case of aborted or colonial modernity. Without belittling the value of these reinterpretations, I think it is fair to say that the construction of India in terms of this and other failures represents a foundational view. While it highlights the paradoxes of "renaissance" in a colonial context, the interpretation of these events as aborted or failed modernity defers the conclusion of the modernization narrative but does not eliminate the teleological vision. We are thus led to see the "third worldness" of India in its incomplete narrative and unfulfilled promise, which invites completion and fulfillment.

A somewhat related interpretation has emerged also in recent social history writings that place modern Indian history in a world historical framework. Like Marxist historiography, these social histories have dislodged the undivided and essential India of the Orientalists and nationalists. From works in this genre, the Indian nation appears as a recent and tenuous creation whose artificiality, shown by the earlier "Cambridge school" historians in the intrigues and strategems of the nationalists,[28] is quite evident in eighteenth-century history. Descriptions of that century by these social historians decompose India into coasts that look outward and face the Indian Ocean, and hinterlands composed of regional systems of social and political interests, trade, and agriculture. Coasts and hinterlands connect and disconnect, fragment and rejoin; but the multiplicity of interests and perspectives disallows the articulation of a unitary India. C. A. Bayly's study is perhaps the most complete and original work in this genre.[29] His work revises, with a wealth of detail and insights, the older notion of eighteenth-century India as a period of chaos and decline in which the British just stepped in to pick up the pieces. Instead of explaining the conquest as the victory of a technologically superior and stronger Britain over a backward and weaker India, he offers a persuasive account of how the tendencies within North Indian society interacted with the East India Company's activities in creating an empire. Stressing parity rather than disparity in technological level and economic organization, he analyzes the British conquest as a conjunctural combination of social, economic, and political conditions and interests. In this story, the rise of the Indian nation appears not as an eruption of a previously existing entity but, rather, as a historical creation attributable to the transformation of the late eighteenth-century empire into a classic colonial relationship by the mid-nineteenth century.

There is no denying the richness of Bayly's narrative and the importance of its revisionist insights. Other studies have added support to this story, and a more explicitly Marxist elaboration of this interpretation has been offered;[30] and although it differs from the Marxist accounts on many substantive issues, it provides a more fully developed and substantiated version of the transition story than that formulated in the older Marxist accounts. Whereas the Marxists write from the position of engaged critics and thus stress domination and struggle, historical sociology underplays conflict and traces the development of structures. We have the echoes here of the now familiar contrast between agency and structure. More significant than this contrast, however, is their common immersion in foundational historiography. For both of them, writing history implies recapturing the operation of classes and structures, with the usual caveats about the historian's biases and ideology. I do not mean by this that this historiography makes simple-minded claims to objectivity, and I do not intend to get bogged down in a sterile debate over subjective versus objective accounts; rather, when I call this form of historical writing foundational, I refer to its assumption that history is ultimately founded in and representable through some identity— individual, class, structure—that resists further decomposition into heterogeneity. From this point of view, we can do no better than document the agency and effects of these founding subjects of history, unless we prefer the impossibility of coherent writing amidst the chaos of heterogeneity. Any change in historical writing becomes primarily a matter of interpretive shifts—new concepts replace old and unworkable ones.

The difficulty with an approach that regards history as a record of such founding agents as modes of production and class structures is that it begs the next series of questions: How was class signified? By what discursive logic did the identification of class interests lead the chain of signification to economic relations? If such a logic was cultural (or historical), then how do we account for its formation and its hegemonic position? The point here is not that class and structural analyses are unimportant but that to regard them as originating causes and subjects of history is to neglect an important question: namely, how did class, or any other subject for that matter, come to acquire the status of an originating subject? Of course, we can complicate the notion of class, as historians of India often do, by adding caste, religion, language, region, and, more recently, gender. But these additions end up illustrating only that none of the categories is self-sufficient; they all spill into each other and the gesture of adding more categories betrays the nonfoundational character of them all.

I have lingered on the issue of foundational writings in order to highlight that while Marxist and social historians have unsettled the unitary status of India, their vision excludes a critical return to the scene of writing history and carries with it an objectivist bias, however provisional. Take, for example, the narrativization of Indian history in terms of the development of capitalism. For Marxists, this is an obviously critical question. But how is it possible to write a critical account of capitalism unless we also enstrange, disfigure, and deconstruct its colonization of history? Does this not require the displacement of capitalist development as a privileged theme of history and necessitate the defamiliarization of the bourgeois political economy? Or, to take another example, how can the historians of India resist the totalizing claims of the contemporary nation-state if their writings represent India in terms of the nation-state's career? This question is easier for most people to handle because nationhood can more easily be shown as "imagined" and fictive.[31] The decomposition of the autonomous nation into heterogeneous class, gender, regional, linguistic, and cultural divisions is easy to show.

Refusing foundational categories that construct the theme of global modernity, however, has proved difficult. But the tenuous presence and the very historicity of class structures that anchor the transitional narrative cannot be fully acknowledged without the rejection of the stability occupied by the theme of transition in the discourse of historians. Without such an acknowledgment, Marxist and social historians can only envision that India's "third worldness" consists of its incomplete or underdeveloped development. India, which is seen in this history as trapped in the trajectories of global modernity, is doomed to occupy a tragic position in these narratives. Such a vision cannot but reproduce the very hegemonic structures that most historians find unjust and occlude histories that lie outside the themes privileged in history.

Toward Postfoundational Histories

The preceding account of how the "Third World writes its own history" makes clear that historiography has participated in constituting shifting positions. The nationalists, who were opposed to the Orientalist representation of India as a separate and passive Other, gave it autonomy and a national essence. Cultural anthropology and area study programs in the postwar period, particularly in Europe and the United States, orientalized this essence in terms of the cultural concept and left an undivided India intact. Marxists and social historians broke up this entity in terms of founding class and structural subjects, but narrativized India in contemporary hegemonic terms. If nothing else, these multiple positions suggest how the third world subject escapes being fixed. Lest this recognition of nonfixity be appropriated as another form of fixing, I hasten to add that the gesture that frames the endorsement of heterogeneity refuses the language of fixing. By way of elaborating and concluding my account of the post-Orientalist Indian historiography, I will refer to Edward Said's *Orientalism* as an argument for an antifoundational history and discuss examples of attempts in this direction.

Several scholars have noted that Said's work rejects an essentialist reversal of Orientalist constructions and calls attention to the discrepancy in the Orient-Occident binary opposition.[32] He does not envision the task of post-Orientalist scholarship as consisting of substituting the "real" Orient for the "myth" of the Orientalists; instead, his work outlines a post-Orientalist interpretive position that traces third world identities as relational rather than essential. This rules out a mere inversion of the Hegeliah dialectic so that, instead of the Orientalist's assertion of the Occident's primacy, the Self-Other opposition could be used to assert the autonomous presence of the Orient. In its place, a post-Orientalist historiography visualizes modern India, for example, in the relationships and processes that have constructed contingent and unstable identities. This situates India in relationships and practices that organized its territory and brought it under an international division of labor, assembled and ordered cultural differences into a national bloc, and highlighted it as the religious and spiritual East opposed to the secular and materialist West. I am not suggesting that Indian historiography has yet to study these relational processes. On the contrary, as my account has noted, Marxist and social historians, for example, have shown in considerable detail that the global history of capitalism has articulated the identity of modern India; but such historical writings do not explore and expose the alterity that underlies this identity—other than calling it precapitalist, protoindustrial (or feudal and semifeudal as opposed to capitalist), unfree labor (as opposed to free labor), and traditional (not modern).[33] This strategy cannot historicize the emergence of a modern, colonial-capitalist Indian nation because it does not displace the categories framed in and by that history. The historicization of this process requires (as Said, for example, accomplishes in his study of the Orientalist essences) unsettling these identities, disrupting their selfsame presence.

The most prominent example of such an attempt in Indian historiography is to be found in the volumes of *Subaltern Studies,* a series of fiercely combative historical accounts written by a group of Indian and British Marxist historians scattered between India, Britain, and Australia—almost all of them having had first world academic training or experience.[34] Arguing that much of the existing historiography reproduced the colonial, nationalist, and Marxist teleologies, the *Subaltern Studies* group aims at recovering the history of subaltern groups. In doing so, it disrupts, for example, the nationalist narrative that considers all colonial revolts as events in the becoming of the Indian nation and contests the older Marxist accounts that see these episodes as preludes to the emergence of full-fledged class consciousness. In carrying out this project, several essays in the series employ the familiar "history from below" approach. Furthermore, the teleological effects of the Hegelian dialectic that they employ, as well as the notion of recovering and restoring the subaltern that they use, do not mesh very well with their structuralist decoding of the sign systems.[35] These limitations, however, should not be allowed to obscure what is truly novel and theoretically refreshing in their work—the deployment of the concept of subalternity. This concept is particularly defined and used most fruitfully in the work of Ranajit Guha, the editor of the series, who, in place of class as an essential object, views subalternity as an effect of power relations expressed through a variety of means— linguistic, economic, social, and cultural.[36] This perspective, therefore, breaks the undivided entity of India into a multiplicity of changing positions that are then treated as the effects of power relations. The displacement of foundational subjects and essences allowed by this also enables Guha to treat histories written from those perspectives as documents of counterinsurgency—those seeking to impose colonial, nationalist, or transitional (modernizing) agendas. Writing subaltern history, from this point of view, becomes an activity that is contestatory because of its insurgent readings.

If the use of the concept of subaltern as an identity dependent on difference suggests that the *Subaltern Studies* shares some of the structuralist and poststructuralist critiques of the autonomous and sovereign subject, this does not mean that the two are identical. There is no denying the explicit influence of French and Soviet structuralist semiotics in some of the writings; and a recent collection consisting of selections from several volumes aims at making an explicit connection with Michel Foucault's writings.[37] Notwithstanding these connections, the subaltern project is also different because, while it rescues the subaltern from the will of the colonial or nationalist elite, it also replaces one autonomous subject (the nation) with another (the subaltern). This feature, however, is not as straightforward as it sounds: if the assertion of the subaltern's unified consciousness, on the one hand, unravels elite projects, the claim for the subaltern's autonomous agency is rendered impossible, on the other hand, by the very definition of subalternity as a position in relation to that of the elite. Gayatri Chakravorty Spivak calls this self-contradictory attribute a *"strategic* use of positivist essentialism" and endorses its difference from the antihumanist decentering of the subject in the West because it affirms the heterogeneity of contexts.[38] In addition, she recommends the claim for "a *positive* subject-position" as a "strategy for our times" because it pinpoints and displaces the simultaneous constitution and effacement of the Third World by European imperialism—a process that the critical apparatus of the antihumanist discourse leaves unexamined when it fails to recognize that modern forms of power include not just disciplinary (in clinics and prisons) but also representational forms with which European territorial imperialism created and erased colonial subjects. According to Spivak, this means that while the antihumanist writing of histories without subjects (as recommended by Louis Althusser) may be an adequate oppositional practice in the West for unmasking those operations of power that masquerade as triumphs of human will and freedom, such a strategy cannot suffice for the Third World. Critical practice in the Third World must posit the subaltern as a subject in order to dethrone Europe's implantation as the universal subject of history by territorial imperialism, even as this strategy—falling prey to its own procedures—turns the autonomous agent (the subaltern) into a positionality consisting of effects.

The similarity and difference that Spivak reads between the structuralist and poststructuralist critiques of the autonomous subject, on the one hand, and the *"strategic* use of positivist essentialism," on the other, suggests persuasively that heterogeneous discursive contexts produce and require not a homogenous internationalism but discrepant discourses. But the very fact that Spivak finds the critical value of the *Subaltern Studies'* variety of heterogeneous discourse through an "against the grain" reading indicates that its essentialism contains problems despite the fact that its privileging of culture and "communal" modes of power is not simple minded but complex, "strategic," and politically enabling. These problems are compounded by the pervasive influences of cultural pluralism and the anthropological traditions of cultural relativity, both of which regard differentiations produced in history as expressions of immutable diversity of essences. The enduring strength of these influences can easily freeze the dynamic of differentiation into a sterile diversity of autonomous attributes, and turn essentialism, howsoever strategic, into an "authentic" third world attribute. This possibility also arises from what Spivak identifies as one of the ways in which the radical intellectual in the First World approaches and appropriates the Third World: grant it an essential position while regarding it as improbable. To realize that essentialism carries an enormous risk, even when it takes the self-cancelling form, one has to only recall how anthropological studies in the 1960s ended up rejuvenating nineteenth-century Orientalist images when they sought and found various "authentic" traditions. The critical force of *Subaltern Studies* lies in its disruption of such enduring colonialist and nationalist essentializations as the unitary Indic civilization and the nation; the assertion of the subaltern autonomy or the resurrection of culture and tradition as an originary ground for contestation, on the other hand, while challenging the projection of elite (colonialist and nationalist) interests as "general interests," fails to deconstruct the nativist and populist suppression of asymmetrical differences. Such an approach is not novel—the "history from below" writings have been there before. Nor is it necessary to posit the subject-agent *I* prior to its concatenation in effects because it limits the potential for prespectival critique offered by the concept of subalternity as a positionality.

If the force and the discursive contextuality of the *Subaltern Studies* lie in the challenge that it throws at colonial and nationalist discourses of history, this critique is extended further by the new, post-Orientalist historiography. With a somewhat different focus than *Subaltern Studies,* it takes forms of knowledge, culture, and "traditions" canonized by colonial and hegemonic Western discourses as issues of inquiry; it examines precisely those anthropological and historical constructions that sometimes surface unexamined in *Subaltern Studies* scholarship. In part, this critical thrust arises from the fact that much of such studies are being written in the first world academy where the power of the hegemonic Western discourses in the knowledge produced about India appears palpable. This is not to say that the influence of such discourses does not extend beyond metropolitan centers; but outside the First World, in India itself, the power of Western discourses is concealed and operates through its authorization and deployment by the nation-state; deeply sedimented in the national body politic, the knowledge generated and bequeathed by colonialism neither manifests itself nor functions exclusively as a form of imperial power.[39] In the West, however, the production and distribution of Orientalist concepts continue to play a vital role in projecting the First World as the radiating center around which others are arranged. Confronted with the first world academy's involvement in such a configuration of knowledge and power, the new, post-Orientalist scholarship has found the poststructuralist decentering of the West enabling and influential.

Obviously, it would be a mistake to see the formulation of critiques of Orientalist dichotomizations as products entirely of the recent dissolution of such hegemonic subjects of the West as Man, freedom, and progress just as it would be incorrect to see the two as unrelated; the current literature exemplifies the two as energized by each other while pursuing their different aims. Even when the poststructuralist suspicion of centers is not the driving force, it can nevertheless be read in critiques of foundations that Orientalism institutionalized—East-West, masculine-feminine, tradition-modernity, freedom-unfreedom—in its operation as a discursive organization of power. This can be seen in many recent historical writings: examinations of the nineteenth-century reformist attempts to suppress and outlaw the institution of widow sacrifice (*suttee*), for example, reveals the formulation and use of gendered ideas by the colonial rulers and Indian reformers in enforcing new forms of domination even as they questioned the burning of widows; a study of criminality points to power relations at work in classifying and acting upon "criminal tribes" even as threats to life and property were countered; and an inquiry into labor servitude depicts how the freedom-unfreedom opposition concealed the operation of power in the installation of free labor as the human destiny while it provided a vantage point for challenging certain forms of corporeal domination.[40] The disclosure of histories that history and historiography excluded is not the only effect of these studies' revelation of that which is concealed when issues are posed as traditional, reactionary, and oppressive treatment of women versus their modern and progressive emancipation; as crime versus law and order; and as freedom versus bondage. Rather, they reveal the politics of knowledge involved in the construction of these binary oppositions and trace their canonization as seminal historical events not just because they were so regarded in the past but in order to interrogate the past as the history of the present.

The emerging historiography, as the preceding account makes evident, can be located at the point where poststructuralist, Marxist, and feminist theories intersect, converge, and diverge. In understanding this scholarship, however, it is not enough to trace its links with these theories. Equally relevant is some of the earlier historiography. Take, as examples, Romila Thapar's searching scrutiny of Orientalist and nationalist constructs in her work on ancient India and Bernard Cohn's historicization of cultural forms essentialized during colonial rule.[41] Such earlier work of clearing and criticizing essentialist procedures anticipated the contemporary trend of making cultural forms contingent and of highlighting the complicity of colonial and nationalist knowledge in constituting the objects of inquiry. The work by Nicholas Dirks illustrates this point.[42] Like earlier scholars, he also traces the genealogy of a widely accepted idea—namely, that the caste system was primarily a religious phenomenon that encompassed the political; but his argument is framed by contemporary theories in showing that British rule depoliticized the caste system, which then gave rise to the idea that it was primarily a religious entity. Thus, he historicizes the conventional notion of caste by showing its shifting position in a South Indian kingdom. This unstable and changing position of caste and kingdom is accentuated, in turn, by the repeated interruptions of the narrative and its movement in and out of different historical periods and disciplines. The overall result forces the reader to reflect upon the procedures and rhetoric of academic disciplines in which the book is located.

This historiography's critical focus on epistemological procedures and institutional interests makes it somewhat different from the *Subaltern Studies*. While the *Subaltern Studies* scholars see themselves targeting and disrupting the colonialist and nationalist wills directly and recovering the subaltern consciousness, the postcolonial perspective of the emerging historiography seeks to disclose the archaeology of knowledge and analyze the sedimentation of academic disciplines and institutions in power. Although both ultimately aim critical reflections upon discursive formations, the emphasis is clearly different. In view of the role that Western academic institutions play in studying and marginalizing the Other, it is not surprising that post-Orientalist historiography targets academic disciplines. It is also precisely for this reason that, as disciplines devoted to representing the Other, Indology and area studies in Europe and North America have been less than enthusiastic, if not hostile, to Said's interpretation. Because the demystification of India as an undivided and separate object calls for the decomposition of the undivided and autonomous West, disciplines instituted to extend the East-West binary logic are understandably reluctant. Interestingly, it is in these fields not associated with Indology—such as literature—and in institutions without strong programs in South Asian area studies that Said's book has stimulated much new work; but even traditional centers of Indology are beginning to take account of challenges posed by critiques of Orientalism.[43]

The story of Indian historiography that I have been telling has certain evident themes. First, the "third worldness" of India has been conceived in a variety of different ways by historiography. These shifting concepts testify to the changing history of India and locate historiography in that history, contributing to as well as being a part of it. This rules out the comfort of assuming that India, or the Third World, will finally speak in a voice that will render all previous ones inauthentic. Second, the identification with the subordinated's subject-position, rather than national origin, has been the crucial element in formulating critical third world perspectives. Of course, as subordinated subjects, Indian historians have obviously developed and embraced the victim's subject-position more readily; but because the experience and expression of subordination are discursively formulated, we are led back to the processes and forces that organize the subordinate's subject-position. Third, the formation of third world positions suggest engagement rather than insularity. It is difficult to overlook the fact that all of the third world voices identified in this article speak within and to discourses familiar to the West instead of originating from some autonomous essence. This does not warrant the conclusion that the third world historiography has always been enslaved, but that the careful maintenance and policing of East-West boundaries has never succeeded in stopping the flows across and against boundaries, and that the Self-Other opposition has never quite been able to order all differences into binary opposites. The Third World, far from being confined to its assigned space, has penetrated the inner sanctum of the First World in the process of being "third-worlded"—arousing, inciting, and affiliating with the subordinated others in the First World. It has reached across boundaries and barriers to connect with the minority voices in the First World: socialists, radicals, feminists, and minorities. If these third world voices have spoken before or speak today in languages that appear to be of the First World, this repetition does not mean replication—a point that the nationalist reversal of the Orientalist problematic clearly establishes. If the insistence on hybridity and discrepancy and the crossings and interruptions of boundaries seems more insistent now, the turmoil in the field and attempts to write post-Orientalist histories are not new. Historians of India have previously questioned and unsettled dominant paradigms. Fine examples of non-Orientalist histories already exist; to think otherwise would mean attributing a totalizing power to Orientalism. The existence of earlier precedents, however, does not mean that the present historiography is completing the tasks left unfinished and that we are now witnessing the end of Orientalism; such a perspective entails the notion of a continuous history and assumes an essential similarity between different historiographies. Neither entirely new nor completely the same, the specificity of the present ferment is owed to the ways in which a new, post-Orientalist scholarship is being conceived, from its difference from previous contexts; and the particular insights generated by the emerging historical writing can be attributed to the larger field of social experience articulated in discourses.

The present critical appraisal of concepts, disciplines, and institutions associated with the study of South Asia forms a part of contemporary challenges to beliefs in solidly grounded existence and identities, if not their loss. Jacques Derrida's disclosure of the "metaphysics of presence" and Michel Foucault's genealogical accounts of the disciplinary constitution of criminal and sexual subjects have certain general affinities with Edward Said's analysis of Orientalism's suppression of difference in favor of stable and hierarchical East-West identities. These resemblances, which do not diminish significant differences among them, arise from their common espousal of certain decentering methods. It is argued that these methods theorize what was practiced earlier by literary and aesthetic modernism (such as the latter's break from the belief that language was a transparent medium) and that the kinship with modernism accounts for its obsessive concern with language and writing, which displaces political questions to the aesthetic arena.[44] While the trace of modernism's transgressive impulses may well be discerned in poststructuralism's de-centering methods, the current prominence of these theories is better understood as a moment in the postmodern valorization of blurred genres and off-center identities. Fashioned by denials of grand totalizing theories, postmodernism defies and refuses definition. Only a laundry list of conditions can be offered—television images, fashion magazines, Salman Rushdie, Talking Heads, challenges to universalist and essentialist theories, architectural irreverence and playfulness, transnational capitalism . . . The list is endless and without a beginning or end; any gesture toward classification and distillation would be contrary to postmodernism, which exists only as a combination of conjunctural conditions.[45] If this poetics of pastiche is capable of arousing a pluralist fantasy of escape from power, the juxtaposition of First and Third Worlds, of "modern" and "premodern," can just as easily highlight the asymmetrical conjoining of territories, political institutions, economies, and cultural forms; while the postmodern may be used to assimilate discrepancy and inequality into some sort of good-intentioned liberal universe of cultural relativity, the conjunctural combination of difference also directs our attention to precisely those unevennesses and asymmetries that the universal march of civilization, progress, and history was supposed to eliminate but actually advanced. In its latter form, as what Hal Foster calls a "postmodernism of resistance,"[46] the juxtaposition of asymmetrical differences reveals that which the modern constituted and subordinated as its Other. The insistence on disclosing these unevennesses forms as much a part of the contemporary context as the conflation of the postmodern with liberal pluralism. If poststructuralist theories have confronted and given shape to this contradictory context by displacing such unitary essences as the "individual" with decentered and differentiated selves, the postcolonial perspective in third world scholarship has approached and influenced this context somewhat differently. Concerned not so much with decentering the individual as a founding subject, it has nevertheless forced a crisis in universalist ideologies and provoked a genuine confrontation of discrepant histories and cultures by taking a combative stance with respect to the legacies of the application of such parts of the "Western tradition" as reason, progress, and history to non-European cultures.

This repudiation of the post-Enlightenment ideology of reason and progress distinguishes the present historiography from the anti-Orientalism of nationalism. Earlier, when nationalism challenged Ori-

entalism, it staked the subjected nation's claim to the order of reason and
progress by showing, for instance, that India had a history comparable
to that of the West; that it, too, had produced a protorepublican political
order; and that it had achieved economic, cultural, and scientific progress.
The older Marxist historiography, as well as the more recent studies by
social historians, broke up the nationalist's undivided India into an entity
permeated with class conflict, but their global mode-of-production narratives did not fully confront the universalism of the post-Enlightenment
order of reason. What we are witnessing now in the post-Orientalist
historiography is a challenge to the hegemony of those modernization
schemes and ideologies that post-Enlightenment Europe projected as the
raison d'être of history, an assault on what Ashis Nandy calls the "second
colonization." This is because, as Nandy argues,

> modern colonialism won its great victories not so much through its
> military and technological prowess as through its ability to create
> secular hierarchies incompatible with traditional order. These hier-
> archies opened up new vistas for many, particularly for those exploited
> and cornered within the traditional order. To them the new order
> looked like—and here lay its psychological pull—the first step towards
> a more just and equal world. That was why some of the finest critical
> minds in Europe—and in the East—were to feel that colonialism, by
> introducing modern structures into the barbaric world, would open
> up the non-West to the modern critical-analytical spirit. Like the
> "hideous heathen god who refused to drink nectar except from the
> skulls of murdered men," Karl Marx felt, history would produce out
> of oppression, violence, and cultural dislocation not merely new tech-
> nological and social forces but also a new social consciousness in Asia
> and Africa.[47]

Today, the ideologies of science, progress, and hypermasculinity that the
Age of Reason brought to the Third World riding on the back of colonialism have lost their seductive appeal; but in reflecting on that history
when Descartes defined rationality and Marx defined social criticism, we
must, Nandy argues, listen to voices contained therein and write
"mythographies" that we did not write before. This is not only a plea
for a recognition of the plurality of critical traditions but a claim for
the liberating nature of the victim's discourse, particularly for that of
the colonized. Although both the colonizer and the colonized have been

the victims of colonialism, the colonized have a special story to tell because they had to not only confront the West in its own terms of robust hypermasculinity but also construct and connect with the other subordinated selves of the West. This call for a writing of mythographies, therefore, provides an appreciation not only for the colonized's construction of their subjected selves but also the colonized's appeal to and affiliation with the subordinated selves of the colonizer. Such mythographic accounts revealing the previously hidden histories of the subordinated selves of the First and Third worlds will also expose the mythic quality of colonial and national fables of modernity. This invocation of the mythic in disclosing the fablelike character of "real" history calls to mind Salman Rushdie's fabulous history of postcolonial India and Pakistan in *Midnight's Children*.[48] In the novel, Saleem Sinai, a child fathered by history, melts the apparent solidity of history single-handedly—and through his long nose, face, casual talk, and telepathy—causing border wards, violent demonstrations, and ethnic riots. The very extravagance of myths, dreams, and fantasies elicits belief in its truthfulness and defamiliarizes the real. While Rushdie spins his tale around pepper pots and spittoons, Nandy's mythography of history has unheroic heroes—the saintly Gandhi and the comical Brown Sahibs—and it is through these unlikely figures that the tragic tale of colonialism is told, its alliance with psychopathic technologies exposed, its fantastic quality revealed.

Such a strategy of privileging the "mythic" over the "real" has turned the historiographic field topsy-turvy. The foundations upon which South Asian studies were based—all the antinomies implied by the opposition of "India" and the "West"—can no longer be unquestionably accepted as entirely separate and fixed. After all, if Gandhi's saintliness and nonviolence—those quintessential "Indian" qualities—had counterparts in the "West" (albeit marginalized); if the Brown Sahibs' imitation of the British was an "Indian" strategy of survival and even resistance; and if, in spite of its clearheaded realpolitik, modern anticolonial Indian nationalism fell prey to "second colonization"; then what is left of the neatly separated "India" and the "West"? Such destabilization of identities and crossing of carefully policed boundaries promise a new, third world historiography that will resist both nativist romanticization and Orientalist distancing. This postfoundational move, implicit in the emerging writings, affiliates the new, third world historiography with post-structuralism, and together they both echo the postmodernist decentering of unitary subjects and hegemonic histories.

This common articulation of the postmodern condition, however, cannot be taken to mean that the fragmentation and proliferation of identities, histories, cultures, and the failure of representations and the existence of ironic detachments do not have regional configurations and contextual resonances (American? French? Parisian? German? Continental philosophy? Marxist?). This being so, post-Orientalist scholarship, while sharing certain common features with poststructuralism and postmodernism, cannot but be different from them. This is particularly important because the Third World was defined as marginal from the very beginning. The new, post-Orientalist scholarship's attempt to release the Third World from its marginal position forms a part of the movement that advocates the "politics of difference"—racial, class, gender, ethnic, national, and so forth.[49] Obviously, all of these are discrepant with one another and the relationships among them are forged rather than inherent in some epistemological solidarity. This discrepancy and the necessity for negotiated relationships are made all the more insistent by two tendencies: first, by the proliferation of histories, cultures, and identities-in-difference arrested by previous essentializations; and second, by the refusal to erect new foundations in history, culture, and knowledge. While these tendencies may suggest that the postcolonial perspective and the politics of difference evince impulses similar to what is generally referred to as cultural criticism, we should not make too much of this resemblance; cultural critics have different concerns in that their principal aim is to unlock the "closures" in "high" literary and philosophical texts, releasing meanings trapped by beliefs in essences, and provide a multiple reading of the "Western tradition";[50] their interests are not often directly focused on political questions and they sometimes demonstrate an aestheticist bias. Feminist theorists and the advocates of the politics of difference, on the other hand, are concerned with the poetics of power shaped by "Western tradition" and by different aesthetic styles. The post-Orientalist historiography also is directly concerned with the question of domination because its very subject—the Third World—is defined by its dominated status.[51] The attempt to unlock history from the "closures" is thus not so much a question (for these scholars) of taking pleasure in the revealed Bakhtinian carnivalesque but an issue of engaging those relations of domination. This involves a relentless disfiguration of themes—the development of nationhood, the transition to capitalism—that come to us as accretions of history open only to interpretation, not displacement. This disfiguration cannot stop with the themes that have served domination: it must extend to the processes that project and authenticate history as interpretation. Since the existing corpus of records and historical writings have participated in just such authenticating projects, historiography has always been a contested field and its politics is once again undergoing scrutiny. The representation of India as an Other defined by certain essences—tradition, spirituality, femininity, otherworldliness, caste, nationality—is now contested and these contests involve the maintenance and the subversion of the relations of domination discursively reproduced by the lack of a clear break from the legacies of Orientalism, nationalism, and the ideologies of modernization.

History's power to constitute what exists and has existed makes the writing of histories a profoundly "worldly" activity—a fact recognized by most historians although they regard the questions it raises as issues of inevitable biases and subjective interpretations that require disclaimers, nothing more. But surely this is not the most significant conclusion to be derived from the awareness of historical writing as a political practice. If history as a "worldly" activity has participated in "worlding" the Third World, then it follows that a contestatory practice demands the disfiguration of those patterns of history that have served the relations of domination. Such a clearly political vision characterizes recent post-Orientalist historical accounts and distinguishes this historiography in a context in which the Third World is widely recognized as a signifier of cultural difference but is rapidly appropriated and commodified as cultural surplus (the Banana Republic stores being the most offensive contemporary example in this respect);[52] or serves as an Other in a hermeneutic exercise devoted to the exploration of blurred genres and decentered realities validated by postmodernism.[53] Enabled by, but also in resistance to, these contemporary and contradictory postmodernist tendencies, the self-consciously political visualization of history writing as a site of contest acquires its distinct significance from the efforts to rethink the Third World out of its historical enclosures. Undoubtedly, the postmodern conjuncture and the consequent problematization of the "Western tradition" lend some strength to these efforts and account for the attention currently paid to how the "Third World writes its own history." These enabling conditions, however, also threaten to envelop the Third World in the larger project of dislodging the "Western tradition," rendering and celebrating it as just any other fragment, and thereby reinscribing the West as the universal subject of history. If such a mutually consolidating embrace between pluralism (the world as a cultural garden of fragments) and universalism (the essential homogeneity of fragments) occurs successfully in the present flurry of conferences and seminars on the Third World, we will lose sight of the crucial fact that the "Western tradition" was a very peculiar configuration in the colonial world; and the old axiom—that the Third World is a good thing to think with about the West—will once again be proven correct. Such a turn of events will bring post-Orientalist historiography's promise to contest hegemonic structures and reveal new histories to an ironic end.

NOTES

This is a revised and expanded version of the article published in *Comparative Studies in Society and History* 32, no. 2 (1990): 383–408, and it was originally presented as a paper in a panel entitled "After Orientalism: The Third World Writes Its Own History" at the American Historical Association's annual meeting in Cincinnati, December, 1988. I am thankful to Carol Gluck, whose imagination and organizational efforts made this panel possible, and whose invitation prompted me to think about these broader questions. Remarks by others on the panel—Ervand Abrahanian and Edward Said in particular—and the questions and comments from the audience clarified the issues involved. The present version developed in response to the following: comments from Nicholas Dirks, Joan Scott, and Carol Quillen; criticisms and suggestions offered at the workshop on "Colonialism and Culture" by *Comparative Studies in Society and History* at Ann Arbor, Michigan, May, 1989, particularly by Roger Rouse and Vicente Rafael; and reactions to the paper at the Social Science seminar, Institute of Advanced Study, Princeton, in February, 1990, and at the Rutgers-Princeton conference on "History Today—And Tonight," in March, 1990.

    1. It is this affirmation of history's supremacy that lies behind Frederic Jameson's well-intentioned but first world declaration that all third world texts must necessarily be national allegories. See his "Third World Literature in the Era of Multinational Capital," *Social Text* 15 (Fall, 1986): 65–88; Aijaz Ahmad, "Jameson's Rhetoric of Otherness and the 'National Allegory,'" *Social Text* 17 (Fall, 1987): 3–25, and Jameson's reply (26–27).

    2. Edward Said, *Orientalism* (New York: Vintage, 1979).

    3. Peter De Bolla, "Disfiguring History," *Diacritics* 16, no. 4 (1986): 49–58.

4. On these Orientalist writers, see Bernard S. Cohn, "Notes on the History of the Study of Indian Society and Culture," in *Structure and Change in Indian Society*, ed. Milton Singer and Bernard S. Cohn (Chicago: Aldine, 1968), 7. On Halhead, see Rosane Rocher, *Orientalism, Poetry, and the Millenium: The Checkered Life of Nathaniel Brassey Halhead* (Delhi: Motilal Banarasidass, 1983). For a discussion of Persian historiography and for more on the early British treatments of how eighteenth-century British writings dealt with pre-British history, see Mohibbul Hasan, ed., *Historians of Medieval India* (Meenakshi: Meerut, 1968).

5. Wilhelm Halfbass, *India and Europe: An Essay in Understanding* (Albany: SUNY Press, 1988), 69–83. See also Ronald Inden, "Orientalist Constructions of India," *Modern Asian Studies* 20, no. 3 (1986): 401–46.

6. Martin Bernal, *Black Athena: Afroasiatic Roots of Classical Civilization* (New Brunswick, N.J.: Rutgers University Press, 1987), 227–29, 330–36.

7. James Mill, *The History of British India* (1817) rpt. (Chicago: University of Chicago Press, 1975). On missionaries, see Ainslee Thomas Embree, *Charles Grant and British Rule in India* (New York: Columbia University Press, 1962).

8. On how European ideas were applied to India, see Ranajit Guha, *A Rule of Property for Bengal: An Essay on the Idea of Permanent Settlement* (Paris: Mouton, 1963); Eric Stokes, *The English Utilitarians and India* (Oxford: Clarendon Press, 1959).

9. Richard Saumarez Smith's "Rule-by-Records and Rule-by-Reports: Complementary Aspects of the British Imperial Rule of Law," *Contributions to Indian Sociology,* n.s. 19, no. 1 (1985): 153–76, is an excellent study of this process in Punjab.

10. See Inden, "Orientalist Constructions," on the use of representation in Orientalism. Timothy Mitchell's *Colonising Egypt* (Cambridge: Cambridge University Press, 1988) contains a fascinating interpretation of representation in British and European knowledge about Egypt.

11. Cited in Smith, "Rule-by-Records," 153.

12. Nicholas B. Dirks's *The Hollow Crown: Ethnohistory of an Indian Kingdom* (Cambridge: Cambridge University Press, 1987) is a powerful argument against this thesis. See also Inden, "Orientalist Constructions."

13. Cf. Partha Chatterjee, *Nationalist Thought and the Colonial World— A Derivative Discourse?* (London: Zed Books, 1986), 38.

14. Much of this account is based on Romila Thapar's excellent "Interpretations of Ancient Indian History," *History and Theory* 7, no. 3 (1968): 318–35, which contains a critical discussion of these nationalist historians. For more on this phase of historiography and on individual historians, see S.P. Sen, ed., *Historians and Historiography in Modern India* (Calcutta: Institute of Historical Studies, 1973).

15. Jawaharlal Nehru, *The Discovery of India* (New York: John Day, 1946), 65.

16. Interestingly, Marx and Engels's writings in the *New York Daily Tribune* on the 1857 revolts were put together and published in the Soviet Union as *The First Indian War of Independence 1857-59* (Moscow: Foreign Languages Publishing House, 1959).

17. R. C. Dutt's *The Economic History of India* (1901), 2 vols., rpt. (London: Routledge and Kegan Paul, 1950) is the classic of this genre. For a detailed treatment of this line of nationalist historiography, see Bipan Chandra, *The Rise and Growth of Economic Nationalism in India* (Delhi: People's Publishing House, 1966). For a debate on the "deindustrialization" question, see M. D. Morris, Bipan Chandra, and Tapan Raychaudhuri, *Indian Economy in the Nineteenth Century: A Symposium* (Delhi: Indian Economic and Social History Association, 1969).

18. Chatterjee, *Nationalist Thought,* 30, 168-69.

19. The list is huge, but for some representative examples, see Frederick J. Bailey, *Caste and the Economic Frontier* (Manchester: Manchester University Press, 1957); M. N. Srinivas, *Social Change in Modern India* (Berkeley: University of California Press, 1966). David G. Mandelbaum, *Society in India,* 2 vols. (Berkeley: University of California Press, 1970) summarizes and cites much of the scholarship on caste. Fine historical studies of caste include the following: Ronald B. Inden, *Marriage and Rank in Bengali Culture: A History of Caste and Clan in the Middle Period Bengal* (Berkeley: University of California Press, 1975); Frank F. Conlon, *A Caste in a Changing World: The Chitrapur Saraswat Brahmans, 1700-1935* (Delhi: Thomson Press, 1977); Karen I. Leonard, *Social History of an Indian Caste: The Kayasths of Hyderabad* (Berkeley: University of California Press, 1978).

20. Louis Dumont, *Homo Hierarchicus* (Chicago: University of Chicago Press, 1970); McKim Marriott, "Hindu Transactions: Diversity without Dualism," in *Transaction and Meaning: Directions in the Anthropology of Exchange and Symbolic Behavior,* ed. Bruce Kapferer (Philadelphia: Institute for the Study of Human Issues, 1976), 109-42; Michael Moffatt, *An Untouchable Community in South India* (Princeton: Princeton University Press, 1979). Although Dumont's work no longer enjoys the influence it did in the 1970s, its formulation that ritual hierarchy defines India continues to draw adherents. For example, Donald E. Brown's *Hierarchy, History, and Human Nature* (Tucson: University of Arizona Press, 1988) employs the Dumontian essentialization of caste and hierarchy to explain the absence of "real" historiography in India.

21. See, for example, James Silverberg, ed., *Social Mobility in the Caste System of India* (Paris: Mouton, 1968).

22. James Clifford, "On Ethnographic Surrealism," in *The Predicament of Culture* (Cambridge, Mass.: Harvard University Press, 1988), 117-51.

23. Cf. Dirks, *Hollow Crown,* 3-5. For other critiques, see Arjun Appadurai, "Is Homo Hierarchicus?" *American Ethnologist* 13, no. 4 (1986): 745-61, and "Putting Hierarchy in Its Place," *Cultural Anthropology* 3, no. 1 (1988): 36-49.

24. Johannes Fabian, *Time and the Other: How Anthropology Makes Its Object* (New York: Columbia University Press, 1983), 47.

25. The notable examples include: P. C. Joshi, ed., *1857 Rebellion* (Delhi: People's Publishing House, 1957), which tried to reclaim the 1857 revolt as a moment in the popular revolutionary movement; A. R. Desai, ed., *Peasant Struggles in India* (Delhi: Oxford University Press, 1979) interprets revolts and movements spread over two centuries as part of a wider struggle of the dominated; and Irfan Habib's masterly *The Agrarian System of Mughal India* (London: Asia Publishing House, 1963), which argues that peasant revolts led by the local notables plunged the Mughal empire into a paralyzing crisis in the eighteenth century.

26. D. D. Kosambi's works on ancient India mark the beginning, and remain stellar examples, of a professional Marxist historiography of this genre. See his *Culture and Civilization of Ancient India in Historical Outline* (London: Routledge and Kegan Paul, 1965).

27. See Sumit Sarkar, "Rammohun Roy and the Break with the Past," in *Rammohun Roy and the Process of Modernization in India,* ed. V. C. Joshi (Delhi: Vikas, 1975), 46–68; Barun De, "The Colonial Context of the Bengal Renaissance," in *Indian Society and the Beginnings of Modernization ca. 1830–1850,* ed. C. H. Philips and Mary Doreen Wainwright (London: School of Oriental and African Studies, 1976), 119–25; Asok Sen, *Iswar Chandra Vidyasagar and His Elusive Milestones* (Calcutta: Rddhi-India, 1977).

28. See John Gallagher, Gordon Johnson, and Anil Seal, eds., *Locality, Province, and Nation* (Cambridge: Cambridge University Press, 1973); David Washbrook, *The Emergence of Provincial Politics* (Cambridge: Cambridge University Press, 1976).

29. C. A. Bayly, *Rulers, Townsmen, and Bazaars: North Indian Society in the British Expansion, 1770–1870* (Cambridge: Cambridge University Press, 1983).

30. For example, David Ludden, *Peasant History in South India* (Princeton: Princeton University Press, 1985); Muzaffar Alam, *The Crisis of Empire in Mughal North India: Awadh and the Punjab 1707–1748* (Delhi: Oxford University Press, 1986). For a Marxist version of this narrative, see David Washbrook, "Progress and Problems: South Asian Economic and Social History," *Modern Asian Studies* 22, no. 1 (1988): 57–96.

31. See Benedict Anderson's *Imagined Communities: Reflections on the Origin and Spread of Nationalism* (London: Verso, 1983). The brilliance of its insights is somewhat marred by a lapse into sociological determinism and by its overemphasis on "print capitalism."

32. See James Clifford, "On Orientalism," in *The Predicament of Culture* (Cambridge: Harvard University Press, 1988), 255–76. See also Rashmi Bhat-

nagar, "Uses and Limits of Foucault: A Study of the Theme of Origins in Edward Said's 'Orientalism,'" *Social Scientist* 158 (1986): 3–22.

33. My *Bonded Histories: Genealogies of Labor Servitude in Colonial India* (Cambridge: Cambridge University Press, 1990) shows how the free-unfree opposition appropriated and reorganized different forms of labor.

34. Ranajit Guha, ed., *Subaltern Studies,* 6 vols. (Delhi: Oxford University Press, 1982–85). The reference to national origins and to the first world site of academic training and experience is not meant to be invidious; rather, my intention is to show that national origin is not a necessary requirement for the formulation of a post-Orientalist position.

35. Rosalind O'Hanlon's "Recovering the Subject: *Subaltern Studies* and Histories of Resistance in Colonial South Asia," *Modern Asian Studies* 22, no. 1 (1988): 189–224, argues persuasively that an essentialist and teleological thinking also exists in their work. For an "against the grain" reading that attempts to capture what is novel and contestatory in *Subaltern Studies,* see Gayatri Chakravorty Spivak, "Subaltern Studies: Deconstructing Historiography," in *Subaltern Studies,* 4:330–64.

36. See, in particular, Ranajit Guha, *Elementary Aspects of Peasant Insurgency in Colonial India* (Delhi: Oxford University Press, 1983).

37. Ranajit Guha and Gayatri Chakravorty Spivak, eds., *Selected Subaltern Studies* (New York: Oxford University Press, 1988). The last section, for example, is called "Developing Foucault."

38. Spivak, "Subaltern Studies," 342–45.

39. Cf. Lata Mani, "Multiple Mediations: Feminist Scholarship in the Age of Multinational Reception," *Inscriptions,* 5 (1989), 1–23, esp. 9–10.

40. Veena Das, "Gender Studies, Cross-Cultural Comparison, and the Colonial Organization of Knowledge," *Berkshire Review* 21 (1986): 58–76; Lata Mani, "Contentious Traditions: The Debate on Sati in Colonial India," *Cultural Critique* 7 (Fall, 1987): 119–56. These constitute only a small sample of refreshingly new studies of gender that are accumulating at a rapid pace. See, for example, Mrinalini Sinha, "Manliness: A Victorian Ideal and Colonial Policy in Late Nineteenth-Century Bengal" (Ph.D. diss., SUNY–Stony Brook, 1988). For criminality, see Sanjay Nigam, "The Social History of a Colonial Stereotype: The Criminal Tribes and Castes of Uttar Pradesh, 1871–1930" (Ph.D. diss., London School of Oriental and African Studies, 1987); for servitude, see Prakash, *Bonded Histories.*

41. See Bernard Cohn, *An Anthropologist among Historians and Other Essays* (Delhi: Oxford University Press, 1987); Romila Thapar, *Ancient Indian Social History: Some Interpretations* (Delhi: Orient Longman, 1978).

42. Dirks, *Hollow Crown.*

43. In 1988–89, the South Asia Regional Studies Department, University of

Pennsylvania, held a year-long seminar entitled "Orientalism and Beyond: Perspectives from South Asia."

44. Andreas Huyssen, *After the Great Divide: Modernism, Mass Culture, Postmodernism* (Bloomington: Indiana University Press, 1986), 206–16.

45. Andrew Ross, "Introduction," in *Universal Abandon? The Politics of Postmodernism,* ed. Andrew Ross (Minneapolis: University of Minnesota Press, 1988).

46. Hal Foster, ed., *The Anti-Aesthetic: Essays on Postmodern Culture* (Seattle: Bay Press, 1983), xi–xii.

47. Ashis Nandy, *The Intimate Enemy: Loss and Recovery of Self under Colonialism* (Delhi: Oxford University Press, 1983), ix.

48. Salman Rushdie, *Midnight's Children* (New York: Avon Books, 1980).

49. For a recent statement of this position from a feminist perspective, see Joan Wallach Scott, *Gender and the Politics of History* (New York: Columbia University Press, 1988). This politics of difference is called "minority discourse" by Abdul JanMohamed and David Lloyd in their "Introduction: Minority Discourse—What Is to Be Done?" *Cultural Critique* 7 (Fall, 1987): 5–17.

50. These concerns are stated, for example, in Dominick LaCapra's *Rethinking Intellectual History: Texts, Contexts, Language* (Ithaca: Cornell University Press, 1983), and *History and Criticism* (Ithaca: Cornell University Press, 1985).

51. See Gayatri Chakravorty Spivak, "Can the Subaltern Speak?" in *Marxism and the Interpretation of Culture,* ed. Cary Nelson and Larry Grossberg (Urbana: University of Illinois Press, 1988), 271–313, in which she argues that even politically oriented Western poststructuralists, such as Foucault, are marked by a certain blindness to the reality of imperialist domination.

52. See Paul Smith, "Visiting the Banana Republic," in Ross, *Universal Abandon?*, 128–48.

53. Stephen A. Tyler's "Postmodern Ethnography: From Document of the Occult to Occult Document," in *Writing Culture: The Poetics and Politics of Ethnography*, ed. James Clifford and George Marcus (Berkeley: University of California Press, 1986), 122–40, exemplifies this tendency. Note, for instance, that he conceives postmodern ethnography's task as invoking "the fantasy reality of a reality fantasy," and "the occult in the language of naive realism and of the everyday in occult language." This invocation, according to him, "provokes a rupture with the commonsense world and evokes an aesthetic integration whose therapeutic effect is worked out in the restoration of the commonsense world" (134). In this view, the off-centering of the ethnographer, as in the cover photograph of *Writing Culture,* becomes the purpose of postmodern ethnography.

Contributors

MICHAEL ADAS is Professor of the Comparative History of Colonialism at Rutgers University. His books and articles have focused on various aspects of the history of European imperialism in Africa and Asia, from peasant protest movements to the impact of Western science and technology on colonized peoples. His most recent work is *Machines as the Measure of Men: Science, Technology, and Ideologies of Western Dominance* (1989).

FREDERICK COOPER is Professor of African History at the University of Michigan. He is the author of *Plantation Slavery on the East Coast of Africa* (1977), *From Slaves to Squatters: Plantation Labor and Agriculture in Zanzibar and Coastal Kenya* (1980), and *On the African Waterfront: Urban Disorder and the Transformation of Work in Colonial Mombasa* (1987) and the coeditor, along with Ann Stoler, of a special issue of *American Enthnologist* (November 1989) on "Tensions of Empire: Colonial Control and Visions of Rule." Currently, he is completing a book on "Decolonization and African Society: The Labor Question in British and French Africa."

NICHOLAS B. DIRKS is Professor of History and Anthropology at the University of Michigan. He is the author of *The Hollow Crown: Ethnohistory of an Indian Kingdom* (1987) and other essays on colonialism, culture, and historical anthropolgy. Currently, he is working on the relation of colonial anthropologies to postcolonial politics in southern India.

RICHARD HELGERSON is Professor of English and department chair at the University of California, Santa Barbara. He is the author of *The Elizabethan Prodigals* (1976), *Self-Crowned Laureates: Spenser, Jonson, Milton and the Literary System* (1983), and *Forms of Nationhood: The Elizabethan Writing of England* (1992).

DAVID LUDDEN is Associate Professor of History and South Asia Regional Studies at the University of Pennsylvania. His *Peasant History in South India* (1985) was reprinted in paperback in 1989. His forthcoming volume for *The New Cambridge History of India* is entitled *Agriculture and Indian History*.

389

TIMOTHY MITCHELL is Associate Professor of Politics, New York Univeristy. He is the author of *Colonising Egypt* (1988) and an editor of the journal *Middle East Report*. He is currently conducting research in rural Egypt for a book about the discursive production of the Third World since World War II. Parts of this research have already been published in *Middle East Report* and *International Journal of Middle East Studies*.

GYAN PRAKASH is Assistant Professor of History at Princeton University. He has published *Bonded Histories: Genealogies of Labor Servitude in Colonial India* (1990), edited *The World of Rural Labourers in British India* (1991), and coedited, with Douglas Haynes, *Contesting Power: Resistance and Everyday Social Relations in South Asia* (1991).

VICENTE L. RAFAEL is Associate Professor of Communication, University of California, San Diego. He is the author of *Contracting Colonialism: Translation and Christian Conversion in Tagalog Society Under Early Spanish Rule* (1988) and other essays on culture and politics in the Phillippines. Currently, he is working on Filipino nationalist discourse during the late Spanish and early American colonial regimes.

ANN LAURA STOLER is Associate Professor of Anthropology, History, and Women's Studies at the University of Michigan. She is the author of *Capitalism and Confrontation in Sumatra's Plantation Belt, 1870–1979* (1985) and has edited (with Frederick Cooper) "Tensions of Empire: Colonial Control and Visions of Rule," a special issue of *American Ethnologist* (1989). She is currently completing a book, *Carnal Knowledge and Imperial Power,* on the sexual politics of racial thinking in colonial Southeast Asia. She is on the editorial boards of *Politics and Society, American Ethnologist,* and *Journal of Peasant Studies*.

MICHAEL TAUSSIG teaches in the Performance Studies Department of New York University and has carried out research in and on Colombia since 1969. His work includes *The Devil and Commodity Fetishism in South America, Shamanism, Colonialism, and the Wild Man: A Study in Terror and Healing,* and *The Nervous System*.

Index